AMERICAN ELEGY

The University of Minnesota Press
gratefully acknowledges the generosity of the

David L. Kalstone Memorial Fund

of the Department of English of Rutgers University,
which contributed to this book.

American Elegy

The Poetry of Mourning
from the Puritans
to Whitman

Max Cavitch

University of Minnesota Press

Minneapolis
London

Excerpts from "Kaddish," by Allen Ginsberg, copyright 1984.

An earlier version of chapter 2 appeared as "The Man Who Was Used Up: Poetry, Particularity, and the Politics of Remembering George Washington," *American Literature* 75, no. 2 (2003): 247–74.

Published by the University of Minnesota Press
111 Third Avenue South, Suite 290
Minneapolis, MN 55401-2520
http://www.upress.umn.edu

Library of Congress Cataloging-in-Publication Data

Cavitch, Max.
    American elegy : the poetry of mourning from the Puritans to Whitman / Max Cavitch.
        p.   cm.
    Includes index.
    ISBN-13: 978-0-8166-4892-4 (alk. paper)
    ISBN-10: 0-8166-4892-1 (alk. paper)
    ISBN-13: 978-0-8166-4893-1 (pbk. : alk. paper)
    ISBN-10: 0-8166-4893-X (pbk. : alk. paper)
    1. Elegiac poetry, American—History and criticism.   2. American poetry—History and criticism.   3. Mourning customs in literature.   4. Grief in literature.   5. Death in literature.   I. Title.
    PS309.E4C38 2007
    811.009'3548—dc22
                                                                                2006026217

Printed in the United States of America on acid-free paper

The University of Minnesota is an equal-opportunity educator and employer.

12 11 10 09 08 07   10 9 8 7 6 5 4 3 2 1

Contents

Acknowledgments

To own the debts accrued in writing this book is delightful. Michael Warner was the first, best reader of many of these pages. Countless felicities of thought and expression are his, and the value of the example he has set for the conduct of life is similarly incalculable. Richard Poirier, Myra Jehlen, and Virginia Jackson have been tough and inspiring critics; it matters deeply to me that they be pleased with this book. For their late readings of the entire manuscript, I owe special thanks to Chris Castiglia, Mary Loeffelholz, and Matthew Parr, as well as to certain lips unknown. I hope they have not found me too incorrigible. My book and I have also thrived on the many good offices of Nancy Bentley, Lauren Berlant, Stuart Curran, Colin (Joan) Dayan, Dennis Debiak, Wai-Chee Dimock, Jim English, Michael Gamer, Daniel Harris, Amy Kaplan, Sean Keilen, Christopher Looby, Michael Meranze, Meredith McGill, Michael Moon, Elisa New, Barry Qualls, Esther Schor, David Shields, Frank Shuffelton, Emily Steiner, Julia Stern, Susan Stewart, and David Wallace. I have been extremely fortunate in my teachers at Yale and Rutgers and in my colleagues and students at the University of Pennsylvania and at the McNeil Center for Early American Studies. My research and writing have been materially supported by the Massachusetts Historical Society, the Woodrow Wilson National Fellowship Foundation, and the Penn Humanities

Forum. I am very grateful to Richard Morrison, Mary Keirstead, Laura Westlund, Adam Brunner, and their colleagues at the University of Minnesota Press for taking such good care of my book, and to the David L. Kalstone Memorial Fund for easing the cost of its publication. It is a great honor to have David Kalstone's still vital memory associated with this book about the vitality of remembrance. The staffs of the Rare Books and Manuscripts department at the University of Pennsylvania's Van Pelt Library (especially John Pollack and Daniel Traister) and of the Library Company of Philadelphia (especially James Green, Connie King, and Phil Lapsansky) have been surpassingly generous with their time, resources, and advice. The Local History and Genealogy Division of the Central Library of Rochester and Monroe County, New York, provided indispensable information at the last minute. For encouragement and forbearance I thank my parents, Joanna and David; my sister Elizabeth and her husband, Kevin; my friends Maggie Robbins and James Meyer; and especially Matthew Parr.

INTRODUCTION
Leaving Poetry Behind

> What living and buried speech is always vibrating here, what howls
> restrain'd by decorum.
>   —WALT WHITMAN, "SONG OF MYSELF"

Elegies are poems about being left behind. They are poems, too, that are themselves left behind, as literary and even material legacies. Their heritage helps constitute the "work" (both process and artifact) of mourning—a form of psychic labor that is also fundamental to the work of culture.[1] Ranging from dull repositories of borrowed affect to dynamic traces of the struggle to fix ineffable loss, they measure out the distance between emotion and convention, between local disruptions of bereavement and long traditions of resignation. In their figures of death, elegies seek to apprehend the ultimate, most unknowable condition of privacy, while pointing, in their language of loss, toward the sheer commonality of human experience. Elegy is a genre that enables fantasies about worlds we cannot yet reach, even as it facilitates investments in a world that will outlast us. It prompts ambitious engagement with one of the oldest and most distinguished verse traditions, and it also provides ample literary journeywork for the industriously maudlin. To this day elegy remains a capacious, flexible, widely practiced poetic genre. It figures prominently on the contemporary scene: in the work of formalist and experimental poets and in the accumulating effusions of Web site memorialists. It is well represented in revisionist as well as unreconstructed literary canons. Indeed, in its reflexive appeal for remembrance, in its frequently self-conscious ordering of poetic lineages, in its framing of questions of inheritance and continuity, and in its availability for imitation to nontraditional authors, it continues to be a genre crucial to the making of literary histories.

Elegy also has an unbroken history in English-speaking North America from the earliest years of British settlement. Yet beyond its Puritan phase it has received no comprehensive treatment. The genre has itself been, as it were, left behind in the attempt to narrate the very history it helped to make. This gap in the narrative of American literary history represents more than a deferral of recovery. It reflects the genre's loss of susceptibility to self-narration in the American context. For the heightened self-reflexiveness of elegiac convention—the tendency, for example, to figure acts of mourning in terms of poetic competition, to discover solace in the perpetuation of poetic communities, and to assimilate the object of mourning to the poetic vocation of the mourning subject—often faltered in late-colonial and early-national cultural climates generally inhospitable to literary institutions and careerism, whether aristocratic or bourgeois-professional. Sustained as an important commemorative resource in the tightly controlled mourning culture of the New England Puritans, the consolidating force of elegiac tradition became increasingly attenuated under countervailing pressures of migration and encounter, pluralization and secularization, war and independence.

Yet Americans did not stop writing elegies. During the early and mid-eighteenth century, elegies continued to number among the most abundant contributions to the pages of colonial newspapers. In 1790, Philip Freneau remarked that "No species of poetry is more frequently attempted."[2] And in 1866, Lydia Sigourney found it impossible to take the full measure of the nation's investment in memorial and consolatory verse; the number of entreaties and commissions for elegies she had received was simply too large to calculate.[3] Disparate classes of people in eighteenth- and nineteenth-century America—the self-consciously literary and the barely literate, the devout and the worldly, the politically powerful and the socially dead—left behind thousands of elegies in broadsides and the penny press, books, magazines, and diaries, and in the records of coteries and public performances. This body of work has been difficult to recognize as such, not simply because the genre ceases after Cotton Mather, its last great Puritan exponent, vividly to commemorate a single, relatively coherent local tradition, but also because it simultaneously and variously begins to resist, revise, and further recontextualize received emplotments of vocation and inheritance from the classical-European tradition.[4]

The history of American elegy is difficult to trace because it is itself part of the story of Americans' periodic frustrations with both the oppressiveness and the inefficiency of routes and mechanisms of transmission. From Creole resistance to imperial consolidation, to Puritan cries of declension; from opposition to primogeniture and to the matrilineal inheritance of slave status, to the poor traction of utopian and millenarian movements; from fitful evangelical revivals, to repeatedly contested citizenship claims; from linguistic standardization, to geographical instability; from uneven technological advancement, to the invention of a national literature—in relation to all of these conditions, elegy continued to be a highly adaptive discursive resource, not just for mourning the dead but for communicating and managing anxieties in contexts of survival.

The thematic and formal diversity, as well as the sheer volume, of eighteenth- and nineteenth-century American elegies makes the genre difficult to historicize. Yet the fact that such a history has been unattempted by literary scholars is surprising when one considers the significance of elegy in Western literary history—not to mention the allure of a largely unworked field. Nevertheless, while criticism continues to recognize elegy as a major literary genre and an essential agent of literary tradition, and while elegies of other periods and places have been studied intensively as objects of sociohistorical as well as aesthetic interest, eighteenth- and nineteenth-century American elegy has been virtually ignored.[5]

Indeed, for the most part it remains quarantined within the space of disparagement carved out by two trenchant and memorable satires. At one end, Benjamin Franklin's seventh Silence Dogood letter (1722) helped make elegy a kind of running joke about cultural provincialism and institutional hypocrisy. "For the Subject of your Elegy," Franklin recommends in his "receipt" or recipe,

> [t]ake one of your Neighbors. . . . Having chose the Person, take all his Virtues, Excellencies, &c. and if he have not enough, you may borrow some to make up a sufficient Quantity: To these add his last Words, dying Expressions, &c. if they are to be had; mix all these together, and be sure you strain them well. Then season all with a Handful or two of Melancholy Expressions, such as, Dreadful, Deadly, cruel cold Death, unhappy Fate, weeping Eyes, &c. Have mixed all these ingredients well, put them into the empty Scull of some young Harvard; (but in Case you have ne'er a One at Hand, you may use your own,) there let them Ferment for the Space of a Fortnight, and by that Time they will be incorporated into a Body, which take out, and having prepared a sufficient Quantity of double Rhimes, such as, Power, Flower; Quiver, Shiver; Grieve us, Leave us; tell you, excel you; Expeditions, Physicians; Fatigue him, Intrigue him; &c. you must spread all upon Paper, and if you can procure a Scrap of Latin to put at the End, it will garnish it mightily; then having affixed your Name at the Bottom, with a Maestus Composuit, you will have an Excellent Elegy.[6]

At the other end, Mark Twain's *Adventures of Huckleberry Finn* (1885) condensed a wide range of sentimental lyric and consolatory verse into the lugubrious antebellum figure of Emmeline Grangerford and her "Ode to Stephen Dowling Bots, Dec'd." Emmeline's brother Buck tells Huck that she could

> rattle off poetry like nothing. She didn't ever have to stop to think. He said she would slap down a line, and if she couldn't find anything to rhyme with it she would just scratch it out and slap down another one, and go ahead. She warn't particular, she could write about anything you choose to give her to write about, just so it was sadful. Every time a man died, or a woman died, or a child died, she would be on hand with her "tribute" before he was cold. She called them tributes. The neighbors said it was the doctor first, then Emmeline, then the undertaker—the undertaker never got in ahead of Emmeline but once, and then she hung fire on a rhyme for the dead person's name, which was Whistler. She warn't ever the same, after that; she never complained, but she kind of pined away and did not live long.[7]

These satires are so familiar, and in some ways so akin to one another, that it is easy to elide the historical and literary distance between them.

Critics and anthologists continue to do so, disregarding in the process the abundance and variety of elegiac poetry produced in the interim and the complexities of the cultural work undertaken therein.[8]

Yet part of the work and the reward of reading these poems is an evaluation of the cultural consequences for mourning of a series of profound social and psychological shifts. From the Puritans to Whitman, they span the rise of capitalism in Protestant North America and its transformation into the consumer society of the late-nineteenth-century United States. They trace the concomitant reconfiguration of interior life, as older, Calvinist modes of introspection gave way—first, in the time of Franklin's satire, to rationalist practices of self-control, and then, in the time of Twain's, to increasingly singular experiences of interiority, of personal identity as an ongoing and individuated process within a fin-de-siècle society of mass consumption and mass democracy. In reacting against formulism and piety both satires reflect sociocultural aspirations for individuality—in the early eighteenth century, as the subject of reason operating in the sphere of morality, and by the late nineteenth century, as the emancipatory project of personal autonomy. During this period, American elegy bids its long farewell to the soul and steps up its hailing of the unconscious. Far from being an undifferentiated series of conventional laments, as casual readers of Franklin and Twain often conclude, these poems track broad cultural changes framed, rather than collapsed, by the two satires' kinship.

Nowhere should this be more evident than in Franklin's and Twain's respective treatments of the reciprocal relation between gender and mourning. Proscriptions against the mourning of women, and against mourning *like* women, are among the most common and enduring in the history of regimentation of Western deathways. From ancient Athens to eighteenth-century Boston, authorities have variously adopted what Nicole Loraux calls "measures against feminine excess."[9] Initially, there was little extravagance in the funereal practices of seventeenth-century New England. Absent a belief in purgatory or in any possibility of efficacious intervention on behalf of the dead, rites were kept simple, even austere. Until midcentury, graves were often left unmarked. The simple obsequies were much more about those who remained alive—about the opportunity to the living such occasions provided for repentance of one's own sins and for expressions of joy at the presumed "happy Change," the departed's salvation.[10] Immoderate grief suggested a lack of faith, and ministers such as Samuel Willard warned against imitating the inconsolable mourner, citing the cautionary example of Rachel weeping for her children and refusing to be comforted. Willard further explained to readers of the Book of Jeremiah that the call there to engage professional "mourning women [to] take up a wailing for us, that our eyes may run down with tears, and our eyelids gush out with waters" (9:17–18) was not a recommendation of this ancient practice, but rather, on the contrary, a figure "used Rhetorically to signifie the desperate miseries" that the sins of the Judeans—inured to evil and incapable of authentic spiritual mourning—had called down upon them. "These women," Willard writes, "were, by their bruitish howlings; and formidable ejulations, accustomed to represent sorrow Tragically, and raise the affection in the mourners; which ought rather to have means used with it, whereby it may be rectified and moderated."[11]

The last line on the title page of Willard's book, *The Mourner's Cordial against Excessive Sorrow* (1691), reads "Very Suitable to be given at Funerals" and thereby attests to two realities of late-seventeenth-century New England memorial culture. First, immoderate mourning was on the rise, manifesting itself not only in elegiac appeals to emotionalism but also in more and more elaborate and expensive funerals. Second, the increasingly rich material culture of New England funerals—special gloves sent as invitations, elaborate mourning attire, souvenir rings etched with winged death's heads or skeletons, and broadside elegies—ironically included Willard's own book, written in reaction against such extravagance (see Figures 1 and 2). By the 1720s, the decade of Franklin's first appearance in print as Silence Dogood, the provincial assembly in Boston began passing a series of acts meant "to Retrench the extraordinary Expence at Funerals."[12]

Less directly, such acts provoked (even as they sought to retrench) extraordinary imaginings as well. Excessive mourning had become, in Loraux's words, "a threat to be contained, but also one to be fantasized about."[13] Franklin's satire demonstrates this. His female persona

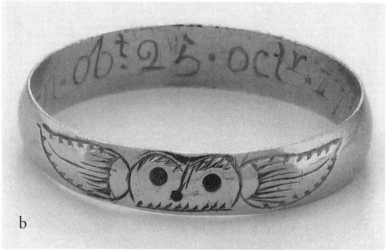

Figure 1. Two mourning rings. (a) Jeremiah Dummer, gold mourning ring commemorating the death of James Lloyd, Boston, 1693. Diameter ¾ inch (19 mm). Courtesy of Winterthur Estate. (b) Jeffrey Lang, gold mourning ring commemorating the death of the young son of Edward and Freke Kitchen, 1736. Diameter ¾ inch (19 mm). Courtesy of Yale University Art Gallery, Mabel Brady Garvan Collection.

A Pindarick ELEGY Upon the Renowned,

Mr. Samuel Willard,

Late Reverend Teacher of the South Church in *Boston*, and Vice-Prefident of *Harvard College* in *Cambridge* ;

Who Deceafed *September* the 12th. 1707.　　　　*Ætatis Anno* 68.

ENdited by an Heart with Grief repleat,
My Verfe doth *Homage* at his *Mourners* Feet :
Is a Juft Mourner too : It's Grief fo Loud :
Louder the Caufe : Invading ills fo crowd.
In trembling Airs, its feather'd Arrow flys ;
But not fo High, nor half fo Swift, as doe our Deftinys.
It fpies, big with Portentoufnefs and Dread,
Amazing Signs advance their Lofty Head :
Views, how fierce Lightnings doe *our Steeples ftrike*
　　　　And Temples Batter,
　　　　And their moft Sacred Riches Scatter.
Victims, and Priefts in flames afcend alike,
Moft wondroufly ; fuch horrid Carnage make
Heav'ns fiery Bombs, when they fo fall & break.

It views our choiceft Treafures made a Prey ;
　　　　Death Triumphs them away :
But fo much for to lofe, altho' no more,
Would Beggar Nations, make Rich Empires Poor,
The High & Mighty States a Begging fend,
Or Borrowing at leaft ; But where are they can lend ?
It fees, (and Sighs,) Hereby we were Undone,
　　　　Hereby Alone ;
So much choice Gold is Buried in this Grave ;
But that it fees our Mines no Bottom have ;
Mines that for Profelyted Rebels, lie
　　　　Within the Treafury
　　　　Of Grace Ador'd,
Of our Dear Saviour and Afcended Lord.
'Twill yet, to Gain fo much, take a long Day,
For choiceft Pioneers to dig, and Pray ;
And Get again what we have forfeited away.

In Crimfon Flood, wade Thoufands to his Tomb,
Swell'd Big with *Heroe's* Blood, like *Trojane* Womb ;
　　　　Troy were forgot,
　　　　But for our Parallel Lott ;
Ah ! Woful Day ! One Conquering Horfe of Fate
Severe & Juft, Enter'd our Opened Gate ;

　　　　Nay 'Twas a Troop,
　　　　Enough to Seize, and fwallow up
Long horded Stores that made Us Rich, & Proud,
That many Scores of Plenteous years had bounte-
　　　　oufly beftow'd.
Such Lofing *Bankrupts* We ; *'Twould break Heaven too*
But that it's Wealth is Infinite, to Set us up Anew.

Let all *New-England*, and let *Bofton* know,
How much they do to CHRIST for *Willard* owe :
Chrift's Precious *Blood* produc'd this Copious *Good*,
(In all Its worth) not fully underftood.
Harvard! I'le call thy Head (for tis no Treafon)
　　　　Mafter of Reafon ;
Mafter of all the Wifdom of the Sages,
　　　　That's handed down to later Ages :
Mafter of Tongues ; Mafter of Policy's
So much Admir'd ; And in Theology's
Doctrines & Truths, which moft Myfterious Are,
His Learned Mind might fafely take the *Chair.*
He *Liv'd* and Wrought in the *Oraculous* Flame,
　　　　'Till he an Oracle became ;
　　　　Whereat when many did Enquire,
They had the mind of *Chrift,* to their Defire
So ftrong in *Chrift* his Pen, Thoufands do know
　　　　And ftouteft foes have found it fo,
That when he pleas'd to Conquer, he was able,
Chaftiz'd the Rafh, and fettled the Unftable.

One of the King of *Ifrael's* Mightys he,
　　　　Of the Firft Three
Full of the Holy Ghoft : (Wou'd fo were we.)
His Virtue's Roll's fo large, Th' Ocean's fo Deep ;
My Verfe could do no more, but only creep
And Spy, and Speak a little on the Brink :
And thus much he muft fay who will fpeak leaft :
　　　　But of the Reft,
Bright Angels may, and fuch as They
　　　　with Juft Amazement Think.
　　　　　　　　John Danforth.

is an orphan and a widow. However, she tells her readers that she has none but imaginary afflictions, "as nothing is more common with us Women, than to be grieving for nothing, when we have nothing else to grieve for" (*Writings, 6*). Silence Dogood's reticence about her own losses contrasts sharply with the prolific work of local elegists, of which she takes notice in her self-appointed role as civic conscience. "Our soil," she writes in the seventh of her fourteen letters on civic virtue to *The New-England Courant,* "seldom produces any other sort of Poetry," and, to make matters worse, most of the elegies are "wretchedly Dull and Ridiculous" (21). She is therefore eager to alert her readers to what is ostensibly an exception: "a most Excellent Piece of Poetry, entituled, *An Elegy upon the much Lamented Death of Mrs.* Mehitebell Kitel" (19). After an appreciation of its supposed merits, she encourages "our Poets" to take advantage of the instructions for producing just such an elegy, the "receipt" left to her "as a Legacy" by her late husband (21).

This provincial scene of cultural transmission mocks the waning authority of Puritan elites over New England's burgeoning print culture, and the success of Franklin's ruse helps mark the merging of female authorship into the public discourse of the colonies' increasingly diversified marketplace of information. Nevertheless, the inhibition of women's speech and writing continued as a strong imperative amid the proliferation of print media. A popular guide to family life, for example, warned women against going "idling and tatling abroad, neglecting their household affairs."[14] Among those affairs was, upon the death of a family member, the preparation of the corpse for viewing and burial. Intimate handling of the dead remained a common part of domestic life, especially for women, before the rise of the mortuary industry in the latter part of the nineteenth century. A real-life Widow Dogood would have laid out her husband's corpse. But a brother minister would most likely have written his elegy.

A real-life Widow Douglas, on the other hand, would stand a fair chance of having written the elegy for Mr. Douglas herself, and Twain's target in his satire is not Harvard-trained ministers but an obsessively morbid teenage girl, reminiscent of such short-lived antebellum prodigies as Lucretia Maria Davidson. In the poetic corpus of Emmeline

Grangerford, Huck's periodic melancholy silences find their profusely verbal other.

By the time he and Jim set off down the Mississippi, Huck, like Silence Dogood, is an orphan (though he does not find out until the end of the book). Unlike Silence, however, who hints she is looking for a new husband, Huck eschews the primary source of identity in antebellum America by repeatedly electing to remain aloof from traditional family groups. The singular exception is his sojourn with the Grangerfords, into whose home and daily routine Huck slips without any apparent reluctance, despite his earlier protests against living indoors, regular mealtimes, and most clothing. He spends much time alone in the parlor, admiring its cleanliness, perusing its library (reading "considerable" in *Pilgrim's Progress*), and marveling at the gewgaws and the patriotic prints on the walls (*Mississippi Writings,* 724). Hung alongside the Washingtons and Lafayettes are drawings made before her death by the Grangerfords' daughter, Emmeline—drawings imitating the stitched and painted memorial pictures and mourning samplers that decorated the parlor walls of middle-class homes throughout the antebellum United States (see Figure 3). The pictures give Huck "the fan-tods." But he is deeply moved by the scrapbook full of newspaper obituaries and the elegies Emmeline has written "after them out of her own head" (725). Indeed, it is the time he spends alone in her old bedroom, reading from the scrapbook, that seems to attach Huck most strongly to the Grangerfords. He insists that he "liked all that family, dead ones and all, and warn't going to let anything come between us" (726–27). His sympathy with Emmeline extends so far that he even tries to write an elegy for her, "but I couldn't seem to make it go, somehow" (727). Huck's inability to engage in what Twain considered to be a debased sentimental tradition of versified lament is a hallmark of his authentic feeling as well as of his characteristic evasion of customary forms. It may also be a sign of the innocence that saves him from being swept up in the wrath that overtakes and destroys his new family. Forced to watch helplessly as Grangerfords and Shepherdsons slaughter each other in the name of a forgotten grievance, Huck cannot seem to "make it go" when he later tries to describe the experience and mourn his friends:

I ain't agoing to tell *all* that happened—it would make me sick again if I was to do that. I wished I hadn't ever come ashore that night, to see such things. I ain't ever going to get shut of them—lots of times I dream about them. (737)

Huck recognizes, in his own way, that trauma does not simply undermine narrative capacity. It alters our perspective on the narrative capacities that remain. It makes narrative risky; it makes us wary of occasions for storytelling.

That poetry may provide a legitimate refuge for this wariness is a thought Twain's burlesque of elegy mercilessly refutes. The credit is all to Huck, the one who *cannot* write such a poem. Yet the thought returns to Twain after the death of his daughter Olivia in 1896, prompting him to write an elegy for her, on the first anniversary of her death,

Figure 3. Elizabeth Abigail Leavitt, mourning embroidery, including verses on the orphan's loss of her parents, Portland, 1823. Silk, chenille, pencil, paint, and ink on silk. Courtesy of the Hingham Historical Society, Hingham, Massachusetts.

in which he departs dramatically from temporal order. For the real time of loss, Twain substitutes the remote order of myth. The poem begins: "In a fair valley—oh, how long ago, how long ago!" In this valley, "[s]hut from the troubled world, a nameless hamlet drowsed," and, near this hamlet, a temple. The temple is Olivia, projected far back in time, yet marmoreally rendered as if she were already a monument to her own death. The temple is served by "adoring priests . . . who lived by day and night submerged in its immortal glow." One day ("'Tis ages since it chanced"), the temple disappears. By and by, the people of the hamlet grow reconciled to its loss; some refuse to believe that it was ever there. For the priests, however, the memory of the loss can barely be assimilated:

> They stand, yet, where erst they stood
> Speechless in that dim morning long ago;
> And still they gaze, as then they gazed,
> And murmur, "It will come again;
> It knows our pain—it knows—it knows—
> Ah, surely it will come again."[15]

Twain projects himself into both the hamlet-folks and the priests. The former enable the consolatory anticipation of a long retrospect on grief dulled and half-forgotten. The latter enable the story of the loss to be forever postponed, in the desperately held conviction ("it knows—it knows") that the pain of separation will be healed and the beloved restored.

It is a remarkable poem, coming from the man who, in *Huckleberry Finn* and elsewhere, generally did everything he could to discredit mourning's "sweet drapery of verse."[16] It not only attests to the powerful attractions of a genre that offers an anodyne to some of the painful demands of narrative but also provides a glimpse of the regretful shadow cast by the Grangerford satire itself. For satire, too, is an elegiac genre; its critical outlook always has reference to some prior order against which the present is unfavorably measured. One has only to consider the abundance of death, traumatic experience, and symbolic loss in *Huckleberry Finn*—the book is a monument to unaccomplished mourning—to recognize in Twain's satire his own lament for the loss of an expressive resource. That he later rediscovered this resource is not the worst reason to consider more carefully its long and dynamic history in American literature.

A further reason to be surprised that this has not already been done is the great size and relative availability to scholars of this poetic archive, which ranges from anonymous, highly occasional verses to well-known canonical poems by major American authors—poems, like William Cullen Bryant's "Thanatopsis" and Ralph Waldo Emerson's "Threnody," that have rarely received sustained critical treatment. The fate of elegy is representative: the history of early American poetry generally remains both undernarrated and poorly integrated with the history of other discursive forms. Roy Harvey Pearce's *The Continuity of American Poetry* (1961) is still the comprehensive standard, and poetry remains at the margins of Americanist criticism. Indeed, even as the canon of early American poetry is being vastly expanded, it still constitutes one of the last truly "separate spheres" in the study of American culture.[17] This critical tradition of neglect and distantiation has been considerably refined since Leslie Fiedler, in *Love and Death in the American Novel* (1960), proclaimed that the "classical poetic genres revived by the Renaissance had lost their relevance to contemporary life before America entered the cultural scene."[18] Yet, despite the avowed centrality of their concern with representations of grief and mourning, important recent works of Americanist criticism by Neal Tolchin, Mitchell Breitwieser, Julia Stern, and Susan Mizruchi overlook the mourning genre—elegy—widely and diversely practiced by successive generations of Americans, including most of the authors whose prose writings are treated in those studies.[19]

Thus *American Elegy* is both the history of a particular genre and a study of the place of genre in American literary history. It ends where most commentaries on post-Puritan American elegy tend to begin: with Walt Whitman's "When Lilacs Last in the Dooryard Bloom'd" (1865). It does so in order both to foreground the earlier elegiac tradition obscured by that poem's reception history, and also to refocus attention on the work of poetic genres in early American culture—work greatly overshadowed by Whitman's legacy of iconoclasm. For the reception of

"Lilacs" has been for the most part structured by the effective interdiction of the American elegiac tradition in which Whitman participates. Scholars continue to observe and even to reinforce the poem's importance (including its importance as a specifically "American" elegy[20]), although the poem itself is a relatively infrequent subject of sustained analysis. For example, in the wake of various critical notices to the effect that "Lilacs" has inspired "few comprehensive readings,"[21] one valuable and far-ranging collection of recent work on Whitman and American culture makes but two passing references to "Lilacs." The editor's introduction suggests that the poem receives no real attention in the volume precisely because it has been canonized—and thus, presumably, rendered less amenable to contemporary critical transformations—by virtue of its formal coherence.[22] To dwell on the relative formal coherence of "Lilacs" does to some extent risk minimizing Whitman's strangeness as a poet and as a dispersive force struggling against the normativistic formal arrangements of nineteenth-century American poetry. Yet it is ironic that the prizing of "Lilacs" in the absence of a full interpretive tradition also has the effect of further removing Whitman from his American contexts—facilitating his poem's assimilation to the more conventional canon of Anglo-European elegy and obscuring the poetics and politics of elegy in the nineteenth-century United States, with which Whitman was distinctively engaged.

The chapters of this book illuminate elegy's contribution to a range of American cultural projects that remain active into Whitman's time: assessing the relation of sincerity and aesthetic merit, revising masculinized tropes of inherited tradition, constructing and deconstructing a national heritage, reconciling claims of republicanism and liberalism. The chapters proceed as a series of interlinked arguments rooted in and achieved through close reading. And they labor under a multiplicity of aims: to document the history of American elegiac practice, to trace aspects of the careers of particular elegists, to interpret the genre and its permutations in relation to the history of colonial and national sociality and institutions, to illuminate the mutually generative relation between certain political and psychoanalytic accounts of mourning, to explore how expressivity in contexts of loss helps constitute social as well as individual experiences of memory and anticipation, to evaluate elegiac responses to a specific ethical task—one that prizes resistance to the reduction of grief to grievance—and to suggest how these responses help variously to configure, legitimate, and disrupt national identifications by both crossing and articulating divisions of class, race, gender, religion, sexuality, and politics.

So many aims could not be fulfilled by one book. And readers will recognize other aims as well in the pages that follow—aims that are not wholly susceptible to rigid subordination, one to the next. But *American Elegy* should not be difficult to read and to use on that score. Rather, it should be of greater use not only to those who wish to read it as a comprehensive literary history, but also to those who are interested in individual poems, particular poets, and shorter periods within the book's more-than-two-hundred-year span. The textual idiosyncrasies and surprising developmental turns of literary history rarely accede to any overarching line of contention—unless, of course, they are forced to do so—and the history recounted here is not one in which every aspect points in a single direction. Nevertheless, it should be useful at the outset to articulate, as one organizing principle or ethos, the idea that all elegies—indeed all mourning arts—are about the struggle to make the most out of some sign of the inarticulable, the trace of the loss that abides in our mostly inaccessible lives. For me, the term *unconscious* well names—thanks chiefly to its elaboration in object relations theory—this inaccessible life.[23] But one need not have a psychoanalytic worldview to experience mourning, either one's own or that of others, as the mute agony of incorporation, whereby we keep the dead inside ourselves, so to speak, in tangles and hollows that figurative language can only strain to reach. This reaching is not only a source of pain (such as overworked muscles experience through the accumulation of toxins) but also evidence of a fundamental sort of aspiration, or will, that may manifest itself—that we may make manifest—in creative living. In a sense, mourning is a parapraxis of will, by which I do not mean to denigrate or trivialize mourning (or will), but rather to emphasize how commonly loss leads us astray in ways that turn out to be integral to the social imaginaries we construct and to how we inhabit them.

Social imaginaries, to modify the abstraction developed by Charles Taylor, are those ways in which psychic life crosses externalized will in intersubjective experience.[24] They are the intersections at which we meet (or miss, or collide with) one another as we go about the business of world building. They are the intersections at which we forge institutions and at which we stand the best chance of recognizing and understanding institutional changes on every scale, from individuals to families to markets to ecclesiastical polities to secular nation-states to eschatological visions of a world to end all worlds.

American Elegy—to offer another organizing principle—is the story of how different poems and their writers and readers get *caught*: between social structures in which genre transmits normative values (such as belief in an afterlife, or speaking well of the dead, or promoting the continuity of patriarchal authority) and individuated efforts to imbue poems and persons with the value of more idiosyncratic perceptions. In eighteenth-century Anglo-America, social structures come increasingly to be developed and understood in relation to modes of collective action directed against external, essentially imperial encroachments. These modes of collective action are enabled, because legitimated, by a widely shared and remarkably stable faith not only in the value of liberties locally cultivated, but also in regularly augmented elected assemblies to identify, strengthen, and protect those liberties. Thus, in chapter 1, I reject the declension narrative—one at least tacitly accepted by *every* other scholar of early American elegy—in which the genre is driven into desuetude and irrelevance by the attenuation of Puritan culture in the early eighteenth century. To the contrary, I argue that the genre does not merely survive this attenuation, but indeed that it accumulates new kinds of interest and relevance for North American populations, some of whose idiosyncratic perceptions were *becoming* normative values, and some of whose perceptions of value were changing the ways in which different kinds of lives were mourned and, indeed, whether certain lives would be mourned at all. Elegy is central to the emergence of local and ultimately of national identities in eighteenth-century Anglo-America, shaping historical self-understanding in works by authors as diverse as Cotton Mather, Benjamin Franklin, Richard Lewis, Annis Boudinot Stockton, Phillis Wheatley, and Philip Freneau. By marshalling such a wide range of examples, chapter 1 provides the first broad account of elegy's history from the waning of American

Puritanism to the Revolution and its aftermath, highlighting the challenges war and nationalization posed to conceptions of time, inheritance, and continuity.

Chapter 2 takes up the problem of national mourning and the making of national subjects by interpreting the enormous outpouring of elegies for George Washington at the turn of the nineteenth century—elegies ranging from anonymous newspaper verses to poems by established literary figures like David Humphreys, Susanna Rowson, and Charles Brockden Brown. Recalling the imperative of legitimate succession in colonial elegy, the literary mourning of the nation's first president contributed in unprecedented ways to contemporary debates over the heritability of political values and institutions.

In the ensuing decades, increased immigration, territorial expansion, racial and cultural assimilation, and continued secularization and democratization all work further to reduce the authority of traditionalism in American life, thereby challenging elegiac resourcefulness. Chapter 3 explores how elegy develops in this period both as a form of conservative custodial remembrance and as an oppositional resource for the historically overlooked or maligned. I also examine at length how William Cullen Bryant's major and minor poems exemplify elegiac resourcefulness by linking exploration of the genre's formal and conceptual limits with the retrospective narration of national heritage—and in particular with the deadliness to Native Americans of Jacksonian expansionism.

In chapter 4 I follow the proliferation of what has become the most abjected form of elegy on the contemporary critical scene: the much-mocked, tepidly celebrated child elegies that overwhelmed the genre's popular development in the antebellum period. I have chosen to focus chiefly on the depression years of the late 1830s and 1840s because they were years of such profound social and cultural change, during which many Americans underwent crises of identity and faith and, with extraordinary frequency, shaped their anxieties in the figure of the lost child. I begin with child elegies by Lydia Sigourney, Henry Wadsworth Longfellow, and other poets who tend to measure the loss of children in conventional terms. Then I offer an extended analysis of Ralph Waldo Emerson's "Threnody," his elegy for his son Waldo, as an instance of radical skepticism about patterns of generational continuity and cultural transmission that nevertheless cannot simply transcend the antebellum crisis in the economic value of the child.

Whereas Emerson seeks to escape the dead weight of generations, African-American elegists must struggle to preserve traces of the severed affiliations from which they suffer disproportionately. For many, and especially for slaves, to mourn publicly at all was to consecrate ties of feeling and of blood that often lay under the heaviest interdictions. Chapter 5 offers an unprecedented survey of African-American elegy from the late eighteenth century to the Civil War. In addition to elegies by slave and free-black poets, this chapter also explores elegiac treatments of blacks by white poets, contrasting the compensatory discourses of national mourning with the politically articulate voices of the socially disprized. My analysis of poems by authors black and white, known and unknown—including Phillis Wheatley, George White, Joshua McCarter Simpson, Grace Greenwood, Daniel Alexander Payne, Julia Ward Howe, George Moses Horton, and Frances Harper—demonstrates elegy's cultural importance to their critique of patriotic propaganda, while revealing their political radicalism to be itself conditioned by the seductions of death.

American Elegy concludes, in chapter 6, with an extended reading of Walt Whitman's "When Lilacs Last in the Dooryard Bloom'd" as a critique of elegy's ability to reenact the national community of sympathy whose loss Whitman and other Lincoln elegists deplored. Whitman extends the efforts of American poets to develop a politically relevant elegiac practice by introducing a radical, eroticized vision of improved relations among the living as well as between the living and the dead. In his liberatory practice, dependent as it is on the staggering costliness of the Civil War, Whitman nevertheless manages to approach more nearly—more nearly perhaps than any elegist before or since—a way of mourning free from deformation by grievance against the past for not having been otherwise.

"Lilacs" did not immediately stand out for Whitman's contemporaries. Commenting on the literary qualities of James Russell Lowell's "Commemoration Ode" in 1868, James B. Thayer adduced Emerson's 1846 "Threnody" as the closest, comparably fine memorial poem.[25] And it was Whitman's own "O Captain! My Captain!" that appealed immediately and lastingly to popular taste as what Matthew Brown calls "a communal rhetorical strategy, appealing in its memorizable simplicity to a broad base of listeners."[26] Indeed, "O Captain!" continues to be one of the most frequently memorized poems in U.S. schools, and much of the best recent criticism on Whitman himself continues to read genre fairly straightforwardly as a mechanism of consensus—a mechanism that Whitman seeks variously both to preserve and to cancel through the unfolding of lyrical subjectivity. Less well remarked is Whitman's location of lyrical subjectivity in the figure of the elegist: the "lone singer, wonderful, causing tears."[27] In "Lilacs" especially, the historical tension between "communal rhetorical structure" and lyric subjectivity appears reflexively as the problem of genre—what Jacques Derrida calls "participation without belonging."[28] For Whitman, genre is, like death, at once the condition of and inspiration for individuation; like genre, the figure of death—especially as a bequest of literary tradition—represents both the consciousness of limitation (there will be neither world nor time enough) and the urge toward transcendence (to expatiate in the life to come). Whitmanian elegy establishes the theme of death in American poetry as the potential solvent of compulsory poetic arrangements, political as well as formal. Death is Whitman's prescription for poetry—"that remedy," according to Allen Ginsberg, "all singers dream of."[29] This prescription has its own long background, one that Whitman's reception history has largely forgotten.

To uncover and illuminate this background, *American Elegy* relies on genre's power to classify and organize texts and thereby to delineate literary traditions. It seeks to do so in a way that takes advantage of genre criticism's fundamental methodological challenge: reconciling the demands of historicism and formal analysis. Once, genres were thought primarily to fix or objectify relations among texts. Now, we tend to treat genres as objectifications not of textual constituencies but rather of the processes of change that texts undergo historically within categorizing institutions, such as the school or the marketplace. Generic thinking is still understood at once to fuel and to gratify the need for classification, the urge to identify unidentical things. But the interest taken in texts by most varieties of contemporary genre criticism and theory is, thankfully, no longer what Hawthorne's Custom-House officer called "the saddened, weary, half-reluctant interest which we bestow on the corpse of dead activity."[30] No longer taken to be the inert residue of some instance or version of the struggle over the relation between particulars and universals, genre now refers to the struggle itself. In this book, genre is understood not as a strictly substantive term but also as a processual one. The "work" of genre, like the work of mourning, refers here to a dynamic activity as well as to a cultural artifact.

The dynamic relation *between* mourning and genre is itself largely overlooked in twentieth-century criticism and theory. At the beginning of the twentieth century, Benedetto Croce painted genre criticism (especially its anatomizing and classifying activities) as the mortal enemy of literature: "division annihilates the work . . . turns the living being into a corpse."[31] He fetishized an organic and unambiguous singularity, hoping that would be an adequate defense against modernity's ever-accelerating homogenization of value. In the intervening century, the idea that organic being, specifically personhood, is what anthropologist Igor Kopytoff calls the "natural preserve for individuation" has lost even more of its presumptive force.[32] And as a corollary development with the philosophical deconstruction of the subject, most recent thinking on genre tends variously to refute the ideal of the incarnate text.

Nevertheless, genre theory and criticism—from Alastair Fowler's family resemblance model to Julia Kristeva's work on (and in) the novel—attest to the continued viability of the biological analogy for a wide variety of rhetorical, discursive, historicist, and materialist approaches that invariably reject essentialism. Michael McKeon has recently written that genres "have a historical existence in the sense that they come into being, flourish, and decay."[33] Like Fowler, who also speaks of genres in terms of their "dying," McKeon employs the biological analogy as a sign of his commitment to a diachronic conception of genre and *not* to invoke a fixed-species model that biology's own historical turn has long since obviated.[34] They continue to conceive of genres as the engines of literary history, just as biologists continue to regard species as the "engines of evolution."[35] And throughout Kristeva's corpus, the novel—imagined as a "critical, incarnate, sensory narrative"—is a privileged site for her endeavor, in the wake of what she calls "necrophiliac" language philosophies, to bring the speaking body back into discourse.[36]

The biological analogy, as the citations of Croce, Fowler, McKeon, and Kristeva indicate, is commonly signaled by images of mortality ("corpse," "decay," "dying," "necrophiliac"). I take this to be a reflection of the extent to which thinking about genre is also a way of thinking about human loss. For example, approaches to genre as otherwise diverse as those of Northrop Frye and Henry Louis Gates Jr. are nevertheless both inspired by a desire to speak with and to the dead. For Frye, this commitment is expressed through an archetypal criticism that seeks to reveal, as Fredric Jameson puts it, "the continuity between our psychic life and that of primitive peoples."[37] For Gates, studying the canon-defining work of African-American genres ("the repetition and revision of shared themes, topoi, and tropes") means recuperating for contemporary African-American life lost human constituencies. His attachment to generic history and criticism is poised in opposition to what he considers an unwarrantable disavowal of social identity—an overscrupulous devotion to theories of social constructionism—in present life as well as in the study of the past: "You can't," he insists, "opt out of a Form of Life."[38]

At the opposite end of the historico-materialist spectrum, Paul de Man identifies generic thinking as a form of "resistance and nostalgia" opposed to "true" or "non-elegiac" mourning.[39] For de Man, genre mistakenly presumes the intelligibility of the literary object (I know what "Lycidas" is), and the elegiac mistakenly presumes the intelligibility of the object of mourning (I know who it is I am grieving for). By these lights elegiac, or "false," mourning would seem, ironically, to be akin to the Crocean arrogance of assuming the critic can know the text apart from its various and inevitable iterations. Whitman, for one, keeping poetic vigil over the corpse of a nameless young soldier, knew better: "I think we shall surely meet again," he writes in an elegy that has little to do with pious visions of posthumous personal reunion.[40] He means they will meet again in other poems and other deaths. The present study proceeds from the Whitmanian understanding that the singularity of any text, and of any object of mourning, can only be approached via its repetitions, transferences, and reiterations—by what Derrida calls "the traversal of discourse toward the unique."[41] The work of genre and the work of mourning are homologous, and thus inspire thoughts of one another, in that they are both enactments of this "traversal." They are ways of seeking to understand the relation between the singularity of an event (a poem, a death) and its inevitable repetition—a relation that takes contingent forms: *Justa Edouardo King,* "Vigil Strange I Kept on the Field One Night," "The Deaths of Roland Barthes."

What is at stake for the claim to genericity is, to borrow some language from Louise Fradenburg, "the *creation* of a series of distinctions, whose instability is nevertheless apparent."[42] Why, asks the critic or theorist who rejects generic distinctions, should we want to hold that instability at bay? Isn't the effort to do so merely nostalgic: a defense, ultimately, against the loss of an ideological commitment to transcendence? Shouldn't we, in our study of the mourning arts, as in our pursuits in medicine and philosophy, be seeking always, as Henry Staten puts it, "to peel away every transcendental mystification of our erotic and organic fate"? Doesn't generic thinking conservatively affirm what Staten calls the "unthinkability of nontranscendence"?[43] The answer, I believe, is that the claim to genericity is pragmatic rather than conservative: whether or not nontranscendence is unthinkable, it is certainly unlivable. It may be that our lives really are nothing more than the residue of our psychic refusals to credit the reality of our present dissolution. Yet Freud's famous observation that it is impossible to harbor an unconscious belief in one's own mortality was not a prescription for the disavowal of culture. The knowledge (as evermore dramatically confirmed by the history of science) that everything we think of as belonging to our proper persons is continuously being engulfed and relinquished by the world should render even more valuable whatever it may yet be possible to learn about our sustainable cultural fictions of difference and relationship. Genre is one such fiction; mourning is another.

Genre is only mistakenly apprehended as a simple fiction of sameness and identity. The expectations and norms genericity produces educate taste in the pleasures of the available (what has been and what freshly is), which means, among other things, helping readers to adjudicate the relation between repetition and novelty. Mourning offers a similar education in the relation between the lost object and its so-called substitutes. There really are no substitutes, as Freud conceded in a 1929 letter to his friend Ludwig Binswanger. There is only "something else."[44] Fradenburg eloquently reflects on this letter and on the concept of substitution as it pertains to mourning theory:

> if we try to de-essentialize this concept, we might focus instead on the problem of how we become attached to—how we develop bonds and relationships with—*particulars.* What makes grief agonizing is precisely that when someone or something particular has been lost, it cannot recur. Thus in the concept of substitution there continues a defense against the loss of the particular, hence against the advent of the new as well as the end of the old. If the particular cannot be repeated, it remains forever lost; and this is why there can be no final closure to mourning. There can only be, *alongside* of mourning, learning to love new particulars.[45]

"Alongside" here must be understood, I think, as a metaphor for a kind of cleaving: not separate and parallel, but simultaneously split off from and adhering to one another. "Mourning" and "learning to love new particulars" can never be fully differentiated. That is, "learning to love new particulars" is a meaningful characterization of the work of mourning. It is also a meaningful characterization of the work of genre. Through a textual object's genericity, we learn to recognize and value its difference from what we have been taught to desire. Genre is the way eros manifests itself in the literary-critical imagination. By reading elegies as reflexive expressions of the need to learn to love new particulars, we can understand them better in aesthetic, psychological, and historical terms.

As a genre fundamentally concerned with the relation between limitation and transcendence, elegy has an elaborate politics as well. Elegies counsel submission to various forms of authority, order the speech and silence of grieving subjects, and establish hierarchies and communities of abjection within and against which alliances and identities are worked out. For Fradenburg, developing a properly political reading "of the elegy, of theories of elegy, and of elegiac theory" is an explicitly utopian project:

If we can grieve for our particular losses, *and* admit futurity to our interpretations, we can perhaps begin to outline an alternative to the hermeneutics of transcendence. In doing so we could perhaps recognize that the seeking of community in the form of undifferentiated unions or of unions predicated on identity can never be anything other than a defense against loss; we could also consider the possibility that historical community might be re-imagined as the promise of relationship between irreducible particularities.[46]

Fradenburg's project for studying mourning discourse proposes ultimately to return us, once again, to the Crocean fetishization of unambiguous singularity ("the promise of relationship between irreducible particularities"). This utopian promise could, in its actual social or discursive fulfillment, only be chaos. Yet this promise, as what E. M. Cioran calls an "extravagant idea," helps implicitly to guide the political reading of elegy to which the present study aspires.[47] For, if one aspect of the work of genre is to enforce and normativize certain forms of subjective identification, another is to enable and sustain social and transgenerational alliances that may disrupt or improve such forms.

The extravagant idea of this book is that the telos of American elegy is not consolation for the deaths of others, but fulfillment, rather, of a specifically political, shared happiness that "loss" misnames. In a recent meditation on the American response to terror—that most radical disruption of alliance—Judith Butler reminds us that even under extreme conditions of alienation and fear loss makes "a tenuous 'we' of us all." Even when driven violently toward a humiliated and powerless solitude, grief may bring "to the fore the relational ties that have implications for theorizing fundamental dependency and ethical responsibility."[48] To live and, especially, to own that dependency in a state of emergency are something most Americans will rarely if ever have to do. This is obviously part of our great fortune; less obviously, it is part of our particular obligation to learn to mourn, as Butler puts it, "in global dimensions."[49] This obligation has a very long history.

Consequently, this book holds at bay the instability of a series of distinctions called "elegy" in order to better appreciate the role it has played in acting out and clarifying Americans' relational ties, both synchronically and diachronically. I therefore examine elegy in a number of its socio-literary contexts, such as the congregation, the patrilineal family, sororal literary networks, abolitionism, racial and sexual minority cultures, inheritance law, and the nation. The titular contextual designation "American" is itself, of course, an unstable series of distinctions. It includes, for example, what Benedict Anderson has called the "imagined community" of the modern nation-state. In *American Elegy,* I treat the nation not as a prescriptive idealization but as yet another sustainable fiction of difference and relationship—one that was of considerable historical (which may also mean proleptic), cultural, and psychological importance to the elegists under discussion, and one that, as Anderson reveals, is fundamentally concerned with death and immortality.[50] This does not mean that the nation is the ultimate horizon of American literary history, nor need it point to an incapacity to mourn in any other than nationalist terms. (This is especially important to emphasize at a time when the way we allocate grief tends so unreflectively to favor American lives and to sanctify American losses.) One of the most exciting and transformative developments in recent Americanist cultural criticism has involved various translinguistic and transnationalist revisions of the disciplinary concept "American." I hope that the present study might suggest ways in which such revisionary practices could be brought to bear on the study of genre—for example, in connection with Native American death songs or with the Creole funerary traditions of the Caribbean. The present focus on English-language elegy in eighteenth- and nineteenth-century North America is but one, and hitherto untold, story among many about the cultural history of alterity in American mourning literatures.

In other words, the horizontal ambitions of *American Elegy* are at once historico-political and ethico-literary. It remains, as it was initially conceived to be, a project toward the recovery and reinterpretation of a vital and critically underserved corpus of early American poetry. It enhances our understanding of the role played by the commemorative arts in Americans' social and political lives. And for specialists and nonspecialists alike, it establishes this corpus of early American elegy as a crucial site for studying the literary-historical development of one of the most urgent questions facing criticism today: What are the possibilities for imagining and inhabiting a future that need not be understood as a set of grievances against the condition of its arrival? This is an especially important question now for Americanist literary and cultural critics. Americanist criticism has never been more scrupulously and hopefully devoted to two essential tasks: the ideological critique of literary histories, and the recovery and interpretation of new canons of early American writing. At the same time, however, criticism continues to display signs of becoming a largely accusatory enterprise against the past, a game of seek and condemn, as if literature were merely a repository for evidence of the faults and crimes of earlier generations. This often has the unintended and unfortunate effect of hampering rather than enhancing possibilities for both renewed aesthetic pleasure and enlightened political inquiry in the present. This book argues that elegy—a genre essential to the making of literary histories and to the cultural production of knowledge about the past—has long addressed the same fundamental tension between accusation and understanding, between aggravated memory and possibilities for world building. One of the broadest claims of *American Elegy* is that this poetry often works to sustain the goal of achieving a prizable, meaningful diachronic relation to others that is not based merely on personal or collective grievances against the past. The struggles these poems enact help teach us how our burdensome feelings of indebtedness, remorse, and hostility might be mitigated by more freely chosen allegiances—allegiances not only to the dead but also among the living. This, I believe, is what makes the story of American elegy one of the most important untold stories of American literature.

Yet if the story of American elegy has gone untold, it has not gone unanticipated. "To undertake a study of American elegy," Peter Sacks writes in his epilogue to *The English Elegy* (1985), "would be to open yet another book." He tries to suggest in his concluding remarks "some of the ways in which our approach to the genre might be brought to bear on American elegies."[51] And, indeed, his psychosexual analysis is a crucial starting point for later readers of "Lilacs" like Michael Moon. Some of Sacks's remarks on Whitman even hint toward fascinating potential revisions of his own work on British elegy. For example, reading Sacks on Whitman puts one in mind of elegies such as Marvell's "Poem upon the Death of His Highness the Lord Protector" and Tennyson's

"Ode on the Duke of Wellington," elegies that do not figure in Sacks's book but that participate, with Whitman's "Lilacs," in a tradition of republicanism in English-language elegy, in relation to which the assertion of distinct national strains would make stronger persuasive sense.

In his remarks on American difference, however, Sacks takes a less persuasive tack. For behind his assertions of distinctiveness ("these poems do differ from their English counterparts") lie presumptions of a "compulsion toward originality and privacy" and a "more nakedly expressive style" that could not withstand a genuinely comparative analysis.[52] One reads the word *counterparts* and scratches one's head. What are the American "counterparts" to the elegies Sacks analyzes: to "Astrophel" and "Lycidas" and "To the Memory of Mr. Oldham"? These poems were widely read and imitated in British America, of course. But Sacks is not suggesting that any poems of comparable interest or influence were produced there—at least not until Whitman's "Lilacs," which is where Sacks, in his adumbration of an American countertradition in elegy, looks first. "Lilacs" seems to fit well the pastoral-vocational paradigm upon which Sacks's canon depends. But whatever representative quality the poem possesses as an *American* elegy has less to do with Whitman's relation to earlier pastoral poets than with the way it treats its political subject as a condensation of the fundamental problem of personhood.

Indeed, the characteristics by which Sacks would seek to recognize an American countertradition in elegy could not be said to mark a specific local style. Far from having a "compulsion toward originality," for example, large numbers of British *and* American elegies surrender readily—and often strategically—to inherited form and expressive convention. As for privacy, even the most sophisticated and skeptical elegists find ways of prizing the consolations of received form—including the consolation (so crucial to Whitman's own practice) of the reader's participation in what Kenneth Burke calls "public, or communicative structure."[53] The "more nakedly expressive style" Sacks attributes to American elegy is frequently renounced by Whitman himself, who often displays a markedly Tennysonian investment in the grieving heart's modesty and the wracked soul's reticence. The works of both poets make clear that one of the elegist's characteristic gestures is to embrace the contrived and the banal—to interpolate expressions of mourning that may even seem to lack relevance or emotion altogether. They know that the voice of loss, especially at first utterance, rarely sounds original or even exigent. "Laments," says Freud, "which always sound the same and are wearisome in their monotony nevertheless take their rise each time in some different unconscious source."[54] Elegy, before and after Freud, teaches us that contemporary criticism continues to have a too complacent view of convention as the antithesis of sincerity. "Grief," writes Amy Clampitt in her elegy for John Lennon, "is original, but it / repeats itself: there's nothing / more original that it can do."[55] An important point that goes missing in Sacks's theory of elegy is that even when elegiac gestures themselves seem unrigorous or psychologically inauthentic, they may reward patient criticism with insights into the pressures that maintain form as well as those that distort or subvert it.[56]

"I *mind* them," Whitman says of such pressures in "Song of Myself," pinpointing his place at the turning of modern lyric away from the social institutions in which poetry's meanings had hitherto commonly been received.[57] That is, he *heeds* them even though they *offend* him, for he recognizes that the decorousness by which their efficacy is registered ("howls restrained by decorum") is still a serious, constitutive mode of the world he inhabits. It is a world in which decorousness still makes sense and is of value—not just to sentimentalists, but to morally daring readers like Emerson and Dickinson as well. What generally comes across as Victorian-American priggishness in reactions against Whitman's work is symptomatic of deeper anxieties about the possible failure of sublimation as the basis of a legitimate and transmissible post-Christian culture.[58] Such anxieties are not limited to the American context, but they do have a long history in that context, forcibly emerging in New England Puritanism and influencing subsequent transformations in late-colonial and early-national mourning culture. In *American Puritanism and the Defense of Mourning,* Mitchell Breitwieser observes that Puritanism was "in large measure an attempt to sublimate mourning, to block and then redirect its vigor," and that this sublimation may be understood to reappear in American culture as a "legacy of social technique."[59] But he is quick to point out that sublimation entails the possibility—the risk—of other experiences and representations of mourning. Against the explanatory cogency of accumulating Puritan narratives of providence and exemplarity, Breitwieser reads Mary Rowlandson's story of loss as a textual landscape pocked with eruptions of dissonant grief—eruptions that signal *generic* as well as psychological pressures. He "look[s] at the genres that she faces—conversion narratives, funeral sermons, and scriptural typology, primarily—to describe her narrative as a collision between the costs and potentialities of these genres on the one hand and the perplexing area of history that afflicted her on the other."[60]

Elegy's absence from Breitwieser's constellation of relevant genres—despite its importance as a supplementary resource for Puritan mourners, including female mourners like Rowlandson who were barred in so many ways from literary culture—marks an opportunity for extending his analysis of the psychology of form in American literature. For Breitwieser, both the "costs and potentialities" of mourning genres lie in our various allegiances to the notion that a proper discursive universe is one that subsides out of sheer intensities. The chief liability of such genres is a misleading emphasis on the denouement of psychic struggle in a triumph of regimentation over chaos, a "sufficient culmination for grieving."[61] Their chief potentiality is to measure the cost of this illusion—the toll it exacts both upon ideological systems (such as Puritanism or genre) and upon individual persons or texts. The other (prose) genres Breitwieser "looks at" are also among the most heavily brokered genres in New England culture; they exemplify the social management of discourse in ways that elegy, as a poetic genre, does not. That is, elegy represents an alternate form of vigilance, not only in the formally exaggerated vigilance of the metrical line (poetry actively displays its competence to measure[62]), but also by virtue of poetry's special set of relations to discursive commerce and diachronic transmission, for example, its unsurpassed susceptibility to imitation, its relative separability from the technology of the book and the ideology of print culture, and its synecdochal enshrinement as the "literary."

In literary history, as in all other protocols of remembrance, enshrinement may function as a form of banishment as well as celebration. Elegies, like the persons by whom and about whom they are composed, make bids for immortality and thus require and help sustain various techniques of memory. Some techniques advertise, others enshroud. Elegies are among the persistent cultural expressions of the impulse to survive—literally, to live beyond—death's assaults upon the human (or textual) body and consciousness. Yet survival may also mean terrible privation, as Melville—a stern and innovative elegist—observed in the voice of Babbalanja, perhaps in relation to his own posthumous reputation. Asked how best to perpetuate one's name, Babbalanja replies: "Carve it, my lord, deep into a ponderous stone, and sink it, face downward, into the sea; for the unseen foundations of the deep are more enduring than the palpable tops of the mountains."[63] Melville understood that his own cultural survival would mean awaiting reintroduction into the restrictive economy of remembrance. Recovery projects, such as those that have recently generated such a large number of anthologies of early American poetry, for example, are at best preliminary to such reintroductions.[64] The history of anthologies, after all, is for the most part a history of periodic, celebratory re-sequestrations. The inclusion of certain poems in an anthology—for example, the dozens and dozens of elegies for the confederate dead assembled in Sallie Brock's *Southern Amaranth* (see Figure 4)—may contribute to the process whereby it is forgotten that they were once far more present to the living, in closer parlance with the world, through manuscript circulation and periodical reprinting. In her preface, Brock pushes the point well beyond the limits of analogy:

> The design of this work was conceived in an individual desire to offer a testimonial of gratitude to the memories of the *brave men* who perished in the late ineffectual effort for Southern Independence; as well as in a wish to render to my Southern sisters some assistance in gathering up the remains of the Confederate Dead, from the numberless battle-fields over which they were scattered, and placing them where the rude ploughshare may not upturn their bleaching bones, and where sorrowing friends may at least drop a *tear,* and lay a *flower* upon the grass-covered hillocks that mark their resting-places.[65]

For Brock, to anthologize is to mourn. The elegies gathered from hither and yon are not *like* the remains of the dead; they *are* the remains,

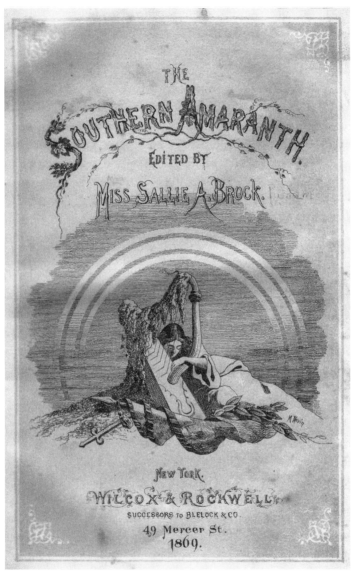

Figure 4. Title page of Sallie A. Brock's *The Southern Amaranth* (New York: Wilcox and Rockwell, 1869), an anthology of elegies and other memorial verses.

picked up from the numberless pages of newspapers, magazines, diaries, and letters where they had been scattered, and placed, ironically, where they will be safe from disturbance by the archetypal instrument of peace and poetry: the ploughshare, forged from the retired sword, that inscribes the earth with lines in its turnings (verses). Brock literalizes the image of the anthology as cemetery, a dedicated realm apart from living discourse and, except perhaps on certain occasions or when we fall into certain moods, apart from the discourse of the living. Brock's understanding of her anthologizing practice is not atypical, even among peace-time anthologists. For John Keese, the compiler of an 1844 anthology of American elegies, "bind[ing] together these Gems of Consolation" was itself an act of mourning. Keese put his book together "at a moment of intense family bereavement, when he felt himself impelled to the relief herein suggested."[66]

The varieties of relief suggested if not always achieved through the production and consumption of eighteenth- and nineteenth-century American elegies are coveted in relation to a world of loss, from Keese's "moment of intense family bereavement" to moments of social catastrophe—moments that elegy is, for reasons outlined earlier, well suited to bring together in relation to the genre's attempts to figure its own history of permanence and change. Thus it is, as I will show in the following chapters, an especially politicized literary genre in the double sense of being "on the spot" for history: not only present to witness (elegy may be the originary "occasional" form) but also implicated in ongoing social struggles over memory and meaning. Elegies seek to extend the lives of individuals and of groups, augmenting personal remembrance and collective heritage. But the production of shared memories also entails exclusions and amnesias. Elegy is a way of dealing with being left behind. But it may also be a way of leaving others behind and thus often yields resentment and ideological violence along with consolation and beauty. Chapter 1 begins to assess the multiple legacies of particular eighteenth-century American elegies for the local and protonational contexts in which they emerge.

CHAPTER I

Legacy and Revision in Eighteenth-Century Anglo-American Elegy

Some—Work for Immortality—
The Chiefer part, for Time—

—EMILY DICKINSON

Until the eighteenth century, the history of American elegy was by and large a function of Puritan resource and resolve. The funeral elegy, adopted from their English counterparts by New England Puritans in the 1640s, was practiced assiduously for almost a century, constituting what Robert Henson calls "our first coherent body of verse."[1] A few seventeenth-century elegies from colonies outside of New England survive, including two on Nathaniel Bacon reproduced in a contemporary account of the 1676 rebellion in Virginia.[2] But it would be another fifty years before elegies written in the middle and southern colonies, such as those by Maryland poets Ebenezer Cook and Richard Lewis, would start to appear in significant numbers.[3] The New Englanders' archival proclivity, combined with their early acquisition of print technology, meant that the history of seventeenth-century American poetry in English would essentially belong to them.

Puritans shaped this history and contributed to the elegiac accent in American poetry by writing and, just as important, by preserving the ephemera of memorial culture, such as broadside elegies. William

Scheick insists that ceremonial practice trumped archival consciousness for many Puritan mourners, who often pinned elegies to coffins before they were buried, "funerating" the poems along with their
nominal subjects: "Printed on broadsides, elegies were attached to the
hearse, thrown into the grave, or at best distributed among the mourners to be read on the occasion. Extrinsically or intrinsically, they were
not designed to survive this occasion, and that they did not is evident
from their scarcity today."[4] Yet while it is true that relatively few of
the earliest imprints survive, we know this in part because so many of
the texts were preserved in other forms, for instance, by contemporary
historians like Nathaniel Morton. Intrinsically, the poems are often
highly self-conscious of their traditionality, their more-than-occasional
implication in matters of familial, communal, and cultural continuity.
And the *relative* abundance of elegies among surviving broadsides of
the later seventeenth and early eighteenth centuries strongly suggests
an extrinsic, artifactual significance.[5]

Michael Warner reasons that it was in part through their thematiza-
tion of death that broadside elegies acquired the value of heritability,
helping them to survive where other popular forms did not. People
saved elegies and passed them on as a kind of heritage, that is, both
as a cultural tradition and as property.[6] A writer for *The New-England
Courant,* which published a number of satirical pieces on elegy in the
1720s, alludes to just this sort of dual heritage as an aspect of the genre's
alarming ubiquity:

> Nor is there one Country House in Fifty which has not its Walls garnished
> with half a Score of these Sort of Poems, (if they may be so call'd,) which
> *praise the Dead to the Life,* and enumerate all their Excellencies, Gifts
> and Graces. I have trac'd this Spirit of Elegy among us for an hundred
> Years back, and find that it came in with the first Planters. *New-England's
> Memorial* furnishes us with several Elegies made long since by our Fore-
> Fathers, which our modern *Elegiac* Writers imitate.[7]

Elegies, according to "Hypercriticus," are treated as important household belongings—not just part of the furniture but a kind of heraldic
memory. They "garnish" the walls of rustic homes like a verse counterpart of portraiture, in which the dead are praised "to the Life." His
research discovers them also to be the substance of a New England liter-

ary tradition. While ridiculing the provincial appeal of such poems, "Hypercriticus" nevertheless acknowledges, in his references to cultural transplantation, historiography, and the much-imitated elegiac activity of "our Fore-Fathers," the genre's role as a literary genealogy that also engages wider social and discursive contexts.

Exemplary in this regard is the elegy Cotton Mather wrote in 1682 for Harvard president Urian Oakes. Eager to embrace responsibility for preserving the memory of past worthies, Mather begins the poem (his first published work) by enthusiastically attaching himself to a procession of New England elegists:

> Cotton *Embalms great* Hooker; Norton *Him*:
> *And* Norton's *Herse do's* Poet-Wilson *trim*
> *With Verses*: Mitchel *writes a poem on*
> *The Death of* Wilson; *And when* Mitchel's *gone,*
> Shepard *with fun'ral Lamentations gives*
> *Honour to Him: and at his Death receives*
> *The like from the* (like-Maro) *Lofty Strain*
> *Of admirable* Oakes! *I should be vain*
> *To thrust into that gallant* Chorus . . .[8]

The "Chorus" Mather assembles here is composed of men who are both writers of elegies and members of New England's spiritual and political elite. The New England literary tradition he identifies is also identified *with* a hereditary rendering of the effort to conceive and secure a Puritan community.

Adopting the pose of the initiate, Mather invokes with conventional gestures of modesty the authority of classical and biblical precedents (Virgil, David, Christ) that both suggest the scale of his ambition and legitimize the displacement of glorified predecessors. Succession and potency are overtly and continuously at stake. He seeks condolence in what Joseph Roach calls "the rejuvenating imperative of legitimate succession."[9] In "*thrust*[ing]" himself, as Mather puts it, "*into that gallant* Chorus" of elegists at the beginning of his career, he also anticipates his own death and subsequent memorialization by some future elegist—some younger poet-minister's retrospective attribution of meaning to the life Mather has yet to lead. As he says toward the end of the poem, his elegy for Oakes is unfinished business:

>   after my *Encomiastick Ink*
>   Is all run out, I must conclude (I think)
>   With a *Dicebam,* not a *Dixi*!

That is, with an "I was speaking" rather than an "I have spoken." There is more to say—more, as he puts it a few lines later in a hortatory apostrophe to the sons of Cambridge, "To *publish* both in *Print* (as well as *Life*)."[10] Your ink, he says to them, will do for me what I now do for Oakes. The poem's easy shift from self-directed to communal exhortation is characteristic of Puritan elegies, which—printed and distributed as broadsides, recited and ritually interred at funerals, calling not only for mourning but also for action in the present and into the future—have as much to do with public life as with private reflection. Indeed, it is the life of the community that is often the clear object of such poems.[11] It is in the community's life to come, celebrated in elegies like Mather's, that the influence of a Urian Oakes will live on after his death.

By the same token, the community needed its immortals in order to endure, and Mather tended eagerly to the afterlives of those upon whose continuing example the life of the community seemed to depend, doing so most notably in the monumental biographies of American Puritan worthies he went on to publish in his *Magnalia Christi Americana* (1702). These prose memorials find a precedent in Mather's elegy for Oakes, the principle behind which is that there is a kind of immortality that is socially allocated, bestowed by one elegist upon another, in celebration of the local. Indeed, mourning prompts Mather to rethink cultural allegiance. At the end of his biography of Jonathan Mitchell (architect of the Half-Way Covenant and Harvard fellow) in book 4 of *Magnalia,* Mather revises his decision to adapt, as a poetic tribute, some lines from Richard Blackmore ("the best of *Poets* in the *English Nation*"). "But what need I travel, as far as *Europe,*" Mather asks by way of introducing homespun verses by an author named Drake, "for an *Elegy* upon this Worthy Man? Let it be known, that *America* can *Embalm* Great Persons, as well as *Produce* them, and *New-England* can bestow an *Elegy,* as well as an *Education* upon its *Heroes.*"[12]

The relation alluded to here between mourning and pedagogy was mediated by Harvard College, from which came many departed New England ministers *and* many surviving New England elegies. David Shields points out that "the predominance of college men as composers of surviving texts indicates that the sons of Harvard effectively exercised control over the public memory to keep recollection of their own alive."[13] To do so meant exercising control over Harvard as well. Along with their world-canceling appeals to divine judgment, Puritan memorials solicit future generations to continue the work and the institutions of the present—like Harvard—in the name of the departed. "Let not the Colledge droop, and dy!" (418) is both Mather's prayer to God and his challenge to readers at the end of the Oakes elegy. Indeed, Puritan elegies tend to be preoccupied not with eternity but with personal fame and institutional continuity.

As Puritanism's promise for societal longevity fades, however, the authority of the genre seems to diminish along with that of its representative institutions. The literary tradition sketched by Mather ("that gallant Chorus") and the community in which it developed were not, of course, isomorphic. But their connection was such that they have seemed to scholars necessarily to share a common end. Ivy Schweitzer suggests that Mather was "the final link [in] an unbroken chain of clergymen's deaths and poetic eulogies,"[14] and Kenneth Silverman writes that "by 1720 the vogue of the New England communal elegy was effectually ended. By that time it could no longer focus in the fact of death so many issues crucial to the Puritans' life in the new world." The congruence of literary tradition and the genealogy of power that Mather illustrated so well in his elegy for Oakes was no longer even a tenable fiction. The genre seemed defunct, and in Silverman's account it is consigned to a postmortem fate of continued popularity in "sub-literary circles throughout the neoclassical era."[15]

But the point at which the perceived coherence of a unitary generic tradition unravels is precisely where the story of American elegy starts to gather new kinds of interest. Examples of failed nostalgia for Puritan modes prompt elegists to rethink the relation between mourning, poetry, and cultural vigilance. New England, mid-Atlantic, and southern elegies increasingly reflect distinct styles and eschatologies.

Manuscript networks create new contexts for mourning and sociability. Women write and publish elegies prolifically. Native Americans, slaves, and other casualties of America's imperial history become increasingly prominent in the literary language of loss. And the British empire in America itself begins a process of dissolution that helps to shape eighteenth- and ultimately nineteenth-century elegiac writing.

Because this accumulation of interest has gone largely unexamined, its history could be very long to tell indeed. But instead of writing a massive developmental history, such as John Draper, for example, chose to pursue in his magnificent account of *The Funeral Elegy and the Rise of English Romanticism* (1929), I have concentrated more selectively on what are among the most representative texts, the most memorable episodes, and their most problematic interstices. The remainder of this chapter, like the book as a whole, combines chronicle and close reading in a way that resists retrospective remediation of historical complexity. At the same time, though, it holds to the fundamental thesis that elegy continues, from the Puritans to Whitman, to be a vital expressive resource for those who in the aftermath of loss get stuck in their aspirations toward creative living. The immobility of illness (melancholy), or political rage (grievance), or the burden of history (anxiety) is also a dark opening, a necromimetic opportunity for the revival or reinitialization of creativity. Elegies are the expressive record of such opportunities and of the personal and collective failures and triumphs against which their shared history must be read. Here, then, at the moment of immobility fixed by previous accounts of early American elegy, is where the new stories of that expressive record begin.

First of all, within and beyond New England, the energy and inventiveness of satirical assaults on elegy during the 1720s and 1730s belie the genre's ostensibly dwindling relevance. Read apart from the tradition to which they respond, satires on elegy by Benjamin Franklin, Joseph Green, Joseph Breintnall, and others have been very successful at diverting attention from the genre's continued authority. Yet the success of any satire is misapprehended without a sense of its object's own power or troublesomeness. Inspired by Franklin's seventh Silence Dogood letter (1722), correspondents of *The New-England Courant* used its pages to wage war on elegy for more than two years. One of them—Hypercriticus, cited earlier—not only bemoaned (like Franklin) a provincial, Harvard-bred fondness for outworn elegiac conventions but also implicitly challenged the hundred-year-old archive of New England elegies as an illegible record and as a contemporary mnemotechnique of limited usefulness. It is "beyond my Capacity," he wrote, "to unfold the Mysteries contained in these dark Expressions."[16] Meanwhile, however, the *Courant* continued to publish elegies submitted by its readers, and Bostonians did not hesitate—for example, in a nearly contemporary letter on nonconformism published in *The Boston News-Letter*—to cite "forefather" elegies as authoritative texts.[17] When the *Courant* met its demise in 1726, the paper itself was mourned in an elegy by Harvard poet (and nephew of Cotton Mather) Mather Byles.

This was, as David Shields points out, an "exquisite piece of irony," not just because Byles was the quintessential Harvard verse-monger, but also because, as such, he assumed the role of unofficial laureate and state elegist, helping to sustain the institutions—proper institutions like Harvard College as well as literary "institutions" like elegy—whose cultural authority the *Courant* sought to undermine.[18] In keeping with his connections to the Mather dynasty and to the colonial administration (Massachusetts Governor Jonathan Belcher was another of his uncles), Byles was devoted in his elegiac practice to lineage-based hierarchies. For example, in his elegy for George I, "A Poem on the Death of King George I and Accession of King George II" (1727), he embraces the consolation of a kind of genealogical resuscitation: "Let *Britain's* Sorrows cease, her Joys enlarge, / The *first* revives in thee the *second* GEORGE."[19] To commemorate the death of Queen Caroline, George II's wife, Byles addressed an elegy to Belcher, who functions in the poem as a metonymy of courtly grief and power:

> *Belcher,* first in grief as in Command;
> With early zeal you kist her beauteous hand;
> Your honours to the destin'd queen you paid,
> Ere the crown flash'd, far-beaming, on her head.
> The muse reluctant, by your order sings,
> Else had she silent wept, and broke her strings.
> What fame to *us* reports, by *you* were seen.[20]

Byles serves his patron by figuring his close relation to the London court. At the same time, however, he signals his own attenuated relation, as a colonial subject, to the hierarchy his elegiac practice commemorates by acknowledging the poem's basis in secondhand reports of Caroline's personal virtues ("What fame to *us* reports, by *you* were seen"). In the 1727 elegy cited above, the extension to Boston of "Britain's Sorrows" over the death of George I and its "Joys" at the accession of George II is asserted rather than taken for granted: "Ev'n our far Shores," Byles writes, "confess the big Delight." Byles laments the king's passing with insistence from the periphery, implicitly mourning his own absence from the culturally legitimating metropolitan center.

Eager to expand his reputation beyond the literary confines of America's "far shores," Byles found his ambition anticipated and undermined in the prestigious *London Magazine* by fellow Bostonian Joseph Green. Green's satirical elegy "The Poet's Lamentation for the Loss of his Cat, which he used to call his Muse" (1733) was the chief glory of a subversive campaign, begun by Green in the late 1720s, against Byles's laureateship.[21] In the poem, Green emphasizes what he sees as Byles's debasement of literary ambition by foregrounding the reflexive relation between elegy and poetic vocation: the poet mourns his muse, upon whom depend his own prospects for literary immortality as a producer of elegies. These prospects, Green suggests, were marked by transience even before the death of Byles's "muse," for instance, with respect to a poetic lineage already vitiated by his plagiarism:

> But when my dullness has too stubborn prov'd
> Nor could by *Puss's* musick be remov'd,
> Oft to the well-known volumes have I gone,
> And stole a line from *Pope* or *Addison*.[22]

Implicitly allied with the poetic lineage Byles debased through his very efforts to sustain it are the lineages of colonial authority he praised self-servingly in his commemorative verses—stealing lines from Pope's "Elegy to the Memory of an Unfortunate Lady" in his elegy for Governor Belcher's brother-in-law, and in his elegy for Belcher's wife, stopping just short of figuring the coattails to which he clung:

Mean time *my* Name to *thine* ally'd shall stand,
Still our warm Friendship, mutual flames extend;
The Muse shall so survive from age to age,
And BELCHER'S name protect his *Byles's* page.[23]

These couplets conclude what is both an elegy commemorating the strength of the patronage relationship, and a memorial poem on the passing of a patron system upon which Byles's own art anxiously recognizes itself to depend.

Another view of the tenuousness of the patron system emerges in the elegiac practice of Maryland poet Richard Lewis, whose 1732 elegy for his friend and patron Governor Benedict Calvert reveals strains not only on the patronage relationship but also on the economic basis of the British empire in America. Dissatisfied with imperial policies he felt were inimical to colonial Maryland's trading economy, Lewis obliquely registers his impatience with proprietary foot-dragging through a conventional elegiac protestation of modesty:

T'advance our Trade, Employ'd his Daily Thought
By various ways our Happiness He Sought.
But why do I presume in Humble Verse
His Actions, as a Ruler, to Rehearse?
Let History to those Extend her Care,
While I his Mild Domestic Life Declare.[24]

The elegist's recoil ("But why do I presume") from a more particular "rehearsal" of trade policy couches his disapproval in a scrupulousness about genre; that matter is for "History," not for elegy. Yet the "domestic" frame here deemed appropriate to elegy is violated elsewhere in the poem without compunction. Indeed, the elegy is structured by expansions and contractions of provincial consciousness that show Calvert's "Mild Domestic Life" to be merely incidental to their articulation.

The elegy opens with a portrait of Calvert as a talented young student and gentlemanly traveler. Returning to his "Native Isle," he is quickly drafted into service by his brother Charles as governor of Maryland, where Lewis makes his acquaintance. At the margin of empire, Calvert regales him with descriptions of Roman antiquities and treasures of the Vatican museum. "If I had Travell'd," Lewis insists, "I should scarce discern, / More than my Ears from Benedict might Learn."[25] In Calvert's person—more specifically through his eloquent voice—the course of empire has taken its westward way. But his final peregrination reverses the direction of the *translatio* motif crucial to American efforts at self-differentiation. Sick and dying ("How Chang'd, alas! from whom I once had known!" Lewis writes, alluding, it would seem unthinkingly, to Satan's horrified recognition of Beëlzebub in book 1 of *Paradise Lost*), Calvert heads back to England to recuperate but dies during the journey home. After making the more decorous Miltonic allusion to Lycidas's death at sea, Lewis identifies as Calvert's fitting memorial the financial legacy he has bequeathed to the colony's Prince William School. "Some Greatfull Youth," he predicts,

> warm with Poetic Fire,
> Thy School Annapolis in Time shall Raise;
> Justly to Sing her Benefactors Praise.[26]

Against the apparent attenuation of the genre's authority, Lewis's elegy extends the traditional pastoral-vocational model through his own allusive practice and the anticipated, mutually reinforcing relation between commemorative verse and emerging local institutions.

Yet, as in New England, mid-Atlantic elegists witnessed a challenge to the cultural authority of the genre's traditionalism through satirical disruptions of local poetic genealogies. As master of the Annapolis school and poet of considerable local reputation, Lewis was himself elegized by one "W. Byfeild" upon his death in 1734. The elegy was presented to Franklin's *Pennsylvania Gazette* accompanying a satirical letter by Joseph Breintnall (Franklin's friend and member of his original Junto), the subject of which was the problem posed for elegy by the relation of sincerity and aesthetic merit. Breintnall writes that he was at first "offended" by the "blundering unnatural Rhymer's publishing his Elegy on the Death of a fine Poet." He claims to have grown more tolerant, however, upon reflection that it was "real Affection" and "the Sincerity of his Love" that led the elegist to "expose his own Weakness." He concludes with the modest proposal that, in future, all elegies be vetted by committee—the good ones to be published, the bad ones to be paid for generously out of a "publick Fund" and then *"carefully lock'd up."* Archly recalling the burial of Puritan broadside elegies, this literary entombment would protect inferior poets from "having their Works publickly exposed, to the Dishonour of them and the Place where they reside."[27] Like Franklin's Dogood satire and the two-year assault on elegy sustained in the pages of *The New-England Courant* a decade earlier, Breintnall's letter reflects a provincial sophisticate's assumption of a cosmopolitan attitude toward local literary culture.

It is also suggestive of what would over the next century come to be the profound penetration by emerging market systems of social relations predicated upon mourning. Byfeild's fault in subjecting the public to an offensively poor piece of verse, Breintnall implies, derives from his failure to consult his own "Self Interest." His solution is an ironic appeal to self-interest for the public good: an elegy-subsidy by which the elegist would be rewarded for producing something in excess of or counter to public need. In Franklin's *Autobiography,* Samuel Keimer's composition "in the Types" of his elegy for Aquila Rose not only reinforces his characterization as a provincial hack but also interferes with the commerce of his printing house by holding up production.[28] As for Keimer, so for Byfeild too, according to Breintnall, elegiac verse-mongering represents a lost opportunity, if not for direct profit, then for protecting the future value to himself of his reputation as a poet. It further depicts Byfeild as out of touch with a communal ethos no longer predicated upon shared feeling. Sincere expression of grief is admirable, but if its literary representation does not comport with changing notions of aesthetic value, it should remain unpublished ("lock'd up").

Each of the satires by Franklin, Green, and Breintnall attests to elegy's significance as a staging ground for ongoing contests of literary accomplishment within provincial culture. They also reflect a period of uncertain transition from piety to skepticism in eighteenth-century attitudes toward death—a period during which satirical wit anticipates the energy with which later elegists would seek to suit elegiac conventions to changing social and existential needs. Satirical critique is a negative index of the period's commitment to elegy's significance, even as the terms of death's significance began to shift, alternately favoring renovated, increasingly individualized pieties and a skeptical, sometimes defiant rationalism. Franklin, Green, and Breintnall all express dissatisfaction with their culture's persistent attachment to a mourning resource whose conventions have come to seem thoroughly evacuated of emotional authenticity and commemorative power. In their satires, the cultural authority of elegy does not disappear, but rather takes a kind of refuge from convention-thwarting pressures, such as the growing secularism that makes the consoling pieties of a Mather Byles morally as well as aesthetically unpersuasive.

Though often under the historical cover of satires like Franklin's influential Silence Dogood letter, a vital elegiac impulse nevertheless persists in eighteenth-century American poetry. There is, for instance, Franklin's own enduring interest in elegiac forms. An elegiac ballad, he notes in his *Autobiography,* was one of his earliest compositions.[29] He had a particular penchant for epitaphs, incorporating them liberally into the pages of his *Poor Richard's Almanack* and composing them in a variety of tones and styles for his parents, a squirrel, Thomas Penn, and, most notably, himself. With the exception of the epitaph for Josiah and Abiah Folger Franklin, which their son had inscribed upon their tombstone around 1754, these epitaphs were never meant to be a part of funerary practice. They are also to be distinguished from the classical tradition—vigorously sustained in Puritan elegy and still practiced widely in the eighteenth century—of concluding funeral elegies with formal epitaphs. Like his Dogood satire, Franklin's literary epitaphs announce a kind of closure to traditional elegy, while continuing to draw critical attention to generic hierarchies and commemorative practice. For instance, in his letter accompanying the epitaph he wrote for Georgiana Shipley's pet squirrel (1774), Franklin explained his decision to write "in the monumental Stile and Measure, which being neither Prose nor Verse, is perhaps the properest for Grief; since to use common Language would look as if we were not affected, and to make Rhimes would seem Trifling in Sorrow."[30] The eighteenth-century taste for pet elegies, exploited by Joseph Green in his satirical elegy on Mather Byles's cat, is here indulged in by Franklin with a kind, avuncular irony. But the question of what stands between common language and trifling rhyme in his society's poetic negotiations with the dead is one that continued to be posed in earnest.

Part of that earnestness, as Franklin had long recognized, had to do with the importance of elegiac verse in negotiations among the living. His self-epitaph dates from 1728 (the year Cotton Mather died), and it announces, as Michael Warner has noted, "not his death, but his intentions for his career"[31]—a career not simply as a printer but as a man who would find both life and afterlife in print:

> The Body of
> B. Franklin,
> Printer;
> Like the Cover of an Old Book,
> Its Contents torn out,
> And stript of its Lettering and Gilding,
> Lies here, Food for Worms.
> But the Work shall not be wholly lost:
> For it will, as he believ'd, appear once more,
> In a new & more perfect Edition,
> Corrected and amended
> By the Author.[32]

Despite a similar emphasis on surviving in print, Franklin's self-epitaph works against Mather's earlier deployment of the trope. To imagine the remembrance of one's own death is to attempt some control over the meaning of one's life. In his elegy for Oakes, Mather implicitly relinquishes an important measure of that control to the elegist—one of the sons of Cambridge—who will follow him in the tradition he has entered. Franklin, however, makes personal continuity a personal endeavor.

Yet while Franklin seeks to manage his own postmortem future directly, bypassing Mather's filiopious chorus of elegists, his version of personal continuity depends profoundly on a vision of community in a way that Mather's does not. Puritan elegy is at best an interim management of temporary lives and deaths that hover precariously between election and eternity. It helps build a community in which—through constant self-examination and the scrutiny of acts and behaviors that might signify election—an unascertainable but nevertheless certain judgment is anticipated and rehearsed. However, for post-Calvinist Franklin and the increasingly plural Enlightenment America he comes to represent, doom has more to do with dissolution than with judgment. Indeed, in his 1725 *Dissertation on Liberty and Necessity, Pleasure and Pain,* he expresses the conviction that while the soul endures beyond bodily death, it retains no imprint of personality. Thus, while it is

> not impossible that this same *Faculty* of contemplating Ideas may be hereafter united to a new Body, and receive a new Set of Ideas . . . that will no way concern us who are now living; for the Identity will be lost, it is no longer that same *Self* but a new Being.[33]

For Mather, immortality binds the future to the past; the immortal soul is the interim soul. He can find internal and external assurances of his election, but he cannot alter prior divine judgment. For Franklin, immortality means a continuity between past and future contingent upon the recruitment of communal approval. His strategy of self-transcendence is one of public persuasion. That which transcends his proper self is what Mitchell Breitwieser calls "the emulating acclaim of future generations."[34]

Mather's and Franklin's elegiac verses speak to their common need not to revisit the past but to develop a satisfactory vision of the future. At one point, Mather contemplated an epitaph of his own. In the preface to his *Bonifacius*—whose running title, *Essays to Do Good,* Franklin remembers in the name of his first journalistic persona—Mather likens the book to a tomb upon which he will refrain from self-aggrandizing inscription. He compares himself to a man who "would not have so much as his name in his epitaph; he would only have, *Hic jacet, umbra, cinis, nihil.*" Thus, writes Mather, referring to his decision to publish the book anonymously, "[t]here shall be no other name on this composure; *hic scribit (vel Scripturire studet et audet) umbra, cinis, nihil.*"[35] Because he acknowledges elsewhere in the preface the inevitability of his authorship's becoming known, Mather seems here to anticipate Franklin's use of strategic self-effacement—his "usual Rule," as he puts it in the *Autobiography,* of "avoiding as much as I could . . . the presenting myself to the Publick as the Author of any Scheme for their Benefit."[36] But there is a sharp difference. For, finally, the intended beneficiary in Mather's scheme is not the community but God, whose glorification is the end of any and all efforts to do good. "We may *now* praise God," Mather writes in an early sermon, "as *Parents,* as *Masters,* as *Officers* in the Church or Common-Wealth. All those Capacities will *dy* with us."[37]

For Mather, a satisfactory vision of the future is the ultimate dissolution of communities, and of the relational selves that inhabit them, in God. His style of self-effacement in *Bonifacius* is a way of practicing being-in-God. Franklin's self-epitaph, on the other hand, is a way of practicing being-in-print—a kind of citizenship that might go on being his even after death, thus preventing his absolute removal from a community imagined as continuous but with no transcendent fate. His goal is the ongoing production, rather than the dismantling, of his social being. In his elegy for Oakes, Mather had conceived of a model for continuous community in his articulation of a New England elegy tradition—a tradition with which Franklin, in his Dogood satire and in his self-epitaph, seems emphatically to break. Franklin's modernity consists not so much in his challenge to the received forms of a particular tradition, however, as in his challenge to the isomorphism of tradition and community as figured in the Oakes elegy. With Franklin, traditionality in Anglo-American literature becomes increasingly a means for the transmission not of a particular social structure but of the value of self-production.

The cultural transvaluation of individuality was of course by no means an exclusively secular or secularizing process in eighteenth-century Anglo-America. And if the consciousness of personal limitation best represented by death helped to inspire individualism in the skeptical, it was also fundamental to the individuated piety of evangelical movements. "In the new religious experience," writes Harry S. Stout in his biography of George Whitefield,

> piety was no longer something inextricably bound up with local community and corporate spirituality. The emphasis shifted to a more individualistic and subjective sense of piety that found its quintessential expression in the internal, highly personal experience of the "New Birth." Indeed, the individual experience of regeneration, detached from a particular place and time and existing within the self came to be the badge of religiosity and true piety in Whitefield's revivals.[38]

Along with this doctrine of a "New Birth" came a new kind of death, not just for revivalists but for post-Puritan Calvinists of many stripes.

While rhetorical emphasis on the terror and uncertainty of death persisted (for example, in the fire-and-brimstone imagery of some of Whitefield's funeral sermons), the general sentiment waxed optimistic.[39] The elegiac hymn Whitefield composed in 1764 "to be sung over his own Corps" begins with the line, "Ah! lovely Appearance of Death."[40] And in one of the earliest known references to Franklin's self-epitaph, Whitefield shared with his friend a sense of confidence in an afterlife of personal aggrandizement:

> I have seen your *Epitaph*. Believe on JESUS, and get a feeling possession of GOD in your heart, and you cannot possibly be disappointed of your expected second edition, finely corrected, and infinitely amended.[41]

His tone clearly adjusted to suit Franklin's temperament and the requirements of casual correspondence between friends, Whitefield's exuberant assurance ("you cannot possibly be disappointed") is nonetheless startling, coming as it does from a lifelong Calvinist who consistently rejected Arminian conditionalism.

In his good-natured capitulation to the self-realizing ethos of Franklin's epitaph—which Franklin circulated as an advertisement not of his piety but of his wit—Whitefield suggests his appreciation of the complex relation between individual and corporate histories that, later on, his own death on September 30, 1770, would highlight. Mourning for the first transatlantic culture-hero was so energetic and pervasive that it raised serious misgivings about public attachment to Whitefield's person.[42] Ambivalence about the apparently universal sense of personal loss often found expression in elegy, a genre strongly characterized by competing tendencies toward individuation and deindividuation. The very form of certain elegies for Whitefield figures the tension between particularity and abstraction—between Whitefield the man and Whitefield the avatar of sainthood. For example, an acrostic elegy called "The Saint's Death Warrant" embraces Whitefield's particularity by foregrounding the meaningfulness of his name. Yet it promotes abstraction by avoiding biographical detail and by using the letters of Whitefield's name to spell out a primer of sainthood.[43] Such devices as acrostics and anagrams, abundant in Puritan elegies, continued to be widely practiced among eighteenth-century elegists. By no means an exclusive feature of American verse, the acrostic elegy nevertheless appropriately links Whitefield's memorialization with a long tradition of poetic engagement in America with the problems of material textuality and representative personality. The formal echoes of New England Puritan elegy in the elegies for Whitefield help to preserve his memory as the enterprising spirit of a renewed American "Puritan errand" to Europe.[44]

At the same time, the widely shared experiences and expressions of grief for Whitefield helped elegists in the closing months of 1770 further to articulate the intercolonial identity coalescing around recent events, such as March 5th's Boston Massacre. One anonymous poet pictured Whitefield, in his dying hour, heaving "a last, a dying pray'r" for the victims of tyranny in "Nov-Anglia."[45] Another elegist wrote of being

> left behind to mourn the heavy Loss,
> Both to our selves, and all AMERICA—
> No WHITEFIELD now, with tears to plead our Cause![46]

In these concluding lines, the elegy evokes Whitefield's famously lachrymose preaching style (by all accounts he made a rhetoric of weeping) and transmutes the sorrowful tears of Whitefield's mourners themselves into emblems of subrational public persuasion.

In the elegy that launched her own transatlantic career, Phillis Wheatley, an enslaved West African teenage girl brought to colonial Boston on the eve of the Revolution, links grief with protonational feeling as she recalls Whitefield's lifelong attachment to the American colonies:

> When his AMERICANS were burden'd sore,
> When streets were crimson'd with their guiltless gore!
> Unrival'd friendship in his breast now strove:
> The fruit whereof was charity and love
> Towards *America*—couldst thou do more
> Than leave thy native home, the *British* shore,
> To cross the great Atlantic's wat'ry road,
> To see *America*'s distress'd abode?[47]

The emphasis here on fateful transatlantic crossings and the break with Britain—the movement "Towards *America*" given added point by the uncommon enjambment of the fourth and fifth lines quoted above—

recalls the incipient colonial tensions expressed in Richard Lewis's crossing-themed elegy for Benedict Calvert. It resonates chiefly, however, with the crossing motifs that abound in Wheatley's verse, from the worldly trafficking of "On Being Brought from Africa to America" to the spiritual crossings figured in so many of her other elegies, which constitute the lion's share of her verse (and are discussed at length in chapter 5).

It is ironic that Wheatley achieved an international voice with her elegy for Whitefield, who sought anxiously to circumscribe the speech of black Christians. Like many black evangelicals inspired by Whitefield's example, Wheatley ignored the exhortations to silence he directed at his black auditors.[48] If, however, Wheatley refused to "keep the door of my lips, that I may not offend with my tongue"—an exhortation she and other black followers would have found in Whitefield's "Prayer for a poor Negroe"—she nevertheless affirmed with her poetic voice Whitefield's sense of the special gratitude the slave owed to God "for bringing me over into a Christian country."[49] Wheatley's subjection to coerced migration undergoes transformation, through Whitefield's evangelism, into the grateful acknowledgment of providence in "On Being Brought" that has saddened and enraged so many readers from Wheatley's day to our own. With her trip to London in 1773, Wheatley got a taste of the astonishing free mobility that characterized Whitefield's circumatlantic ministry. But prior to that momentous trip, she had already begun to imagine, with the elegist's characteristic, if unconscious, grandiosity, taking Whitefield's place:

> Hail happy Saint on thy immortal throne!
> To thee complaints of grievance are unknown;
> We hear no more the music of thy tongue,
> Thy wonted auditories cease to throng.
> Thy lessons in unequal'd accents flow'd!
> While emulation in each bosom glow'd.

There is an implicit logic of substitution at work here, whereby Whitefield's death—his silencing—enables the music of the poet's tongue to seek "auditories" of its own, perhaps the same auditories, reassembled and differently addressed by the emulating African voice that Whitefield had sought to stifle.

There is also a logic of difference at work. It takes form most obviously in the protonational form of intercolonial identification, galvanized by events like the Boston Massacre. The reference in the 1770 broadside (see Figure 5) to streets "crimson'd with . . . gore" is excised from the 1773 London version, along with various other political and local references in a number of different poems.[50] Yet the sense of unifying grievance persists even in the expurgated version, where Wheatley continues to refer to "we *Americans*" as a bereaved collective, mourning Whitefield specifically as an advocate who "long'd to see *America* excel."[51] On one hand, Wheatley's self-identification as an "American" speaks to her sense of Whitefield's desire—however compromised by racial anxieties—for universal conversion and spiritual emancipation, and of the contribution Whitefield's intercolonial American ministry made to the emergence of revolutionary ideology. On the other hand, Wheatley's circumscription, within as well as beyond the world of religious revivalism, by racial ideology grounds the "grievance" and "complaints" of her Whitefield elegy in an experience of loss barely articulated but palpably felt, for example, in the references to "guiltless gore" and "the ORPHAN'S smart." It is hardly necessary to read such references as consciously subversive of American hypocrisy to recognize signs of unvoiced rage in Wheatley's images of the violence and political upheaval of late-eighteenth-century colonial America.

Yet the debate over Wheatley's conscious intentions continues to polarize and thereby hamper the critical discussion of her work. Wheatley's elegies have been read both as a subtle imaginative assault on the white European canon and as the subliterary impertinence of an African girl who found in vicarious mourning a means of gaining qualified social acceptance. She could have chosen no genre in which to specialize that would have accommodated better such divergent readings of her literary-historical significance. And the coincidence of her anomalous literary career with the emergence of U.S. nationhood fortuitously highlights elegy's place at the intersection in America of poetic traditions and national communities. For if Wheatley's singular status as a published black woman elegist isolates her achievement within what was in many ways a continuous eighteenth-century Anglo-American literary culture—one that survived even as it registered the rupture of

An ELEGIAC

POEM,

On the DEATH of that celebrated Divine, and eminent Servant of JESUS CHRIST, the late Reverend, and pious

GEORGE WHITEFIELD,

Chaplain to the Right Honourable the Countess of Huntingdon, &c. &c.

Who made his Exit from this tranfitory State, to dwell in the celeftial Realms of Blifs, on LORD's-Day, 30th of September, 1770, when he was feiz'd with a Fit of the Afthma, at Newbury-Port, near Boston, in New-England. In which is a Condolatory Addrefs to His truly noble Benefactrefs the worthy and pious Lady Huntingdon,---and the Orphan-Children in Georgia ; who, with many Thoufands, are left, by the Death of this great Man, to lament the Lofs of a Father, Friend, and Benefactor.

By Phillis, a Servant Girl of 17 Years of Age, belonging to Mr. J. Wheatley, of Boston :---And has been but 9 Years in this Country from Africa.

HAIL happy Saint on thy immortal throne !
   To thee complaints of grievance are unknown ;
We hear no more the mufic of thy tongue,
Thy wonted auditories ceafe to throng.
Thy leffons in unequal'd accents flow'd !
While emulation in each bofom glow'd ;
Thou didft, in ftrains of eloquence refin'd,
Inflame the foul, and captivate the mind.
Unhappy we, the fetting Sun deplore !
Which once was fplendid, but it fhines no more ;
He leaves this earth for Heaven's unmeafur'd height :
And worlds unknown, receive him from our fight ;
There WHITEFIELD wings, with rapid courfe his way,
And fails to Zion, through vaft feas of day.

When his AMERICANS were burden'd fore,
When ftreets were crimfon'd with their guiltlefs gore !
Unrival'd friendfhip in his breaft now ftrove :
The fruit thereof was charity and love
Towards America-----couldft thou do more
Than leave thy native home, the Britifh fhore,
To crofs the great Atlantic's wat'ry road,
To fee America's diftrefs'd abode ?
Thy prayers, great Saint, and thy inceffant cries,
Have pierc'd the bofom of thy native fkies !
Thou moon haft feen, and ye bright ftars of light
Have witnefs been of his requefts by night !
He pray'd that grace in every heart might dwell :
He long'd to fee America excell ;
He charg'd its youth to let the grace divine
Arife, and in their future actions fhine ;
He offer'd THAT he did himfelf receive,

A greater gift not GOD himfelf can give :
He urg'd the need of HIM to every one ;
It was no lefs than GOD's co-equal SON !
Take HIM ye wretched for your only good ;
Take HIM ye ftarving fouls to be your food.
Ye thirfty, come to this life giving ftream :
Ye Preachers, take him for your joyful theme :
Take HIM, " my dear AMERICANS," he faid,
Be your complaints in his kind bofom laid :
Take HIM ye Africans, he longs for you ;
Impartial SAVIOUR, is his title due :
If you will chufe to walk in grace's road,
You fhall be fons, and kings, and priefts to GOD.

Great COUNTESS ! we Americans revere
Thy name, and thus condole thy grief fincere :
We mourn with thee, that TOMB obfcurely plac'd,
In which thy Chaplain undifturb'd doth reft.
New-England fure, doth feel the ORPHAN's fmart ;
Reveals the true fenfations of his heart :
Since this fair Sun, withdraws his golden rays,
No more to brighten thefe diftrefsful days !
His lonely Tabernacle, fees no more
A WHITEFIELD landing on the Britifh fhore :
Then let us view him in yon azure fkies :
Let every mind with this lov'd object rife.
No more can he exert his lab'ring breath,
Seiz'd by the cruel meffenger of death.
What can his dear AMERICA return ?
But drop a tear upon his happy urn,
Thou tomb, fhalt fafe retain his facred truft,
Till life divine re-animate his duft.

Sold by EZEKIEL RUSSELL, in Queen-Street, and JOHN BOYLES, in Marlboro'-Street.

Figure 5. Phillis Wheatley, *An Elegiac Poem, On the Death of . . . George Whitefield* (Boston: Ezekiel Russell, 1770). Broadside. Courtesy of The Library Company of Philadelphia.

political independence—it also puts her at the beginning of an African-American countertradition in U.S. literature.

The complexity of the relation between such countertraditions and the continuity of poetic vocation gets expressed around, as well as in, Wheatley's elegiac practice. For instance, in a 1771 elegy for Whitefield, Jane Dunlap cites Wheatley's already famous poetic performance in terms that both accentuate its singularity and enroll it in a conventional discourse of competition among elegists: "Shall his due praises be so loudly sung," Dunlap asks, "By a young Afric damsels virgin tongue? / And I be silent!"[52] When Wheatley herself died in 1784, one pseudonymous elegist, "Horatio," praised the internationally known poet and prolific memorialist in terms of a conventional elegiac reproach: "shall the honour, which she oft apply'd, / To other's reliques, be to hers deny'd?"[53] Like Dunlap's competitive stance, this sort of challenging query is common in mourning poetry. Yet the application of literary honors to Wheatley remained an uncommon and gingerly proceeding, turning, as it had for the socially prominent Bostonian men (Mather Byles and Joseph Green among them) who vetted the initial publication of her book, upon questions of ownership and attestation:

O that the muse, dear spirit! own'd thy art,
To soften grief and captivate the heart,
Then should these lines in numbers soft array'd,
Preserve thy mem'ry from oblivion's shade.

Here Horatio quietly wraps the matter of literal ownership—not only of "thy art" but also of Wheatley's person—within an apostrophe that explicitly elevates Wheatley above the poet and his muse, and that also more subtly "owns" his debt to her through the use of the word *captivate,* one that Wheatley favored strongly for its enfolding of slavery and imagination.[54]

Horatio's imitation of Wheatley is a modest rejoinder to the pervasive, often overtly racist accusations of her formal imitativeness—accusations shortly to be encapsulated by Thomas Jefferson in *Notes on the State of Virginia.* Later in the poem, Horatio addresses more directly the racial bias of her critics:

What tho' her outward form did ne'er disclose
The lilly's white, or blushes of the rose;

> Shall sensibility regard the skin,
> If all be calm, serene, and pure within?

In the culturally specific problem of what particular bodies are imagined to reveal (the virtuous "lilly's white," the moral transparency of
"blushes"), Horatio's elegy locates the genre's perennial and fundamental concern with disclosures of "outward form"—with the relation,
that is, between generic convention and expressive authenticity. When
Jefferson, in *Notes*, pronounced this relation to be abrogated in poetry
by blacks like Wheatley, he was not only revealing a color consciousness grounded in the contemporary distinction between reason and
emotion but also framing notions of literary value and canonicity that
depend markedly on the corporeal:

> Misery is often the parent of the most affecting touches in poetry.—Among
> the blacks is misery enough, God knows, but no poetry. Love is the particu-
> lar oestrum of the poet. Their love is ardent, but it kindles the senses only,
> not the imagination. Religion indeed has produced a Phyllis Whately; but
> it could not produce a poet. The compositions published under her name
> are below the dignity of criticism. The heroes of the Dunciad are to her, as
> Hercules to the author of that poem.[55]

This passage—from the chapter in which Jefferson seeks to rationalize the political and juridical excision of non-whites from the national
body—is strongly characterized by images of generativity and embodiment: in its assertion of a genetic relation between misery and poetry,
in its explicit linking of sexual drive ("oestrum") and poetic production, and in its crushing analogy between Wheatley's poetic talent and
Pope's famous physical deformity.

Such language suggests that it is not Wheatley's conformity and
imitativeness as an elegist but rather her surprising appearance, as a
black woman, within the purview of criticism that troubles Jefferson,
prompting both his pompous assertion of criticism's "dignity" and
his illogical swipe (given his argument's investment in Wheatley's authorship) at the authenticity of the "compositions published under her
name." To condemn her verse, he discounts her misery. "Their griefs
are transient," he says of blacks earlier in the paragraph, and then goes
on to locate in Wheatley's body a barren misery—one without a proper

or lasting poetic issue. Jefferson's insistence upon the homology of grief and poetry is an index of elegy's important role in what Betsy Erkkila calls "one of the earliest instances of the politics of canon formation in post-Revolutionary America."[56] For the successful (intelligible, persuasive, authoritative) articulation of "misery" by a black woman threatened the representational politics of disembodied individuality upon which white male authority largely depended. In her elegies—focusing not on her own losses and privations but rather on those of white acquaintances and public figures—Wheatley invited and performed sympathetic identifications across racial boundaries.

Anxieties over the boundedness—formal as well as authorial—of elegy are nothing new, owing in large part to the genre's occasional and improvisatory nature. Its history in English is a compendium of verse forms and socioliterary aims, and adaptivity has been a salient feature of its traditionalism since its classical origins. Dennis Kay observes that elegy "had from ancient times been recognized as a form in which consciousness of tradition, repetition, translation, and imitation was inseparable from innovation and invention." The genre's development during the sixteenth and seventeenth centuries accentuated this self-reflexive principle and compounded elegiac proteanism with popular appeal. It became, says Kay, "a form which any educated person would have wished to try."[57] In the early life of the American colonies, the states of rhetorical and literary instruction, professional authorship, and literary theory were less conducive to self-conscious experimentation than they were in Britain, and elegy's historical importance in seventeenth-century New England culture as an instrument of communal stability and the consolidation of civic authority continued to obscure the genre's role as an instrument of literary and social change. Yet by the time "Hypercriticus" came to trace the American "Spirit of Elegy" in 1722 it had ceased to be (as the archive suggests it had been) the province of a Harvard-trained, ministerial elite: "there is scarce a Plow-Jogger or Country Cobler that has read our Psalms, and can make two Lines jingle, who has not once in his Life at least, exercised his Talent this way."[58] This satirical claim is, in itself, no reliable index to a lost archive of something like incipient proletarian elegy. But it suggests, at the very least, a vexed consciousness on the satirist's part of the genre's wide appeal and availability for imitation to nontraditional authors.

With respect to elegies by women, such vexation had already been surfacing in Anglo-American literary culture for decades. The Puritans especially, motivated by fears of declension, revived the ancient civic grievance against feminized mourning—against, that is, the politically disruptive affect and conduct of mourning women and also of men who, as Plato puts it in the *Republic,* "play the parts of women . . . possessed by grief and lamentation" (3.395d-e). For example, in his 1677 elegy for Thomas Shephard, Urian Oakes—himself shortly to become the vehicle of Cotton Mather's entry into a self-consciously male elegiac tradition—seeks to distinguish his effort from the ostensive triviality and insincerity of a female countertradition:

> Ah! Wit avails not, when th'Heart's like to break,
> Great griefs are Tongue-ti'ed, when the lesser speak.
> Away loose rein'd Careers of Poetry,
> The celebrated Sisters may be gone;
> We need no *Mourning Womens* Elegy,
> No forc'd, affected, artificial Tone.[59]

Oakes arrogates responsibility for expressing and mitigating the cardiac peril of "Great griefs" to the embattled eloquence of a similarly elevated or intensified style—a style he clearly wants to distinguish from female mourners' "lesser" techniques of complaint. However, the overlapping gendered hierarchies of sensibility and genre that structure Oakes's defense of fraternal elegy are unstable from the start. His own elegy affects to strain after the excess its control and conventionalism belie, and the authorizing model he cites repeatedly throughout—David's dirge for Jonathan in 2 Samuel 1—was also a frequent model for female elegists, including Anne Bradstreet.

To a great extent, the existence of a significant body of elegiac verse by seventeenth-century American women writers—who had comparatively little opportunity or encouragement for publication—must be inferred from comments like Oakes's. The foremost exception is the poetry of Bradstreet, the singularity of whose achievement was stressed, even by some of her encomiasts, as a way of shoring up distinctions between male and female literary traditions. Cotton Mather, for instance, reaches back to remote figures of female achievement such as the martyred mathematician Hypatia of Alexandria, Pindar's rival poet Corinna of Tanagra, and the Empress Eudocia of Byzantium in order to rarify a poet who herself directly engaged a far more relevant and proximate tradition.[60]

In her elegies for European poets, for instance, Bradstreet discovers a troubled consciousness of cultural circumstance that has only partly to do with gender. In contrast to Mather's local pride in not having to "travel as far as Europe for an Elegy," Bradstreet seems to feel the thread of her Englishness slipping away as she belatedly mourns the national poet-hero Philip Sidney. Although she refers in her elegy for Sidney to "our British land" and "our British tongue," and is concerned that "none disallow of these my strains / Whilst English blood yet runs within my veins," she nevertheless finds that the link between mourning, writing poetry, and being English is difficult to maintain for a poet writing in America. "So," she concludes, "Sidney's fame I leave to England's roles, / His bones do lie interred in stately Paul's."[61]

Because it comes after the staging of the poet's expulsion from Parnassus, where hostile muses are enraged by her effort to praise Sidney, Celeste Schenck reads this demurral as evidence of Bradstreet's inability to triumph over elegy's "patriarchal constraints," specifically the genre's function "as a ritual of poetic consecration during the course of which a new poet presents himself as heir to the tradition." Citing as evidence such lines as "Thy fame and praise is far beyond my strain," Schenck argues from Bradstreet's example that "early female elegists deplore their own inadequacies."[62] But Schenck is too quick to assume that a female poet's self-consciousness about gender, which does of course constitute important *materia poetica* for Bradstreet, is the ultimate meaning of all protestations of inadequacy. Such gestures abound in elegies by men as well—in Spenser's elegy for Sidney, for instance, and in the same tribute to Shephard that contains Oakes's attack on "*Womens* Elegy." The modesty topos is a convention whose adoption itself often constitutes part of the ritual entry into elegiac tradition for male and female poets alike. Bradstreet's use of it could reasonably be read as a sign of her sense of *adequacy* to that tradition. It is a tradition into which she writes herself by successfully adapting generic conventions to the potentially disqualifying specificity of female authorship.

Bradstreet's example may have helped to make female authorship itself a qualifying aspect of elegiac performance. In 1733, *The New-England Weekly Journal* published "*A Lamentation &c. On the Death of a* Child" with the following prefatory remark:

> The following Lines, (compos'd by a tender Mother, not far from this Place,) on the Death of a most forward, amiable and hopeful Child, was lately left with us for a Publication, without her Knowledge, and without the least Alteration.[63]

The stated circumstances of the poem's composition and publication strongly suggest those of Bradstreet's own verses, and the poem itself seems in many of its tropes and images to hearken back to Bradstreet's elegies for her grandchildren. In turn, the appearance of increasing numbers of poems by women in early-eighteenth-century newspapers and magazines undoubtedly encouraged others to write and to publish. Yet even as the development of periodical culture helped augment the archive of colonial women's poetry, the conventional anonymity of print complicated the significance of women's authorial roles. For with its authorship unconfirmed, the "Lamentation" may be read not only as the authentic expression of "a tender Mother" but also as an act of literary impersonation. Regardless of who wrote it, the poem's appearance in a newspaper helps endow women's writing as such with public importance, while at the same time reinforcing associations of domesticity and passivity ("without her Knowledge") that delimit women's literary emergence.

Eighteenth-century male elegists contributed both to the accelerating pace of this emergence and to the policing of women's social roles by writing more and more elegies about female subjects. For example, while Cotton Mather publicly celebrated women's literacy and virtue in his elegies for Mary Brown (1703) and Sarah Leveret (1705), he also used these occasions to remind parents of their duty to raise pious and tractable mates for the "*Sons* of Men."[64] The opening lines of his elegy for Brown announce (somewhat archly to be sure, as if he cannot help himself) the need for men—those "Monopolizing HEE's"—to step out of the limelight generated by their own mutual praise and make room for exemplary women. Women's worth, though, continues to be measured against an ideal of fitness for domestic service in patriarchal households ("the Skill an House to *Guide & Feed*").[65] Nicholas Noyes addresses his 1710 broadside elegy for Mary Gerish to an explicitly female audience. The poem begins, "Fair Ladies see, (if you can see for Teares) / How Death regards not either Sex, or Years," as if simultaneously to own the importance of female readers and to warn them not to take the sheltered domesticity of "Daughter, Sister, Wife of Youth, and Mother" for granted.[66] Along with such admonishments, the authority of speech and the voice of print are evermore likely to be features of memorial tributes to women. Thus, in his 1713 broadside elegy for Elizabeth Hutchinson, John Danforth alerts his female readers to the proximity of death through a prosopopoeia of his subject: "from the very *Tomb*; / She calls aloud; 'LADIES, BE READY.'"[67] And in his 1724 broadside elegy for Susanna Thacher, feminine virtue is endowed with documentary authority: "A Practick Transcript of the Heav'nly Volume; / Each Line and Letter Bright, in every Column."[68]

Female elegists, too, traded more and more on the authority of the female voice—their own and that of other women—with mixed responses. For example, when Benjamin Tompson, the renowned poet and prolific elegist, died in 1714, his half-sister Anna Tompson Hayden wrote an elegy for him, preserved in their brother Joseph's journal. Joseph appended a note to his transcription of the poem, saying that he had kept it "not for the poetry, but for the love & spirit of Christian spirit breathing in them." The gratuitous judgment now has the effect, of course, of driving the reader back to the poem, determined to discover unrecognized felicities. And while the poem is meager (as are many of her brother's), Hayden does not entirely disappoint. For in her effort to characterize and entwine the social manifestations of death and of quotidian parting, she comes up with an arresting couplet: "Thus we daily drop away & take our flight / Both from each others Company & sight."[69] There is an artful and exquisite tension here between the routine effortlessness of "daily drop away" and the preparatory alertness of "take our flight." Which is the better metaphor for death: relinquishment or escape? And with what profit might we attend more closely to our innumerable rehearsals for that final flight from man to God? How might poetry serve the need for intensified attention?

Memento mori is the implicit epigraph of all elegies. (The phrase is also often found carved into woodcut illustrations at the head of broadside elegies.) But the shared, or collective, memory of death—the mindfulness of dying—is contingent rather than transhistorical. It depends, for example, on the shifting relation between what Paul Connerton calls incorporating practices (characteristic or socially appropriate postures of the body) and inscribing practices (durable, transmissible artifacts of memory that do not require the body's presence).[70] Traditionally, women have been more closely associated with incorporating practices of mourning (recall Samuel Willard's allusion to the professional mourning women who are called upon to weep over the destruction of Jerusalem). In the early eighteenth century, the societies of British North America were trying to establish acceptable limits to women's participation in the inscribing practices of mourning from which they had been traditionally excluded.

The consequences of this historical shift in the way death is remembered were mixed, especially for women. For if, as the subjects as well as the authors of increasing numbers of elegies, women realized some of the dignity conferred by memorialization, they also became increasingly visible as figures of alterity and disruption. By the mid-nineteenth century, the reciprocity of death and femininity would form the basis of one of antebellum culture's most notorious aesthetics: Poe's claim in "The Philosophy of Composition" (1846) that "the death . . . of a beautiful woman is, unquestionably, the most poetic topic in the world."[71] For teenaged Benjamin Franklin a century earlier, the thanato-erotic inflection is absent, and the aesthetic stakes are considerably lower. Yet his own satirical criticism of elegy also links representations of gender and mourning to social anxieties about women's roles. Indeed, the vantage of liberated widowhood from which Franklin, writing as Silence Dogood, blasts the New England elegy's weak submission to outworn conventions is implicated in the more significant constraints of the genre's patriarchalism. The seventh Dogood letter is but one installment in an extended critique of Puritan institutions and colonial authority, at the center of which is the exclusively male elegy-factory of

Harvard College. The satire's blunter edge is directed at student poet-izers, whose "empty Sculls" are said to be the proper mixing pot for the clichés, tears, and latinisms that seemed requisite to elegiac perfor-mance. But by choosing an elegy for a woman, rather than one for a man, as the object of a woman's ridicule, Franklin enables subtler forms of satire as well. For instance, by homing in on the elegist's "Threefold Appellation" of Mrs. Kitel, Franklin exposes the bathos of her aggran-dizement while also poking fun at the trinitarian mystery:

> [The poet] gives his Reader a Sort of an Idea of the Death of *Three Persons,* viz.
>> —*a Wife, a Daughter, and a Sister,*
> which is *Three Times* as great a Loss as the Death of *One,* and consequently must raise *Three Times* as much Grief and Compassion in the Reader.

The trivialization of women's roles is, through Franklin's imposture, inseparable from his female persona's trivialization of what is not only a fundamental Christian doctrine but also a spiritualized image of male self-sufficiency, a divine masculine parthenogenesis.

Winking once again at female assertion in the "*RECEIPT to make a* New-England *Funeral ELEGY*" (supposedly bequeathed by her late husband the country minister), Dogood notes the formula's applicabili-ty to female subjects, "*provided you borrow a greater quantity of Virtues, Excellencies,* &c."[72] The association of femininity and borrowed virtue teases contemporary apprehensiveness about women who, like the sub-ject of Pope's "Elegy to the Memory of an Unfortunate Lady" (1717) and like Silence Dogood herself, do not conform to social or religious norms. "To emphasize the paradigm of the 'virtuous woman,'" writes Cheryl Walker in her study of images of women in early American poetry, "is to suggest the fear of what unvirtuous women could bring to pass: the destruction of hierarchy, collapsing of distances, erasing of distinctions."[73] Short of imagining such apocalyptic consequences of fe-male waywardness, Franklin's satire challenges assumptions about gen-der roles, anticipating the problems gender asymmetry would pose for an increasingly plural and secular society on the verge of nationhood.

Even within an earlier Puritan worldview, such apocalyptic conse-quences never seemed creditable to female *literary* waywardness. Women like Ann Yale Hopkins—who according to John Winthrop had "fallen into a sad infirmity, the loss of her understanding and reason, which had been growing upon her divers years by occasion of her giving herself wholly to reading and writing"—hurt *themselves* by reading and writing.[74] They represented a tear in the social fabric rather than the threat of its systematic unraveling. Yet, as Mitchell Breitwieser notes, with emphasis on the coercive dimension of the "separate spheres" metaphor, women's "confinement to the minor" persisted in New England literary culture from the seventeenth to the nineteenth century.[75] To the extent that the metaphor of confinement holds, it might be thought to designate not a pristine "separate sphere" but a kind of cell network across which the pressures of gender asymmetry get articulated.

For example, recent work on eighteenth-century women's poetry in America suggests that the printed—and thus usually anonymous or pseudonymous and often authorially suspect—exempla of the particularity of women's tradition are less significant than the evidence of active networks of manuscript circulation among known poets like Susanna Wright (1697–1785), Hannah Griffitts (1727–1817), Annis Boudinot Stockton (1736–1801), and Elizabeth Graeme Fergusson (1737–1801).[76] Such "sororal networks," according to Carla Mulford, not only encouraged women's literary development but even "served to create for them a sense of community in an eighteenth-century world that left them largely isolated on farms or family estates, a world in which their actions, outside the home, would almost always be called into question."[77] The familiar presence of death and the privations of loss colored and intensified such isolation in ways that were commonly expressed through elegies—elegies that, in turn, helped to sustain and extend social bonds among survivors, and to figure the expanded social and civil roles that death and mourning, ironically, opened up for many women.

The elegies of Annis Boudinot Stockton are a case in point. Between 1757 and 1791, Stockton wrote at least three dozen elegies, most of which fall into three general groupings based on subject: at least seven are for her husband, Richard Stockton; twice that many are for female friends and relations, including Frances Ramsey and Rachel Wilson; and another handful are for male public figures like General Montgomery and Benjamin Franklin. But Stockton's elegiac practice also frustrates these

descriptive conveniences. For instance, one untitled elegy for her husband, taking the form of a pastoral dialogue between Stockton and her
friend Elizabeth Graeme Fergusson, makes it a matter of doubt whether
the chief cause for lamentation and rebuke is Richard Stockton's death
or the alienating effects upon friendship of grief for a spouse.[78] In her
elegies for female friends, Stockton not only reflects upon the affective
life of "sororal networks" but also often strongly identifies with their
widowed husbands, many of whom played prominent political roles in
the drama of national formation. And her elegy for Franklin figures a
sentimental vision of political community in a poem that memorializes
both a shared national "forefather" and Stockton's childhood next-door
neighbor.

Indeed, Stockton's elegiac practice highlights the genre's tendency to
defy presumptive literary boundaries between public and private, male
and female, rational and sentimental. Such distinctions remain far
less fully deconstructed with respect to early American poetic genres
than, say, the novel—to take the most obvious and important counter-
example. The record of Stockton's practice strongly encourages consideration of what gets left behind in currently neglected poetic forms, like
elegy, and how and to what end it might be recovered.

The memorialization of Richard Stockton was an elegiac project
that occupied his widow for at least a decade—one in which her own
and her husband's legacies are intricately bound together.[79] Her elegies figure the couple's relationship as, in large part, a history of relinquishment and self-denial in the service of nationalizing interests,
highlights of which include her husband's ambivalent conversion from
loyal subject to revolutionary, the war's hastening of his death, her own
experience of the disruption of domestic life, and her abandonment of
her manuscripts under threat of British invasion. Annis Stockton memorializes these and other aspects of their personal histories as part of
the drama of nation formation. In doing so, she also meditates on how
much like uncompleted grief work the experience of nationalism feels.
The dynamics of individual and collective mourning figured in her poetic project—dynamics later given more precise formulation in psychoanalytic theory—anticipate parallel developments in the theory of
nationalism, from Walter Benjamin to Benedict Anderson to Zygmunt

Bauman, for all of whom nationalism seems to function less like a political ideology than like a new style of mourning.[80]

This new style, so to speak, got entextualized in old genres, among
them elegy: at once the most elite and demotic of mourning genres in
the Revolutionary and early national periods. It was a kind of poetry
that involved—both as reading matter and as something to venture
writing oneself—virtually all reasonably literate people, both for its
classical authority and for its popular appeal. Stockton's spousal elegies
remember the past and contract with the future in a variety of ways: as
testaments to the sufficiency of personal memory as well as to the need
for public memorialization, as highly occasional remembrances and as
less event-oriented meditations, as printed texts and as manuscripts intended for more limited circulation, as contributions to emergent communities of women writers and as entries into an ancient and highly
patriarchal genre, and as both literary and artifactual legacies.

All of these mechanisms of transmission come together in the 1782
newspaper printing of an elegy for Richard Stockton in the *New Jersey
Gazette*. The poem is prefaced by a brief note, probably by Stockton
family friend Aaron Burr:

> The following little ode, written by a lady on the anniversary of her hus-
> band's death, tho' it deserves a more lasting remembrance than a Gazette
> can give it, yet, in the mean-time, may serve to entertain your ingenious
> readers. Sent to me as a friend, I have to beg her excuse for thus exposing
> her grief to the eyes of the publick, while I wish to shew it her wit.[81]

This breezy meditation on the temporality of fame is full of ambivalence
about the text it introduces. It reveals both the impulse to hold apart
the aforementioned categories—public/private, male/female, rational/
sentimental—and the difficulty of doing so. It calls the poem a "little
ode," implying with a clearly gendered inflection something at once
trivial and grand. The writer registers his exposure of the poet's grief as
his personal betrayal of her private communication, yet he also claims
justification for his act in the public exhibition of "her wit." The poem
"deserves," he says, "lasting remembrance." But it will serve, "in the
mean-time," as light entertainment for newspaper readers.

Remarkably, publicly managing the *poem's* remembrance (for that is the task he has taken on) seems to have nothing to do with the person the poem remembers: Richard Stockton, an important royal appointee turned revolutionary, and a signer of the Declaration of Independence. Why should there be no mention of his name nor any more direct allusion to his status? Burr *does* seem still to feel some duty to protect the identity of the poet whose confidence he has betrayed. And, of course—"in the mean-time" of newspapers and revolutions—many contemporary readers of the *New Jersey Gazette* would easily have recognized an elegy for Richard Stockton, one of the region's most socially and politically prominent citizens. Burr's reticence about the identity of the elegy's author and subject is surely in part an unremarkable effect of the pressures of literary convention and social decorum. In 1780s mid-Atlantic U.S. culture, their identities would have been an open secret. Thus there would have been no need for him to name the Stocktons directly in order to take advantage of their local and even national celebrity to draw attention to the poem. Yet Burr also predicts, in his appeal for "lasting remembrance," the need for a different kind of fame management—one that would *not* depend on the poem's embeddedness in local history.

Annis Stockton's poem itself anticipates this need. It is, most plainly, a pastoral elegy—full of that mode's conventional displacements away from historical concretion and topicality—and thus it makes its own generic appeal for lasting remembrance independent of historicist reading. It aspires to traditionality and to the temporal stability of the mourning space opened up by pastoral convention. This aspiration to traditionality resulted in a series of elegies composed by Annis Stockton at regularly spaced intervals. Memorializing her husband was, as I have said, an elegiac project that occupied her for over a decade, resulting in at least eight extant poems, several of which, like this one, were written on the anniversary of his death. In this first anniversary poem, Stockton organizes both her experience of mourning and the poetic utterance that gives shape to it around the cyclical performance of a private act of remembrance:

Oh! on this day may each revolving year,
Be mark'd by nature's sympathetic groan!

Nor sighing gales, deny the pitying tear,
While at his tomb, I make my silent moan! (25–28)

Here, the seasonal revolutions of "each revolving year" impose a kind of order and continuity upon the naturalized images of political upheaval (howling tempests, screaming winds, dreadful blasts) with which the poem begins. Stockton's family was thrown into crisis during the war. In 1776, they were forced to flee their home, which was subsequently ransacked. And later that year Richard Stockton was imprisoned by the British for several months under appalling conditions of hunger and exposure. These circumstances probably contributed significantly to his long, agonizing death from cancer of the mouth between 1778 and 1781. But by naturalizing the historical forces with which she and her husband contended, the elegy makes Richard Stockton seem to have died out of the national history he helped to engender.

That is, the suppression of Richard Stockton's historical role might seem to be the cost of "lasting remembrance" for the poem that remembers him. Yet the economy of memory here is even more complex than that, in part because Annis Stockton depicts her *own* relation to historical time as one subverted by the self-reflexiveness of mourning. She represents herself as suffering from terminal reminiscence:

What avails my sorrows' sad complaint,
While in the grave my Lucius breathless lies?
The turf enshrines the dust; the skies the saint;
But left behind the hapless mourner dies. (13–16)

"Left behind," Stockton produces a sequence of poems that, taken together, constitute a self-conscious narrative of what she calls "resignation." The final elegy we have by Stockton for her husband is titled "Resignation," and the word *resign* figures punningly throughout the sequence as a way of joining together images of relinquishment, stoic acceptance, and writing, or signing.[82] Indeed, Stockton's trope of resignation quietly enfolds her husband's ascriptive identity as "signer." It mutes the privilege of this historical identity, and it fashions a mode of relation to her dead husband, as well as to poetic production, that does not depend on public act or public response.

What Timothy Sweet calls pastoral's interdiction of history may well have been one of Stockton's aims in writing a pastoral elegy for her husband, in order both to figure some sort of stable posthumous relation to him and to ensure a future for the poem that seeks to repair his loss.[83] But Stockton's relation to history, too, remains destabilized by the circumstances of her mourning. For example, alienation from historical time is, in a sense, a condition of her poetic mourning as a female elegist. The pastoral elegy tradition whose conventions she wields is resolutely male-centered; indeed, it often seems predicated on a kind of literary-masculine parthenogenesis linking older and younger male poets. Thus, pastoral elegies by and about women frequently express a consciousness—sometimes arch, sometimes dispirited—of the masculinization of literary tradition. In Annis Stockton's place and time, the gendering of literary traditionalism was also implicated in the gendering of political and revolutionary discourse. Her honorary membership in literary Princeton's Whig Society, for example, was an unprecedented concession made to her gender in thanks for her aid in keeping some of their politically sensitive papers out of the hands of British troops during the war. Despite some real progressivism in republican thinking about gender relations, nation formation in the Revolution's aftermath continued to depend on models of transgenerational survival that shored up the idea of male control, for example, by circumscribing or disqualifying a biologically determined role for women in the fashioning of sociopolitical continuity. Linda Kerber has described this exclusion of women from historical time as the "inherent paradox of Republican Motherhood."[84]

At one point in Stockton's elegy, grief for her husband registers explicitly as something that interferes with maternal responsibility:

No change of circumstance, no varying scene,
Can draw the deep, envenom'd, barbed dart:
Tho' care maternal, prompts the look serene;
The anxious sigh, still wrings the mother's heart. (21–24)

Here, proper solicitousness for her children—including the son, Richard, who had already inherited the family estate upon his father's death—seems to require that mourning not obtrude upon her relations with them. "Care maternal" is a reminder both of how the pressures of Revolutionary history impinge on Stockton's mourning and of the extent to which, in contemporary narratives of women's lives especially, children conventionally trump other possible forms of personal survival. Her 1787 anniversary elegy naturalizes her own displacement by the person of young Richard, to whom it is inscribed. When Stockton herself shall be, as she puts it, "hid beneath the turf clad ground," her son, not her poetry, will secure the future for her husband:

> All that a mothers fondest hopes require—
> I find in him, and now my heart revives—
> The *genius Form* the *virtues* of his Sire—
> And in Alexis all my Lucius lives.—[85]

There are two dramas being played out here, as they are throughout Stockton's cycle of elegies for her husband: reciprocal dramas of revivification ("my heart revives") and recuperation ("my Lucius lives"). Stockton seeks to recover in two senses: to get rid of the grief that plagues her, and to get hold of the person she has lost. The apparent cost of this dual recovery in the poem is the sacrifice of the possibility of her own personal survival. Her husband "lives," while she lies "hid beneath the turf clad ground."

A decade earlier, as British troops descended on Princeton, Stockton had apparently elected to sacrifice quantities of personal papers—including some of her manuscript poems—in order to save the papers of the nearby Whig Society, which she preserved by hiding them "beneath the turf clad ground" in her backyard. This anecdote of recovery, presented thus in a variety of sources, shows Stockton participating in historical time through the rescue of public documents at the cost of her own writings.[86] There is an economy of inheritance implied, both in the Stockton mythology and in her own elegiac poetry, in which to preserve something for the future entails the abandonment of something else, and her 1782 elegy for Richard Stockton concludes with a stanza on his place within the analogous economy of nationalism:

> In times when civil discord holds her court;
> And vice triumphant, keeps his ancient post:
> When most is needed, such a firm support,
> They mourn with me, their friend and patron lost. (45–48)

For Stockton, the circumstances of personal grief adjust themselves to the distress and instability of the civic body, which in turn finds mourning not only a socializing process ("They mourn with me") but also a nationalizing one. Grief perpetuates national affiliation in the face of "civil discord" at the cost of departicularizing individual deaths and individual griefs; Richard Stockton becomes, for one and all, the "friend and patron lost."

In her 1787 anniversary elegy, Annis Stockton defines mourning as the perpetuation of the wish to "exclud[e] woes that cluster thick behind." This is an apt definition in its recognition of the endless antagonism between the pressure to remember particular losses and the pressure to move, in a less encumbered way, into the historical future. It is also an apt definition of nationalism—one that anticipates an important strain in later theoretical work on the temporality of nationalism specifically. In Stockton's 1782 elegy she represents that temporality as the time frame of mourning Richard Stockton: "When most is needed, such a firm support, / They mourn." The nation, like Stockton, exists, in other words, within the "mean-time" of mourning. Much later, Freud would recognize—without ever feeling he had solved—the problem of the "mean-time."

One of the puzzles Freud confronts in "Mourning and Melancholia" is the fact that reality testing is never immediately successful. Respect for reality comes by and by. Indeed, for Freud, mourning does not just happen *in* but essentially *is* "the meantime [during which] the existence of the lost object is psychically prolonged."[87] With the mediating influence of Walter Benjamin's "Theses on the Philosophy of History," Benedict Anderson tropes upon Freud's psychological insight and develops a historical insight of his own regarding the modern emergence of a new experience of what he calls "temporal coincidence," or "simultaneity." Anderson emphasizes the importance of the newspaper and the novel as providing the technical means for representing this new simultaneity (this "meanwhile," as he also calls it) as the imaginary condition of national experience.[88]

Anderson's enormous influence on American studies has thus helped to solidify the novel's paradigmatic status in most contemporary narratives of American literary history. A consequence has been to overlook other kinds of American literature and the ways in which they might enhance our understanding of early national experience. Annis Stockton's elegies are an excellent example. For her, nationalism inheres in the mean-time, rather than existing as a "meanwhile." Instead of Anderson's "simultaneity," her strongest experience is of an acutely attentive *suspension between*: something closer to what Zygmunt Bauman has called "vigilance," or "national nervousness," and which is also a sharp characterization of the desperate idealizations of mourning. "In a perverse way," Bauman writes,

> nationalism's universalistic disguise is a tribute which the group's selfishness must pay to the humanity of its members. Yet the inner contradiction which results makes of all nationalisms endemically unfulfilled—and in all probability unfulfillable—projects. Nationalism must be forever unsatisfied with every concrete sedimentation of its past labors.[89]

Annis Stockton's series of elegies—each one motivated by the somehow unsatisfactory nature of the earlier poems, ever to be revised and replaced until death—would seem to constitute a very non-novelistic narrative of national experience: an uneasy tribute that she pays, perhaps, to her imagined national community for joining her, however selfishly, however futilely, in her attempt to "exclud[e] the woes that cluster thick behind."

In post-Revolutionary America, Stockton was by no means the only person for whom the experience of nationalization frequently meant mourning the loss of the particular. The contradictions of the past and the idiosyncrasies of the present continuously threatened the imaginative coherence and cohesion of the new national community. As a ground of meaning and a mechanism of community, sympathy with the bereaved and with the dead themselves took on increasingly pervasive and explicit importance, fostering radical as well as conservative impulses. This was true in England as well, of course. But in America, the national capacity for sympathizing with the dead seems to have been haunted more tenaciously, more presently, by the casualties of its imperial history. In American elegy, the pressures of unavowed mourning often get figured in the oblique or particularized relations to the genre of the displaced and the destroyed, of the civilly and socially dead. American Indians, for example, get filled with meaning in lieu of death. In American elegy, Indians often serve as the imaginative correlative of the political war nationalism wages against difference.

The assertion of distinctly American interests in the Revolutionary era depended in large part on strategic acts of reversal whereby Englishman and Indian alike were rendered alien. In his inspirational first *American Crisis* essay, published at the end of 1776 when Washington's army was at its weakest, Tom Paine draws a parallel between the British troops who threaten the "home counties" and the Indians who threaten the "back counties."[90] Both are depicted as invaders from without, rather than as groups that have themselves been displaced. Americans are those who will defend the newly independent states against the incursions of strangers. After the war, new political contexts for these anxious encounters, such as the Treaty of Paris and the federalization of Indian policy, helped to rationalize and reduce the instabilities of conflict. Poets of the early national period faced the challenge of developing new imaginative contexts for these encounters as well—imaginative contexts that would give form to chaotic experience at both the real and ideal frontiers of a new society.

Death, of course, is the ultimate frontier problem. It can be approached and tamed through religious or philosophical inquiry. It can be represented in art. It can even be pushed back by medical science. Franklin, along with Enlightenment peers like Condorcet, anticipated quantum improvements in healing technologies and wondered if the human life span might not be increased indefinitely.[91] But not even these apostles of progress imagined a world that was not trimmed with black borders like a broadside elegy. As Hamlet lamented, there would always be an undiscovered country, and the Enlightenment emphasis on the idea of death's constructedness helped refocus attention on the reportable realm of human culture.

In eighteenth-century British America, Indians were kept at the margin of that reportable realm. Approached and tamed through inquiry, represented in art, they were also pushed back by violence and disease. Eschatologists of various stripes might fantasize about the death of death, but Indian extinction was a real and seemingly inevitable effect of European settlement. As Indian societies receded, however, they left behind evidence of their own symbolic relation to death and immortality. More than simple memento mori, Indian grave goods and burial sites were the physical residuum of the metaphysics of Indian hating. They stood, as perhaps no white graveyard could, for the dead's estrangement from the living. Writing of the fresh graves of Revolutionary soldiers in his 1781 elegy "To the Memory of the Brave Americans," Philip Freneau embraces fellowship with the departed "patriot band."[92] But unlike this nationalistic meditation on death, which ends with images of happiness and sunshine, Freneau's 1787 "Lines occasioned by a visit to an old Indian burying ground" foregrounds the difference of Indian deathways and ends by projecting a future of "shadows and delusions."[93]

Yet rather than depicting a place where the reciprocal figures of death and the Indian might be thoroughly othered and contained, Freneau's poem enacts a blurring of borders that reflects its historical moment. The previous decade's struggle for independence had involved rebelling colonists in various assertions of disjunction and estrangement from the living populations—English as well as Indian—they sought to displace. In the aftermath of separation, these assertions faltered before cultural allegiance to England and the complexity of jurisdictional disputes with Indian societies. At the same time, dreams of national continuity were interrupted by nightmares of dangerous, erratic activity, as when Revolutionary veterans launched an internal rebellion in western Massachusetts.

Under such circumstances, artifacts of Indian mortuary practice were perhaps especially likely to provoke certain intense strains of thinking regarding the primal encounter from which ideas of continuity stem: that is, the encounter with the dead.[94] Freneau's "visit" to an Indian burying ground inspires thoughts about the relation between the dead and the living that are further complicated by the unsettlement of the Indian dead. In this setting, he does not, for example, share that sense of fellowship in death enjoyed by the speaker of Thomas Gray's "Elegy Written in a Country Churchyard." Gray's churchyard reflects an entire social—indeed national—order. But Freneau's Indian burying ground is a far less stable metonymy for the newly independent United States. In Gray's churchyard, the "rude Forefathers of the hamlet sleep" in eternally regimented rows,[95] while in Freneau's poem, the Indians he refers to as "the ancients of these lands" (5) are restless and unconstrained. In death as in life, they seem to lack a settled relation to the land, a shortcoming conventionally ascribed to Indians and used as a legal justification for their dispossession. Imaginative dispossession, Freneau's poem suggests, will be harder to achieve.

The "visit" Freneau refers to in his title may or may not have occurred in fact. As a Philadelphian he lived in proximity to various Delaware tribal cemeteries, but there is no evidence that his subject is a particular site or even a particular tribal culture. Indeed, one possible source for the poem is the account of Sioux burial practices in Jonathan Carver's *Travels*.[96] Freneau's tendency to dwell on the problem of human mortality led him to respond strongly to literature from which knowledge of the dead and of deathways could be derived—not only descriptive accounts like Carver's but also imaginative works that made no claim to veracity, such as Joseph Warton's 1748 poem "The Dying Indian" and its many British and American successors in the genre. Freneau's encounter with the dead in his Indian burying ground is largely, if not wholly, mediated by literature. Indeed, it is the representation of an encounter embedded in European conventions of noble savagism and pastoral elegy.

Yet amid these fanciful conventions, the strangeness of fact asserts itself. That Indian burial practices are different from European ones is the distinction with which the poem begins. But it is really a double distinction, one that complicates from the start our sense of the speaker's relation to both Indian and European culture:

> In spite of all the learn'd have said,
> I still my old opinion keep;
> The posture that we give the dead,
> Points out the soul's eternal sleep.
> Not so the ancients of these lands . . . (1–5)

In these lines, the speaker positions himself between and in contrast to two theories of the soul's activity after death: one identified with European or colonial thought, the other inferred from North American Indian burial practices the poem goes on to describe. In the Indian burying ground, possible skepticism regarding orthodox views of the afterlife meets the progressive impulse to treat human experience comparatively. Freneau professes to adhere to his "old opinion" as to what European burial customs signify—"the soul's eternal sleep"—despite learned assurances of the soul's posthumous activity. Where orthodox theology fails, however, Indian deathways succeed at least in jostling his doubts about personal immortality to the extent that they inspire a poem about another culture's belief in a vigorous afterlife, in a dream of continuity.

The confused temporality of the poem's first five lines is symptomatic of Freneau's ambivalence. His *old* opinion seems logically to precede what the "learn'd have said," yet his is the newer, Enlightenment position—at once preoccupied with and skeptical of the doctrine of immortality. And the Indian *"ancients,"* whose remains, at least, have resisted dispossession, were also Freneau's contemporaries, predecessors who endured still and who continued even after the Revolutionary War had ended to interfere with colonial Anglo-America's smooth transition to independent nationhood. The resistance to diachronic arrangement revealed in the opening lines of Freneau's poem finds a much more confident counterpart in the writings of those architects of transition, like Jefferson and Paine, who had a taste for disjunction. "We are brought at once," Paine wrote with reference to the American Constitution, "to the point of seeing government begin, as if we had lived in the beginning of time. The real volume, not of history, but of facts, is directly before us, unmutilated by contrivance, or the errors of tradition."[97]

The Constitution itself, "unmutilated by contrivance, or the errors of tradition," is for Paine a kind of origin, and origins, for him, are a matter of presentation, "of facts . . . directly before us." Freneau—who was virtually silent about the Constitution as it was being drafted and debated—is interested in texts that, despite contrivance and error, reveal a correlative tendency. Death can only be a matter of representation, and, like its British elegiac antecedents, Freneau's Indian burying ground poem depends for its illusory encounter with the dead upon an image of difficult reading. The epitaphic, monumental text within the text of the poem is "a lofty rock,"

On which the curious eye may trace,
(Now wasted half by wearing rains)
The fancies of a ruder race. (22–24)

The faded inscriptions of one's forebears (the "dusty heraldry and lines" of George Herbert's 1633 poem "Church-Monuments," for example) become here the hieroglyphics of another race. The stranger's "curious eye" may "trace" but presumably cannot discern and read these "fancies." He cannot, as Herbert's speaker learns to do, "spell his elements" or "find his birth" written in them.[98]

He might, however, fancy that he could—fancy that the tracings on the Indian burying ground's "lofty rock" could sound out for him a new and necessary lineage. Fancy, in fact, competes with reason's estrangement in the poem to supply the place of available traditions. Initially, Freneau's speaker presents himself as an advocate both for the burial artifacts themselves and for the integrity of the culture they represent:

Thou, stranger, that shall come this way,
No fraud upon the dead commit,
Yet, mark the swelling turf and say,
They do not lie, but there they sit. (17–20)

Borrowing the language of epitaph—the hailing of the stranger—he is already in some sense speaking in place of the dead, as though the poem itself were a kind of Indian gravestone—a substitute for the "lofty rock" with its illegible tracings as described in the following stanza. The speaker makes these tracings legible again by associating the "fancies" he imagines depicted by them with the operations of poetic fancy in the poem. Pastoral conventions like the "aged elm," "the children of the forest," the "midnight moons" and "moist'ning dews," along with the uncanny image of the "restless Indian queen," which looks forward to Brown's Queen Mab in *Edgar Huntly*—all of these comprise a catalog of elements, beginning with the "lofty rock," seen or imagined by the speaker as part of the landscape. At the same time, due to the ambiguity of Freneau's language, the scenes described can be understood as "fancies" depicted "here" upon the rock itself.

Freneau's use of the deictic *here,* which occurs four times in the poem, seems initially to be in keeping with the emphasis it receives in classical and European pastoral elegy, where poets create tangible, substantial worlds in which sorrow can, consolingly, be "placed."[99] Yet Freneau evades the comforts of this gestural rhetoric by stressing the sense of imminent loss in the landscape itself ("Here, *still* a lofty rock . . ."; "Here, *still* an aged elm . . ."), as though these features had somehow exceeded expectations of their durability. The landscape grows increasingly chimerical, becoming finally a place of pure fantasy:

> And long shall tim'rous fancy see
> The painted chief, and pointed spear,
> And reason's self shall bow the knee
> To shadows and delusions here. (37–40)

These final lines make the poem difficult to interpret as a scene of savagism thoroughly othered and contained. Is "tim'rous fancy" a feature of Indian superstition, or is it human fancy? Does reason genuflect to "shadows and delusions" only "here," that is, among Indians? Or here more generally? The poem's deictics are hard to orient throughout, and Freneau's final "here" may take in the burying ground, "these lands" referred to in line 5, and the poem itself, blurring the distinctions between them to the extent that all of the poem's realms become potentially immune to reason's sway.

Despite his apparent lack of interest in the Constitutional Convention and his reiterated defenses of the imagination, Freneau joined his republican peers in supporting the rule of reason. In 1784, in a poem called "On the Emigration to America and Peopling the Western Country," he jubilantly proclaimed that the Enlightenment project to liberate the mind would be realized on American soil. There, he wrote, "Reason shall enforce her sway" and in the future may even "over death prevail." Not, however, until

> The unsocial Indian far retreats,
> To make some other clime his own,
> When other streams, less pleasing, flow,
> And darker forests round him grow.[100]

Freneau's echoing of Milton's "Lycidas" jars with his expansionist theme and signals a notable moment of amnesia in the poem. For whereas the allusion to Milton's vision of "other groves, and other streams" suggests that death involves only the gentlest of changes,[101] Freneau elsewhere demonstrates his awareness of the violence that attended Indian removal, not simply to "groves" just beyond the latest European encroachment but to another country altogether. The "false surmise" of a happy beyond was necessary to the rationale for extinction,[102] while the triumph of reason itself *was* the rationale.

In his Indian burying ground poem, Freneau took a harder look at this paradox, even as the New World rationalism was being entextualized at Philadelphia. The framers of the Constitution did not need to articulate a theory of death, for their new government did not depend on a hereditary social order. Such a dependence would have jeopardized the self-reproducing nature of the envisioned state. Jefferson, for example, watching the proceedings from afar, was especially anxious regarding the tenure of the chief executive, which he was afraid would be extended to life, making the fate of the president's person too momentous.[103] In 1799, the massive cultural response to George Washington's death was also a celebration of political continuity, which had already been peacefully preserved in the first transition of presidential power. Unlike many of the traditional societies it displaced, the United States, as figured in the Constitution, made no provision for the restoration of political legitimacy after the death of a leader. Continuity was a corporate, not a personal, phenomenon.

Yet even in a constitutional democracy individuals still die, and if the Revolution and its legitimation in the Constitution demonstrated that liberation from the past was possible, the new United States could not free its citizens from the reality of a future in which they would no longer exist. Furthermore, the Constitution's silence about death is rendered problematic by the lethal consequences of its representational politics for "free persons," "Indians not taxed," and "three fifths of all other persons" (Article I, section 2). The Constitution's obliqueness with respect to Indian extinction and to slavery preserves it from extremes of irrationality while confirming its limitation as an instrument of reason. Freneau's Indian burying ground poem offers a contemporary commentary on this obliqueness. For, insofar as the poem has a politics, it reveals an anxiety over the exclusions that condition liberal rationalism in late-eighteenth-century America. Against what Paine saw as a happy, rational beginning, Freneau suggests the desirability of a more complex view—one that is characterized to the point of being riven by the contradictions for which "reason's self" creates a space.

Looking back from the nation's self-constituting moment, Freneau sees a space destined to remain open and marginal—a space in which retrospective remedies for incoherence will not work—and he wonders about national identity here at what Joseph Roach would call "the outer limits of imagined community."[104] He wonders, that is, how a national subject will endure the contradictions of that identity, and he begins, in his Indian burying ground poem, to endow this national subject with something like an unconscious—a locus of unresolved contradictions with which any retrospective narrative of national coherence must contend.

Looking back from this nationalizing moment in the history of American elegy, it has been tempting for literary historians to imagine they saw a kind of poetic void, within which certain individual poems might be located but which amounted to little more than a realm of accumulation, a kind of potter's field of poetry, as if each elegy marked its own grave and nothing more. The retrospective project of this chapter has been not simply to locate more of these graves but to reveal their emplacement in complex patterns of cultural transmission, of legacy and revision. Behind these patterns, as we have seen, there are contradictions. Elegies often express commitments to particular social and political orders while nevertheless celebrating, prospectively or retrospectively, release from those temporal orders. These poems trade in the dubious finality of death, which seems to settle scores and determine outcomes while also tending to unfix and disperse social arrangements. Elegies often seem to promote the view that the past and the future are *both* better alternatives to the present. They exploit death's fascination and its repugnance. And they encourage the sense that one's losses are intelligible and shared, even as they exclude certain groups or classes of persons from memorialization. Some elegies go so far as to challenge, confusingly, the propriety of individuated mourning. Indeed, one of the contradictions increasingly characteristic of American elegy as the eighteenth century drew to a close stems from republican attachment to what Ernest Becker calls "the living myth of the significance of human life"[105]—an experience of contradiction best exemplified in elegiac responses to the death of George Washington at the turn of the nineteenth century, which is the subject of the following chapter.

CHAPTER 2

Elegy and the Subject
of National Mourning

In the meantime were employed two pretty copious bleedings, a blister
was applied to the part affected, two moderate doses of calomel were
given, and an injection was administered, which operated on the
lower intestines. [It was agreed] to try the result of another bleeding,
when about 32 ounces of blood were drawn. . . . Vapours of vinegar
and water were frequently inhaled . . . succeeded by repeated doses of
emetic tartar . . . with no other effect than a copious discharge from the
bowels. The power of life seemed now manifestly yielding to the force
of the disorder. . . . Speaking, which was painful from the beginning,
now became almost impracticable; respiration grew more and more
contracted and imperfect, till half after eleven on Saturday night, retaining the full possession of his intellects—when he expired without
a struggle.

—JAMES CRAIK AND ELISHA C. DICK

By 1799, the young nation had already caught dramatic glimpses of
itself in the mirror of mourning. From the start of the Revolutionary
War to the end of the century, the deaths of soldiers, patriot noncomba-
tants, illustrious citizens, and noncitizen subjects had inspired a wealth
of elegies that reflected back to their audience various images of a country in tears. Such idealizing images encouraged members of what was
in reality a riven and uncertain populace to understand themselves as

representatives of a nationally unified mourning subject. They exhorted a people to weep itself into being.

In the process, the exaltation of the dead generated political anxieties at the heart of national life. On April 21, 1790, during the first year of George Washington's presidency, an estimated twenty thousand people joined Benjamin Franklin's funeral procession and burial ceremony at Philadelphia's Christ Church Burial Ground.[1] The House of Representatives, acting the next day at the behest of James Madison, resolved to wear mourning badges for one month in Franklin's honor. The Senate, however, refused to pass an equivalent resolution, and this refusal moved Secretary of State Thomas Jefferson to call upon George Washington for a counteractive gesture from the government's executive branch. "I proposed to General Washington," Jefferson later recalled, "that the executive department should wear mourning; he declined it, because he said he should not know where to draw the line, if he once began that ceremony."[2] The misgivings generated by Franklin's death regarding national mourning for a private citizen—"an honor," according to Benjamin Vaughan, "not shown to any person before out of office"[3]—were greatly enhanced by the French response, beginning with Mirabeau's galvanic address to the National Assembly, which "touched off," as Julian Boyd reports, "a whole series of proceedings in the French capital that amounted to nothing less than a republican apotheosis of Franklin."[4]

The pressure to respond to French enthusiasm only deepened American divisions over republican theory and practice, thus helping to set national mourning on a course of ambivalence well illustrated by Philip Freneau's own sharply contrasting pair of Franklin elegies. The first, published in New York's *Daily Advertiser* on April 28, is a fully pious declaration of collective sorrow at the loss of a quasi-deific political and intellectual leader—one who "seiz'd from Kings their sceptr'd pride, / And turn'd the lightning's darts aside."[5] The second, however, published in the same newspaper almost a month later, ventriloquizes Franklin himself, speaking "from the other World" in utmost contempt for all the florid elegies that have been produced since his death. He attacks the pathetic fallacy and the sheer conventionality of its application in verses that, he finds, also misrepresent national mourning as uniform (even if the skies *had* wept in Pennsylvania, "In Carolina, all was clear") and forget the egalitarian current of the Revolution ("That day on which I left the coast, / A beggar man was also lost; / If nature wept, you must agree / She wept for him—as well as me"). Freneau's satiric reaction against the shortcomings of national elegy opens with the spectral Franklin's apparent rejection of the poetic enterprise altogether. "Love for your tribe I never had," he says in the opening stanza, and in the third asserts that "To better trades I turn'd my views, / And never meddled with the Muse." Yet the poem ends not with a denial of poetry's place in national life but rather with an appeal for poetic innovation, particularly with regard to the pathetic fallacy. In its final lines it encourages future elegists when employing the device of "Dame Nature" in their poems to "Make her do some—uncommon things."[6] In the national hero's posthumous voice, Freneau asks for a recommitment to the development of an aesthetically and politically adequate elegiac practice when mourning those figures most strongly identified with their new, most uncommon nation.

As Freneau and many others found, the best chance for evaluating the potential for and consequences of such a recommitment came a decade later with the death of George Washington. Indeed, the profusion of literary memorials to Washington in the weeks and months after his death, on December 14, 1799, constitutes the first draft of a work of mourning that is still under revision. Washington continues to symbolize a national cultural process of postrepublican transformation—a process to which he himself contributed preposthumously in his Farewell Address. The address, cowritten with Alexander Hamilton and delivered in 1796, is one of the earliest and most complex statements on the legacy of the eighteenth century's disembodiment of political power in modern nationalism.[7] No person, no *body,* may in this conceptualization of political tradition interpose itself between citizen-subjects and their self-actualizing polities. Nevertheless, more than two centuries after his near-liquefaction at the hands of well-meaning surgeons, it would seem that Washington's *disjecta membra* remain touchstones of national subjectivity for many who are otherwise unconscious of or repelled by vestiges of monarchal fetishism in their experience of democratic state sovereignty. Washington's false teeth, bits of his hair, and other personal relics circulated not long ago among the nation's cultural institutions in honor of the two-hundredth anniversary of his death—among the latest in a series of efforts to assess the visibility and value of Washington's posthumous image in the changing contexts of its manipulation.[8]

As part of this ongoing construction, writers of fiction, like so many historians, biographers, and exhibit curators, have sought to portray a Washington more personally compelling than the abstract or monumental figure he commonly strikes, a Washington not yet purged of singularity, a Washington of depth, interiority, even edginess. For example, at one point in Thomas Pynchon's novel *Mason & Dixon,* the title characters visit Washington at home and are invited by him to sample Mount Vernon's newest cash crop: a small patch of marijuana he has planted in back. Washington gives signs that he has already done so as he stares deeply into the shiny buttons of Jeremiah Dixon's coat. He also has a vision, which he relates to Charles Mason, of the British surveyor being hunted down and eaten by backcountry Presbyterians. Mason is nonplussed. "Ever so kind," he replies, declining the weed, "to imagine for me my death in America."[9]

Since Washington's death, novelists including Cooper, Thackeray, Gertrude Stein, and Gore Vidal have preceded Pynchon in taking up the challenge of imagining his historically oblique character.[10] The novel's special relation to the problem of character may help account for this perennial interest in Washington, the notorious rigidity of whose public persona undoubtedly heightens the appeal of Pynchon's bent depiction. For beyond the superficial satisfactions of irreverence, Pynchon's Washington helps gratify a deeper skepticism that manifests itself in the reiterated need for a Washington who seems close, visible, idiosyncratic. Indeed, this is what modern novels teach us that character should be. Consequently, we tend to reject characterizations that seem in comparison flat or idealized.

This novelistic thinking about character is one reason, at least, for the minimal attention paid by literary and cultural historians to the vast poetic response to his death. Michael Gilmore, for instance, invests these poems with all the uniformity and banality of his own characterization of early national poetry:

> Verses on Washington's death resembled most contemporaneous poems in that they were pedagogic and rhetorical, summoning listeners to draw a lesson or pursue some action. Apart from being in meter and rhyme, poetry did not seek to differentiate itself from other forms of discourse. Verse was the servant of morality and politics.[11]

A more attentive reading of these poems—one attuned, for example, to the differentiating effects of "meter and rhyme," and to contemporaneous confidence in what E. P. Thompson calls poetry's "historical rights among other intellectual disciplines"[12]—would acknowledge the palpable, if awkward, and thus frequently idiosyncratic, vibrancy of their engagement with other "pedagogic and rhetorical," moral and political, discursive forms. The sheer quantity of elegies for Washington helps mark his death as a watershed event in the history of nationalist commemorative practices in the United States. But my contention here is not simply that the Washington elegies are essential to that history. Once seen as important sites for the operations of fellow feeling, or sympathy, in the early republic, they should help sharpen our appreciation of poetry's role in the formation and deformation of national subjects.

In making this argument I take an unsympathetic view of a salient feature of Americanist cultural criticism, namely, its marginalization of poetic forms and its correlative commitment to the novel as a metonymy of literary culture. Lurking here, therefore, is a disciplinary argument about literacy: Americanists need to read more poetry. I will admit to this as long as it is understood that I am not trying to defend a revanchist formalism or to fetishize poetic genres as such. Instead, by focusing attention on elegy's importance within early national culture, I seek to address what Bakhtin calls the "novelization of genre," which has made certain questions—including questions about the novel—less likely to be asked in Americanist cultural criticism.[13]

Some of the most subtle recent work on early American novels focuses on the ways in which they figure and facilitate operations of sympathy in literary as well as broader cultural terms. For instance, in her book *The Plight of Feeling,* Julia Stern seeks, as she puts it,

> to reveal an unappreciated level of novelistic creativity—one that expresses a dialectic of inclusion against exclusion, thereby enacting and to various

degrees discomposing the way an elitist culture contains the dissent at its margins. The constitutive power and simultaneous unraveling of sympathy as an operative cultural fantasy become the abiding metaphors through which eighteenth-century American fiction figures problems of social and political cohesion.[14]

That these metaphors seem to have been wielded largely by novelists with a kind of exclusive power is an impression to which Elizabeth Barnes also contributes in her critique of the sentimental novel's seductive conservatism—its power to unite readers in circuits of convention and conventional feeling, to link them as "respondents to rather than performers of language."[15]

Lots of people in the early United States read novels, but very few wrote them. Poetic forms, on the other hand, were at least as widely produced as they were consumed—and they were consumed voraciously. The basic point I want to make—the point that leads me to my discussion of the Washington elegies—is that whatever people were learning from reading novels about how to enter into the feelings of others cannot be very well understood apart from their own various public and private enactments of the relation between literary and affective conventions—enactments that included the composition, imitation, transcription, recitation, and audition as well as the closeted reading of poetic genres like elegy. This point applies to elegists with all kinds of relations to literary culture, including elegists who also wrote novels. Thus, in what follows I have tried to represent a wide range of elegiac activity, while also devoting considerable attention to elegies by two of the period's best-known novelists, Charles Brockden Brown and Susanna Haswell Rowson. The point in doing so is not to accede uncritically to the novel's greater cultural authority but rather to help mark that authority as part of our current retrospective.

As word of Washington's death radiated outward from Mount Vernon in late December 1799, the famous and the obscure began to produce verses that would not only be circulated in a variety of print media but would also be spoken or sung at civic processions, religious services, and commercial theatricals around the country.[16] They were written by seasoned authors and by one-time versifiers; by editors, lawyers, and politicians; by New England schoolmistresses and Masonic grand-masters; by Congregationalists, Episcopalians, Deists, and Quakers; by members of Washington's intimate circle and by strangers who had not always been well-wishers. The elegies are formally diverse, includ-ing odes, hymns, sonnets, acrostics, ballads, and even prose poems in Ossianic measure. Many elegies were brief and epitaphic. Others were comprehensive verse eulogies hundreds of lines long. "It would seem," one contemporary observer noted archly, "as if the nine Muses were encreased to nineteen; and they had all agreed to disperse and compose, according to their respective ingenuities."[17]

Yet the pressure to represent grief as a national affect, distributed among particular but not isolated persons, resulted in a remarkable expressive homogeneity. A shared idiom of woe supported assertions of fellow feeling that reached from the centers to the margins of national life. In Boston, Thomas Pemberton noted that a local paper

> mentions the following as an additional evidence of the universality of the grief excited by the death of Washington. . . . At the Funeral honors or-dered by [General] Pinckney at the United States garrison at South West Point—Nine principal Chiefs of the Cherokees & a large number of the common Indians appeared in the funeral procession and testified by their deportment [and] by sighs & death songs that they felt that their highly respected Father Washington is no more.[18]

This report from the Tennessee frontier, where perceptions of radi-cal difference between Indians and whites would lead to the grief of Cherokee removal, renders sameness of affect plausible through vague-ness. Given "Father" Washington's history of paternalistic benevolence toward the Cherokees, their representatives no doubt "felt" his loss, es-pecially in the presence of federal troops no longer under Washington's command. But the question of what specifically they might have felt—what particular sentiments might have prompted their "sighs & death songs"—is carefully avoided.

In the "death songs" of white Americans, too, the claim of grief's universality sometimes hinged upon its ineffability in problematic ways. Alluding to the mourning bands and clothing Americans were offi-cially urged to wear in Washington's memory, as well as to the words in which writers dressed the nation's sorrow, a South Carolina newspaper elegy, signed "Myrtilla," maintained that "Dark mourning weeds but ill express / The poignant grief that all confess." The convention of pseudonymous publication adopted by the author, Philip Freneau, reinforces a sense (compounded by cross-gendering) of the transitivity of public expression. But the poem also seeks, somewhat discordantly, to retain a sense of delicacy regarding the privacy of sentiment: it tells us, for instance, that *all* hearts congeal with "secret" woe, and that tears "steal" down *each* pale cheek.[19] If authorial anonymity is often a condition of generalized publicity in republican print culture, it is also a frequent token and guarantor of privacy in the elegiac tradition within which Freneau writes. His difficult goal is to establish grief's authorizing universality without compromising its authenticating reticence.

This difficulty is compounded for Freneau by the tension between his impulse as a republican to resist particularized heroization and his commitment as an elegist to his subject's individuation. Such a commitment, always in competition with the genre's parallel commitments to exemplification and sublimation, and with the deindividuating tendency of literary and social conventions, posed special problems for Washington's elegists. Throughout the 1790s, against a backdrop of faction and uncertainty, Washington provided a welcome ground for fellow feeling and, increasingly, a link between the revolutionary past and the national future. The monumentalist response to his death celebrated this effect, but it also prompted questions about the basis of one man's enduring hold over the national imagination and about his unique relevance to the continuity of union. Americans' overwhelming investment of value and significance in the person of George Washington pointed to the persistence of royalist mentality and sentiment, while concern over the Caesarian tendencies of the republican hero—a concern at the very heart of Washington's Cincinnatus role—conflicted with any truly particularized heroization and thus with the elegist's task of individuated mourning. The childlessness that delinked biology and paternity in popular conceptions of Washington as national father enabled a diffusion of family feeling crucial to a sense of unity among national subjects—including noncitizen subjects.[20] Yet the very disembodiment that made his image a powerful force for the elision of difference and conflict also made it an awkward site for authentic mourning.

At the same time, the anonymity of republican print culture and the national premium on fellow feeling as an index of social coherence discouraged elegiac self-display: as one poem exhorts, for General Washington, a "general grief."[21] Many of the elegies bear titles like "America in Mourning" and "Columbia's Distress" and are full of depersonalized sentiments: the "general sorrow," the "People's grief," the "country's woe."[22] Such figures are common to the poetry of public mourning, including the elegies Anglo-Americans had written only a generation earlier for King George II.[23] But grief in a republic ought to be different, as an editorial writer for New York's *Commercial Advertiser* insisted in defense of Washington's effusive mourners: "It is not the ostentation of fashion, or the admiration of a stupid multitude, staring at the glitter of a crown; it is the heartfelt grief of a nation for the loss of great public and private virtues."[24] Tocqueville draws a sharp distinction between what he calls "instinctive" and "reflecting" patriotism, associating the former with monarchism and the latter with republicanism.[25] But the experience of forms of sentimental and rational attachment portrayed in the Washington elegies does not readily conform to this opposition. Rather, it confirms the dialectic of historicism and traditionalism that generates and sustains patriotism in modern nations, where death, as Benedict Anderson observes, stands for a range of fatalities that must be given continuity and meaning.[26]

Washington's death was more than an occasion for ceremonial remembrance, for establishing a past from which the future could depart. It was an opportunity to define a new style of relation to the dead—a style that could encompass the potentially conflicting ideals of personal freedom and civic duty. Washington himself endured this conflict famously and self-consciously throughout his life, and many of the elegies stress his sad willingness to yield to the people's claims upon him. In his "Poem on the Death of General Washington," David Humphreys describes Washington's acceptance of the presidency:

> To the first office call'd by every voice,
> His will submissive to his country's choice;
> By reason's force reluctance overcome,
> Behold him meekly leave his darling home;

> Again resign the calm of rural life,
> Again embarking on a sea of strife![27]

These lines echo the characterizations of sacrifice in many Puritan elegies, where the call to public office is depicted as both a challenge to piety and an opportunity to do good. For Washington, love of domestic retirement takes the place of the Puritan inward calling to redemption in its conflict with the call to civic duty. He seeks not redemption but the privacy American independence makes possible: a withdrawal from political action consistent with patriotism. "I have the consolation to believe," Washington wrote in his Farewell Address, "that while choice and prudence invite me to quit the political scene, patriotism does not forbid it."[28] Posthumously, he is commiserated with by fellow citizens like Humphreys who are at the turn of the century themselves learning to think of patriotism privately cultivated as an alternative to virtuous public action.

Humphreys, as minister to Spain, delivered his 860-line elegy as a Fourth-of-July oration to an audience in Madrid. The poem is largely the story of Washington's career, with special attention given to the war years. In his Advertisement to the published version of the poem, he expresses his fear that the events of the Revolution are "in danger of becoming unknown to posterity," and he affirms his faith in poetry as both a repository of the past and as an inducement to virtuous behavior in the present.[29] Yet in a letter to Martha Washington he describes the poem as "a representation . . . of my melancholy sensations,"[30] and it is in fact full of assertions of Humphreys's distinctiveness as a mourner. He seems to have felt that his personal relationship with Washington distinguished his pain from the sense of common loss taken for granted here as elsewhere:

> Though duty calls and friendship leaves no choice,
> Unutterable feelings choak my voice—
> For sensibilities I bring, not less,
> And greater grief than others, to express. (21–24)

He speaks of his wish privately to "indulge the luxury of grief" (52), though he insists two lines later that it is "Grief not confin'd to nation, sex, or age" (54). His elegy offers a forum for both sensibility and public virtue, but it does not yet mediate critically between the two.

The requirement that public grief be—and be seen to be—universally sincere made the subject, as well as the object, of republican mourning a site of conflict. Indeed, the pressure to embody a "nation's grief" could easily become insupportable, as the celebrated actor Thomas Cooper discovered during his recitation of a Washington elegy written by Charles Brockden Brown. Brown produced the elegy to help solemnize the reopening of New York's Park Theatre. The theater, which had closed on December 20 when news of Washington's death reached New York, resumed its season ten days later with an adaptation of Boutet de Monvel's melodrama *Clémentine et Désormes.* Before the play began, Cooper, one of its stars, attempted to deliver Brown's poem, with results described the next day in the New York *Spectator*:

> He came on, with a bow not the most graceful in the world, but with a countenance that seemed to say, *"If you have tears prepare to shed them now,"* and in truth never was an audience more predisposed to harmonize with *"sorrows saddest note."* His tongue, however, soon counteracted every such emotion, for he began to speak in [tones] artificial and declamatory. . . . [H]e had hardly exceeded thirty lines when . . . his words stuck in his throat, and he lost all power of recollecting a line further. . . . He edged a little nearer the prompter, caught his cue and went on—stopt again—moved on a word—stopt again—the ladies cast down their eyes—he caught another word, and went on—stopt again—the Pit groaned aloud, and a small hiss began to issue from the gallery—when some good honest fellow got up and clapped his hands, which encouraged [him] to start once more, and to go quite through the piece . . . much to our own as well as his relief. To add that he pronounced it very ill [is] unnecessary, as no man can ever speak with propriety and effect, whose whole attention is constantly occupied in the sole business of recollection.[31]

Cooper's performance renders the audience's dream of sympathy his own perfect nightmare. Instead of uniting the spectators in a shared consideration of their situation as mourners of George Washington, Cooper finds himself confronted with their pained consideration of the lack of sympathy with which his own situation is attended. He fails not only to project elegiac sincerity but also to achieve the theatrical dissimulation of sorrow with which his audience is "predisposed to harmonize."

Ironically, Brown's elegy begins by promising the audience it will be spared the trappings and the suits of woe:

> No mimic accents now shall touch your ears,
> And now no fabled woe demand your tears;
> No Hero of a visionary age,
> No child of poet's phrenzy walks the stage.
> 'Tis not my office, now, in such a cause
> As erst, to cheat you of your dear applause.
> 'Tis no phantastic fate of Queens or Kings,
> That bids your sympathy unlock its springs.[32]

These lines refer most directly to the plays (including the Monvel adaptation, Henry Brooke's *Gustavas Vasa,* and Shakespeare's *Hamlet*) with which Brown's poem was meant on various subsequent evenings to share the bill. But they also initiate a complex assault on modes of soliciting fellow feeling, including aspects of his own gothic fictions. Negative constructions fill these opening lines and dominate the rest of the poem as well. Brown describes the audience's grief ("No passing grief it is, no private woe" [11]), its object ("Not for your children's friend your tears must fall" [17]), its scope ("Not singly we, who haunt this western shore" [19]), its propriety ("No cause there is that may demand a tear" [30]), and its lasting monuments ("Not built with hands" [88]) all in terms of what they are *not*. In doing so, he seems often to echo the virtuous self-denial of civic republicanism, while also anticipating a bourgeois spirit of self-control. Indeed, in a kind of proleptic defense against the conflation of political and domestic spheres, the poem aggressively cancels the domestic scene of sentimentalism:

> You are not call'd to view, bereft of life,
> By dread convulsion seiz'd, your child or wife,
> To view a parent's feeble lamp expire;
> But *Washington is dead,* his country's sire!
> Not for your children's friend your tears must fall;
> For *Washington is dead,* the friend of all! (13–18)

Washington's death matters because it is like a personal loss ("parent"/ "sire"; "children's friend"/"friend of all") *and* because it transcends the sentimental ties of consanguinity and checks the unregulated indulgence of grief. The conflict manifest within the poem turns on Brown's wish to stage grief as a collective, specifically national experience rather than a domestic one: home and nation are not yet the same thing. The paradox of national sorrow is encapsulated in the poem's insistently repeated reminder to the audience, "This woe is yours," which it cannot possibly be if they need to be reminded of it.

At the same time, as Thomas Cooper found, there is a price to pay for a too exclusive devotion to the "sole business of recollection"—a price that the poem's distantiating formalism ought to have indemnified him against. Like the figure of Washington within the elegy—who is there described as guiding, steering, teaching, subduing, and fixing—the poem itself is a model of regulation, its conventional form contrasting sharply with the chaotic mimeses of vexed subjectivity in some of Brown's fictions. If Cooper had been given a page from Brown's novel *Edgar Huntly* to memorize and recite, his incoherence and forgetfulness would have been at least dramatically consistent with the material. But Brown's elegy presents no comparable stylistic challenges and gives little evidence of its hasty composition. On the contrary, it offers numerous aids to memorization and recitation. Its rhymed iambic pentameter couplets are fairly regular; its syntax and diction are never outlandish; it engages frequently in the repetition of key words and phrases; and it follows a familiar elegiac pattern of lamentation, praise, and consolation. Yet the professional, celebrated actor still could not remember it—could not, that is, piece it together in and as an embodiment of national sensibility. The poem, like the woe, simply was not his.

Many other such poems were also originally produced for public reading, their direct appeal to communal expression itself a kind of civic action. Even without Thomas Cooper to give them special life, the contradictions these poems embodied as disciplinary instruments of spontaneous, shared feeling tended to emerge at the nexus of orality and print—captured in the performance details that often accompanied the text of an elegy as it made the rounds in the press after its spoken debut. The Georgetown *Centinel of Liberty,* for example, was one of several newspapers to reprint an "Elegiac Ode" from Fredericktown, Maryland, with the following prefatory remarks:

> Last evening, the Youth of our Academy joined in the general unexampled sorrow of their country, in delivering, at the close of their Eloecutionary

> Exercises, the following Elegiac Ode, on the death of the ever to be revered WASHINGTON, to a very melancholy and deeply affected audience. It was spoken by three young gentlemen in deep mourning, by alternate Stanzas or divisions, as it is written—and was accompanied by Solemn Music.[33]

The "very melancholy and deeply affected audience" is offered to newspaper readers as evidence of the poem's ability, through its young speakers, to rouse and direct the emotions of its listeners. It also reinforces the implicit exhortation to such readers to join in "the unexampled sorrow of their country." In the poem that follows, references to the patriot's "sympathizing groan" and "raptur'd ear" seem intended to inspire what they portray: the very practice of nationalism that David Waldstreicher locates in the "reciprocal influence of celebrations and print."[34] Yet the prefatory description, in attempting to set an imaginary stage for the private reading of the printed poem, also helps ensure that its rhetorical excesses will ring false. For its plaintive exclamations ("Ah! Mourn!"; "For ah! Alas!"; "On earth ah! Heard no more") and tolling laments ("Ah! Gone!—gone!—gone!"; "Now Dead!—Dead!—Dead!") rather adroitly test the reader's ability to imagine it being "spoken as it is written."[35] That is, they seem to interfere with possibilities for affective consent by feeding into contemporary distrust of rhetorical ornament and stylistic affectation.

Yet these same features, through their very conventionality and stylization, open up a space between text and reader for the representation and solicitation of a depersonalized, national sensibility. For this rather straightforward reason, it seems to me that these sorts of poetic texts are improperly understood—or rather too quickly dismissed—by literary scholars of the period as irrelevant to discussions of what is these days mysteriously referred to as "sentimental form."[36] A further example helps make the point. It is an elegiac hymn for Washington that was widely reprinted with the following framing account of its initial performance:

> A stranger who attended divine service, on Sunday, at the 1st Episcopal Church in this town, upon entering was struck with reverential awe and affected even to tears at the testimonials of affliction there exhibited. The pulpit, chancel, organ, gallery, and state pew were hung in black. A discourse,

worthy of the author, was delivered by the Rev. Mr. [James] FREEMAN; the subject the illustrious WASHINGTON. After which the following "Occasional Hymn" (having been previously distributed) was sung.

I.
ASSEMBLED round the patriot's grave,
Pity, O Lord, a nation's sighs:
We mourn our chief, the warrior brave;
Low in the dust the hero lies.
II.
By thee inspir'd with warlike art,
He urg'd the fight, or bade it cease:
Not less he fill'd the statesman's part;
Our guide in war, our head in peace.
III.
His country happy, great, and free,
Hail'd him her father, hope and pride;
But fix'd, O God, his hope on thee,
He liv'd thy friend, thy servant died.

At the first line, the whole congregation actuated by one sentiment, immediately rose and joined in the singing.[37]

By combining the text of the poem's broadside version with an account of its incantation, this newspaper item encourages a sympathetic reading through a fantasy of participation. The text begins by smoothly interpellating the reader as a "stranger" in a way analogous to that in which epitaphic inscriptions conventionally hail the "stranger" or "traveler": by reaching out, in this case, not from the dead to the living but from the local to the extralocal.[38] At various removes—temporal, geographical, denominational—readers could enjoy the sense if not the sensation of being "struck with reverential awe and affected even to tears," of being "actuated" by a single sentiment shared not just by the King's Chapel congregation but by an entire nation. Readers are invited, along with the congregation, to participate, to "rise" and "join" in a liturgical enactment of unity. Everyone sings, everyone mourns. The conventions of Protestant hymnody, adapted to the political occasion, appear in this newspaper account as a republican counterpart to the Reformation doctrine of the priesthood of all believers; voicing the new civic liturgy is an expression of the national right to interpret republican principles. The alleged involuntariness with which stranger and congregant alike submit to the scene's coercive sentimentality ("upon entering," "at the first line") does not suggest a mere uniformity of feeling. It suggests—through both descriptive and conscriptive methods that include the unifying and distantiating effects of poetic form—a prior uniform disposition to be moved that should enable the newspaper reader readily to inhabit the phrase "We mourn."

But the nation was a unified subject only in fantasy, and along with proliferating assertions of affliction came increasing evidence of a general unwillingness to credit the genuineness of those assertions. A flood of skepticism and Juvenalian satire kept pace with the flood of tearful elegies. Often, the cries of insincerity were politically motivated. The pseudonymous "NO TORY," for example, railed against the "crocodile" elegies of the Federalists, while New York's *Commercial Advertiser* opined that in order to estimate the "sincerity and value" of "Jacobin" accusations of Federalist idolatry, "we must wait till some Jefferson shall die."[39] Party rancor was the most overt, commonly shrill expression of a strong cultural preoccupation with representations of sensibility free from threatening vagaries of interest and subjectivity—threats at the heart of contemporary fears about the novel's ability to collapse the distance between text and reader. "Far from a mere literary trend," David Waldstreicher observes, the cult of sensibility "was a cultural imperative of international dimensions."[40] Yet, as a literary trend, it occupied the attention not only of powerful newspaper editors but also of the current steward of federal feeling—President Adams—who was by no means above faking it. In the midst of writing thank-you notes for the Washington tributes that inundated the executive mansion at Philadelphia, Adams seems to have been estimating his own chances for lasting fame when he expressed the hope that "[we] no longer disturb his ghost with fulsome adulation."[41]

Adams's impatience with the mourning contest Washington's death inspired probably had more to do with personal ambition than with the critique of sentimental forms. He nevertheless read many of these tributes with specifically literary interest. He took notice, for instance, of an elegy by a young poet named Charles Love and wrote him a detailed response. Praising Love's poem for its "invention & judgment," as well as for its successful imitation of Milton, Adams honored what he called a "talent worth cultivating" with both criticism and compliments: "The versification," he wrote, "is in some places negligent & wants labor. The heart which appears in it is pure & amiable in a high degree."[42] From Alexandria, Love whipped back a long reply full of youthful gratification, self-absorption, and ambitiousness. He thanked Adams for his salutary criticisms but was especially pleased with the president's endorsement of his sensibility: "He," Love ventured, "who in his writings displays the 'Pure Heart' the chaste sentiment—can not be said to have written in vain."[43]

The Adams-Love exchange reads more like one between teacher and student than between president and citizen. It is a sign that the sentimentalization of virtue was a lesson Americans were still learning, from the schoolroom setting of the Frederick Academy to King's Chapel to the home of the president. With a strong civic tradition in colonial Anglo-America and a foundational connection to contemporary poetries of sensibility, elegy was, unsurprisingly, a common tutelary genre.[44] But even for more experienced poets, elegy was a challenging venue for the expression of fellow feeling. Despite the codes of anonymous or generalized mourning and the political pressure to conform to such codes, the very conventions of elegiac tradition also, ironically, encouraged elegists to argue for their own uniqueness and special sincerity. David Humphreys, for example, recognized the legitimating force of both generality and self-assertion, and struggled in his Madrid elegy to mediate between the two.

Self-conscious about this struggle within the poem, Humphreys prefaced the published version with not one but two dedicatory letters to Martha Washington, whose public status as a mourner was no less complex for being self-evidently legitimate. As Washington's widow, hers was acknowledged to be the "greater grief," but as the symbol of a "widow'd country," as another elegist put it, her grief was also deemed representative.[45] As Washington's widow, she was a political figure, subject to partisan identification and attack, but as a woman she was excluded from the realm of political representation. Like the widely circulated images of Columbia weeping, Martha's image feminized national affect but was also deployed as a model for the regulation of private feeling—its subordination to the common interest located in a general, genderless sympathy.

One sees this sort of deployment in author-identified elegies by prominent poets like Humphreys and Richard Alsop, where Martha is invoked as a figure of silent, inviolable grief, illustrating the "convergence of femininity and the unrepresentable" that Eva Cherniavsky locates in the early national discourse of sympathy.[46] One sees it also in a cheap anonymous broadside elegy called "Lady Washington's Lamentation for the Death of Her Husband," a dramatic monologue in which Martha anatomizes her own sorrow only to reject its particularity in the final stanza:

> But why with my own single grief so confounded,
> When my country's sad millions in sorrows are drowned,
> Let me mingle the current that flows from my bosom,
> With my country's vast ocean of tears while they lose them.[47]

Now, one can easily point to the sheer awfulness of rhyme here. Indeed, we have to strive pretty mightily to ignore the ludicrousness of "bosom"/ "lose them" in order to read this poem with the respectful attentiveness we have learned customarily to bring even to the tinniest prose. Which is to say that we require ways of distinguishing between stylistic defects that seem to verge on self-parody and formal effects of distantiation that the novelization of genre militates against. In contrast to the "one sentiment" supposed to unite the King's Chapel congregation in spontaneous public display, Martha's "single grief" represents individuated affect literally out of touch with collective sorrow. The imprecision of the former helps ensure its generalizability; the particularity of the latter leads to a vexed ("confounded") interiority. To regulate her feeling (her "grief unconfined") and to join the national body, the broadside Lady Washington commits herself to the solvent tears of "sad millions."

Yet as Martha narrates her own dematerialization in the text of the elegy, the accompanying cut depicts her as strikingly embodied (see Figure 6). Though recognizable as children, the four surrounding figures' relative size makes the seated Martha appear monstrous in the crude carving. As the children—two boys and two girls—buzz about her with their open books, she seems to stare quietly past them. The image prompts the recollection that Martha had borne four children in her life—Daniel Parke Custis's two sons and two daughters—all of whom, by this point, were dead. Indeed, Washington's celebrated status as the country's father begs the question of the significance of

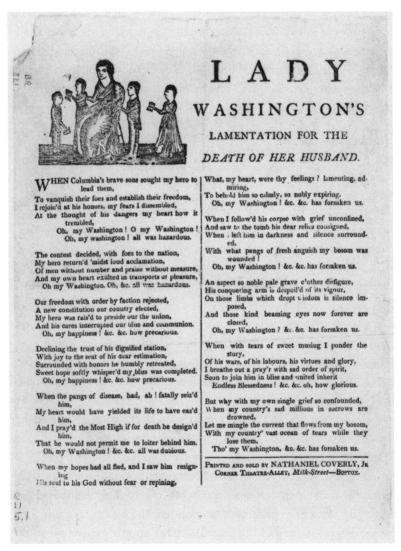

Figure 6. *Lady Washington's Lamentation for the Death of Her Husband* (Boston: Nathaniel Coverly Jr., 1800). Broadside. Photograph courtesy of the Peabody Essex Museum, Salem, Massachusetts.

Martha's motherhood in the context of national mourning. As if in response, the broadside's text and image conflate individual and collective mourning, maternal embodiment and political abstraction, reflecting the complexity of the period's feminization of loss.

Recent criticism associates this phenomenon most strongly with sentimental fiction—crucially with what Julia Stern calls the "sentimental *ur*text" of the 1790s, Susanna Rowson's *Charlotte Temple,* against the sympathetic vision of which Brockden Brown's novels, most notably, would offer a gothic (and arguably feminist) dissent.[48] As we have seen, Brown's elegy for Washington also reveals skepticism about the authenticity of collective grief even as it registers the success of sentimental literature not merely in depicting but even inspiring just that sort of powerful, collective feeling. *Charlotte Temple* may well have been on Brown's mind as he attempted in composing his elegy to construct Washington as an object of shared, active mourning. Rowson's novel is famous, after all, for having inspired its own cult of memory; it moved masses of readers to visit the supposed grave of a fictional character.[49] Indeed, as the new century began, the cults of George Washington and Charlotte Temple vied for national attention, helping to blur the distinctions—including gendered distinctions—between real and fictional embodiments of national self-understanding. Stern notes that despite the distance between Washington's "exalted masculinity" and Temple's "degraded femininity," their two cults functioned similarly, "channeling both political and sentimental affect."[50] While readers found in Charlotte Temple a kind of postrevolutionary catharsis, girls at schools like Rowson's Young Ladies' Academy circulated Washington elegies in their letters and diaries, and learned needlework by copying the Washington memorial prints that were part of a lucrative commercial industry fueled by his never-ending apotheosis.[51]

Indeed, any simple distinction between Washington's "exalted masculinity" and Temple's "degraded femininity" is untenable when we consider, on the one hand, the dignity conferred upon Charlotte's abjection by her popularity and by the novel's commercial success, and, on the other hand, the incongruity of merchandizing Washington—the very image and pattern of self-sacrifice—in the service of economic self-interest.[52] Whether as an opportunity for moving masses of souvenir handkerchiefs or as an inspiration for sentimental verses, Washington's memorialization was by no means consistent with popular notions of masculine virtue. In the elegies, one encounters repeated suggestions of an odd passivity in relation to other men. Kind hands hold him powerless, for example, in one of the most widely reprinted elegies, where he is a superannuated spirit "lead, enrapt" by the ghosts of thronging generals who died in their prime.[53] And Humphreys's elegy emphasizes the pathos of enforced self-denial; he refers to Washington as "submissive," "overcome," "meek" (588–90). Furthermore, if Washington's attenuated presence in the whole range of elegies for him is a function of sound republican mourning practice, it also contributed to fears that the virtues with which he was associated would be "obscured [rather] than rendered more [vivid and] impressive."[54]

Brown himself reviewed many of the Washington elegies and apprehended motivation, not dullness, behind their decorous abstraction. Yet that very decorousness also provoked him to expressions of ambivalence and aggressivity. In a long review of an elegy by Charles Caldwell, he wrote:

> We wished to find, under a mantle of such glossy texture and luxuriant folds, a body, graceful, vigorous, and well proportioned. A meager, distorted, tottering and limping frame, covered with tissue and embroidery, is always a mournful, and sometimes a disgustful spectacle. The mind is shocked by the incongruity between the vestment and the wearer, and our displeasure is increased by our disappointment. A crazy body is expected to accompany rags and rents, and its garment may be threadbare and dingy with impunity; and yet may it not be said, that a shewy garb is of more value to the skeleton than to the perfect man? The latter may shew himself, unbedecked, with more advantage than the former; and where the form beneath is disgustful or ridiculous, may we not thank the taylor who has thus dexterously covered up deformity, and afforded us, at least, the spectacle of a magnificent outside?[55]

This passage, in its allegory of the dialectical relation between style and form, has left far behind the particular elegy under review. Indeed, Brown goes on to say that he does not mean to imply that Caldwell's poem is in any way "disgustful" or "loathsome." Yet the elegy is his occasion for a complex critique of decorousness that reveals concern about Washington's "exalted masculinity." Brown is alarmed at the incongruity that decorousness might just as readily reveal as conceal. It is difficult, for example, not to hear in this passage anxiety about the mournful spectacle of Washington's body—once famously "graceful, vigorous, and well proportioned"—now distorted in the public imagination by age, illness, and death.[56] One also hears the gothic novelist's preoccupation with depth and interiority—his anxiety that interiority is itself a kind of deformity that delineations of character, however decorous their surface, risk revealing.

Brown's outburst dramatically confirms his ambivalence about the Washington elegies. As a literary critic, he faults certain poems for failing to honor elegy's commitment to individuation, while seeming to fear the spectacle such a commitment might entail. Devoted in his major novels to detailing psychological complexity, Brown's own elegy falls substantially in line with Washington's prescriptions for his notoriously opaque public image. As an elegist, Brown participates in the awkward but widespread poetic effort to reconcile protoliberal ideals of individuation and republican ideals of depersonalization. Yet he maintains an antagonistic distance from sentimental fiction's parallel effort to generate sympathy through the representation of affect unmediated by complexities of character, as in the case of Rowson's Charlotte.

Indeed, one could infer from their respective fictive strategies for representing character that Washington would have been a more suitable subject for Rowson than for Brown. She is in fact credited with writing a number of Washington elegies and dirges, two of which were set to music by the contemporary composers Oliver Holden and Caleb Carr. Of more certain attribution is the "Eulogy to the Memory of George Washington," published in her 1804 *Miscellaneous Poems.* Like Brown's "Monody," it depicts an abstract, depersonalized Washington. But in other respects it is a very different kind of poem. It lacks, most obviously, the other elegy's uneasy penchant for negation. Furthermore, whereas Brown's elegy was produced for public reading and circulated (after its disastrous debut) as a kind of approximation of public remembrance, Rowson's seeks not merely to reproduce but to transform the experience of hearing a poem recited. Her elegy subjects the motif of civic action to imaginative introjection and makes the spectacle of mourning Washington an episode of inwardness.

Capitalizing on Washington's famous impulse toward withdrawal from public life, she opens the poem by imagining her own retreat to the romanticized precincts of Mount Vernon:

> Where the Patomac, with majestic wave,
> Washes the borders of Virginia's shore;
> Once the retreat of him most wise most brave,
> Our sainted hero! now, alas, no more;—
> Oft has my fancy took delight to stray,
> Pensive, beneath the high cliff's craggy side;
> List to the dashing of the foaming spray,
> Or undulating murmurs of the tide.[57]

In this setting, she is approached by "visions" (11) and "airy forms" (12), whose dreamlike procession offers a private alternative to the parades, ceremonies, and theatrical gatherings so widely enacted and reported on in the early months of 1800, some of which may have featured Rowson's own earlier verses:

> a celestial band appears;
> Some bearing wreaths, with cypress twin'd,
> Others with measured step and slow,
> Drest in the sad habiliments of woe,
> Whose brows funereal honours bind,
> And others lingering far behind,
> With veils that flutter in the wind,
> Conceal the mournful face, and dry the gushing tears. (19–26)

The pageant, led by "Fancy," includes personifications of the "Social Arts," "Bellona," "Death," "Wisdom," "Poesy," and "Commerce," who speak or gesture to the fantastic crowd as it expands beyond the reach of any human orator's voice.

It is tempting to read this poem, following as it seems to have done several publicly performed dirges by the same author, as an instance of elegiac poetry's withdrawal from civic and even interpersonal realms to a more self-reflexive world of poetic sensibility. Rowson begins by displacing the already vague, lost object of mourning from his place of retirement and transforming the landscape into an amalgam of late-eighteenth-century views of Severn and Snowdon. There, in language borrowed most directly from the elegiac sonnets of Charlotte Smith, she focuses on possibilities for imaginative compensation:

There rapt, entranc'd, each anxious thought, each care,
And each corporeal sense would dormant lay;
While visions, ever bright and ever fair,
In airy forms would round my temples play.
Keen winter's chilling blast is never felt,
While beatific scenes the fancy throng;
The heart in Zembla's frozen clime will melt,
When FANCY leads the fetter'd soul along. (9–6)

While Washington is being "led, enrapt" to his martial heaven, Rowson goes to meet a different kind of rapture and suspension of embodiment. Despite the claim of sensual dormancy, the landscape and Rowson's self-projection into it are palpable, even quietly eroticized. The brilliance of Rowson's poem—that is, what makes it seem at once both supremely witty and strongly predictive—is its transformation of the national-domestic shrine to public self-effacement into the very ground of sentimental subjectivity.

Rowson's encounter with her own fancy has, at one particularly emphatic moment, the force of autoerotic revelation: "She comes! She comes! A stream of light, / Bursts on my aching wondering sight" (17–18). Yet the vision her ecstatic withdrawal gives rise to is of a funeral procession, and the pageant conjured by her "Fancy"—which includes speeches by personifications of various aspects of national life (war, literature, commerce, memorialization)—suggests an expansive rather than contracted range of public commitments, even as the poem maintains its distance from actual scenes of public bereavement. For example, Rowson's own footnote to one of the speeches indicates that part of it was quoted "in manuscript, by Dr. Bartlett . . . in his Oration on the death of Washington."[58] The note confirms the poem's legitimizing connection to civic culture while at the same time drawing attention to the localized and occasional nature of its earlier, partial dissemination. In the context of the poem, the speech is the product of the poet's private reverie and has no other human audience. Yet it is imagined to achieve universal audibility.

Spoken by the figure of "Gratitude," the speech recommends a temperate alternative to sentimental effusiveness, rejecting "useless grief" in favor of the terms of remembrance established by Washington himself in his Farewell Address: a paradoxical combination of "independent mind" (151) and national "unanimity" (153). The speech urges a rational response but does so through the figure of an emotion—gratitude—rather than through the figures of "Wisdom," "War," or "Commerce" that also appear in the poem. The speech appeals to reason—to the idealized rational citizenry that is the implicit universal subject of republican mourning in most of the Washington elegies—but because of its affective basis, counts upon reaching "even savages, untaught and rude" (136), such as the Tennessee Cherokees Thomas Pemberton read about in his Boston newspaper. The poem understands its audibility, and the vision of nationalistic union it promotes, to depend upon this dual appeal.

This sort of self-understanding is typical of the mass of Washington elegies and relocates Rowson within the realm of republican poetics from which she also seems fantastically to depart. Rowson joins her masculinist peers, for instance, in aligning herself explicitly with the oldest traditions of poetry and panegyric. She is mindful of how "ancient poets gain'd immortal fame" (97) and says she need not envy Homer because she has an even "nobler theme" (106) to treat. Yet the framing devices of withdrawal and self-entrancement help distinguish Rowson's elegy from those of her peers to the extent to which it illustrates how the appeal to national sensibility could be made on behalf of imaginative as well as civic action. Her elegy does not seem to have been written for public performance, it was published belatedly in book form rather than hard upon the event in newspapers or broadsides, and it depicts a moment of explicitly private fancy rather than a shared vision. She reaffirms here what she had already argued elsewhere: that the indulgence of fancy is not incompatible with civic-mindedness. In her preface to *Charlotte Temple,* she asks that the book be considered "not merely the effusion of Fancy, but as a reality," and stresses her desire to "be of service" and "of use" to the widest possible readership.[59] Part of that usefulness was to give popular form to the young nation's continued engagements with grief for individual and collective losses. But if Rowson was helping to remake the novel into a kind of mourning genre, through which feelings were solicited for the furtherance of sympathetic union as well as personal edification and satisfaction, then she, her fellow novelists, and countless other professional and nonprofessional writers were also adapting traditions of elegiac poetry to new civic and imaginative requirements, including the rise of sentimental culture and its later emergence as domestic ideology. A proper history of literary mourning in the early United States must consider how elegy, too, helped instruct Americans in the imaginative basis of national self-understanding. As part of such a history, the troubled commemoration of George Washington also helps illuminate the troubled self-constitution of elegy's own national tradition as, under pressure of the nation's postrepublican transformation in the early nineteenth century, the genre adapts to new memorial requirements for its proliferating subjects—from heroic personages to cherished infants, from known individuals to entire groups and classes of the unnamed dead.

Indeed, it is worth remembering, as we turn in subsequent chapters to face some of these other subjects, that they by no means displaced Washington as an object of poetic mourning. Throughout the first half of the nineteenth century, poets including Lydia Sigourney, Thomas Holley Chivers, Samuel Bartlett Parris, Hannah Gould, John Pierpont, and John Brainard continued to write and publish elegies for Washington—elegies that in their perseveration on an increasingly distant collective loss reflect some of the changing conditions of national mourning.[60] For example, Rowson's elegiac enshrinement of Washington within the idealized precincts of a national household gets revisited by later elegists struggling, decades after Washington's death, to reassert ideals of domestic sanctity and unblemished paternal control. Sigourney's "Mistletoe at the Tomb of Washington" frets over the appearance at Washington's Mount Vernon tomb of this parasitic plant due to its pagan, specifically Virgilian associations with Aeneas's passage through the underworld on his way to founding a new imperium:

> What though in tuneful Maro's lore
> To Troy's sad chief thine aid was lent,
> Who dauntless trod the infernal shore
> Where proud and frowning shades of yore
> Their date of anguish spent,
> Yet we, to Pluto's dreary coast,
> Passport to ask of thee, disdain,—

We seek *our hero* mid the host
Where wails no grim or guilty ghost,
On heaven's unclouded plain.

The protest of these lines ("no grim or guilty ghost") suggests that Sigourney's belated elegy for Washington is also a wish for a place or condition in which to shed "the filial tear" that would not already be haunted by the casualties of America's own imperium.

One of the compensations of extended mourning—one of the incentives to persist in maintaining some sort of relationship with the deceased—is the preservation of ideals to which the deceased is linked. As John Bowlby writes, this "persistence of relationship" may help in "maintaining values and pursuing goals which, having been developed in association with the lost person, remain linked with him and can without falsification continue to be maintained and pursued in reference to memory of him."[61] This observation goes some distance toward explaining the repeated exhortations in early-nineteenth-century American culture to remember Washington and to pursue values (such as selflessness) and goals (such as a strongly unified nation) once powerfully associated with him. Yet Bowlby's optimism regarding the fate of such values and goals (the idea that they can be maintained and pursued "without falsification") does not seem readily available to Washington's later elegists, who—removed ever further from the immediacy of grief—give signs of their anxieties over the strength, legitimacy, and durability of those associations. The idealization of Washington becomes more, rather than less, conflicted, as his memory gets bound up with and attached to other, more proximate sources of grief—the deaths of later presidents, for instance (especially those of Adams and Jefferson in 1826, and of Lincoln in 1865), and the ever-darkening spectacle of slavery.

The tendency of idealizations to break down is one of the fundamental psychological insights of republican theory and its revolutionary practice. The overthrow not just of kings but of kingship was a remedial approach to the idealization of leaders on other, more modest terms. Republicanism is not a denial of the destructive impulses that persist even in the absence of dynastic succession. Rather, it is an opportunity to clear a space among envious and persecutory anxieties for something more closely approximating what Melanie Klein calls gratitude, that is, a feeling—a civic feeling—that mitigates the resentment of horizontal and vertical dependencies. Destructive impulses persist; any citizen of a republic can tell you that. But peaceful nondynastic regime change demonstrates that those impulses may be accepted rather than denied or harshly punished and that they may be accommodated without bloodshed. Ultimately, of course, this liberatory experience of gratitude is subject to its own idealization, which, in turn, helps generate and sustain the compensatory discourse known as patriotism. As an incentive to collective mourning, patriotism redirects destructive impulses beyond certain cultural or ideological barriers, like those of nation-states, and toward groups or classes of persons who not only will not be mourned but also might have to be killed. As the following chapter will show, the priority of "taking care of" the dead in the postrevolutionary period of expansion and consolidation not only amounted to a domestic privilege and a civic duty but also channeled undercurrents of violence against the remembrance of those who had been or were to be otherwise "taken care of."

CHAPTER 3

Taking Care of the Dead: Custodianship and Opposition in Antebellum Elegy

What is the use of grief in the economy?
—THOMAS JEFFERSON TO JOHN ADAMS, 1816

Elegy continued to be a popular and widely practiced genre in nineteenth-century America in part because of its traditional role in helping to sustain the idealizations to which mourning is characteristically devoted. These include the idealization of the object of mourning—its elevation to a position of unassailable virtue and undiminishing value—and also of the subject of mourning, who cherishes an image of himself or herself not only as a successful memorialist but also as the departed's worthy remembrancer and heir. Both kinds of idealization depend on a sense of the coherence and durability of relations over time. If the value of both mourner and mourned is to be preserved and even mutually enhanced, then the basis of their connection, the source of their affiliation, must remain intelligible and persuasive. Thus, the attenuation of linkages in early nineteenth-century America between past and present, and between the dead and the living, challenged elegiac resourcefulness. Increased immigration, territorial expansion, racial and cultural assimilation, continued secularization and democratization all worked to reduce the authority of traditionalism in American life and to call more and more into doubt the notion that the dead were the moral and economic creditors of the living. As antebellum America came increasingly to distinguish itself through the social detachment of economic life—an economic life characterized at once by its burgeoning corporate ethos and by the collective violence of its expansionist designs—one consequence was the rapid, market-driven devaluation of the dead and of the past. In response, antebellum elegy rehearsed, sometimes defensively, sometimes more aggressively, a commitment to the idealizations of mourning that was also a law of value: custom, precedent, ancestry, history should be affluent sources of meaning and authority in the present.

Indeed, hundreds of early-nineteenth-century elegies are bound to the repetition of this law. Verses of conservative custodial remembrance proliferate, for instance, in response to the deaths of Presidents Jefferson and Adams. So, too, do poems—such as Lydia Sigourney's tribute to "The Mother of Washington" and Jane Schoolcraft's memorial to Ojibwa chief Waub Ojeeb—that seek to use elegy's traditionalism as an oppositional resource for the celebration of the historically overlooked or maligned.[1] Especially numerous were elegies for young children, whose individual deaths could not readily be deemed historically significant. Against the dehistoricizing energies of contemporary life, the commemoration of personal and collective losses laded the atmosphere. "The air is full of farewells to the dying / And mournings for the dead," wrote Longfellow in an elegy for his infant daughter Fanny. Whether to "keep unbroken," as Longfellow puts it, "[t]he bond which nature gives" between parent and child, or to promote public memorial allegiances to the forgotten and the disprized, antebellum elegists urge memory of the dead upon the living.[2] In doing so, they also urge versions of themselves invested with the authority of the dead and of the values developed in association with them: for example, Jefferson's republicanism, Waub Ojeeb's hereditary valor, Fanny Longfellow's innocence. And further, as elegists, they urge the authority of the genre itself.

Yet the genre is also under pressure to adapt. If elegists must work harder to liberate the individual suppressed and diminished by what Emerson calls the "sheaths and clogs of organization," they must also encompass the aggregate suffering of groups and classes of the unnamed dead.[3] In

an era of corporatism—that is, of society's perceived devotion to com-
binatorial urgencies—the public expression of personal bereavement
can register as a protest against the devaluation of the individual. At the
same time, elegists learn to practice a corporatism of their own, insofar
as collective mourning can model an alternative to the massive social
disavowals of slavery, Indian removal, and other programs of suppression and dispossession. In formal terms, this means that conventional
elegies share space with more obliquely elegiac poems: poems that medi-
tate upon death, that reflect broadly upon relations between the living
and the dead, and that participate in elegiac conventions while often
avoiding the personalism and occasionalism of traditional elegy.

These more obliquely elegiac poems—among which none was more
popular or widely imitated than William Cullen Bryant's "Thanatopsis"—
extended the tradition of graveyard meditations on unspecified griefs
popularized by Robert Blair, Edward Young, and Thomas Gray in
the eighteenth century. They also localized this tradition, supplying
American settings for and emplotments of its more general appeal to
the culturally and psychologically tenacious sensation of being haunted
by the dead. "The dead are there," as Bryant puts it in "Thanatopsis,"
signaling the need for readjustments to the spaces and environments
in which lost objects endure.[4] Whether in the naturalized precincts of
America's new rural cemeteries, or in the proliferating monuments of
national life, or in the morbid excesses of sensational literature, or in
the unsettled, ostensibly solitary expanses of the western territories, the
dead awaited the living amid the shifting memorial requirements and
possibilities of nineteenth-century American life.

Bryant's many elegies and his more obliquely elegiac poems explore
the physical and conceptual spaces in which the dead seem to await the
living: spaces of domestic and national life, of historical density and
apparent blankness, of idealism and retribution. His poems take hold
of death as an occasion not only for commemorative and consolidating efforts but also for the imaginative exploration of individual and
collective aspirations beyond known or assigned boundaries. They are
meditations on death as both a limitation on and a condition of freedom. By challenging the personal dimension of traditional elegy, and
by exploring the limits of received poetic technique and form, Bryant
contributed significantly to the elegiac accent in American poetry in

poems ranging from his frustrated elegy for his father ("Hymn to Death") to the exhortation to death of "Thanatopsis," and from his Indian laments to his Jacksonian version of a Romantic history of death in "The Prairies."

The fact that Bryant's poetic achievement occurred in tandem with his rise to prominence as one of the most powerful voices of liberal opinion in antebellum America particularly encourages attention to what Jahan Ramazani calls the "ethical grounds of recuperative art."[5] Most fundamentally, this means questioning the elegist's aesthetic capitalization on the memory of the dead and on the losses and sufferings of others. What price do the living pay for the idealization of the dead? What price do the dead pay for the self-idealizations of the mourner? Should the elegist's transformation of mourning into poetry depend for its legitimacy upon his or her own experience as a mourner? Is the aestheticization of someone else's grief a kind of theft? When and how does the promise of consolation for unjust losses contribute to the ideological work of oppression? For example, while remaining virtually silent on the violence of Indian removal in his editorial journalism, Bryant wrote elegies from the perspective of Indian mourners—poems that seek to impose naturalistic order and transcendent meaning on mass deaths. Such white-authored Indian laments are among the most common types of nineteenth-century American elegy: a fixture, like child elegies, of the period's incessant rehearsal of compensatory mourning. These elegies perseverate on the possibility of compensation for losses that are also a source of self-recrimination; they seek not only to recuperate some image, semblance, or sensation of what has been lost but also to restore the ambivalent mourner to a world of shared meanings in which the value of particular losses would be stable and readily apparent. If the abundance of elegies and the diffuseness of elegiac practice suggest that antebellum culture gets stuck on its experience of loss, it is precisely because the value of particular losses—and the value conferred on persons by their *becoming* lost—was being thrown evermore into question.

Meditating on the value of the lives they have lived, Thomas Jefferson and John Adams exchanged a long series of letters during the year 1816, at the dawn of what Charles Sellers has called the "market revolution."

Their debate over resurrection and immortality was an occasion not only for their airing of end-of-life anxieties but also for reflection upon the development and sustenance of corporate continuity in a nation whose future they would not live to see and perhaps not even be remembered by. Their remarks on "the uses of grief in the economy" pertain at once to the difficult necessity of assigning value to individual lives ("I cannot," wrote Adams, "weigh Sensations and Reflections, Pleasures and Pains, Hopes and Fears in Money Scales") and to the dangers of doing so.[6] Thus, "I will tease you with another Question," Adams writes in one of his letters. "What have been the Abuses of Grief?" Answering his own query, Adams adduces several examples, both ancient and modern, of grief expressed in the service of corporate interest. He does not forget the astonishing display provoked by the death of the nation's first president:

> The Death of Washington, diffused a general Grief. The Old Tories, the Hyperfederalists, the Speculators, sett up a general Howl. Orations Prayers Sermons Mock Funerals, were all employed, not that they loved Washington, but to keep in Countenance the Funding and Banking Systems; And to cast into the Background and the Shade all others who had been concerned in the Service of their Country in the Revolution.[7]

If the tallying of grief may help measure the value of individual lives, as Adams has been trying to convince his friend, partial or insincere expressions of grief may also devalue or even obliviate such lives. Adams's example goes so far as to tease out the relation between grief and value in specifically economic terms: the grief, or rather the semblance of grief, exhibited by Washington's most voluble mourners had no backing, and thus, Adams implies, it bore a suspicious relation to the inflated currency that Washington and Hamilton's banking system loosed upon the nation—a system both Adams and Jefferson feared would continue to vitiate sound credit and defeat legitimate enterprise in the interest of corporate capital.

Such fears metastasized as industrialism and the rise of corporations seemed increasingly to undermine any positive relation between economic and moral progress. In his *Short History of Paper Money and Banking in the United States* (1833), William Gouge objects to corporations on both idealistic and practical grounds as being "incompatible with equality of rights" and "unfavorable to the progress of national wealth." Not only, Gouge argues, are corporations like the Second Bank of the United States bulwarked against the redress of individuals and even of governments, but they are also immune to the leveling influence to which all individuals, however powerful, must submit. "If a man is unjust, or an extortioner, society is sooner or later relieved from the burden, by his death. But corporations never die."[8] They never die, that is, unless they are made to do so, which is what Gouge quietly advocates and what Andrew Jackson set out more boldly to do in his famous 1832 veto of the bill to recharter the bank. The controversy provoked by the veto and by Jackson's subsequent withdrawal of some federal deposits from the bank was bitter and prolonged, and it resulted in some of the same abuses of grief among the bank's supporters that Adams had derided almost twenty years earlier.[9]

This time, however, the object of mourning was not a person but a corporation, the bank itself, which was being mourned, as William Cullen Bryant reported to readers of the pro-Jackson New York *Evening Post,* in the crocodile elegies of rival newspapers, the "Jeremiads of the Bank journals." "It is heart-rending," Bryant writes,

> to hear their doleful lamentations on the occasion of the removal of the deposits. They lift up their voices and weep aloud. From the depth of their affliction come sounds of sublime denunciation. They grieve with an exceeding great grief over the fallen glory of their temple, and refuse to be comforted.

Bryant's satire on the exploitation of these mourning conventions attributes such displays to pure greed. "Who can wonder," he asks, "that they appear at the head of the funeral train as chief mourners, and raise so loud their solemn wul-wullahs, when he reflects how well their grief is paid for."[10]

Bryant's cynicism finds a youthful, idealistic counterpart in his earlier solicitousness for a culture insufficiently mindful of communal responsibility. Disgusted by the pettiness and insensibility he was encountering as a young western Massachusetts lawyer (in the early poem "Green River" [1820], he writes of being "forced to drudge for the dregs of men" [*Poetical Works,* 1:33]), Bryant sought to remind readers of his 1819 essay "On the Happy Temperament" of the importance of personal relations and their basis in sympathy—the use, that is, of grief in the economy. "To be moved to sorrow by the sufferings of others," he writes,

> and to grieve for calamities of our own, are laws of nature, ordained for sacred and beneficent purposes, and are the moving principles of all that we do for our own happiness, and all the good that we impart to others.[11]

To the extent that feelings of mutual responsibility were based in economic relations, Bryant's age experienced a devaluation of such feelings as economic relations became increasingly depersonalized. The articulation of Romantic subjectivity in Bryant and other contemporary writers conspired with the social detachment of economic life in Jacksonian America. It was not as a commentary upon the times, but it was in keeping with them, that Emerson wrote "our relations to each other are oblique and casual."[12]

In Bryant's day, taking care of the dead was becoming a largely domestic and entrepreneurial rather than civic and communal priority. Religious ties and observances were centered increasingly on the family, graveyards were being relocated from town centers to rural outskirts, and mortuary superintendence was undergoing commercial privatization. The notion of a shared dead was growing less and less tenable. Mourning was becoming an increasingly domestic matter, and it was finding expression in a bourgeoning literature of consolation that often served as a medium for protest against an increasingly market-driven society. Yet mourning literatures were never fully assimilated to the literature of domesticity. Antebellum motifs of death and melancholy ambivalently reflect clashing ideals of personal individuation and national and historical consolidation. Against a backdrop of continental expansion, Indian removal, and literary nationalism, the stakes of custodianship of the dead bore materially on experiences of strife and solidarity among the living. Anticipating his lampoon of the bank elegies, Bryant, for example, had already begun in his early verse to explore the uses of grief and of poetry in the moral and market economies of early nineteenth-century America.

Bryant came to the literary scene with a nationalist's sense of what was possible, confident that the American "Genius" would fail to rival that of Europe only if it sat "idle in the midst of its treasures."[13] Among those treasures was the expanding audience for literature he identified in his 1818 essay on "Early American Verse":

> The fondness for literature is fast increasing, and, if this were not the case, the patrons of literature have multiplied, of course, and will continue to multiply, with the mere growth of our population. (*Prose*, 1:56)

Bryant's trust in the growing ranks of "patrons of literature" reflects his faith in the successful development of new-style markets for literary commodities. Indeed, the audience for his own books and magazine verse grew considerably, so that by 1842, as William Charvat reports, he was the best-known and best-paid American poet.[14]

This distinction, however, did not amount to much in financial terms. Professionally, Bryant was not a poet but a newspaper man, his New York *Evening Post* netting him as much as forty times the amount of money his poetry brought in.[15] Shortly after the publication of his 1832 *Poems,* he told his brother that the book was selling "tolerably well—that is, for poetry, which in this country is always of slim sale. I do not expect, however, to make much by it."[16] He did not. The national literary markets were by that time demonstrably not for poetry but for fiction—a medium through which the new "patrons of literature" could find reflected back their own market orientations.

In more disinterested moments, Bryant found this development hopeful and exciting. Reviewing Catharine Sedgwick's novel *Redwood* in 1825, he insisted that American literature's proliferating consumers were also its worthy subjects, dynamic inhabitants of a "country of enterprise" with characters strongly defined by "ambition and a love of adventure."[17] But if a rapidly growing empire for literature in the New World is often the pride of his journalism, death is frequently the atmosphere of his verse. Instead of the "bustle, and change, and action"[18] he sees all around him as available material for American novelists, Bryant dwells on quieter presences in poetry that is more descriptive than narrative, not romance but elegy. In "Thanatopsis," for example, Sedgwick's "country of enterprise" empties into a realm of somnolent transcendence:

> The gay will laugh
> When thou art gone, the solemn brood of care

Plod on, and each one as before will chase
His favorite phantom; yet all these shall leave
Their mirth and their employments, and shall come
And make their bed with thee. (*Poetical Works*, 1:19)

From the rural Massachusetts of his early verse to the western expanses of "The Prairies," Bryant's poetry and the American landscape it depicts are engrossed by the dead.

While Bryant's earliest manuscript productions include occasional poems on the deaths of relatives and friends, he also aspires to something beyond personal elegism. His meditations on death often seek to maintain a totalizing view, even when the impulse to remember a particular person is strong. Throughout his career, Bryant continued to channel this impulse into conventional elegies for associates and public figures like William Leggett, the elder Channing, and Lincoln. That the personalizing impulse is often suppressed, however, and at considerable psychological cost, is the suggestion of one of his most conflicted poems.

Bryant's "Hymn to Death" begins as a defense—a kind of brief for Death, "slandered" (*Poetical Works*, 1:46) by the world, by a poet whose profession was still the law. It proceeds as an expression of his desire to transcend the dour and lachrymose conventions of elegy ("reproaches . . . cries and prayers" [1:46]) and, instead, to speak Death's praises as a "Deliverer" (1:47) and as "the great reformer of the world" (1:50). Death metes out sorrow, to be sure. The poet himself has "wept / Thy conquests, and may weep them yet again" (1:46). But he is nevertheless inspired with the conviction that universal justice is the recompense for private tears. The conqueror, the king, the tyrant, the extortioner, the perjurer, the sybarite—all the agents of oppression are alike struck down by Death in defense of the weak and to the perpetuation of the principle of goodness.

The poet's rationalization of suffering and his temporizing attitude toward the correction of inequity are themselves struck down after line 133, however, as his father's unexpected death intrudes upon the poem. The celebratory mode suddenly seems inappropriate to Bryant ("It must cease" [1:51]), as if the actual death were too difficult to reconcile with the abstract principle of reform. Earlier in the poem, he had maintained that Death's role was "to free the oppressed / And crush the oppressor" (1:47). But Dr. Peter Bryant belonged to neither category, and the recognition prompted by his death of a skewed moral economy (Dr. Bryant is gone while liars, thieves, and hypocrites are "left to cumber earth") leads to the poet's indictment of his own idealism:

> Shuddering I look
> On what is written, yet I blot not out
> The desultory numbers; let them stand,
> The record of an idle revery. (1:52)

Bryant's scrupulousness about letting stand what he "shudder[s]" to look upon dramatizes an ethical tension that is present but less palpable in most of his reveries about mortality and death.[19] He wants to offer a proper memorial to his father, whose death returns him from abstract musings to the reality of loss (both father and "Hymn" are "cut off / Untimely" [1:51]). Yet his "faltering verse" also expresses a commitment to the depersonalization of death and loss that he will not renounce, even in the face of personal tragedy.[20]

Bryant's fervor to defend death and to rehabilitate its image for the "wise and pure in heart" (1:46) wavers before his more urgent need to make sense of losing his father, a task that is complicated by his idealization of death earlier in the poem. He makes an elegy out of his own irresolution of the problem. Belatedly, the poem seeks to stabilize in memorial fashion an image of the lost father, abandoning as it does so its hymnic effort to glorify death. Yet the entire "Hymn to Death" reflects a complex range of attitudes concerning its nominal subject. In the poem, death is variously a calumniated victim in need of defense and an avenger of the innocent, a familiar interlocutor and an object of fear, a reformer of corrupt individuals and an indiscriminate destroyer, an agent of historical progress and a leveler of temporal distinctions, a violent fate and a tranquil sleep, a biological fact and an ontological necessity.

The poem's inability to present a stable, ideal image of death precipitates its collapse into the personalism of elegy, for which Peter Bryant's death is the bitter occasion. But the desire for such an image—and the poet's identification with it—persists in his decision to let the verses "stand." "Hymn to Death" discovers in the death of the poet's father the intractability of individual losses. Irreconcilable with the poet's vision of a universal justice mediated by Death and with his poetic effort to universalize the experience of loss, his father's death forces the poet to confront both his own political naivete and the inadequacy of his "Hymn" to the occasion:

> This faltering verse, which thou
> Shalt not, as wont, o'erlook, is all I have
> To offer at thy grave. (1:51)

Yet while he regrets not having a better offering to make, he nevertheless elects ambivalently to preserve and conclude, rather than simply to replace, the "Hymn" with an elegiac valediction to both his poem and to the father "who taught my youth / The art of verse, and in the bud of life / Offered me to the Muses" (1:51). By emphasizing this vocational link, and by incorporating a number of pastoral devices and tropes, Bryant ends up locating his poem within the elegiac tradition of younger poets mourning the loss of older poets. In doing so he asserts the durability of elegy as a generic resource. Yet he also clearly still wants to find a way of employing poetically his idealization of Death, despite the exposure of his uncritical relation to political ideals and despite its interference with individuated mourning. "Let them stand" needs to be read as both self-admonishing (I won't suppress the evidence of my naivete) and as ocdipally aggressive (I have killed/replaced my father). But it also defends the verses themselves against being cleared away as a broken memorial to an elegiac practice whose reparative terms could no longer strongly cohere amid the inequities of the new moral and market economies.

As the ambivalent outcome of both reverie and grief, "Hymn to Death" also occupies a position at the historically indistinct boundary between the poetry of elegiac meditation and generic elegy. Indeed, the poem's enactment of a struggle against the tenacity of generic consciousness helps mark Bryant as one of America's Romantic poets.[21] And like so much of Bryant's verse, only more dramatically than most, it also reflects the general uncertainty about the meaning of death that, in its combination of rationality and dread, imagination and orthodoxy, typifies late-Enlightenment Anglo-American culture. In his resistance to received ways of thinking about death, including those ways that generic elegy sometimes enforces, Bryant could not match, even in his best poems, Wordsworth's portrayal in "Tintern Abbey" (1798) of an intimate relation between nature and human imagination, nor did he ever so much as suggest the fatal erotic desperation of Shelley's "Alastor" (1816). Nevertheless, as Shelley was composing his first major work, Bryant was beginning to imagine in American terms the response Whitman would still be calling for half a century later. "In the future of these States," Whitman would write after the Civil War in *Democratic Vistas,* "must arise poets immenser far, and make great poems of death"—death, that is, as an occasion not for grief and fear (there must, Whitman says, be no more "shuddering at death") but for thoughts of limitless possibility, of progress and fulfillment.[22] While Bryant stopped short of Whitman's exorbitant claims for poetry, he nevertheless shared with Whitman a sense of death's power as a poetic motif to express a commitment to the idealization of America's material and ideological advancement. The ambivalence of his "Hymn to Death" reveals him to be far less confident, however, about how to reconcile this commitment with practical existence, with occasions for grief and for reform.

Bryant's idealizing practice gets elaborated in poems that often manifest conflicting orientations toward literary antecedents, and thus toward aesthetic as well as social reform. Forming and reforming American literature meant for Bryant and for other antebellum writers something comparable to what many contemporary political and economic reformers hoped to achieve: a disruption of future investments in past concessions to false or outworn decorums. Would the development of American memory have to proceed in strict relation to ancestral forms? Or rather than submitting grief to their familiar shaping power, could Americans freshly apprehend grief itself as an incentive to new cultural achievements? Would new and ancestral forms alike be devalued and displaced by the ruthless transformational goals of market revolution? Or could new economic and moral environments enhance the innovative and even oppositional potential of mourning conventions?

Bryant remained occupied with these questions throughout his poetic career. One of his earliest elegiac verses is a meditation on Anglo-American literary relations that, in its very title, recognizes itself to be one of America's fresh Romantic ruins. In "The Burial-Place: A Fragment" (1818), Bryant notes that altered circumstances made of mourning a very different ritual for Protestant Americans than it had been for their English forebears. In a new land, certain "gentle rites / Passed out of use"—rites having largely to do with the vegetal adornment of graves. Whereas the somber tones of English churchyards were lightened by the careful placement of "shades" and "blossoms" (*Poetical Works,* 1:28), in America, "[n]aked rows of graves / And melancholy ranks of monuments / Are seen instead" (1:29–30), and it is left to Nature herself to decorate the broken, neglected ground with wild roses and strawberry plants.

The place of abandoned forms, Bryant suggests, needs to be supplied. But his fragment of a poem leaves unfinished the characterization it begins of an American mourning ritual—a ritual yet to emerge from the "fresh virgin soil" along with the "strange flowers" (1:29) that are not only signs of a distinct American topography but also promises of fresh elegiac conventions. "The Burial-Place" is a scene of reading. It enumerates, in its first half, some of the more familiar plants from the pastoral elegy tradition (including yew, willow, primrose, pansy, and woodbine) and also implicitly recalls, in its second half, the history of elegy in America, beginning with the "pilgrim bands who passed the sea" (1:29), for whom elegy was such a prized poetic genre. The contrast Bryant sets up between British and American traditions seems to favor the former. Yet while the bleak regimentation of "[n]aked rows" and "melancholy ranks" in "The Burial-Place" evokes the perceived multiplicity without variety of seventeenth- and eighteenth-century New England funeral elegies, an allusion to "Lycidas" some lines later suggests a distancing from the English pastoral tradition as well. The bramble that grows near the graves "[o]ffers its berries to the schoolboy's hand, / In vain—they grow too near the dead" (1:30). Milton's "berries harsh and crude" are reduced in the schoolboy's superstitious eyes to metonymic extensions of the dead themselves, offering not the immortality of poetic achievement but the fatality of curse or contagion.[23]

But while Bryant cautioned American poets against the "sickly and affected imitation" (*Prose,* 1:54) of their British antecedents, he by no means conceived of a new American poetry wholly immune to their continued influence. Dating the "origin" of American poetry from the moment of political independence (*Prose,* 1:48), he nevertheless maintained that the reading and tutelary imitation of British poets would continue to have a beneficial effect upon the production of homespun works for American literary markets. As a self-consciously nationalistic poet, Bryant wrestles with himself in "The Burial-Place" over what use to make of a British tradition that is at once familiar and alienated and a Puritan tradition that is both native and defunct. As a characteristically elegiac poet, he makes ambivalent gestures of contact with the past as a means of critiquing present usages. In fact, the disposition to commune with extant forms is the complex subject of his most famous poem, in which he loosens the formal and thematic bounds of elegiac poetry.

"Thanatopsis": Poetry, Nature, Politics

Growing up just as the enormous shadow of Pope's influence was lifting in America, Bryant had a special interest in metrical form, particularly in the use of the trisyllabic foot, which was still controversial in the early nineteenth century. One of his earliest critical pieces was a polemic against Augustan regularity, in which he likens metrical features to topographic ones. He writes that when he encounters the improving beauty of some trisyllabics "amid a dead waste of disyllabic feet, their spirited irregularity refreshes and relieves me, like the sight of eminences and forests breaking the uniformity of a landscape" (*Prose,* 1:65). As he was composing his essay "On Trisyllabic Feet in Iambic Measure," Bryant was also practicing the spirited irregularity it espoused in the Wordsworthian blank verse of "Thanatopsis," which begins with the assurance that

> To him who in the love of Nature holds
> Communion with her visible forms, she speaks
> A various language. . . . (*Poetical Works,* 1:17)

Bryant's use of trisyllabics in lines 2 and 3 suggests a connection between the irregularity of natural and poetic forms and indicates that metrical variation will be part of his communion with the reader.

Bryant continues to use trisyllabics throughout "Thanatopsis" as a subtle way of reinforcing meaning. Toward the end of the poem, for instance, he contrasts sound and sense by deploying the faltering rhythm of two consecutive trisyllabics in the phrase "an unfaltering trust" (1:20). Modest as it now seems, this sort of variation on strict iambic meter was fairly daring at a time when liberated rhythms were finding slow acceptance in New England. Eighteenth-century prosodic standards were still being generally upheld.[24] But in his essay on trisyllabics, Bryant offers Edward Young's melancholy classic *Night Thoughts* (1742) as a cautionary example of the price of mechanical conformity to ideals of "point" and "sententiousness," which he says injured the "fine flow" of Young's imagination and of his verse. "It was," Bryant writes, "like setting the Mississippi to spout little *jets d'eau* and turn children's waterwheels" (*Prose*, 1:63).

This fanciful comparison suggests that Bryant held Young, for all his flaws, in high esteem. Indeed, Bryant's inclination to dwell on the problem of human mortality led him to respond strongly to the loose tradition of poets, ranging from Young and Robert Blair to Thomas Gray and Wordsworth, who focused their attention on what it means to die and on what it means to experience the death of another. "Thanatopsis" incorporates some motifs and images from this tradition in its opening admonition to the reader:

> When thoughts
> Of the last bitter hour come like a blight
> Over thy spirit, and sad images
> Of the stern agony, and shroud, and pall,
> And breathless darkness, and the narrow house,
> Make thee to shudder, and grow sick at heart;—
> Go forth, under the open sky, and list
> To Nature's teachings. . . . (1:17)

Such "sad images," of course, "come like a blight" primarily from various forms of evangelistic and imaginative literature, including the minister-poet Robert Blair's *The Grave* (1743), whose gothic machinery Bryant draws on heavily. While he rejects Blair's Christian orthodoxy in favor of an overtly naturalistic one, Bryant is nevertheless a somewhat reluctant iconoclast, preserving Blair's imagistic vehicles while dropping their Calvinist tenor. The "sad images" remain compelling to him.

Yet images may both precede and outlast what they represent, and Bryant leaves it uncertain whether the "shudder" these sepulchral images produce is the result of their premonitory power or of their contrivance—whether we "grow sick at heart" in terror of death or in loathing of gothic excess. The "shudder" of line 13 recalls the "shuddering" look Bryant casts upon his own verses in "Hymn to Death," where his reaction is not primarily one of fear but of distaste at his own imaginative and moral complacence. He associates something of that distaste with the hackneyed expressions ("last bitter hour," "stern agony," "breathless darkness") that link "Thanatopsis" with its British models and their often shopworn phrases and figures.

Bryant was an early and appreciative reader of *Lyrical Ballads,* and he shared a measure of Wordsworth's dissatisfaction with the artificial language that had, as Wordsworth notes in his preface, "long been regarded as the common inheritance of Poets." "Thanatopsis" registers a "shudder" both for the prospect of death and for that poetic "falsehood of description" Wordsworth famously disavows, in part by asserting his forfeiture of the inheritance best represented for him by the elaborate diction of Gray's elegy for Richard West.[25] If Bryant himself makes no such assertions, he nevertheless seeks to embed his numerous borrowings from Gray and others in a matrix of blank verse, casual diction, prosaic rhythms, republican principles, and American topography.

Like Wordsworth, Bryant affirms a locodescriptive poetics. "I saw some lines by you to the skylark," he wrote his brother John in 1832. "Did you ever see such a bird? Let me counsel you to draw your images, in describing Nature, from what you observe around you. . . . The skylark is an English bird, and an American who has never visited Europe has no right to be in raptures about it" (*Letters,* 1:319–20). Bryant's insistence that there is a "right" to poetic rapture grounded in direct observation seems to confirm Tocqueville's nearly contemporary claim that there is a diminished taste for ideal beauty in democratic societies. "Doubt," he says, "pulls the poet's imagination back down to earth and confines him to the visible and real world."[26] Instead of Shelleyan skylarks, Bryant is careful to populate his poetry with North American species. Indeed, whereas Shelley in "To a Sky-Lark" (1820) is drawn heavenward by the unseen songbird's voice, Bryant's imagination tends to dwell in the more down-to-earth company of birds of industry and predation: hangbirds, brown thrashers, redbirds, vultures, desert eagles, and prairie hawks. While Shelley's skylark seems liberated from the burden of mortality, Bryant's birds are often reminders of death's imminence. The "[l]one wandering" bird in his "To a Waterfowl" (1818), for example, evades not listeners but "the fowler's eye" (*Poetical Works*, 1:26).

Bryant's "right" to be in raptures about the waterfowl is anecdotally confirmed by his biographer, who recounts the story of the solitary evening walk and the sighting of the bird that may have inspired the poem.[27] But there is no mention of the hunter, who nevertheless becomes an emblem in the poem of Tocqueville's "visible and real world," and who may in fact be a sign of Bryant's skepticism about the idealization of nature during a period of promiscuous destruction. The fowler suggests the objectification of nature as commodity or sport. Yet as the agent of death he also stands poised at the threshold of the invisible world conjured by the poem's elegiac tone: "And soon shall that toil end," the poet says of the bird's long flight. "Soon shalt thou find a summer home, and rest" (1:27).

Throughout Bryant's poetry, places of rest—the forest, the prairie's ancient mounds, ubiquitous graves—mark the limits of both experiential and imaginative "communion" with nature's "visible forms." While the speaker of "Thanatopsis," for example, invites the reader to "[g]o forth, under the open sky"—to abandon his "darker musings" and the gothic obscurity of tombs (*Poetical Works*, 1:17)—one nevertheless leaves the tomb only to find it again in nature's forms, which monumentally mask an ineffable reality:

> The hills
> Rock-ribbed and ancient as the sun,—the vales
> Stretching in pensive quietness between;
> The venerable woods—rivers that move
> In majesty, and the complaining brooks
> That make the meadows green; and, poured round all,
> Old Ocean's gray and melancholy waste,—

> Are but the solemn decorations all
> Of the great tomb of man. (1:18–19)

The moral liveliness of these topographic features (the "pensive" vales, the "venerable woods," majestic rivers, complaining brooks, and melancholy ocean), hitherto a sympathetic source of delight, is frozen into mere decorativeness by their association with human death. Bryant here casts nature in the role of the ceremonious undertakers whose discretion is praised in Blair's *The Grave*:

> 'Midst all the gorgeous Figures you exhibit,
> Why is the Principal conceal'd, for which
> You make this mighty Stir? 'Tis wisely done.
> What would offend the Eye in a good Picture
> The Painter casts discreetly into Shades.[28]

Like a painter,[29] Bryant seeks to offer a "prospect of death," which is more or less what the nonce word "Thanatopsis" means.[30] Yet while the "golden sun, / The planets, all the infinite host of heaven, / Are shining on the sad abodes of death" (1:19), the landscape conceals rather than illuminates the poem's principal subject.

Tocqueville considered locodescriptive poetry to be only a transitional phase in the imaginative contest between idealism and skepticism in democratic society. "I am convinced," he wrote, "that in the long run democracy will deflect the imagination from everything external to man in order to fix it exclusively on man himself." His political interpretation of literary history emphasizes the importance to Americans of "what will be," rather than what has been or even what is.[31] This orientation toward the future highlights a sense of structural incompletion that in early assessments of American literature, from Orestes Brownson's incipient socialism to Tocqueville's aristocratic critique, results in a common theme of cultural inadequacy qualified by the promise of greatness to come. "I am quite prepared to admit," Tocqueville wrote, "that the Americans have no poets but not that they have no poetic ideas."[32] Emerson and Poe, and after them Melville and Whitman, would attempt to transform this cliché into the metaphysical center of American aesthetics by elevating unfulfilled possibility to the status of cultural ideal. As both an enabling condition and a limit of this ideal, death was for them a key metaphorical context for forms of transcendence that subverted rather than served the ideological interests of contemporary art and politics.

In "Thanatopsis," Bryant treats death not as a historically conditioned—and thus conceivably surmountable—barrier to political and imaginative freedom but as a necessary destination where struggle against unfulfilled possibility is retroactively rendered meaningless. He likens this destination to the western landscape, where the dead, in the stipulated absence of the living, populate a kind of countersocial vision, a necrotopia:

> Or lose thyself in the continuous woods
> Where rolls the Oregon, and hears no sound,
> Save his own dashings—yet the dead are there:
> And millions in those solitudes, since first
> The flight of years began, have laid them down
> In their last sleep—the dead reign there alone. (1:19)

Losing oneself in the unpopulated wilderness, Bryant implies, means finding oneself in the midst of an ongoing communal project in which social distinctions are obviated.

Bryant retains, however, the language of political power ("the dead reign"), along with a complementary language of renunciation ("laid them down"). Indeed, the gesture of renunciation typifies the stance toward death encouraged by the poem through repeated images of surrender, withdrawal, and recumbence. "Thou shalt lie down," Bryant promises,

> With patriarchs of the infant world—with kings,
> The powerful of the earth—the wise, the good,
> Fair forms, and hoary seers of ages past,
> All in one mighty sepulcher. (1:18)

This easy conflation (patterned after Job 3:13–19) of political ranks in the face of death—the assurance that death, rather than power over life, gives life its meaning—culminates in the famous exhortation with which the poem concludes:

> So live, that when thy summons comes to join
> The innumerable caravan, which moves

To that mysterious realm, where each shall take
His chamber in the silent halls of death,
Thou go not, like the quarry-slave at night,
Scourged to his dungeon, but, sustained and soothed
By an unfaltering trust, approach thy grave,
Like one who wraps the drapery of his couch
About him, and lies down to pleasant dreams.[33] (1:20)

Bryant seems here to confirm his view of death not as a yet-unconquered limit to freedom but as what Herbert Marcuse refers to as an "existential privilege," the "self-chosen end of his living."[34]

The initial spondee of line 73, however, accentuates an imperative ("So live") that equivocates the poem's exhortation to death. To make knowledge of death a consolation rather than a burden, one must not invoke a privilege but adopt a mode of action—one that the poem leaves unspecified. It reveals only that this mode of action, or way of living, is based on "an unfaltering trust," a phrase whose loose metrical underpinnings encourage an at least momentary skepticism. Trust in what? The will of the state? Corporeal resurrection? The voice of the poet? Historical process? In linking immortality to ethical conduct in terms of compliance and submission, Bryant manages to evoke key stages in the history of the idea of death from Socrates and Christ to Wordsworth and Hegel in his own time. Yet it is "trust," rather than any spiritual, anthropological, or historical object of such trust, to which the idea of death is finally reduced.

The poem's blandishment to confidence belies the uncertainty that precipitates the crisis of Bryant's "Hymn to Death." Trust or confidence in the face of death, as the "Hymn" reflects, was increasingly compromised in Bryant's time by complex, often antithetical circumstances, such as the decline of popular interest in formal theology occurring alongside the emergence of the higher criticism of the Bible, the persistence of providential interpretations of natural history in the wake of major advances in geological science, and the growing strength of the evangelical impulse despite the influence of skeptical arguments against the doctrine of the soul's immortality. "Thanatopsis" expertly manages to subdue, in a way that helps account for its enormous popular success, a potentially agitated range of attitudes toward death. It tends to inspire the trust it calls for. Nevertheless, the metrical fillip of the phrase "an unfaltering trust" coming at the end of the poem suggests a view of death that also takes in the faltering of that trust.

As an exhortation to trust, "Thanatopsis" looks forward to various expressions of confidence in forms of self-expansion.[35] But from Jacksonian individualism to transcendentalism, such forms, like the welcome death in Bryant's poem, would entail potentially disturbing requirements for self-renunciation. "Can you not save me," Emerson wrote to Samuel Ward from Nantasket Beach in 1841, "dip me into ice water, find me some girdling belt, that I glide not away into a stream or a gas, and decease in infinite diffusion?" Emerson in need of rescue from a sensual, Keatsian exhalation into death is an excellent caricature of the predicament of American idealism as it awakens, amid the "din and snappish activity and invention and wilfulness" of Emerson's New England, to the possible self-sublimating consequences of its enthusiasms. "I have seen enough," Emerson tells Ward, "of the obedient sea wave forever lashing the obedient shore. I find no emblems here that speak any other language than the sleep and abandonment of my woods and blueberry pastures at home."[36]

Emerson's "obedient sea" recalls the decorative ocean of "Thanatopsis," which along with other natural forms speaks a language of "sleep and abandonment" that displaces the language of political power. The achieved calm of Bryant's poem depends on an idea of death that does not belong, or does not seem to belong, to the realm of political struggle. Indeed, there are many ways in which Bryant's poetic idealism (and his idealism about poetry) supports an unreconstructed view of Romantic apoliticism. Yet the aspiration beyond assigned limits that characterizes the American reception and transformation of European Romanticism also fuels the practical implementation of dreams of market expansion and territorial acquisition. In his elegiac poetry of the 1820s and 1830s, Bryant further explored the consequences of Romantic aspiration not only for the metaphysics of death but also for the morbidity of power.

Bryant's Indian Laments

The number and popularity of Indian laments in eighteenth- and nineteenth-century American poetry reflect the ongoing need of many white Americans to believe in the inevitability of Indian disappearance even as the active and uncertain work of displacement and genocide proceeded. The dissemination of the figure of the dead or dying Indian through such poems both naturalized and anteriorized the fatal consequences of political and military protocols of removal. Lora Romero's observation regarding a cluster of American novels from the 1820s and 1830s also well describes one aspect of the cultural work of the poetic tradition that precedes them: "The elegiac mode here performs the historical sleight of hand crucial to the topos of the doomed aboriginal: it represents the disappearance of the native not just as natural but as having already happened."[37] In more genre-specific terms, the common version of the Indian lament in which the poet adopts the perspective and the voice of an Indian mourner also functions as a kind of white cultural totem against Indian wrath: it projects a recognizable memorial impulse onto the figure of the living Indian and thus, by substituting aesthetic discipline for emotional volatility, helps displace the image of the vengeful savage. The Indian who composes elegies is less likely to seek consolation or redress through violence.

In the 1820s, as the ostensibly inevitable disappearance of native populations and cultures was being effected with the augmented energy of the War Department's new Bureau of Indian Affairs and the push toward the Indian Removal Act, Bryant wrote two elegies from the perspective of Indian mourners: "An Indian at the Burial-Place of His Fathers" (1824) and "The Indian Girl's Lament" (1825). Both poems employ a six-line stanza consisting of a cross-rhymed quatrain followed by a rhymed couplet: a symmetrical, stable structure that reinforces a sense of mournful composure. Each poem opens with additional assurances that the passion of grief has been or will be sublimated by the work of representation. In the first stanza of "The Indian Girl's Lament," the poet-speaker introduces the lament itself by establishing the setting, posture, and mood of the Indian mourner:

> An Indian girl was sitting where
> Her lover, slain in battle, slept;
> Her maiden veil, her own black hair,
> Came down o'er eyes that wept;
> And wildly, in her woodland tongue,
> This sad and simple lay she sung. (*Poetical Works*, 1:68)

Her seated position and veiled, weeping eyes suggest a reaction to grief that is already controlled and interiorized. Within the poem's setting, there is no audience save the mediating poet for her song, and it is in her singing alone that any traces of unruliness abide. The "wildness" with which the poet characterizes her voice is acknowledged only as something already tamed by his translation of her "woodland tongue" into the proffered "sad and simple lay."

"An Indian at the Burial-Place of His Fathers," which begins directly in the voice of the Indian mourner, also depicts the Indian mourner's psychic subdual. For instance, in its first stanza grief already appears to have been formalized by ritual observance: a pilgrimage home to honor ancestral remains:

> It is the spot I came to seek—
> My father's ancient burial-place,
> Ere from these vales, ashamed and weak,
> Withdrew our wasted race.
> It is the spot—I know it well—
> Of which our old traditions tell. (*Poetical Works,* 1:93)[38]

The containment or redirection of the Indian mourner's hostility toward whites is further suggested by the mourner's chastisement of surviving Indians who, he says, "ashamed and weak, / Withdrew." He ascribes a diminished character to other members of his displaced tribe or clan for abandoning this memorial "spot," while submerging any indictment of the white agents of their displacement in the adjective "wasted." Thus, at the outset of the poem, the anger associated with the Indian mourner's grief is made to seem directed not at whites but at Indians like himself. This recrimination of fellow mourners—a conventional feature of elegy that often works to help the mourner avoid self-recrimination—also suggests in its very defensiveness (I, neither ashamed nor weak, have returned to the place you abandoned) the Indian mourner's possible ambivalence about his own responsibility for this forced estrangement from the dead.

Both poems also tame and aestheticize potentially intractable Indian grief by demonstrating their Indian speakers' fluency in the motifs of pastoral elegy. For example, in the tenth stanza of "An Indian at the Burial-Place of His Fathers," such motifs still work to naturalize anti-

Indian violence even though white agency in Indian displacement has become a more explicit theme in the poem. Here is the Indian speaker's description of the fate of his people at the hands of the "pale race":

> They waste us—ay—like April snow
> In the warm noon, we shrink away (1:95)

In these beautifully enjambed lines, displacement and death are figured as deliquescence, and the Indians themselves become, in effect, the mourning tears evoked by the standard elegiac topos of fluidity. Violence is further naturalized and legitimated through its alignment with seasonal change and the regenerative power of the spring sun. In "The Indian Girl's Lament," the speaker lays claim on behalf of her departed lover to the enlivening power of the sun's light: she pulls up the shrubs that grow above her lover's head and breaks away the branches that shroud his grave in shadows so that "[t]he sunbeams might rejoice thy rest" (1:68). Similar acts of vegetal dismemberment abound in pastoral elegy. From the broken boughs of cypress in Spenser's "Astrophel" to the broken sprig of lilac in Whitman's elegy for Lincoln, such castrative gestures often figure the mourner's effort to recover a lost sexual power.[39] Tearing at the vegetation, the Indian girl reenacts the wounding that separated her from her lover, who, in her depiction of his afterlife, has himself become a kind of woodland god, associated with the fecundity of "everlasting autumn" (1:68). Awaiting her death, he prepares a forest bower for their ultimate reunion, through which consolation is figured as the restoration of the severed erotic connection.

Both of these laments unite fictional Indian voices with the conventions of pastoral elegy in order to render the expression of Indian grief familiar and nonthreatening while also working to dissociate the experiences of Indian bereavement from the specificity of an ongoing history of subjugation and genocide. At the same time, the poet's identification of his own voice with the Indian voices enacts an attachment to the bereaved and a longing for the dead akin to what Renato Rosaldo calls "imperialist nostalgia." Linked to the retrospective idealizations of progressive ideology, the expression of "yearning" for the lost or disrupted traditions of other cultures, Rosaldo argues, works to conceal one's complicity with the violent causes of such changes by helping one to "experience transformations of other cultures as if they were personal losses."[40] In this light, the poet may be seen to identify with the bereaved in order to avoid identification with the agents of loss. And, indeed, the persistent cultural rehearsal of the losses of the socially disprized in Indian laments like Bryant's strongly suggests a sense of implication in those losses.

But the origin and nature of that sense of implication, and its specific entailments for the literary expression of mourning in elegy, are only partly accounted for by the dynamics of imperialist nostalgia. Bryant's Indian laments are not only attempts to assuage guilt through sympathetic identification with the aggrieved but also reflections of the social and psychic conditions under which guilt emerges and helps to motivate literary mourning. For Bryant, these social conditions include the preoccupations with race and with generational continuity that come together explicitly in "An Indian at the Burial-Place of His Fathers." In "The Indian Girl's Lament," the psychic condition of melancholy is more overtly linked to erotic loss and ambivalent masculinity, though the former poem, too, is centered, nostalgically, on a figure of idealized manhood.

"The Indian Girl's Lament" figures the dead Indian as an object of love—a love shared by the poet-speaker and the Indian girl. Their voices merge in the expression of the mourner's stated aims of preserving the lost lover (for example, by equipping his corpse for the afterlife and by enhancing the comfortableness of his grave) and of preserving love itself:

> "Yet, oft to thine own Indian maid
> Even there thy thoughts will earthward stray—
> To her who sits where thou wert laid,
> And weeps the hours away,
> Yet almost can her grief forget,
> To think that thou dost love her yet." (1:69)

With the voice of the Indian girl, speaking of herself here in the third person, the poet both does and does not say, "To think that thou dost love *me* yet."

The poet's identificatory relation with the Indian girl is at once deflected and hemmed in by numerous constraints that manifest themselves in the poem's cascading idealizations: feminine decorum in mourning, the faithfulness of the bereaved, death as a peaceful and protected sleep, the lover's powerful and self-sacrificing masculinity, the projected reunion in a personal afterlife, faith in the eternality of love. These idealizations link the poem to culturally dominant traditions of representing Indian grief as, for instance, an aspect of noble savagism, and of depicting non-Indian grief through the salient and overdetermined figure of the Indian. "The Indian Girl's Lament" involves the poet, and through the poet the reader, in the carefully controlled impersonation of a subject that has already been culturally marked for death but temporarily elevated above social abjection. It portrays a distinctly doomed form of subjection, while inviting the reader to take on the melancholy mark of that doom through sympathetic identification. The alert reader seems to have two choices: to succumb, uncomfortably, to the deft management of sympathetic knowledge by the sentimental (the artifice of commiseration), or to reject, impatiently, the elegiac lure of self-idealization (the anxiety of commiseration). Behind this impatience is the more subtle crux of our grievance against Bryant as readers of this and other such poems: his unwillingness to be carried along by his identification with the Indian girl (to be carried along, in this case, by "love") to the sort of disquieting self-recognition that would begin to collapse the distance between cultural ideality and social abjection. We can follow Bryant, in his great poem of the 1830s, "The Prairies," to the very brink of such a collapse.

"The Prairies": American Romanticism and the Power to Kill

The narrator of Bryant's short story "The Indian Spring" (1829) is a type of the American Romantic artist, seeking to enjoy a consciousness of solitude manufactured and sustained through violence. On a ramble through the backwoods of New York, in a region long since "abandoned" (*Prose,* 1:179) by Indians and newly "invaded by the footsteps of civilization," he must arm himself against intrusions:

> I carried a fowling-piece on my shoulder; not that I meant to be the death
> of any living creature that fine morning, when everything seemed so happy,
> but because such a visible pretext for a stroll in the woods and fields satisfies
> at once the curiosity of those whom you meet, and saves you often a world
> of staring, and sometimes not a few impertinent questions. (*Prose*, 1:177)

As the one acceptable "visible pretext" for a walk in the woods, his
gun is a charm against the interruption of his private communion with
the "great natural forest" (1:177). Yet this charm is no proof against
thoughts of the forest's "ancient inhabitant" (1:178), traces of whom remain in the decaying form of an Indian dwelling by which the narrator
lies down to rest. His imagination is overwhelmed in its solitude by the
reflections these remains inspire. He feels "rebuked by the wild genius"
of the place (1:179) and indeed spends most of the rest of the tale fleeing
from the ominous figure of an Indian—"the very incarnation of the
images that had been floating in my fancy" (1:180). Exertion and fear
lead finally to an "interval of insensibility" (1:188), from which he is
roused by a friend, who assures him it was all just a dream. As he tells
his reader, however, he is determined to render an account that would
not depend upon absolute distinctions between illusion and fact.

Like the narrator of "The Indian Spring," Bryant seeks to reconcile
the claims of imagination and experience in a form that would adequately express the "genius" of place. For him that form—indifferent
efforts at fiction notwithstanding—is poetry. Part of its propriety has
to do with its exclusion of "matters which are too trivial and common
to excite any emotion whatever" (*Prose*, 1:13). Yet Bryant was also critical of those archaizing elements in poetry that have "been the destruction of all nature and simplicity" (*Prose*, 1:29). In his 1826 lecture "On
Poetry and Its Relation to Our Age and Country," Bryant condemns
the facile recourse to ancient myth and calls for a poetic revaluation of
the belief in a spirit of place:

> Let the fountain tell me of the flocks that have drank at it; of the village girl
> that has gathered spring flowers on its margin; the traveller that has slaked
> his thirst there in the hot noon, and blessed its waters; the school-boy that
> has pulled the nuts from the hazels that hang over it as it leaps and sparkles
> in its cool basin; let it speak of youth and health and purity and gladness,
> and I care not for the naiad that pours it out. If it must have a religious

association, let it murmur of the invisible goodness that fills and feeds its reservoirs in the darkness of the earth. (*Prose*, 1:29)

This is clearly not a rejection of poetic superstition. Bryant envisions a naturalized mythology, not a poetry of purely naturalistic description. In poems like "Green River," "The Rivulet," "Summer Wind," and dozens of other efforts, Bryant's landscapes—however subdued by his own elegiac reflections—hum with the "murmur" of "invisible goodness."

Indeed, for the most part, one listens in vain for what D. H. Lawrence calls the "hum of destruction underneath."[41] Bryant is largely silent on Indian issues—a silence made all the more emphatic when contrasted with his liberal outspokenness on virtually every other major social and economic question of his day. For example, there is the tepidness of his response to President Jackson's refusal toward the close of his first term to protect eastern Cherokee land from unlawful incursions. During the long and contentious aftermath of this treaty violation, which resulted in the displacement of thousands, Emerson (who unlike Bryant usually confined political complaints to his journals) could not keep from publicly voicing his rage at the federal government's "deafness to screams for mercy."[42] Bryant, however, appears to have been unmoved by the pathos of Cherokee expulsion. Immediately following Jackson's reelection in November 1832, which effectively overturned the Supreme Court's decision that the states had no authority over Cherokee territory, Bryant wrote that he was "glad that a pacific settlement of the Indian question is now certain" and that "civil war with Georgia" would be avoided.[43] Bryant's concern was with the preservation of the Union, and the "hum of destruction" emanating from Georgia and elsewhere—the "screams" heard by Emerson—was overwhelmed in his ears by the sounds of the nation settling into place.

The irony, of course, is that Indian removal both legitimized and accelerated the destabilization of boundaries through territorial expansion, heightening that "ambivalence about boundaries and limits" that Michael Rogin identifies as an aggravating factor in Indian-white relations:

A securely individuated ego requires a stable sense of boundaries between self and environment, and whites insisted America too needed stable boundaries to mature. At the same time mobility and expansion aborted stable environments in America and tied national identity to individual mobility and expansion across the continent. This generated ambivalence about boundaries and limits, and Indians suffered for it.[44]

Indians in fact died for it, and in their dying they were reminders of the extent to which death does belong to the realm of political struggle. In Jacksonian America, even the afterlife was a life of mobility; eternal rest was no more available to the denizens of constantly displaced urban cemeteries in the East than it was to the scattered bones of Indians within the pale of settlement on the western prairie.[45]

At the end of "Thanatopsis," the environment of the grave seems gratifyingly stable. The poem's promise that "each shall take / His chamber in the silent halls of death" answers a wish whose cultural expression was the rural cemetery movement of the 1830s and whose anxious underside is gruesomely revealed in Poe's fantasies of live burial and corporeal dissolution. "The Prairies," however, introduces Bryant's reader to a realm not of boundaries and limits but of dilation and vastness:

> These are the Gardens of the Desert, these
> The unshorn fields, boundless and beautiful,
> For which the speech of England has no name—
> The Prairies. I behold them for the first,
> And my heart swells, while the dilated sight
> Takes in the encircling vastness. Lo! they stretch,
> In airy undulations, far away . . . (*Poetical Works,* 1:228)

At the same time, the reader is introduced to a realm of elegiac reflection and literary allusion. For while Bryant's setting may be one "[f]or which the speech of England has no name," it is one for which the poetry of England—specifically Shelley's elegiac sonnet "Ozymandias" (1818)—has a ready language. Echoing the final lines of the sonnet, where "boundless and bare / The lone and level sands stretch far away," "The Prairies" begins where "Ozymandias" ends and dilates its restricted form into 124 lines of blank verse.[46]

Bryant's speaker—Adamic namer in a new world—is also a kind of American Ozymandias: a creative figure at the center of a boundless solitude, whose inaugural pronouncements about the "Gardens" of a very different "Desert" suggest an affinity with Shelley's tyrannical maker. His swelling heart recalls the passion-feeding heart of Ozymandias, and his sight has a constraining power: it "[t]akes in the encircling vastness." Ozymandias's works have been reduced to nothingness, but, for Bryant's speaker, nothingness contains a métier. "American poets," notes Barbara Packer, "have had to make a Muse of deprivation," and she credits Bryant, along with Thomas Cole and Washington Allston, with the dawning realization that "the difference between our landscape and the landscape of Europe might be made a source of power, not a cause for envy and regret."[47] Yet Bryant comes in "The Prairies" to a much more complex and ambivalent realization about the artist's relation to sources of power, including the power to create the welcome illusion of deprivation.

The speaker's occupation of the boundless prairies is not, as Barbara Packer suggests it is, to "rejoice in a sublimity that makes him unnecessary" but rather to attempt what Wallace Stevens would call in "The Rock" a "cure of the ground."[48] The "ground" in Bryant's case is threefold: at once that of the Illinois prairies themselves, which he toured in 1832; the experiences that inform the poem, also recorded in a series of letters from which Bryant culled phrases and images for "The Prairies"; and the progressive principles of expansion and cultivation that fuel his dissatisfaction—consistently expressed in the letters—with the *un*civilized condition of the land. "It wants turf," he tells his mother, Sarah. "The grass grows thin in the fields and prairies, and the sides of the road and the door yards and immediate vicinity of the dwellings are covered with weeds" (*Letters,* 1:357). It is a far cry, Bryant is saying, from Wordsworth's "pastoral farms, / Green to the very door"—not because of its pristine wildness but because of its imperfect development.[49] The pastoral virtues are also wanting in the people of the place, who still resemble the "semi-barbarous citizens" who populate the frontier in the writings of Crévecoeur and Jefferson.[50] They are, Bryant reports, "principally from Kentucky Tennessee and other slave states. A large proportion of them are ignorant—though often shrewd enough—and are inclined to get drunk and fight on Saturdays" (*Letters,* 1:357). Bryant rarely encounters a prairie that is totally uninhabited. Even where there are no dwellings he is not alone. Describing an excursion north from

Jacksonville, he tells his wife that "every few miles on our way we either fell in with bodies of Illinois militia proceeding to the American camp or saw where they had encamped for the night" (*Letters*, 1:347).

The militia was there, Bryant knew, to fight the Black Hawk War, which had been precipitated by white encroachments upon Sauk and Fox land along the Mississippi River and which was a source of great alarm in the region Bryant was touring. The "Gardens of the Desert" were not only occupied, but they were also being violently contested. Consequently, Bryant's "cure of the ground" begins (as the work of westward expansion continued to begin) with the effacement of human presence. "Man hath no power," his speaker insists, "in all this glorious work" (*Poetical Works*, 1:229). The statement is at once a paean to the sublime and an imaginative fiat. Hazlitt remarks that the "language of poetry naturally falls in with the language of power,"[51] and it is worth noting the extent to which this is true of "The Prairies," which echoes the sense of Andrew Jackson's second annual message to Congress (1830) even as Jackson borrows a topos already heavily exploited by writers of Indian laments:

> To follow to the tomb the last of his race, and to tread on the graves of extinct nations, excites melancholy reflections. But true philanthropy reconciles the mind to these vicissitudes, as it does to the extinction of one generation to make room for another. In the monuments and fortresses of an unknown people, spread over the extensive regions of the west, we behold the memorials of a once powerful race, which was exterminated, or has disappeared, to make room for the existing savage tribes. Nor is there anything in this, which, upon a comprehensive view of the general interests of the human race, is to be regretted.[52]

A similar argument is at the center of "The Prairies," where Indian removal is characterized as part of a natural order of successive displacements. Even the most extreme violence is sanctioned, as in Bryant's account of a lone-surviving mound-builder whose agrarian society has been destroyed by nomadic Indian marauders:

> Haply some solitary fugitive,
> Lurking in marsh and forest, till the sense
> Of desolation and of fear became

Bitterer than death, yielded himself to die.
Man's better nature triumphed then. Kind words
Welcomed and soothed him; the rude conquerors
Seated the captive with their chiefs; he chose
A bride among their maidens, and at length
Seemed to forget—yet ne'er forgot—the wife
Of his first love, and her sweet little ones,
Butchered, amid their shrieks, with all his race.
    Thus change the forms of being. Thus arise
Races of living things, glorious in strength,
And perish, as the quickening breath of God
Fills them, or is withdrawn. (1:230–31)

The moral obliquity of "Thus change" highlights the poem's determination not to locate culpability in a single source. Instead, power over life is distributed over a complex network of relations between victor and victim: the "sense of desolation and of fear" that impels the victim toward a kind of deliverance in death, the "better nature" that inspires the victor to spare the victim from his own suicidal gesture, the assimilation of the "captive" through marriage into the society of the "conquerors," the tug of private memory upon social amnesia.

It is precisely at the moment when the memory of personal bereavement asserts itself ("the wife / Of his first love, and her sweet little ones / Butchered, amid their shrieks, with all his race") that the poem moves to correct its course, having come too close to the question that the Jacksonians sought to quash. What, the poem refuses to ask directly, is the cost of having killed so many? The glimpse of Indian consciousness afforded by the phrase "Seemed to forget,—yet ne'er forgot" is both pathetic and ominous. It recalls, on the one hand, the poignance of Macduff's insistence to Malcolm that he "cannot but remember such things were, / That were most precious to me." Indeed, Bryant's description of the murder of the mound-builder's family seems intended to echo Macduff's grief-stricken response to the news that Macbeth has slaughtered his family ("All my pretty ones? . . . all my pretty chickens and their dam / At one fell swoop?").[53] Yet, on the other hand, one misses in Bryant's mound-builder (in part because the allusion to *Macbeth* is so clear) the sincere *expression* of grief that keeps Macduff within the moral economy of the play—that enables him to join in Scotland's political renewal rather than being the subject of his own revenge tragedy.

The phrase "yet ne'er forgot" implies a pressure of memory that could issue either in commemoration or in vengeance.[54] This ambiguity is a reminder that Indian removal was by no means complete as Bryant was writing. Furthermore, his translation of the present struggle between whites and Indians into a story of past conflict among agrarian mound-builders and nomadic hunters creates a further ambiguity of identification. To whom, in the present, does the burden of memory belong, and how is it to be discharged? How will whites own their perception of Indian removal? And, conversely, how will Indians show whites that they are able to remember?[55]

Initially, the prairie appears to be a place with which no memory is associated. Not only is the speaker of the poem a new arrival on the scene ("I behold them for the first"), but also the scene itself is characterized as having remained innocent of human hands. "The Prairies" begins as the story of Bryant's arrival in a solitary landscape—a space so thoroughly unacted upon that the "speech of England" has as yet no adequate word for it.[56] Yet this landscape in which "Man hath no part" repeatedly throws up signs of human presence:

> Are they here—
> The dead of other days?—and did the dust
> Of these fair solitudes once stir with life . . . ? (1:229)
> All is gone;
> All—save the piles of earth that hold their bones,
> The platforms where they worshipped unknown gods . . . (1:230)

The pressure of other consciousnesses builds, culminating in the persistence of memory that characterizes the "solitary fugitive" whose family was massacred by Indians.

The remainder of the poem restores the reader to the present and reestablishes the poet as the lone figure in a "great solitude" (1:232). Yet having succeeded in suppressing the shadows of former presences, the poet now finds himself confronted with the harbingers of that "advancing multitude / Which soon shall fill these deserts" (1:232). That is, he finds himself in an imaginative predicament that mimics the historical predicament of the Indians, who were made to feel in various ways the vibrations of approach from white settlers.[57] The sound, for Bryant, is not an overtly threatening one. Indeed, he describes it as "the laugh of children, the soft voice / Of maidens, and the sweet and solemn hymn / Of Sabbath worshippers." Yet the origin of the sound gives it a ghostly, macabre quality. It comes up "[f]rom the ground" (1:232), as though it emanated from the same matrons, maids, babes, and sages who are gathered to their graves at the end of "Thanatopsis."

Like "Thanatopsis," "The Prairies" concludes with the image of a dream. But whereas in "Thanatopsis" this image attests to the preservation of consciousness after death, in "The Prairies" the living poet's dreamlike expansion of consciousness is curtailed:

> The low of herds
> Blends with the rustling of the heavy grain
> Over the dark brown furrows. All at once
> A fresher wind sweeps by, and breaks my dream,
> And I am in the wilderness alone. (1:232)

Like Ishmael on the masthead, Bryant is returned abruptly to himself, and if there are no "Descartian vortices" into which he may plunge, there are further depths of solitude to sound.[58] This sort of dramatic, ambiguous ending is rare in Bryant, whose penchant for didactic resolution is often distasteful to modern readers of his poetry. But the fact that "The Prairies" terminates in this way does more than to help make it contemporarily appealing. For if it suggests a familiar Romantic ambivalence about the solitary consciousness as an imaginative goal, it also succeeds in transforming this personal ambivalence into the national appeal of a "fresher" repression of voices from below that would have to be heard not as autochthonous but as political and articulate.

The next two chapters pursue the elegiac fate of voices from below by concentrating on politically marginal populations at the center of antebellum mourning activity: children in chapter 4, and African Americans in chapter 5. For while the figure of the Indian remains fixed to the post of American mourning culture throughout the antebellum period and beyond, the figures of the child and the slave become freshly prominent symbols of the economic problem of mourning under conditions of market revolution. For the first time, the fertile family becomes a site of overproduction, taxing the elegiac imagination both with newly burdensome generations and with specters of the unwanted unborn. And what the population boom did for the ambivalent enshrinement of the dead child, the cotton boom did for the multiplication of slavery-related losses that black and white Americans alike were uncertain whether and how to mourn.

CHAPTER 4

Elegy's Child: Waldo Emerson and the Price of Generation

Have you ever lost a child?
—HARRIET BEECHER STOWE

Because the practice of elegy is fundamentally devoted to the enshrinement of compensatory memory, and thus to a complaint or grievance against the present, elegists frequently seek to project a future that would transcend elegiac salvos of resentment—a future, in other words, that would amount to more than a grievance against the conditions of its arrival. Versions of such a future in antebellum elegy include both Christian and naturalistic visions of posthumous personal reunion, the anticipation of transformed social relations among the living, and exhortations to trust in the principle of change for its own sake. All three of these classes of compensatory projection were for the generations rising in the decades after the War of 1812 rightly perceived to be under assault, for example, by the vast disuniting of families and communities grown too large for intrafamilial stability and intergenerational continuity; by the widening gap between rich and poor; by the antagonisms of sectionalism and sectarianism; by heightened individualism, the competitive pursuit of wealth, and the rise of wage exploitation; by Indian removal; by the disfranchisement of free blacks; by slavery's nineteenth-century rejuvenation and consequent territorial expansion; by the financial crises of 1819 and 1837; and by conservative fears of the unstoppable democratization of an evangelically aroused electorate.

Capitalist transformation, as Charles Sellers suggests, helped ensure that futurity itself would be a source of increasingly cold comfort:

> Radically new imperatives confronted people when they were lured or pushed from modest subsistence into open-ended market production. By the 1820s rapidly spreading channels of trade were replacing an unpressured security of rude comfort with an insecurity goaded by hope of opulence and fear of failure. Within a generation in every new area the market invaded, competition undermined neighborly cooperation and family equality. Ancestral ways and parental example no longer worked. Increasingly individuals had to chart their own chancy courses.[1]

It comes as no surprise that under such circumstances the figure of the child—its sentimentalization as what Serge Leclaire calls "the royal figure of our wishes, memories, hopes, and dreams"—would accumulate cultural significance not only as a vehicle for nostalgia but also as a prop for heavily burdened aspirations of a collective as well as individual nature.[2] That is, the cultish adoration of the child served not merely to oppose symbolically the loss of traditional ways but also increasingly to take the place of adult symbols of the prospect for social stability and civic continuity. And their deaths were mourned accordingly. As Philippe Ariès observes of nineteenth-century American attitudes toward the death of the young, "[t]hese long-neglected little creatures were treated like famous personages." But if, as Ariès also observes, "[i]n middle-class circles in the nineteenth century, the death of the child has become the least tolerable of all deaths,"[3] it is not only, as he implies, because mourning the loss of a child ceremonially bolsters the threatened family ties for which the dead child is also the symbol, but, equally importantly and far more troublesomely, because the death of children has become freshly and appallingly desirable.

Population growth—fueled by human fecundity, lower infant death rates, and massive immigration—had been dramatically exacerbating social decay and alienation since the late eighteenth century. "As the market assailed traditional ways," Sellers explains, "shrinking farms were spawning more people than they could feed." Children grew burdensome to parents, and parents—especially fathers—provoked children's resentment of "a paternal authority that seemed less reasonable as it became less functional."[4] The consequences were momentous:

> The uprooted, insular household found children no longer an asset but an impediment to survival. Their labor on shrunken farms no longer earned their keep; they challenged a paternal authority that could no longer provide them with farms or livelihood; and they required a more rigorous socialization for market competition. Under these pressures Americans inaugurated history's most dramatic and sustained repression of human fertility.[5]

As white birth rates plummeted, new restraints on sexuality exacted heavy psychological costs. Mourning, as it were, for too much life, antebellum Americans sought to evade erotic melancholy by projecting their sense of loss onto the children whose superabundance had caused it. Child elegies proliferated from mothers and fathers as children once had. The infanticidal unconscious enforced and energized a newly expansive mortuary culture in which the image of the dead child seems almost to have amounted to the consummation of a national wish (see Figure 7).

Figure 7. Photographer unknown, unidentified parents with dead child, ca. 1850. Daguerreotype, ¼ plate. Courtesy of Strong Museum, Rochester, New York, 2005.

No elegist coped with that wish more tirelessly than Lydia Huntley Sigourney, whose child elegies number in the many dozens and whose poetic reputation depended on the public perception of her talent for filling the space of inarticulacy generated by ambivalent mourning. In a memoir of her literary career, Sigourney humorously renders the vexed yearning for individuation that so often characterized the antebellum experience of loss generally, and of the loss of children especially. As someone who enjoyed tremendous popular renown as an elegist, Sigourney was barraged with letters imploring her to compose verses on this or that person's death. Having undertaken "at one time to keep a statement of the solicitations that showered upon me," she reports, a "good-sized manuscript book was thus soon filled."[6] Among the many requests Sigourney received for elegiac "custom-work" was one from "a stranger, whose son died at the age of nine months, 'weighing just thirteen pounds, [and who] would be glad of some poetry to be framed, glazed, and hung over the chimney-piece, to keep the other children from forgetting him'" (373). Another came from a father requesting "elegiac lines on a young child, supplying, as the only suggestion for the tuneful Muse, the fact that he was unfortunately 'drowned in a barrel of swine's food'" (373). And yet another stranger wrote, "saying his wife was likely to die, and had a young babe, and wishing some poetry to be written in such a way that it would answer for mother and child, should both be taken by death" (374). The examples Sigourney cites contribute to the impression of a class of mourners seeking far beyond domestic or local spheres of personal valuation for some affirmation of the singularity and value of the person mourned. It is a singularity the mourners themselves seem barely able to apprehend: How can I keep my other children from forgetting their brother? What more can I tell you than that my child was smothered in offal? How might I measure the loss of my second wife against that of my first? Could you possibly differentiate between my wife and my baby in a single poem, were they to die together? It is a singularity these correspondents hope might be made intelligible and enduring by a poet they have never met.

Yet Sigourney's correspondents also tend to understand their requests as existing apart from the impersonal dealings of the market upon which her success and livelihood depended. They tend to view Sigourney not as a professional poet for hire but as a muse of memory, one whose public and prolific sympathies with the bereaved seem to render her an ideal agent of their own conflicted memorial longings. The irony of this confusion is not lost on Sigourney, who admits that she herself has often disregarded the commodity value of her productions in responding to such requests:

> Lacking firmness to say no, I consented so frequently, that the right of re-fusal began to be counted invidious. Those who requested but a few verses considered them, what they appeared to be, a trifle. Yet "trifles make up the sum of human things," and this trifle involved thought, labor, and time. (376)

Would they treat a milliner this way? a carpet-maker? a cook? (377). The material circumstances of her poetic labor, Sigourney feels, should be recognized as belonging to the world of commerce. Yet, because there is "always a degree of pleasure connected with obliging others," she resists the commoditization of her work (377). Her sense of the economic entrapment of personal relations produces uncertainties in Sigourney that remain unresolved in her memoir ("a truce," she writes, "to this diffuse matter of custom-work" [377]) just as they remained unresolved in the poetic practice upon which she is reflecting.

For decades, Sigourney had been particularly influential in linking early nineteenth-century poetry to domestic considerations by dwelling relentlessly on scenes and sentiments of bereavement. The unprecedent-ed industriousness with which at the turn of the century Americans produced memorials to the historical significance of George Washing-ton's death found a counterpart in the consolation literature of ensu-ing decades and its glorification of deaths—particularly those of young children—that could not readily be deemed historically significant. The speaker of Sigourney's poem, "'Twas but a Babe," for example, chastises a "silent" and "tearless crowd" for its refusal to "mete out grief" at a child's funeral:

> I asked them why the verdant turf was riven
> From its young rooting and with silent lip
> They pointed to a new-made chasm among
> The marble-pillared mansions of the dead.

> Who goeth to his rest in yon damp couch?
> The tearless crowd passt on—"'twas but a babe."
> *A babe!*—And poise ye in the rigid scales
> Of calculation, the fond bosom's wealth?
> Rating its priceless idols as ye weigh
> Such merchandise as moth and rust corrupt,
> Or the rude robber steals? Ye mete out grief,
> Perchance, when youth, maturity or age,
> Sink in the thronging tomb, but when the breath
> Grows icy on the lip of innocence
> Repress your measured sympathies, and say
> *"'Twas but a babe."*[7]

In the crowd's estimation, as apprehended by the speaker of the poem, the child's life and death precede not only the standard valuations of the marketplace but also the stages of experience ("youth, maturity and age") that constitute the historical dimension of personhood. It is a child that has, so to speak, died out of time, before becoming available to the crowd as an avowed, valued object of its own "measured sympathies."

The speaker attempts to recuperate the child for general mourning by turning the crowd's attention to the child's parents, particularly the father:

> Go ask that musing father why yon grave
> So narrow, and so noteless might not close
> Without a tear?
>   And though his lip be mute,
> Feeling the poverty of speech, to give
> Fit answer to thee, still his pallid brow
> And the deep agonizing prayer that loads
> Midnight's dark wing to *him* the God of strength,
> May satisfy thy question.

The father's silence indicates his simultaneously acute and decorous sensibility. His refusal to respond in the devalued language of mourning ("the poverty of speech, to give / Fit answer") sets him over and against the crowd's callous reticence, its "silent lip." The speaker appropriates the father's righteous reticence as a "fit answer" to the crowd's conviction that the child amounts to nothing in the "rigid scales / Of calculation."

Yet if the child amounts to nothing in the "rigid scales / Of calcula-tion," it is not clear that it amounts to much more in the "measured sympathies" of Sigourney's blank verse. What is most striking about the poem, particularly as a representative of thousands of similar con-temporary verses—of, that is, the seemingly unreflecting redundancy of child elegy in the antebellum period—is how well defended against fascination with the child both crowd and speaker are. As in so many child elegies—even those that commemorate actual deaths—the child itself remains a departicularized, abstracted *infans,* nothing more than an emblem of undistinguished innocence "just born to mourn."[8] The particular nature of the loss the child might represent to members of the crowd remains the *unattempted* theme of this elegy and of thou-sands like it. The crowd's uninterrupted motion—both the indiffer-ence and fatality of which are nicely enfolded in the phrase "passed on"—helps Sigourney to figure its countermemorial pronouncement upon the child ("'twas but a babe") as a species of evasion. Is it cal-lousness or fear that makes the crowd pass on? To what extent does the crowd's countermemorial pronouncement stand for an aggressive, even murderous act against the figure of the child? Is the speaker's own refusal of fascination with the child a version of the same sacrificial gesture—a sacrifice that cannot be acknowledged as such? And is the father's reticence best understood as a grievance against the social pres-sures that enforce and restrict certain kinds of mourning, or might it also stand for an unavowable protest against the child whose father he remains fated to be?

In the profuse, etiolated leaves of antebellum child elegy—at once the most cherished and reviled of subgenres—Sigourney was the poet who approached these almost unaskable questions most frequently. The poet who approached them most nearly was Ralph Waldo Emerson, whose eloquently voiced grievance against inherited forms came close to choking on a father's tears. The protest Emerson leveled against the Hegelian burden of the past doubled back upon him, so to speak, when he was forced to confront the prospect of a future that would not in-clude the son born to him in 1836.

Among the signs of eroding patriarchal authority and meagerness of patrimony, Sellers notes that well before the 1830s the "general practice of naming first-born sons after their fathers" was rapidly disappearing.[9] Nevertheless, when Ralph and Lidian Emerson's first son was born, on October 31, 1836, the name they gave it was the name by which the father himself preferred to be called: Waldo. Despite Emerson's apostasy and radical individualism, kinship and lineage remained, as Phyllis Cole puts it, "live values" for the Emerson clan throughout the nineteenth century—lineage that had "defined itself as a succession of Massachusetts clergymen," as a history of fathers transmitting their ministerial vocations to sons.[10] Five years before his son's birth, Emerson had announced to his aunt Mary Moody Emerson his intention to resign from the ministry. Her response explicitly recalls and prizes the lineage-based hierarchies that had helped to establish and sustain elegy as the chief poetic genre favored by New Englanders since the early seventeenth century, and it emphasizes the importance to her of a secure ministerial lineage as a consolation for family losses. Her wish, she tells her nephew, is that, as

> an old venerable pastor in the most delightfull spot, you could point to your grand children that within a few miles reposed the ashes of your pious ancestors—who preached the gospel—and that the very place w'h gave you birth & contains your father should wittness your last aspirations after the sovereign Good. It may be that the short lives of those most dear to me have given couler to the hopes of one minister remaining to be enrolled with [the] Mather & Sewells of that venerable City.[11]

Her nephew was not to be that young minister but rather the young champion of a future that could be divested of the fatality of the past, in which the connection between parents and children might be liberated from oedipal violence and rehearsed no longer under the sign of death.

Emerson was largely protected by wealth and circumstance from those vicissitudes of the expanding economy that for many antebellum farmers, mechanics, and clerks made children a new kind of burden and drained parental authority of its legitimacy. And he was freer than Sigourney from the market entanglements that bound her literary professionalism to the infanticidal unconscious. Yet, as he himself observed to an audience of mechanics' apprentices in 1841, when it comes to the base economic relations of the day, "[w]e are all implicated."[12]

Emerson's avowals of complicity are generally lofty ones, though to say so is not to challenge their sincerity but rather to draw attention to Emerson's abiding sense of the heroic demands of living a principled life. Among other things, living such a life meant to Emerson remaining mindful of universal complicity even in the face of devastating loss. The history of his expressive response to such losses is a record of that mindfulness—a record of the painful concessions that even the era's great idealist had to make to contingency in order to answer some of his most pressing questions about death and sacrifice: What is the role of voluntarism in loss? Whose blood, once shed, will ensure the remission of social ills? And, in a principled life, what is the price of generation?

"What is Death?" is the very basic question he asks in an 1837 journal entry. His answer with regard to his own death is pragmatic and assured: "I have nothing to do with it. It is nothing to me. After I have made my will & set my house in order, I shall do in the immediate expectation of death the same things I should do without it." It is "more difficult," he says, "to know the death of another." The expectation is "fearful," and the event is "always astounding." Help from philosophy is sought in vain, so Emerson looks within, which leads him to a surprising inference: "There ought to be, there can be nothing, to which the soul is called, to which the soul is not equal. And I suppose that the roots of my relation to every individual are in my own constitution & not less the causes of his disappearance from me." The power to withstand an incomprehensible loss, Emerson suggests, depends on his ability to identify with the agent of that loss. Although "our philosophy never reaches, never possesses" death, the death of another will not reach and overmaster Emerson if it has already become somehow a consequence of his own action.[13]

This idealizing response to loss "border[s]," according to Barbara Packer, "on the psychotic."[14] Yet Emerson's arrogation to himself of the power to make others disappear introduces him not to madness but to a kind of freedom he associates with the sublime and on the verge of which it seems to him we live our lives. Indeed, for Emerson we are always at the boundary between the quotidian and the sublime. "We are all of us very near to sublimity," he writes in his journal, choosing

as his illustration the sudden vision of Wordsworth's Solitary in Book 2
of *The Excursion*:

> As one step freed Wordsworth's Recluse on the mountains from the blind-
> ing mist & brought him to the view of "Glory beyond all glory ever seen"
> so near are we all to a vision of which Homer & Shakspeare are only hints
> & types and yet cannot we take that one step. It does not seem worth our
> while to toil for anything so pitiful as skill to do one of the little feats we
> magnify so much, when presently the dream will scatter & we shall burst
> into universal power. (*Journals*, 8:51)

Yet the Solitary and the old Man whose "dolorous tale" he is recount-
ing succumb, each in their way, to the force of their respective visions.[15]
For Wordsworth, loss tends to have the depleting, "humanizing" effect
described in the poet's "Peele Castle" elegy for his brother John: submission "to a new control," a withdrawal of power, an enduring, even
insistent, sense of bereavement.[16] Emerson, however, does not find himself similarly absorbed by the debilitating consequences of human loss.
Rather than defeating sublimity with a countertranscendent weight,
the death of loved ones in Emerson is more likely to be associated with
liberating excesses of power and desire.

There are hints of such excesses in Emerson's early, still largely plaintive elegies for his first wife, Ellen—elegies that Emerson himself never
published. In one, he offers a description of "the life / Please God, that I
would lead" in the aftermath of his wife's death. He says he would "quit
this weary town" and withdraw into an "uncouth solitude" of remembrance, where, surrounding himself with instruments of study and observation, he would "aim a telescope at the inviolate Sun."[17] In another
of these elegies, Emerson fantasizes about what frustrated mourning
might mean for self-regulation:

> Teach me I am forgotten by the dead
> And that the dead is by herself forgot
> And I no longer would keep terms with me.
> I would not murder, steal, or fornicate,
> Nor with ambition break the peace of towns
> But I would bury my ambition
> The hope & action of my sovereign soul
> In miserable ruin.[18]

Here skepticism about the continuity of reciprocal relations between the living and the dead prompts visions of an abrogated self-relation ("I no longer would keep terms with me") and consequent violence. The implication and the fear are that Emerson might be capable of doing what he assures himself he would not do—that grief potentially leads to an uncontrolled and dangerous freedom.[19]

The apprehension of power and freedom evident in these early elegies continues to occupy Emerson as he tends more emphatically to abjure conventional mourning, even as the losses accrue. In the poems for Ellen he repeatedly bemoans his separation from her and even berates her for her failure to attend him in her disembodied state. But this mortuary mysticism was of increasingly little use to Emerson as he turned away from consoling conventions like the cult of beautiful death and belief in a personal afterlife—conventions that fostered the notion of a familiar and perfectly preserved relation to the departed individual. In later, published works like *Nature*, "Experience," and "Threnody," he responds with little reassuring sentiment to the disruptions effected by loss. What he finds changed by these "shocks" or "surprises" are arrangements of the self and its relation to the world that have come to seem to him necessarily, even pleasingly, unstable to begin with. The terror of discontinuity informing Wordsworth's elegism is rarely felt in Emerson. Indeed, the "natural piety" by which the poet would bind his days "each to each" in the Intimations Ode is foreign to "Experience,"[20] Emerson's own great meditation on continuity: "Life is a series of surprises, and would not be worth taking or keeping, if it were not. God delights to isolate us every day" (*Essays,* 483).

Yet the surprise that "Experience" foregrounds—the death in 1842 of Emerson's five-year-old son Waldo—is but the latest and perhaps most keenly felt in a series of painful, isolating losses: Ellen in 1831, his brother Edward in 1834, and his cherished brother Charles (the "friend" mourned in *Nature*) in 1836. A month after Waldo's death, Emerson wrote to Thomas Carlyle: "You can never sympathize with me; you can never know how much of me such a young child can take away. A few weeks ago I accounted myself a very rich man, and now the poorest of all."[21] Readers of Emerson's letters and journals have little reason to doubt the sincerity of his anguish over Waldo's death or the exigency of his struggle to find language suitable for its clarification (to himself) and communication (to others), even though here in the letter to Carlyle, as he so often does elsewhere, Emerson employs economic metaphors to characterize his loss in some rather conventional ways. But the letter to Carlyle also startles, because so much of it is concerned with nonmetaphorical matters of commerce. The first half of the letter is all about financial transactions, some executed, some contemplated, in which Emerson's interests in some way join with Carlyle's. The opening sentence refers to a bill of exchange. The subsequent paragraph details arrangements brokered by Emerson with Carlyle's American publishers. And the paragraph after that consists of investment advice: "Our city banks in Boston are in better credit than the Banks in any other city here, yet one in which a large part of my property is invested, has failed, for the two last half years, to pay any dividend, & I am a poor man until next April" (316). Only in the second half of the letter does Emerson come to the impoverishment of grief and attempt to describe for Carlyle the extent of his misery in the moving paragraph from which I have already quoted. And even this paragraph concludes with a reminder to Carlyle to send word about how he wants Emerson to handle further financial transactions. The letter feels dissociative, at least to contemporary ears trained to hear something strongly discordant in the proximity of references to mourning and money-making.

This is no mere matter of tact or sincerity. The question of what Emerson has lost in his son resonates chillingly with American slavery's collapsing of distinctions between offspring and property. Is Emerson, elsewhere so keenly alert to the appalling price of generation under slavery, here simply being callous or obtuse in setting a narrative of mourning for his child in a pecuniary frame? Or is the point (whether consciously intended or not) to present the loss of his most priceless possession as a challenge to the very logic of commoditization that not only made black children into items of trade but also made it more and more difficult for a northern economy in crisis not to tabulate the future cost, and thus the current price, of free children as well?

Emerson had hoped to be sending Carlyle more than bills of exchange. "How often I have pleased myself that one day I should send to you, this Morningstar of mine, & stay at home so gladly behind such a representative! I dare not fathom the Invisible & Untold to inquire what relations to my Departed ones I yet sustain" (317). In this initial expression of reluctance to "fathom the Invisible & Untold," Emerson reveals some of the damage his ego has sustained, along with the untellable gladness of staying at home behind a representative whose destination is not Chelsea but death. And he has also posed a question to himself about his fundamental relation to his son, in response to which he knows he must somehow account for mourning's contingency in the midst of economic crisis.

The question of relation is one Emerson never let drop. He aspired, as he puts it in *Nature,* to have an "original relation" to nature ("the NOT ME, that is, both nature and art, all other men and my own body" [*Essays,* 8]), which means he must have an original relation to "his Departed ones" as well. Consequently, much of the force of Emerson's elegiac writing is generated by the tension between impulses to sustain, on the one hand, conventional relations in conventional forms, and to cast off or transcend, on the other, the economic entrapment of the social self—"that jailyard of individual relations" (*Essays,* 460)—that in his view blocks vital energies of spirit. Many elegists resolve these discrepant impulses in figures of liminality ("Henceforth thou art the Genius of the shore") or anachronism ("The Child is Father of the Man").[22] But Emerson is not satisfied with restitutive tropes of spatial and temporal continuity. He resists recuperation of the mourned object, even though this means there is no release for him from the competing pressures of remembrance and denial, of the material and the ideal. Emerson seeks not to resolve discrepancy but to know the "value," as he puts it in "Experience," of discrepancy itself. "I know," he says, "that the world I converse with in the city and in the farms, is not the world I *think*" (*Essays,* 491).

Unlike the psychotic, Emerson knows there is a difference. But he also knows that the world is not what he thinks it is, and one of the ways he knows this is through his experience of Waldo's death, which prompts the observation that appalls so many readers and that "Experience" seeks unsentimentally to interrogate: "some thing which I fancied was a part of me, which could not be torn away without tearing me, nor enlarged without enriching me, falls off from me, and leaves no scar."

He singles out grief as a false idealization ("it turns out to be scene-painting and counterfeit" [*Essays*, 472]) that cannot carry him "one step into real nature" (473), a phrasing that recalls "that one step" separating us from "universal power" in Emerson's remarks on the sublime. As in the earlier journal entry, Emerson seems here to disavow the efficacy of human action. "Nothing is left us now but death," he wryly observes (473). Yet while he distrusts, as he puts it at the end of the essay, "manipular attempts to realize the world of thought" (492), Emerson's written responses to the death of his son (including "Experience") represent a kind of manipular attempt to bring "the world I converse with" (the world from which Waldo is removed by death) and the "world I *think*" (the world to whose limits Waldo expands in the grieving Emerson's mind) into some sort of accord.

That is, they are attempts to represent an experience of loss without giving over completely the value of discrepancy to emplotments of mourning. "I cannot get it nearer to me," Emerson writes of Waldo's death, even as he forges a compromise with familiar tropes like inheritance (comparing the loss of his son to the loss of a "beautiful estate" [*Essays*, 473]) and with his own literary inheritance, which includes a long elegiac tradition. If, in the letter to Carlyle, he is uncertain about what "relations to my Departed ones I yet sustain," he has nevertheless in referring to Waldo as his "Morningstar" not only suggestively characterized his relation to his son but also, by using such a richly allusive term, implicitly raised the question of his relation to literary tradition and to such literary conventions as inspiration and originality. "Morningstar" aligns Waldo with Phaeton, Christ, and Lucifer, and thus it aligns Emerson with the poet-god Apollo and with the Christian God of Revelations and *Paradise Lost*. It reminds us that Milton, too, is one of Emerson's "Departed ones."[23]

Emerson's elegies for Waldo exhibit a complex irresolution of melancholy and exuberance, particularity and abstraction, guilt and liberation. This irresolution characterizes both his uneasy compromise with language and literary tradition as well as with the figure of his son, whose attachment to himself he would like somehow to sustain but without subordinating it to the possessiveness of memorialization. From the start of his life Waldo provokes in Emerson the excitement of incomprehension, an excitement whose value the grieving father, in the aftermath of his son's death, struggles ambivalently to know.

The Sublimity of Paternity

The most famous American statement of the sublime, in Emerson's 1836 *Nature,* is explicitly counterelegiac:

> In the presence of nature, a wild delight runs through the man, in spite of real sorrows. Nature says,—he is my creature, and maugre all his impertinent griefs, he shall be glad with me. (*Essays,* 10)

But a world filled by loss can only be evacuated of "impertinent griefs" for brief and precarious moments in which conventional human relations—including relations with the dead—are held in abeyance:

> Standing on the bare ground,—my head bathed by the blithe air, and uplifted into infinite space,—all mean egotism vanishes. I become a transparent eye-ball; I am nothing; I see all; the currents of the Universal Being circulate through me; I am part or particle of God. The name of the nearest friend sounds then foreign and accidental: to be brothers, to be acquaintances,—master or servant, is then a trifle and a disturbance. (*Essays,* 10)

Such moments are precarious because in his desire to achieve a vision of transcendence, Emerson is driven to deny his own person and his own attachment to his cherished brother Charles. This pressure of denial is insupportable, and melancholy quickly returns along with the conventional, Romantic images of retreat that affirm Emerson's presence and the strength of his affections: "there is a kind of contempt of the landscape felt by him who has just lost by death a dear friend. The sky is less grand as it shuts down over less worth in the population" (*Essays,* 11).

A "contempt" of nature, motivated by grief, is the enemy of the sublime: "plantations of God" become mere "landscape"; the sky loses its magnificence. At the height of his rhetorical transport, Emerson says he feels "that nothing can befall me in life,—no disgrace, no calamity, (leaving me my eyes,) which nature cannot repair" (*Essays,* 10). Yet he cannot break free of the sense that the world is irreparably diminished by Charles's death. Indeed, in death Charles himself is irreparably diminished. To complete, to verify, to return to Emerson some sense of the "ME" from which the world of nature is to be distinguished is the function Charles's death not only prevents him from serving but also reveals him (through the despondence and self-doubt of the journals he left behind) as having been unable to serve. What reparation can nature possibly make for this catastrophe? What new relation can compensate Emerson for the loss of his closest friend?

Five months after Charles's death, Emerson's first son is born, an event recorded in a spirit that might be called the paternal sublime:

> Last night at 11 o'clock, a son was born to me. Blessed child! a lovely wonder to me, and which makes the Universe look friendly to me. How remote from my knowledge, how alien, yet how kind does it make the Cause of Causes appear! The stimulated curiosity of the father sees the graces & instincts which exist, indeed, in every babe, but unnoticed in others; the right to see all, to know all, to examine nearly, distinguishes this relation, & endears this sweet child. Otherwise I see nothing in it of mine; I am no conscious party to any feature, any function, any perfection I behold in it. I seem to be merely a brute occasion of its being & nowise attaining to the dignity even of a second cause no more than I taught it to suck the breast. (*Journals*, 5:234)

Looking upon his newborn son, Emerson is "stimulated" by the promise of a new and charmed relation. Yet while retaining the "right to see all, to know all, to examine nearly," Emerson rejects the evidence of generation upon which this "right" presumably depends, asserting with cheerful humility, "I see nothing in it of mine." Absent here is the anxiety we would be quick to recognize in the same statement spoken, for example, by Shakespeare's Leontes. Emerson's disavowal is a grateful one—as grateful as Leontes's recognition of his own features in the face of his young son Mamillius.[24] But it is a special sort of disavowal, one that makes possible a kinship with "the Cause of Causes." Like John Locke, Emerson rejects the notion that the mere act of begetting a child makes one akin to divinity.[25] Indeed, he resists the patriarchal logics of possession ("I see nothing in it that is mine") and transmission ("I see nothing in it that comes from me") precisely because they emphasize generation over creation; they emphasize distance from rather than nearness to origins, making them the secular counterpart to the doctrinal insistence upon fallen man's remoteness from God that Emerson had found increasingly inimical to his religious faith.

For Emerson, the right of such nearness to origins is a tenet closely held. This sense of entitlement derives from Emerson's post-Unitarian revision of the Augustinian-Calvinist theory of inheritance—a theory that finds troubled expression in Puritan notions of original sin. The Augustinian conviction that people are not merely heirs to Adam's fall but participants in it is given voice in various Puritan assertions of infant depravity. *The New-England Primer* (c. 1690), for example, instructs that "In *Adam's* Fall / We Sinned all,"[26] and, in his sermon on "The Nature of Early Piety" (1721), Benjamin Wadsworth writes that children's hearts "naturally, are a mere nest, root, fountain of Sin, and wickedness; an *evil Treasure* from whence proceed *evil things,* viz. *Evil Thoughts, Murders, Adulteries* &c. . . . Indeed, as sharers in the guilt of *Adam's* first Sin, they're *Children of Wrath by Nature,* . . . liable to Eternal Vengeance, the Unquenchable Flames of Hell."[27]

Emerson's Unitarian and Transcendentalist peers deplored such views,[28] and nothing could seem farther from Wadsworth's rhetoric of innate evil than Emerson's Romantic effusions over Waldo in the letters and journals. Yet a common discourse of inheritance informs both Wadsworth's hyperbole and Emerson's observation upon his child's birth: "I see nothing in it of mine." Emerson's radical Augustinianism deems Waldo to be not an heir to but already a participant in ("part or particle of") God. Waldo arrives a month after the publication of *Nature* to help fulfill the transcendental fantasy of the transparent eyeball passage, in which grief for Charles interferes with the suspension of ordinary patterns of human relationship.

As Waldo develops, Emerson's stance toward his son continues to be a combination of fond paternal privilege and disinterested wonder. Waldo is his constant companion, permitted access to the study when others are not; a prized interlocutor, whose aperçus are lovingly recorded; and the focus of many mild oedipal dramas.[29] But he also belongs to other, less domestic precincts: "The babe cheers me with his hearty & protracted laugh which sounds to me like thunder in the woods" (*Journals,* 5:371). In the study and the nursery, Waldo remains his child, his wife's boy, his step-grandfather's great-grandson. Emerson's less conventional relation to Waldo takes place in the presence of the sublime, where there is no room for generations:

> This little boy who walks with me to the woods, has no design in his questions, the question which is asked in his mind he articulates to me, over him, over me,—we exist in an element of awe & singleness. (*Journals,* 8:39)

Although his questions have "no design," their effect makes "this little boy" seem to be, at age four, a master of the rhetorical sublime, transporting his listener out of himself and entering with him into an altered subjectivity.[30] Their special relation becomes here a denial of relation, or rather a dialectical transcendence of relation that is also a discursive transcendence of the regressive force of genealogical transmission. To be father or son is worse than "a trifle and a disturbance"; it is an attenuation of divinity to mere patriarchalism. There is little hint of oedipal reversal to salt Emerson's transvaluations of Waldo with the reminder that divinity may be a source of violence and that transcendence is also a kind of loss.[31]

When loss is made palpable by Waldo's death, however, the excitements of self-surpassal are challenged by the experience of personal vulnerability, reflected in Emerson's writing by anxiety over body intactness and his own mortality. Despite memorable assertions of imperviousness, the question of whether Waldo's death is caducous or maiming is not finally resolved in "Experience." The question is active in "Threnody," published two years later, which more plainly dramatizes Emerson's ambivalence regarding his implication in his son's death, that is, his sense both of responsibility and of transformation. Emerson is concerned to know what the nature he has defined himself over and against can and cannot do to him, and he wonders if his son is the price of superiority.

Poetry and Parricide: "Threnody"

The continuities Emerson makes of fatality often come, as in the concluding sentences of his essay on "Compensation" (1841), at the expense of common sentiment:

> The death of a dear friend, wife, brother, lover, which seemed nothing but privation, somewhat later assumes the aspect of a guide or genius; for it commonly operates revolutions in our way of life, terminates an epoch of infancy or of youth which was waiting to be closed, breaks up a wonted occupation, or a household, or style of living, and allows the formation of new

ones more friendly to the growth of character. It permits or constrains the formation of new acquaintances, and the reception of new influences that prove of the first importance to the next years; and the man or woman who would have remained a sunny garden-flower, with no room for its roots and too much sunshine for its head, by the falling of the walls and the neglect of the gardener, is made the banian of the forest, yielding shade and fruit to wide neighborhoods of men. (*Essays,* 302)

According to this doctrine, the death of others is no brutal fact or sad inevitability. It is, at length, an advantage, and the gains are social as well as imaginative. Emerson's ambition to develop new forms of independence and principled living, and thereby to effect the reform of American moral and market economies, repeatedly seems to draw strength from the losses he sustains. Besides his appreciation of the financial freedom Ellen bequeathed him, the journals reveal accesses of energy following the deaths of both Ellen and Charles that lend these deaths a meaning beyond privation.

Emerson's compensatory logic is an affront to the pieties of those who refuse to acknowledge that, whatever it does to the deceased, death alters the relational world of the living. Thus, while Stephen Whicher finds in the "remorseless" lines of "Compensation" a "powerful and chilling idealism," a defensive denial of the reality of evil that results in the "impoverishment" of Emerson's philosophy,[32] Barbara Packer, following James M. Cox, views such assessments as a kind of reaction formation. Resentment at Emerson's failure to be "crippled by his losses" may be understood, she feels, as an expression of unconscious sympathy with his ability to transform "the helplessness of mourning . . . into its polar opposite, a vision of power."[33]

Cox himself goes further, though, suggesting that Emerson's defense against powerlessness is exceeded by "bold assertions of self-confidence [that are] a threat to everyone around him. In the face of prior disasters and griefs, even if we grant him needed assurance for launching himself as a writer, Emerson's assertion of an idealized metaphoric self which, short of blindness, would be impervious to any evil, has about it a ferocious element of provocation." For Cox, the transparent eyeball passage in *Nature* is a reckless challenge—not Waldo's prefiguration but his death-sentence.[34] Emerson says to the universe, "do your worst," and that is precisely what happens. Vestiges of this magical thinking are present at the beginning of "Threnody" where Emerson links Waldo with Hyacinthus, beloved of Apollo, who in Ovid is killed when the god's discus accidentally strikes him and whose blood is transformed into a flower bearing the inscription of Apollo's compunction and grief.[35] Along with the songs in which he vows to commemorate Hyacinthus, the flower is Apollo's survival strategy for one whose death he blames upon himself. In alluding to this myth, Emerson suggests that through his own assertions of divinity and creative power he has caused his son's death and that in "Threnody," his own inscription of woe, he will seek to lend enduring form to Waldo's memory.

Yet from the start of the poem, Emerson seems reluctant to associate Waldo with enduring forms, including enduring forms of human relation. As in the journal entry following Waldo's birth, in "Threnody" Emerson resists bolstering his "right" in Waldo with recourse to the language of property. In the first twenty-nine lines of the poem, he refers to "my empty house" and "my trees" but cannot bring himself to use the possessive pronoun when referring to Waldo (who is never called by that name). Instead, Waldo is "[t]he hyacinthine boy," "[t]he darling," "the wondrous child," "[t]he gracious boy," and "the budding man."[36] When Emerson finally does claim him, it is as "my truant" (30), an incarnation of Waldo that tends to undercut any fixed sense of possession or relation. The number and variety of descriptive epithets used throughout the poem in place of Waldo's proper name suggest both an urgent need and a reluctance to "[n]ail the wild star to its track" (240). From the start of the poem, this calling and recalling works to undo, rather than to bolster, the substantiality of the name of the son he mourns—to free rather than to fix Waldo's memory.

The name of the son he mourns is, of course, his own name—the name he chose first for himself and later for his first child. Gay Wilson Allen explains: "Ralph Waldo Emerson disliked his first name, and his family and friends called him 'Waldo' after he requested them to do so while he was in college. . . . he had *six* cousins named Ralph . . . [making] it difficult for Ralph Emerson to attain an identity of his own." At the same time, "'Waldo' obviously had an emotional appeal for him, probably because his Waldo ancestors were Waldensians who fled to

England in the seventeenth century to escape persecution in Europe for
their Protestant religion. . . . Waldo was continued as a given name in
the Emerson family, and the poet kept it alive by naming his first son
Waldo."[37] Thus, the name "Waldo" is an emblem of both self-bestowal
and generational transmission; it abridges into a word a self-relation
and a relation between father and son.

Emerson's decision not to use this abridgement either in "Experience"
or in "Threnody" suggests, beyond the reticence of grief, a dissatisfaction with the name's proprietary, ancestral, and egotistical associations,
metaphorical limits to his son's transcendence. Yet the urge to preserve
a sense of Waldo's person remains strong. Thus, along with the un-
naming of Waldo comes his incessant renaming in the poem—and
perhaps in "Experience" as well, where the "lords of life" ("Illusion,
Temperament, Succession, Surface, Surprise, Reality, Subjectiveness"
[*Essays,* 490]) are introduced as the "race" of the unnamed "Little man,"
the "Darling" of the essay's prefatory poem (*Essays,* 469). And if in
"Threnody" Emerson avoids the more obvious sort of repetitive elegiac
invocation,[38] he nevertheless attempts through an accretion of detail to
keep hold of Waldo's particularity:

> The painted sled stands where it stood;
> The kennel by the corded wood;
> The gathered sticks to stanch the wall
> Of the snow-tower, when snow should fall;
> The ominous hole he dug in the sand,
> And childhood's castles built or planned;
> His daily haunts I well discern,—
> The poultry-yard, the shed, the barn,—
> And every inch of garden ground
> Paced by the blessed feet around. . . . (82–91)

Familiar objects, scenes, and possessions ground Emerson's memory
of Waldo in what remains behind. Yet he also wants to insist that Waldo
is in no conventional sense his child:

> Not mine,—I never called thee mine,
> But Nature's heir,—if I repine,
> And seeing rashly torn and moved
> Not what I made, but what I loved,

Grow early old with grief that thou
Must to the wastes of Nature go,—
'Tis because a general hope
Was quenched, and all must doubt and grope. (126–33)

In this apostrophe to Waldo, evidence of generation is once again denied (the child is "Nature's heir . . . Not what I made") and denied insistently enough to suggest that even *calling* Waldo his is a lapse in some sort of cosmic propriety to which Emerson nevertheless cannot fully subscribe. This impression is palpable in the exaggerated protest of a manuscript version of the disclaimer quoted above: "Not mine not mine o never mine / But Nature's heir" (*Journals,* 8:453). Emerson mitigates the effect in the final version, but a hint of defensiveness remains, as though he wants to assure himself that fatherly possessiveness will not interfere with his vision of Waldo's (and his own) transcendence.

Still, the pressure of denial is excruciating and builds to a climax of despair:

For this losing is true dying;
This is lordly man's down-lying,
This his slow but sure reclining,
Star by star his world resigning. (162–65)

These lines—which so skillfully combine a feeling of dignified resignation with a sense of exhausting grief—express none of the consolatory power available, for example, to Edward Taylor, through a belief in the postmortem continuity of the parent-child relation. Of his dead children Taylor writes: "I piecemeale pass to glory bright in them."[39] The glory that, on the contrary, it seems to Emerson he "resign[s]" with Waldo's death (the Emersonian pun joining together loss, stoic acceptance, and writing) is the promise of self-surpassal that Waldo seemed to make both manifest and universal. In death, Waldo stands for both personal limitation and failed entelechy:

I am too much bereft.
The world dishonored thou hast left.
O truth's and nature's costly lie!
O trusted broken prophecy!
O richest fortune sourly crossed!
Born for the future, to the future lost! (170–75)

Emerson's expression of disproportionate loss ("I am too much bereft") echoes Ben Jonson's elegy "On My First Sonne," in which he declares, "My sinne was too much hope of thee, lov'd boy."[40] While Emerson is not as explicit here as Jonson is in associating excess with defect (Jonson's "sinne"),[41] he is elsewhere. In "Compensation," for example, he writes, "every excess causes a defect; every defect an excess" (*Essays,* 287), and in "Experience" he associates such excess with the exaggeration of grief:

> People grieve and bemoan themselves, but it is not half so bad with them as they say. There are moods in which we court suffering, in the hope that here, at least, we shall find reality, sharp peaks and edges of truth. But it turns out to be scene-painting and counterfeit. The only thing grief has taught me, is to know how shallow it is. That, like all the rest, plays about the surface, and never introduces me into the reality, for contact with which, we would even pay the costly price of sons and lovers. (*Essays,* 472–73)

Emerson made this discovery during the composition of "Threnody." In the months following Waldo's death, he found himself "courting" suffering in the many senses of the verb given form in the letters and journals: seeking a positive gain from suffering, drawing down further misery, playing the flatterer, even wooing.

In the excess of this "courting" mood he found the defect of the poem he was writing and laid it aside for what may have been as long as two years. This break in composition is reflected in the poem's division into two parts, the first (lines 1–175) spoken by the poet and the second (lines 176–289) spoken by "the deep Heart," Emerson's hortatory projection of sublimity. The deep Heart immediately takes responsibility for Waldo's death and goes on to chastise the poet for his indulgence in what Immanuel Kant calls the "languid" affections, which he says "make the very effort of resistance an object of pain."[42] Through a litany of questions alternately rebuking and coaxing, the deep Heart attempts to cultivate in the poet a Kantian supersensible cast of mind that could grasp the totality Waldo merely betokens. In doing so, the deep Heart revises the poet's eulogistic motifs of inexpressibility (e.g., "all must doubt and grope"), instructing him that it is not grief for Waldo's death but the dynamic wholeness into which he has died that is "'beyond the reach . . . of speech'" (197–98), "'incommunicable'" (200), "'[p]ast utterance'" (203).[43]

Nevertheless, in taking the form of a conversation the poem seems to depend on the communicability of its idealizing alternative to grief, implying (without, however, confirming) the elegist's reception of and assent to the response offered by the deep Heart. The poem is a simpler and starker drama of self-address than the intricate colloquy of "Experience." Yet to call it a "drama" may be misleading, if its effect is to supplant catharsis by transcendence. "Self-address," too, is a reductive characterization, against which Emerson may have sought to defend the poem by calling it "Threnody"—a term that still carries with it the suggestion of multiple voices despite its infrequent and indiscriminate use in English poetry. In classical Greek poetry, *threnos* denoted a formal lament and came to be associated with the choral ode.[44] In English poetry, the distinction between "threnody" and "monody" is largely specious. "Even in elegies that call themselves 'monodies,' such as 'Lycidas,'" Peter Sacks observes, "the voice of the elegist seems to work through several moments of extreme divisiveness or multiplicity."[45] Likewise, English poems that call themselves "threnodies"—though they may, like Dryden's "Threnodia Augustalis," refer to a public or "general Voice"[46]—tend not to figure explicitly a multiplicity or division of voices. Emerson, however, makes such a division the chief structural feature of his "Threnody," giving it a name that bears a sense of the communal, to which its transcendent vision appeals.

Sincerity and Common Sense

The first part of "Threnody" does not end with a clear interrogative. But because the second part is introduced as the response to a question ("The deep Heart answered . . ."), the lag in composition is not felt as a breach of chronological continuity within the poem. Assessments of the poem, however, often dwell on a perceived expressive discontinuity between the first and second parts that is felt to be an effect of the compositional hiatus. In a note on "Threnody" in the centenary edition of Emerson's works, his surviving son, Edward Waldo, writes that the second part "was not written until Time and Thought had brought their healing."[47] Later commentators have stressed the naturalness and spontaneity of the first part, sometimes with excesses of their own. John McAleer, for example, characterizes the first part of "Threnody" as "an authentic expression of grief that becomes not poetry ingeniously contrived but the statement of a mind responding with limpid vitality to the dictates of a sincerely experienced emotion."[48] Gay Wilson Allen also prizes the first part of the poem for its sincerity, maintaining that it "was not a literary exercise, such as Milton practiced in 'Lycidas' or Shelley in 'Adonais.'"[49] Allen's comparison recalls Samuel Johnson's famous dig at "Lycidas" in *Lives of the Poets,* a remark that distilled the eighteenth century's contempt for pastoralism as the enemy of elegiac sincerity. "Where there is leisure for fiction," Johnson wrote, "there is little grief."[50] Yet the first part of "Threnody" traffics heavily in pastoral conventions, even if (like "Lycidas") it does so partly to modify or to challenge them. It also provides abundant evidence of Emerson's careful selection and revision of passages from letters and journal entries, including the letter he wrote to his aunt Mary Moody the day after Waldo's death, which prompted her to comment approvingly on his power so readily to turn affliction into poetry.[51] "Threnody" *was* a literary exercise—one temporarily abandoned in grief, no doubt, but with a more complex sense of the relation between grief and fiction than that implied by a simple standard of sincerity.

Emerson knows there must be leisure for grief as well as for fiction. His concern is not that grief is vitiated by fiction but that grief is itself nothing more than the fictions we imitate in the hope of gaining access to the "reality" we crave and for which we would pay the "costly price of sons and lovers." People grieve, and it is "scene-painting and counterfeit"—theatrical metaphors that link elegy with tragedy and what Kenneth Burke calls the "imitation of victimage."[52] "Threnody" reflects Emerson's impatience with such self-dramatization. An attenuation of grief (Johnson's "leisure for fiction") leads to the interruption of the elegist's voice by the imperious deep Heart—a figure Mark Edmundson deems an "appallingly revised version of the Over-Soul."[53] Presumably, Edmundson is appalled at the cold logic with which the deep Heart begins its response: "'Worthier cause for passion wild / If I had not taken the child'" (177–78). But if the deep Heart is a revision of the Over-Soul, it is a revision toward which Emerson's essay on "The

Over-Soul" tends. In the essay, "common heart" is used repeatedly as a synonym for "Over-Soul" and in its various forms—"heart of nature" (*Essays*, 392), "heart of being" (398), "heart of all" (399)—is the focal point for the soul's ascensions and descensions. Despite its title (now inevitably associated with Nietzsche's own revision), the essay locates value in "depth," which is at the outset associated with "reality" (385) and which characterizes the Over-Soul's expressions: "deep power" (386), "deeps of spiritual nature" (387), "deep, divine thought" (388). The revelation that man needs to receive is that "Highest dwells within him" (399), that he already has, according to the essay's final sentence, "the whole future in the bottom of the heart" (400).

In the despairing lines that end the first part of "Threnody," the future seems to Emerson to have been damaged by Waldo's death ("Born to the future, to the future lost!"). The intervention of the deep Heart at this point recalls the concluding image of "The Over-Soul"—an image of introjection that makes it tempting to read the deep Heart simply as Emerson's own. If the heart conventionally stands for privateness and subjectivity, then the *deep* heart must seem doubly private. But the use in both cases of the definite article rather than the possessive pronoun is significant. In "The Over-Soul" authenticity entails a movement downward through cultural superstructures. "The landscape, the figures, Boston, London, are facts as fugitive as any institution past, or any whiff of mist or smoke, and so is society, and so is the world" (388). Yet while the heart toward which this movement tends is still the center of being, it is also the substance of community. For Emerson, one of the cultural superstructures to be moved through on the way downward to the (not thy) heart is the self-possessive individual. Man, he says, is a "facade" (387).

> And this, because the heart in thee is the heart of all; not a valve, not a wall, not an intersection is there anywhere in nature, but one blood rolls uninterruptedly an endless circulation through all men. (399)

Emerson hastens to remind us that this community is not equivalent with society, that a withdrawal from social existence—"from all the accents of other men's devotions" (399)—is not madness but sanity. "The Over-Soul" nevertheless induces even as it describes a kind of

vertigo—a "shudder of awe and delight" (393)—resulting not from the
proliferating metaphors of high, low, within, and behind that map its
metaphysics, but rather from the condition of simultaneous communion and isolation it asks us to imagine. Despite our commonality of
being, the "things we now esteem fixed shall, one by one, detach themselves, like ripe fruit, from our experience, and fall" (388).

This difficult wisdom is what the deep Heart of "Threnody" demands that the elegist acknowledge and quietly submit himself to in
the aftermath of his son's death, rather than vainly seeking to preserve
sensible attachments:

> "Wilt thou freeze love's tidal flow,
> Whose streams through nature circling go?
> Nail the wild star to its track
> On the half-climbed zodiac?
> Light is light which radiates,
> Blood is blood which circulates,
> Life is life which generates,
> And many-seeming life is one,—
> Wilt thou transfix and make it none?
> Its onward force too starkly pent
> In figure, bone, and lineament?
> Wilt thou, uncalled, interrogate,
> Talker! the unreplying Fate?" (238–50)

Rather than assimilate nature to his own sense of loss, making a mourner out of nature as he does in the first part of the poem, the elegist is
encouraged by the deep Heart both to identify with and to detach
himself from nature's fatality, subsuming its power even as its ultimate
powerlessness to restore Waldo is confirmed. If grief weakly assails the
reticence of fate in a kind of profane, de-idealizing speech (the deep
Heart calls grief "'blasphemy'" [204]) that the poem works to silence,
fate itself is subject to the limitation of its own decrees (193–94).

Not so the elegist, who is potentially able through the operations of
mind to transcend the limits fate would enforce. What Kant calls "reason," Emerson calls "thought" or "intellect," which like the "'servant
Death,'" who "'with solving rite, / Pours finite into infinite'" (236–37),
works to undo what nature has done. Finding a solution in dissolution

is one of Emerson's favorite conceits. He borrows it for "Threnody" from the essays "Intellect" and "Circles" and goes on to use it again in "Fate," where the resilience of matter comes to seem like a mere failure of will, a will that is nevertheless perpetually schooled in "Beautiful Necessity," in the loss of those objects that "detach themselves, like ripe fruit, from our experience, and fall." The Edenic referent is made explicit at the end of "Threnody," where the deep Heart concludes with an image of slightly fevered divinity:

> "Silent rushes the swift Lord
> Through ruined systems still restored,
> Broadsowing, bleak and void to bless,
> Plants with worlds the wilderness;
> Waters with tears of ancient sorrow
> Apples of Eden ripe to-morrow." (282–87)

The tears Emerson weeps at the beginning of "Experience" ("All things swim and glitter" [*Essays,* 471]) yield a "private fruit" (491). But this personal economy of grief waxes mythic in "Threnody," as the poem moves through a series of biblical and Miltonic identifications and ascriptions.

The mythologizing of loss is pervasive in "Threnody." As we have seen, the story of Hyacinthus provides Emerson with a figure for the Ovidian substitution of the aesthetic object for the lost child—a substitution that is both a sign of the poet's devastation and an extension of his creative identity. But the primary figure in the poem for paternal self-fulfillment entailing an innovative strategy for filial survival is Jesus Christ.[54] Christological associations abound in "Threnody," from Miltonic allusion (Emerson's "wondrous child" [11] echoes the "wondrous birth" of Christ in Book III of *Paradise Lost*),[55] to messianic inference ("he died / And wandered backward as in scorn, / To wait an aeon to be born" [147–49]), to explicit reference. The deep Heart tells the poet the boy was sent to him,

> "That thou might'st break thy daily bread
> With prophet, Saviour, and head;
> That thou might'st cherish for thine own
> The riches of sweet Mary's Son,
> Boy-Rabbi, Israel's paragon." (219–23)

In "Threnody," Emerson stands in a variety of metaphorical relations to the Christ-like Waldo: as God, as Joseph, as one of the apostles, even, startlingly, as Mary Magdalene.[56] The multiplicity of associations illustrates the ambivalence of the poet's impulse to identify with divinity, to substitute metaphorically his own presumptive power over Waldo for the power of a son-sacrificing God, to link his own sublimity with the authoritarianism of a powerful, violent father. Emerson's uneasy response to the trauma of Waldo's death is to identify with its unapprehensible cause—not God per se but the external power so designated in Christian mythology, where Christ's sacrifice is the key to human transcendence and the realization of divine will.

This imaginative act of simultaneous submission and overcoming with respect to external power is, in its naturalized form, a hallmark of the Romantic sublime.[57] Thus, Kant locates sublimity in our subjective experience of superiority to nature, a superiority that, according to Schiller, preserves the subject's integrity. One must, Schiller says, be either

> superior to nature as a force, or . . . at one with her. Nothing that she can do to him is violence because before it reaches *him* it has already become *his own action,* and dynamic nature never reaches him, because he has by his own free act separated himself from everything that she can reach.[58]

Yet this integrity (Schiller, like Kant, calls it our "humanity") requires for its maintenance an identification with nature that, paradoxically, separates us from everything that is human, "everything that she can reach." Mark Edmundson, in the remarks on "Fate" that cap his reading of "Threnody," sees something like this paradoxical integrity in Emerson's repeated abrogations of "binding relations to the past . . . figures of authority . . . venerable institutions." According to Edmundson, Emerson works to free himself of these attachments by "subvert[ing] the Freudian category of 'normal mourning,' committing himself to that remorseless activity of self-creation Freud called 'melancholia.'" In his struggle not to be bound to what he has lost or to what is recalcitrant and dead in the present, melancholia becomes Emerson's *via negativa* to a "fresh Romantic sublime," an "unfolding act of self-destroying self-invention, which is at odds with our humanistic ethical principles."[59]

Yet if "Fate" is a clarifying or interpretive extension of the sublime elegism of "Threnody," it is also, as the lead essay of *The Conduct of Life*, one of Emerson's fullest engagements with "humanistic ethical principles." It foregrounds the question, "How shall I live?" and predicates its answer on the assurance that "though we know not how, necessity does comport with liberty, the individual with the world, my polarity with the spirit of the times" (*Essays*, 943). Greatness divines fatality and turns it into a principle of action, an ethic of reform. "Liberation of the will," says Emerson, "from the sheaths and clogs of organization which he has outgrown, is the end and aim of this world. Every calamity is a spur and valuable hint" (*Essays*, 960). Edmundson, following Harold Bloom, turns this liberation ethic into a sublime solipsism, a perpetual self-rebegetting into heroic isolation, a superiority to all attachments and the inscrutable losses they entail.[60] But Emerson is not ready to entrust himself to such a radical view of the private (and privative) character of experience, even as experience reaches the limits of communicability in the face of death. His elegism, whether in the ode to necessity of "Fate" or in the agitated pastoralism of "Threnody," challenges the Bloomian notion that solipsism is the American writer's key to subverting the authority of "unpenetrated causes" (*Essays*, 958).

Elegy and the Demos of the Sublime

Emerson's "fate" is a metaphor for whatever seems to block human will: "a name for facts not yet passed under the fire of thought;—for causes which are unpenetrated" (*Essays*, 958). As such, it is the functional equivalent of the concept of death, which as John Guillory points out is "the slipperiest of signifiers, the most likely to take on the metaphoric task of signifying any blockage, failure, inhibition." Guillory locates this task in Gray's "Elegy Written in a Country Churchyard," where the "invocation of death is the rhetorical mechanism by which the social structure of repression is *abstracted,* rendered subjectless and objectless."[61] Thus, in Gray, the egalitarianism of death works to palliate material inequalities among the living. Death graduates the unequal into the democratic culture of the graveyard, which serves the living as a consoling or humbling reminder of the impermanence of aristocratic divisions even as the poem's pastoralism seeks to stabilize a class structure that is in the process of breaking down.

Wordsworth's pastoralism—for example, in "Michael"—is even more urgent, given the encroachments of technology and the increasing rootlessness that threaten not only Michael and his family but, even more crucially, the imaginative heritability of the landscape. Wordsworth tells Michael's story "for the sake / Of youthful Poets, who among these hills / Will be my second self when I am gone."[62] As one of Wordsworth's Romantic heirs, William Cullen Bryant was inspired by Wordsworth's development of the topographic elegy to write poems like "Thanatopsis" and "The Prairies," in which he rehearsed the lesson of death's equalizing power against a distinctly American backdrop. Bryant was so imaginatively bound, however, to his pre-Romantic and Romantic models that he was unable to exploit the heavy irony of that lesson's apparent redundance in an American context. It took Tocqueville to recognize that in America the "social structure of repression" is abstracted not by death but by democracy.

Emerson had both a better appreciation of the requirements of literary innovation and a keener skepticism about the shallow idealizations of Jacksonianism than Bryant did. Yet he chose in his elegy for Waldo to embrace the structural and thematic conventions and social anachronisms of pastoral elegy. "Threnody" begins with the isolation of bereavement. As a solitary figure in a rural landscape, Emerson looks for the lost boy he knows he cannot find and who has left his house "empty" (9). Although he is aided by a sympathetic nature, "the Day's eye" (21) and "the south wind" (24) are equally unsuccessful in their efforts to locate Waldo. He tells nature "'We are mates in misery'" (103). This sense of shared privation is extended to include shadow figures from Emerson's Concord circle. His longing for Waldo's "household cheer" (36) recalls for him the attentions paid to his son by friends like Margaret Fuller and Henry Thoreau. In the poem they become the "fairest dames" and "bearded men" (43) who, given the chance to play with the boy and to hear his "winsome voice" (51), would "let the world's affairs go by, / Awhile" (47–48).

Such (to echo Milton on Lycidas) is Waldo's loss to Transcendentalist's ear. But it is his imagined loss to the wider world that occupies Emerson most urgently. If I grieve, he says, "'Tis because a general hope / Was quenched, and all must doubt and grope" (132–33). It is as if Waldo was to become what Emerson had in "Compensation" fancied he himself might become—"the banian of the forest"—as a result of the interruption through death of his most intimate relations. Yet this "general hope" was also a general threat to the world's inherent conservatism: "Pregnant with his grander thought," Waldo "[b]rought the old order into doubt" (144–45).

Emerson's quarrel with "the old order" is less political than metaphysical. Yet even as he grew increasingly dismissive of reformers and reforms in the popular sense, his idea of a principled life remained nonetheless bound to an unceasing project of self-reformation that was also a project of societal reformation. In January 1841, he asked a Boston audience of mechanics' apprentices—most of whom were undoubtedly caught up, as Emerson was well aware, in the current social and legal struggles over trade unionism in Massachusetts—to consider how each of them could become "a free and helpful man, a reformer, a benefactor" (*Essays,* 135) in his own right by reconceiving his relation to "the whole institution of property" (138). This reconception touched directly on the theme of filial sacrifice that—long after Emerson had abandoned his ministerial career with his refusal to perform the already largely exsanguinated ritual of the protestant Eucharist—continued to have both expiatory and communal force in his thinking on the relation between moral and market economies. There is all the difference in the world, he tells the apprentices, "between the first and second owner of property." When the father, he explains, who "supplies his own want. . . . comes to give all the goods he has year after year collected, in one estate to his son," they are to the son "not means but masters" and make him into "a puny, protected person, guarded by walls and curtains, stoves and down beds . . . the menial and runner of his riches" (*Essays,* 140–41). Habitual imparting, rather than transgenerational hoarding, Emerson insists, will mitigate the taint of property and inaugurate a society of love: "We must be lovers," he told the apprentices. And again: "Let me feel that I am to be a lover. I am to see to it that the world is the better for me, and to find my reward in the act. Love would put a new face on this weary old world in which we dwell as pagans and enemies too long, and it would warm the heart to see how fast the vain diplomacy of statesmen, the impotence of armies, and navies, and lines of defence, would be superseded by this unarmed child" (148–49). First learn the lesson of self-help and renounce the materialist legacy of infirmity, Emerson exhorts. Then there is an even greater demand. For to refuse or to withhold a degenerative inheritance is merely a prelude to profounder sacrifice. "As the farmer casts into the ground the finest ears of his grain, the time will come when we too shall hold nothing back, but shall eagerly convert more than we now possess into means and powers, when we shall be willing to sow the sun and the moon for seeds" (150).

The pun on "sun" falls hard on the ears of readers of "Experience"— the essay Emerson wrote three years later, after Waldo's intervening death—in which he ventures that, for access to the "reality" masked by grief, "we would even pay the costly price of sons and lovers" (*Essays,* 472–73). Many of the essay's readers (both before and after D. H. Lawrence) associate the phrase "sons and lovers" with family losses—the intimate losses Emerson had already sustained—and therefore conclude that Emerson is obscenely imagining himself to be in a position to sacrifice what he has in fact already lost. Sharon Cameron reinforces this conclusion by asserting that "the disparity between the man's offer and his ignorance of its illegitimacy is all the more shocking when we remember that the sacrifice being contemplated is of a wife and a child."[63] Cameron's claim, however, is imprecise. Whatever the sacrifice being contemplated, it consists not of "a wife and a child" but of multiple "sons" and multiple "lovers." Certainly, we "remember" Waldo's death and also perhaps that of Emerson's first wife, Ellen, in 1831. And to insist on the biographical coordinates is potentially to participate in a pathos that, as Julie Ellison has argued, may be the phenomenological basis for a fresh critical view of antebellum masculine domesticity.[64] But we also remember the "lovers" repeatedly called to account in Emerson's speech to the mechanics' apprentices and the countless "lovers" celebrated throughout his writings, which are found not chiefly in sexual pairings but much more commonly in the diffuse and idealized eroticism of communion—a communion of naturalistic universalism:

> What is man born for but to be a Reformer, a Re-maker of what man has made; a renouncer of lies; a restorer of truth and good, imitating that great Nature which embosoms us all, and which sleeps no moment on an old past, but every hour repairs herself, yielding us every morning a new day, and with every pulsation a new life? Let him renounce everything which is not true to him, and put all his practices back on their first thoughts, and do nothing for which he has not the whole world for his reason. (*Essays*, 146)

A year later—almost exactly a year after exhorting the apprentices to "hold nothing back" in their effort to become free and helpful men—Waldo was dead, prompting Emerson to write in his journal the lines that would later open the published version of "Threnody," lines that note the sharp contrast between the world's inability to restore his dead son and nature's hourly self-remaking. This conventional pastoral motif is an ancient artifact of the fundamental human grievance against mortality, and it is thus a challenge—a challenge "Threnody" takes on—to Emerson's exuberant and hortatory faith in ascesis. It is also a challenge to his bid for literary independence from anterior models. To bring "the old order into doubt" is precisely the task Emerson sets for himself. But "the old order," like the strength of personal attachment to a dead son, is hard to displace. Despite Tocqueville's conviction that democracy "inspires in men a kind of instinctive distaste for all that is old,"[65] and despite Emerson's own surpassing faith in the liberating power of imagination, he readily concedes that objects of thought and affection change "slowly and with pain" (*Essays*, 337).

The pastoralism of "Threnody" may seem like just such a concession, Emerson's implicit acknowledgment in the aftermath of a devastating loss of his need for the heritable fortifications of tradition to mourn a son he was unable to endow with sufficiently empowering fortifications against death. Yet is it really *death* that prevents Waldo from fulfilling Emerson's ambitions, from saving the world? This is the suggestion of the first part of "Threnody," and it is this abstraction by death of the failure of reform that is the poem's chief debt to the tradition of pastoral elegy. If the two parts of the poem are difficult for readers to reconcile, it is not because the second part lacks the putative authorizing sincerity of the first part but because it manages only imperfectly to vitiate that debt.

Indeed, the overall movement of the poem from despair to an offer of consolation is thoroughly conventional. It is, however, in its refusal to ratify even the formless form of consolation the deep Heart makes available that "Threnody" achieves a lurching breakaway from the gravitational pull of its antecedents. Waldo is not in any traditional manner recuperated, sanctified, translated, or stellified. The consolidations of memory effected by the elegist in the first part of the poem are undone by the cooperative dissolutions of thought, nature, and death, which unbind Waldo from the tyranny of his own person ("'too starkly pent / In figure, bone, and lineament'") as well as from the limiting force of the elegist's asseverations of particular loss. The elegist's voice, like the figure of Waldo, is unrecuperated at the poem's end, which may suggest either capitulation or resistance. Indeed, if consolation takes a form in "Threnody" beyond the totalizing corporate abstractions the deep Heart champions, it is the form of the poem itself, through which Emerson sustains the tension between discrepant impulses toward memorialization and transcendence that is for him, finally and terribly, the priceless energy of loss.

Analogous impulses toward individuation and unification characterize the dialectic of the essay "Fate," in which dissolution is also the proper destiny of persons, not to be mourned (*Essays,* 968). "Fate" was published on the eve of the Civil War, when conflicting ideals of individualism and unity were impelling the nation toward its own form of dissolution through brutal killings in the name of filial piety and sacrifice. Five years later, Emerson eulogized the man who held the nation together as "the true history of the American people in his time," emphasizing the achieved eloquence Waldo had only promised.

> Step by step he walked before them; slow with their slowness, quickening his march by theirs, the true representative of this continent; an entirely public man; father of his country, the pulse of twenty millions throbbing in his heart, the thought of their minds articulated by his tongue.

Nevertheless, Lincoln's death seemed to Emerson a true fatality, a providential result that stood for the incompleteness of victory, of "what remained to be done."[66] It remained for Walt Whitman to achieve what Emerson reached for in "Threnody": an extravagant intimacy with the dead that would exceed the reparative terms and residual grievances of more conventional elegy.

In the meantime, the sentimental culture that was rewriting slavery for white readers as the loss of a child slowly made room for texts of black filial experience like Frederick Douglass's autobiography, *My Bondage and My Freedom* (1855), in which Emerson's critique of paternity, sexual doubt, birthright, and inheritance finds its devastating counterpart:

> Slavery does away with fathers, as it does away with families. Slavery has no use for either fathers or families, and its laws do not recognize their existence in the social arrangements of the plantation. When they *do* exist, they are not the outgrowths of slavery, but are antagonistic to that system. The order of civilization is reversed here. The name of the child is not expected to be that of its father, and his condition does not necessarily affect that of the child.

Slave law determined in most cases that the child should follow the condition of the mother. Yet if the slave child was unlikely to know his father, he was no more likely to have an enduring connection with his mother. "I cannot say," Douglass writes,

> that I was very deeply attached to my mother; certainly not so deeply as I should have been had our relations in childhood been different. We were separated, according to the common custom, when I was but an infant, and, of course, before I knew my mother from anyone else.

Douglass deplores this "terrible interference of slavery with my infantile affections" and the difficulty with which he recovered something of his mother's love long after her death:

> After what I have now said of the circumstances of my mother, and my relations to her, the reader will not be surprised, nor be disposed to censure me, when I tell but the simple truth, viz: that I received the tidings of her death with no strong emotions of sorrow for her, and with very little regret for myself on account of her loss. I had to learn the value of my mother

long after her death, and by witnessing the devotion of other mothers to their children.[67]

Emerson apprehended grief for his son as an incentive to question the commonly accepted values of kinship and lineage in white, middle-class society. Widely challenged by market revolution, these values nevertheless persisted to a degree that Emerson found disabling in himself. So he bravely ventured the memory of his adored son in an elegiac bid to escape their reinscription of oedipal violence. Faced with experiences of violence that Emerson would have had trouble comprehending, antebellum slaves and free blacks also engaged elegiac tradition, mourning the loss of kinship and lineage even as they figured acts of infanticide as a viable response to the profound distortion by race hatred of African-American mourning.

CHAPTER 5

Mourning of the Disprized: African Americans and Elegy from Wheatley to Lincoln

When I think of my own griefs, I remember theirs.
—MARY PRINCE

As part of the mourning culture of black Americans, elegy was also part of the racialized drama of sorrow and resistance that characterized American culture more generally and that took shape in related genres like the eulogy, the funeral sermon, the spiritual, and even the minstrel song. An occasional form, commonly devoted to detailing its subjects' lives and connections, elegy sometimes helped to restore a sense of the severed affiliations from which blacks suffered disproportionately. But the forced unsettlement of African-American life and the deracination of slave experience especially meant that particularizing details were frequently difficult to discover or preserve. Many elegies for African Americans are perforce anonymous and typifying. They often resemble elegies for Native Americans in this way—especially those written by whites. To a much greater extent than Native Americans, however, African Americans wrote and published elegies of their own in English, helping to determine the cultural role that mourning would play in the oppositional consciousness of both blacks and whites.

From the late eighteenth century through the Civil War, African-American elegy was a challenge to dominance written under the sign of lamentation. The challenge was sometimes modest and sometimes militant, and it was taken up as well by white poets, who, like their black counterparts, wrote elegies for subjects of both races, contributing to a complex history of identification and remembrance. It is a history of political radicalism but also of faith in transcendence, a history of the idealization of mourning as well as the struggle for emancipation. Elegies by and for slaves commonly generated sympathy and support for the combative, sometimes violent cause of abolitionism. But they also helped articulate an ethos of renunciation, repeatedly discovering in death an end to otherwise insoluble problems of existence. These problems were not limited to the physical and psychological trauma suffered by slaves but included the melancholy and rage of traumatized white and free black populations as well.

For slaves, to publicly mourn at all was boldly to consecrate ties of feeling and of blood that often lay under the heaviest interdictions. Yet despite repressive circumstances, American slaves cultivated and sustained various deathways across generations. Among them were the nighttime funerals favored by slaves both in the South and in the British West Indies.[1] Customary though they were from the seventeenth century through the nineteenth, such funerals were regularly suspected of being pretexts for the organization of rebellion. From Antigua to Virginia to New York, periodic legislative acts restricted or prohibited slave funerals with the hope of forestalling insurrection. In some cases, it was probably a wise precaution; Gabriel Prosser's rebellion in Virginia in 1800, for example, is said to have gained momentum from a meeting held at a slave child's funeral.[2]

Whites who attended such funerals heard black mourners sing English hymns. A favorite was Isaac Watts's "Hark from the tombs a doleful sound" (sung also at Washington's funeral). Whites in attendance also heard, often quite uncomprehendingly, samples of the oral heritage of slave songs that would come to be known as spirituals. Famously linked with "sorrow" by both Frederick Douglass and W. E. B. Du Bois, the songs—transcribed and collected during and after the Civil War—are richly varied in theme and mood. Yet the impression of their sorrowfulness—their apparent reflection of, in Paul Gilroy's words, "the consciousness of the slave as involving an extended act of mourning"[3]—has been hard to dislodge, even though scholars such as Saidiya Hartman have stressed their "complexity and opacity" and have discouraged treating them as "an index or mirror of the slave condition."[4]

Some of the force of these warnings derives from the way in which the songs were collected and preserved, a haphazard and uneven process conducted largely by whites who often lacked basic transcription skills. Thomas Wentworth Higginson, one of the earliest compilers, apologized for his poor approximations of dialect, saying, "I could get no nearer." He admitted to being "bewildered" by one song, and he found another to have "a kind of spring and *lilt* to it, quite indescribable by words." Yet, despite these admitted shortcomings, Higginson's descriptions of the songs as they were sung in the army camps of his black regiment emphasize a familiar "minor-keyed pathos" difficult to surrender wholly to the thesis of "complexity and opacity." Of this pathos Higginson wrote that it "used to seem to me almost too sad to dwell upon, while slavery seemed destined to last for generations; but now that their patience has had its perfect work, history cannot afford to lose this portion of its record."[5] The war, in other words, changed the nature of these songs by obviating their role as antislavery testimony, by altering the terms of the future their lyrics envisioned, and by bringing to an end their solely oral transmission.

Collectors like Higginson were, in a manner of speaking, collaborators on this newly entextualized lyric canon with the long generations of slave singers whom James Weldon Johnson addressed as "black and unknown bards." However intently and respectfully they listened, the collectors would inevitably mishear or misconstrue. They would, as Emerson puts it, "lose ever and anon a word, or a verse, and substitute something of [their] own, and thus miswrite the poem." The songs would even come to be *called* poems on occasion and to be at least partially assimilated into the canon of Western mourning poetry. Jahan Ramazani, for example, in his book on modern elegy, refers to spirituals as "poems of normative mourning." Like elegies, many spirituals stage grief for which they offer consolation, or at least its prospect. They tell of misery and heartbreak but override despair, promising compensation here or hereafter—"Nothing but patience for this life," as Higginson put it, "nothing but triumph in the next," an assessment echoed by Du Bois and reflective of the religious ethos of much European and American elegy.[6]

By way of introduction to his chapter on the elegies of Langston Hughes, Ramazani offers a brief retrospect on African-American elegy. African Americans, he writes with perhaps inadvertent irony, "have mastered the elegy, from Phillis Wheatley in the eighteenth century to Harlem Renaissance poets like Countee Cullen and Langston Hughes."[7] While it is not Ramazani's aim in his book on twentieth-century elegy to tell who these earlier poets were or what their elegies were like, it is nevertheless a breathtaking leap he makes, spanning over 150 years from Wheatley's first poems to Cullen's. Here, my focus is on the first century or so of African-American elegy, from Wheatley's late-colonial Boston through the sudden deaths of the 1860s, when the end of slavery, the assassination of Lincoln, and the transcription of the sorrow songs all helped configure the terminus of the first major phase of its history. Beginning in the latter half of the eighteenth century, literary abolitionism in England and America helped facilitate the appropriation by slaves and free blacks of European-American cultural forms, including the elegy. In turn, white literary abolitionists appropriated the voices of black mourning in their own elegies, eventually assuming the role of post-slavery guardians of the endangered practice of the sorrow songs. These reciprocal appropriations suggest that rather than having "mastered" the elegy, both African Americans and European Americans were using the poetry of mourning to explore the limits, risks, and possibilities of mutually intelligible grief.

What Mourning Over Me

African Americans began composing elegies at least as early as 1746, during King George's War, when Lucy Terry, slave to Ebenezer Wells of Deerfield, Massachusetts, produced a tribute to some Deerfield residents slain in an Indian raid.[8] In the 1770s, Lemuel Haynes's broadside elegy for Asa Burt was published in Hartford, and Phillis Wheatley's breakout poem, her elegy for George Whitefield, was published to acclaim in Boston, New York, Philadelphia, and London. By the time of her own death in 1784, Wheatley had composed at least eighteen other elegies, not counting variants. In the nineteenth century, North Carolina slave poet George Moses Horton was also prolific in the genre, publishing at least seventeen elegies between 1829 and 1865. Other African-American elegists of the early national and antebellum periods include Methodist minister and former slave George White, abolitionist Sarah Louisa Forten, essayist and teacher Ann Plato, A.M.E. preacher Daniel Alexander Payne, bootmaker Joseph Cephas Holly, barber and colonizationist James Monroe Whitfield, lawyer and professor George Boyer Vashon, and lecturer and reformer Frances Ellen Watkins Harper.

The subjects of Wheatley's known elegies, most of whom have been identified, all appear to have been white. This means that George White's untitled 1810 elegy for a young New York slave named Mary Henery may be the earliest extant American elegy by a black author for a black subject. White published the poem, along with a redaction of the funeral sermon he preached for Henery, as part of the narrative of his own "Life, Experience, Travels, and Gospel Labours." White portrays Henery as an exemplary convert to Methodism, full of praise for God even in extremis and exhorting others with her dying breath. Both of Mary's parents were at her side when she died. White preached the funeral sermon at their request, and he addresses them directly in the final stanza of the subjoined elegy:

> Grieve not, ye parents, give your sighing o'er:
> The deep felt cause will soon be felt no more.
> Your daughter lives in pleasures ever new,
> On Zion's hill, where she looks out for you.[9]

The exhortation not to grieve, the assurance of the departed's happiness in Heaven, the promise of posthumous reunion—these conventions of European-American elegy seem to transcend racial difference. Indeed, there is no indication whatsoever in the sixteen-line poem of Henery's race or her slave status, or of the author's identity. Of course, these identifications are readily enabled by the surrounding text. But the elegy's lack of particularizing detail is a sign of more than mere poetic economy or the universalizing language of mourning. Embedded within his own story of slavery, childhood trauma, itinerancy, sectarian conflict, and serial loss, White's elegy for Henery seems emptied of particularity in part to make room for the indirect expression of his own uncompleted mourning. His narrative opens with his early separation from his parents. Except for a brief reunion with his mother at age nineteen, his later efforts to find and reconnect with them are unsuccessful. The fact that George and Sarah Henery were both present at their daughter's deathbed and that they were the ones who asked White to deliver the funeral sermon suggests a kind of surrogacy whereby White takes Mary's place in the poem and reassures himself in a promise to his own absent parents that they will be reunited after death.

The absence of particularizing detail and the corollary prizing of exemplarity in White's elegy for Henery are common features of elegiac poetry. Read out of context, White's elegy would be hard to distinguish from hundreds of other early-nineteenth-century child elegies, such as those later assembled in William Simonds's anthology *Our Little Ones in Heaven*.[10] But elegies that resemble one another in their departicularization of the mourned may each originate in or reflect dramatically different circumstances of mourning. Among European-American elegists, for example, the discoverability and durability of kinship relations across generations were still commonly taken for granted. By contrast, the kinship relations of slaves and free blacks were profoundly and repeatedly disrupted. In African-American elegies, departicularization enables a form of reflexivity based on a shared experience of deracination. They perform threatened continuity as a form of identity.

It is likely that a sentimental view of this identity is behind John Greenleaf Whittier's comment on an elegy by George Moses Horton. Horton, a slave himself, wrote the elegy for a young slave named Rebecca and published it in his first collection of poems, *The Hope of Liberty*, in 1829. Reviewing the collection twenty years later, Whittier quoted at length from "On the Death of Rebecca," and wrote that "[t]here is something deeply affecting in this dirge for a slave, by a slave."[11] Behind the liberal condescension, one hears in Whittier's comment a quiet awe, not at Horton's handling of the form (he is somewhat dismissive of Horton's technical skill) but at the poem's reflexivity ("for a slave, by a slave") and its evocation of the doubled displacements of slavery and death.

For the elegist in this case was also dead—socially dead, in the specific sense likely recognized by Whittier and later described by sociologist Orlando Patterson as "natal alienation." By this Patterson means that all of a slave's social relations, such as might exist with parents, children, siblings, spouses, fellow workers, or coreligionists, for example, "were never recognized as legitimate or binding."[12] Often such relations—indeed the very conditions necessary for such relations to emerge—were violently disrupted. The most dramatic form of this disruption was kidnapping and transportation, such as Phillis Wheatley experienced as a young West African girl. Torn away from her parents and from all claims and obligations, Wheatley became what Patterson calls "a genealogical isolate":

> Formally isolated in [her] social relations with those who lived, [she] also was culturally isolated from the social heritage of [her] ancestors. . . . Slaves differed from other human beings in that they were not allowed freely to integrate the experience of their ancestors into their lives, to inform their understanding of social reality with the inherited meanings of their natural forebears, or to anchor the living present in any conscious community of memory. That they reached back for the past, as they reached out for the related living, there can be no doubt. Unlike other persons, doing so meant struggling with and penetrating the iron curtain of the master, his community, his laws, his policemen or patrollers, and his heritage.[13]

Wheatley did try to reach back. According to her first biographer, she held onto, and shared with others, an early memory of her mother engaged in some form of morning libation.[14] And in a poem addressed to the Earl of Dartmouth, she imagined her father's grief at losing her: "What pangs excruciating must molest, / What sorrows labour in my parent's breast?"[15] But these plaintive questions seem to mark the limit of Wheatley's approach to natal ties. Her extant writings reveal a scant retrospect on her African past. Offered the chance in 1774 to return to Africa as a missionary, Wheatley demurred in terms that suggest the extent of her deracination: "how like a Barbarian Should I look to the Natives."[16] After her manumission and the wartime dissolution of her former owner's family, she reached out and found John Peters, a free black, whom she married and with whom she had three children. But none of the children outlived Wheatley. According to Vincent Carretta, the last one died with her mother on December 5, 1784, and three days later they were buried together in an unmarked grave.[17]

For the most part, when throughout her life Wheatley reached back for the past or reached out for the living, what she grasped was not a social heritage of her own but rather a wealth of opportunities for surrogacy, for the elegiac expression of the heritage of whites. To become an elegist, Wheatley took advantage of the exceptional opportunities for study that Susanna Wheatley and her daughter Mary provided for their slave. She published her first poem in 1767, and only three years later, not yet out of her teens, she wrote her celebrated elegy for Whitefield. Whitefield's great fame tends to overshadow the social status of the subjects of Wheatley's other elegies, a roster of, for the most part, prominent and closely affiliated New England elites.[18]

As a slave, and later as a free black, Wheatley remained marginal to the complex genealogies in which these people, their families, and their larger communities were involved. Her incorporation, first as a possession and later as an author of renown, was never more than liminal. Cut off from all natal ties and ineligible for integration into the world of her captors, Wheatley found that freedom itself—her release from slavery on the eve of a war fought in the name of liberty—was but another (in some ways a worse) form of marginality and privation. By the late 1770s, Wheatley had been cast loose not only from the social moorings her owner's family had provided but also from the community of memory she had helped, from the sidelines, to construct with her elegies.

In the elegy, Wheatley discovered possibilities for managing the unmitigated alienation of slavery and the ungrievable—because largely unknown—losses she sustained as a stolen child. She wrote her elegies on behalf of other mourners radically unlike herself in the clarity of their losses and in the social recognition they received. Not recognized as a mourner, perhaps not even by herself, Wheatley set about acquiring the means of recognizing and managing the mourning of others. She identified the expressions of grief that were intelligible to those around her, and she used them to create a conscious community of memory in which, though a socially dead person herself, she could nevertheless relate to the living with a measure of authority.

Signs of this authority appear throughout her poems, as she assumes the elegist's customary prerogative of chastening other mourners for their lapses or excesses. "Cease your complaints," she writes to a grieving set of parents.[19] "Suspend the sigh, dear Sir, and check the groan," she recommends to Thomas Hubbard in her elegy for his daughter.[20] In most of Wheatley's elegies, she calls on mourners to suppress or relinquish sorrow and moreover to adopt a stance of resignation toward what should ultimately be seen as a happy event: the departed's entry into Heaven. For example, to the weeping, groaning parents of a five-year-old girl who wish to have their daughter back, Wheatley responds:

> No—bow resign'd. Let hope your grief controul,
> And check the rising tumult of the soul.
> Calm in the prosperous, and adverse day,
> Adore the God who gives and takes away.
> Eye him in all, his holy name revere,
> Upright your actions, and your hearts sincere,
> Till having sail'd through life's tempestuous sea,
> And from its rocks, and boist'rous billows free,
> Yourselves, safe landed on the blissful shore,
> Shall join your happy babe to part no more.[21]

From the dramatic metrical emphasis of the caesura-riven spondee, "No—bow," to the theological admonishment and the outlining of conditions for posthumous reunion, Wheatley wields moral as well as poetic authority, taking it upon herself not only to chasten but also to warn the girl's parents that they must conduct their own lives well if they wish to be reunited with their daughter by and by. Such a warning inflects Wheatley's voice not only with the sounds of a cultural tradition, before which generations of mourners had learned to be silent and receptive, but also with something of the force of clerical pronouncement. Being an elegist does not redeem Wheatley from her social isolation as a slave, but it does create out of her liminal status—her social death—opportunities to mediate relations between the living and the dead and among the living mourners she seeks repeatedly to console and chasten.[22]

Some of these opportunities are also occasions for glimpsing the conditions of Wheatley's own mourning and the possibility of recognizing her own losses. In her elegy for Samuel Marshall (a Boston doctor related to Susanna Wheatley), Wheatley enrolls herself in the ranks of filial mourners, describing him as "[t]he common parent, whom we all deplore." More striking is the penultimate stanza, in which she brings herself close to an identification with Marshall's unborn child:

And must not then our *Aesculapius* stay
To bring his ling'ring infant into day?
The babe unborn in the dark womb is tost,
And seems in anguish for its father lost.[23]

This astonishing image of a womb as something that resembles the dark, sea-tossed hold of a ship is as close as Wheatley ever comes in her writings to her experience of the Middle Passage. The textual history of the poem suggests that Wheatley was to some degree conscious of the force of this image and its bearing on her own early trauma. The phrase "the dark womb" in the 1773 version quoted above was a substitution for "dark confines" in an earlier version.[24] Whatever Wheatley may have intended by the change, the greater obstetric specificity of the later version only intensifies the chill of these lines, which suggest both the vengeful imaginative consignment of the Marshall child to the hold of a slaver and Wheatley's recognition, in the image of a life that has no history prior to captivity, of her own deracination. One cannot but recall that she was named after the slaver *Phillis* that brought her to Boston as a child.

Wheatley's only infamous poem, "On being brought from Africa to America," asserts that it was God's "mercy," rather than the literal slaver, that transported her.[25] It is a poem many readers find intolerable because it seems to bear no trace of the anger that they themselves so reasonably feel on her behalf. But it is not hard to understand why Wheatley took hold and clung so tightly—and so publicly—to the consolations of Christianity. For one of its consolations was an otherwise unrealizable social status predicated upon the work of consolation itself. And in that work of consolation, at the hems of a social world frequently outfitted in mourning black, Wheatley may have found the means of conveying some of her anger, as well as a limited authority among freewheeling Boston elites. For example, to the widowed lieutenant-governor of Massachusetts, Wheatley vaunts the "resistless pow'r" of "[a]ll-conquering Death," and, while acknowledging her limited ability to depict for Andrew Oliver his wife's heavenly reward,

insists that he attend to her: "Nor canst thou, *Oliver,* assent refuse /
To heav'nly tidings from the *Afric* muse."[26] In the Christianized conventions of elegiac consolation, Wheatley discovers her authority as a
mediatrix. It is not surprising that where she interposes herself between
the world of her captors and the world of the dead, there—whatever her
intentions—her anger would accompany her.

Any elegy, any figuration of loss, has an element of wish. One cannot represent a death without in some figurative sense causing that
death to occur once again. Indeed, all of our remembrances harbor
aggressivity of one sort or another. Very commonly, a range of ambivalent feelings toward the dead, and toward the living that remain,
is brought into sharper relief by the social and psychological pressures
that attend on loss. We marshal our anger as we mourn. Consciously or
unconsciously, Wheatley employed elegiac conventions to manage and
direct her anger at the injustice of the society she served, the injustice,
that is, of her own ungrieved, unacknowledged losses. Thus, in each
memento mori, the vengeful trace. She advises Samuel Eliot and his
wife to "[p]repare to join" their dead son. "Haste to join him," is her
recommendation to Mrs. Boylston on the loss of her son. Hearkening
to the heavenly voice of yet another dead child, she tells James Sullivan
and his wife: "Methinks I hear her . . . Invite you there." To the parents
of "J. C." she relays the admonition of an angel: "Prepare to meet him."[27]

Through her child elegies, Wheatley had access to the hearts and
consciences of parents. Like George White in his elegy for Mary
Henery, she may have found in these elegies an opportunity to speak
to or on behalf of her own parents, thereby surreptitiously enshrining
their mutual loss and her anger at them for losing her. Each vicarious elegy was in this sense a step toward articulating her own dimly
remembered history of loss. As that childhood history inevitably receded, however, Wheatley moved closer to personal freedom. Ironically,
it was shortly after her 1773 manumission that Wheatley's hitherto
unbridled freedom to mourn others' losses was sharply curtailed by
the person who had been her closest remaining link to the maternal.
Wheatley had cut short her visit to London and hastened home to be
near Susanna Wheatley's sickbed, where her former mistress lingered
until her death on March 3, 1774. No elegy was forthcoming. "It ap-

pears," writes Margaretta Odell, "that on her death-bed she requested that nothing might be written upon her decease. Indeed, Phillis was forbidden this indulgence of her grief."[28] This prohibition seems to have been extended to include the other members of Wheatley's immediate family as well. We have no elegies by Phillis for Susanna's husband, John, who died in 1778, or for her daughter, Mary, who died later that same year, or for her son, Nathaniel, who died in London in 1783, the year before Phillis's own death. Although Wheatley's many elegies had enabled her liminal incorporation into white society, the absence of any elegies for those whose name she shared keeps her place at the margins of that family and its society well marked—which may or may not have been among Susanna Wheatley's dying intentions.

Phillis gave up the Wheatley patronymic when she married, and thus published her last poems—including the last elegy she wrote—under the name Phillis Peters. The final elegy was for Samuel Cooper, pastor at Brattle Street Church to many of Boston's political and financial elite, including John Hancock, John Adams, and James Bowdoin. In the summer of 1771, Cooper had been filling in at Old South Church after the death of Joseph Sewall, and thus it was he who baptized Wheatley into that congregation. Cooper was an important avuncular figure in Wheatley's life. Not only did he support her literary efforts (he was one of the signers of the letter of attestation prefacing her 1773 *Poems*), but he also facilitated Wheatley's spiritual rebirth as part of her incorporation through baptism into the life of the church. Cooper stood, symbolically, at a key point of rupture in Wheatley's life. For the ceremonial confirmation of her new religious affiliation was a stage in Wheatley's deracination as well as a basis for her liminal incorporation into her owner's society. With Cooper's death, the severing of other ties—her ties with the Wheatley family—was confirmed by the appearance in print of Phillis's new name, "Phillis Peters," at the head of her elegy for him.

Just under a year later, her own death prompted the pseudonymous elegist "Horatio" to consider the African-American poet's place in the genealogical imagination. Titled "Elegy on the Death of a late celebrated Poetess," the fifty-four-line poem names its subject only once, in an extended comparison with Orpheus:

As Orpheus play'd the list'ning herds among,
They own'd the magic of his powerful song;
Mankind no more their savage nature kept,
And foes to music, wonder'd how they wept.
So PHILLIS tun'd her sweet mellifluous lyre;
(Harmonious numbers bid the soul aspire)
While AFRIC'S untaught race with transport heard,
They lov'd the poet, and the muse rever'd.[29]

The absence of both the Wheatley and Peters surnames may reflect Horatio's evasion of a difficult choice: should one use the name she was best known by as a celebrity author, or the married name under which she had most recently published? But "Phillis" would be recognized regardless, and the more important effect here is the combination of classical and African references. On its own, the given name Phillis, which means leaf or foliage, suggests a pastoral world and indeed recalls Virgil's Phyllis from the *Eclogues*. At the same time, set in full capitals, the name is strongly linked visually to "Afric's" two lines later. It is the only other word in the poem set in full capitals, as if the racial or geographical designation (Wheatley herself commonly used "Afric" to mean either "Africa" or "African") were a kind of substitute surname or epithet, as in "Phillis the African." But Horatio is also identifying an audience, "Afric's untaught race," and associating them, in part through the pun on "heard," with the "list'ning herds" that gather round the mourning Orpheus in Ovid's *Metamorphoses*. Horatio imagines Wheatley as an Orphic poet with an as yet uncultivated African readership, one that might bridge the oldest classical traditions of poetic mourning and an emergent tradition of African-American elegy.

However, later black poets would seldom remember Wheatley explicitly. There are few elegies for her—none that I have found between the unidentified Horatio's in 1784 and John Willis Menard's in 1879.[30] To Horatio's question—"shall the honour, which she oft apply'd, / To other's reliques, be to hers deny'd?"—the answer was apparently yes.[31] Nor did she become like Orpheus, as Horatio had fancied her, a figure "close to the consciousness of most elegists."[32] Though considered by many literary historians to be the root of an African-American poetic genealogy, Wheatley's almost complete disregard by later elegists makes her seem more like "a branch that from the tree is torn," as she put in "On the Death of J. C. an Infant."[33] One seeks in vain for Wheatley's posthumous incorporation into anything like the pattern of interlinked elegies she helped create for her owners and their associates.

Instead, for poetic memorials to Wheatley, one must look, ironically, to the reprinting of her own poems, in later editions of her 1773 *Poems,* in American and British periodicals, and in early anthologies. Wheatley's poetry was praised and reprinted particularly widely, for example, in the abolitionist press of the 1830s. Toward the end of that decade, abolitionist Isaac Knapp published Wheatley's poems together, for the first time in book form, with the work of another black poet. The volume was called *Memoir and Poems of Phillis Wheatley, A Native African and a Slave. Also, Poems by a Slave* (1838). The second, unnamed slave in the title was George Moses Horton, and the book reprints the contents of his 1829 volume *The Hope of Liberty* (retitled *Poems by a Slave* in its 1837 Philadelphia reissue), including the poem "On the Death of Rebecca" Whittier would later admire.

Whittier is able to appreciate the poem's reflexivity ("for a slave, by a slave") because the poem itself identifies Rebecca as a slave. But her relationship to Horton is unknown. Indeed, whatever knowledge might be recuperated about many of the subjects of his elegies is limited both by their minimal detail and by the relative obscurity into which Horton himself has descended. By his own account, he was born a slave, the sixth of his mother's ten children by different fathers.[34] He married another slave in the 1830s, with whom he had at least two children, Free Snipes and Rhody Snipes, who survived late into the nineteenth century. But "nothing more," according to Joan Sherman, "is known about Horton's wedded life or his descendants." He was active as a poet from the 1820s to the end of the Civil War and his consequent emancipation, when, as Sherman points out, reliable knowledge of his life and possible further literary output stops.[35] He thus shares with Wheatley, his fellow slave elegist, who died in straitened circumstances shortly after the Revolution, the sad distinction of a poetic career launched in slavery and truncated by a larger national-historical movement toward freedom.

Exceptionally liberal circumstances allowed Horton, like Wheatley before him, to develop his poetic talent and even, at length, to derive a regular income from the sale of his poems. He was able to purchase his own time from his master out of the money he made, in part, by writing love poems for amorous but unpoetical college boys at the University of North Carolina.[36] Thus, for Horton, too, poetic surrogacy for whites enabled a liminal incorporation into free society. Like Wheatley, Horton wrote a number of elegies for white public figures, including three for Abraham Lincoln. But, unlike Wheatley, he also wrote elegies for black subjects. Indeed, he is one of the first African-American poets to do so. Along with Ann Plato, Joseph Cephas Holly, and other black antebellum poets, Horton began to explore the elegy as a transmissible cultural heritage and as a site for the development of the African-American genealogical imagination—as a space where what he called the "vital stars of memory" could shine.[37]

This exploration was tentative, of course, but it was in its uncertain approach to forms of heritability that it generated some of its most interesting and moving poems. In Horton's short elegy "On the Death of an Infant," for example, it is not so much the disruption to generational continuity as the recognition of the illusory nature of a slave's parental rights that informs the lament. In the title and in the body of the poem, indefinite pronouns ("an Infant," "a sad parent") suggest that the mourner has had to learn a protective detachment from the lost child, to which in the same vein he refers repeatedly as "it." Later in the poem, the origin of this detachment is figuratively revealed:

> With pleasure I thought it my own,
> And smil'd on its infantile charms;
> But some mystic bird, like an eagle, came down,
> And snatch'd it away from my arms.[38]

The pathos of the retrospect is in his having "thought it my own," a mistake conventionally ascribed by elegists to bereaved parents (e.g., you thought the child "yours," but in fact he was only lent to you by God, etc.), but here given special force by the elegist's slave status. Horton may or may not have written this poem about a child of his own, and that uncertainty only redoubles its pathos as a reflection of the deracination of slave experience.

Uncertain too is the possible borrowing from Wheatley in the fourth

line quoted above. Wheatley uses the verb "to snatch" in multiple contexts, including her own kidnapping, as she imagines it in her poem to
the Earl of Dartmouth:

> I, young in life, by seeming cruel fate
> Was snatch'd from *Afric's* fancy'd happy seat:
> What pangs excrutiating must molest,
> What sorrows labour in my parent's breast?[39]

Horton's use of the word "snatch'd" echoes this scene of paternal loss,
and it also helps mark the beginnings of an African-American literary
inheritance. For it is a word with uncommon resonance as a linking
trope among texts of black experience—as an image of the sudden and
irrevocable action of death, as a term for the illicit seizure of human
chattel, and as a manner of confiscating reading and writing materials.
These negative associations also have their positive counterparts—in
the surprising but welcome release of death, in unexpected liberation or
victory, and in "stolen" hours of reading and writing. In "To Maecenas,"
Wheatley asserts she will "snatch a laurel" from her patron's head.[40]
In a poem heralding "The Doom of Slavery," Alfred Gibbs Campbell
urges lovers of liberty to "snatch from Slavery's brow the crown."[41] T. T.
Purvis's poem about the rescue of a runaway from some slave traders
recounts the abolitionist heroine's satisfaction at having "snatched from
them their prey."[42] In a poem celebrating the end of slavery, Joshua
McCarter Simpson observes that millions were thereby "snatched from
their graves."[43] And both James Madison Bell and Harriet Jacobs read
and write "during hours snatched from other occupations."[44]

That elegy was a staple of black reading and writing may be inferred
from the genre's prominence in early black and antislavery newspapers—
newspapers such as those, perhaps, that Sophia Auld "snatch[ed]" from
the hands of Frederick Douglass in Baltimore in the 1820s and 1830s.[45]
Had Douglass been reading *The Liberator* in 1832, he could have found
every elegy from Wheatley's 1773 *Poems* reprinted in its pages between
February and December. He and other antebellum readers would have
found an abundance of work by other black and non-black elegists as
well in the pages of *Freedom's Journal, The Colored American, The Anglo-
African Magazine, The National Era, The Liberty Bell,* and, beginning
in 1847, in Douglass's own newspapers, *The North Star* and *Frederick*

Douglass' Paper. Among the elegists published in these periodicals were many familiar names: John Greenleaf Whittier, William Lloyd Garrison, Sarah Louisa Forten, Lydia Huntley Sigourney, Eliza Lee Follen, Thomas Holly Chivers, James Russell Lowell, Jones Very, and Frances Ellen Watkins Harper. Greatly exceeding their poems in number were elegies by the obscure, the pseudonymous, and the anonymous.

Like the poets themselves, the subjects of their elegies were diverse. They included prominent blacks such as Richard Allen, Jeremiah Gloucester, and Isaiah G. de Grasse. Many elegies were written for the abolitionist martyrs Elijah Lovejoy and John Brown, and for other white abolitionists and philanthropists such as Stephen Van Rensselaer, John Quincy Adams, Elizabeth Heyrick, Margaret Fuller, and Thomas Clarkson. Several elegies were published for the fictional character Eva, from *Uncle Tom's Cabin.* Countless elegies appeared for Abraham Lincoln. Countless more appeared for the unknown and the unnamed—the "deceased friend," the "young man," a "sister," a "slave mother," all poised by their respective elegists on the brink of oblivion, neither distinctly remembered nor wholly forgotten.

These antebellum newspapers made possible the regular appearance, in generally uncertain proportion, of black and non-black elegists, who were themselves writing about a similarly uncertain proportion of black and non-black subjects. To some degree, this uncertainty compounds our sense of black deracination—of a population not yet well able to name and preserve a recuperable relation to its forebears, not yet fully successful at adapting the elegy genre to its long-frustrated needs for restored genealogies and transmissible heritage. However, this uncertainty also contributes to the impression of a collective endeavor—of a community of mourners in which blacks mourn whites, whites mourn blacks, and the unknown mourn the unknowable. The elegies written and read by both blacks and whites, in the widely circulated pages of newspapers with both black and white editors, may thus constitute one of the earliest cultural manifestations in North America of a shared, interracial past.

Slavery Chain

Apart from Wheatley and Horton, the identifiable African-American elegists of the early national and antebellum periods were almost all freeborn. Their being freeborn, of course, helps make them identifiable, in part because it also meant that they were much less likely to have experienced the extreme forms of assault on family and community ties—on bonds with the past and with the future—that generally characterized slave experience. Their ties were more visible to begin with, and they helped increase their own visibility as genealogical non-isolates by writing elegies. Daniel Alexander Payne, for example, freeborn in Charleston in 1811, begins his elegy for his infant daughter Julia with the following stanza:

> Another painful blow is struck,
> The golden chain again is riv'n,
> The link which bound my heart to earth
> Is broke, and fasten'd now to heav'n.[46]

From the outset of the poem, we know we are in a world of multiple losses. Julia's death is one in a series ("Another painful blow") in which the elegist already finds himself and in which he wishes to locate the reader as well. It may be that Payne has lost other children of his own. But it is also clear that he seeks to join his loss to the losses of others, thereby establishing, at least in fantasy, a collectivity of mourners to stand with him against an isolating melancholy.

The initial impression of serial losses ("Another," "again") is also a reminder of elegiac tradition—of Milton's "Yet once more" and the consolatory power of oft-repeated, highly familiar conventions. Payne adopts the convention of repetition, and he adapts the common symbol of the chain to suit both the resonance of elegiac tradition (the "vital chain" linking body to soul in Johnson's elegy for Dr. Levet, Shelley's expression of regret at being still "chain'd to Time" in his elegy for Keats, etc.) and the peculiar terrors of his own place and time.[47] Indeed, the symbol of the broken chain locates Payne, like Wheatley before him, at a meeting point of classical and African-American traditions. For Payne's image evokes both the ancient notion of a rigidly hierarchized "chain of being"—a symbolic chain profoundly impeding social mobility—and the literal chains of slavery. Born free of the literal chains, Payne was nevertheless born into a world in which, to many people, the naturalized inferiority and servility of blacks still made philosophical as well as economic sense. The chain in Payne's elegy for Julia, transmuted into gold and refastened to heaven, suggests not privation or servitude from which he seeks to be released, but rather a coveted connection, a link between the generations, and an assertion of his and his daughter's rightful place at the top, rather than the bottom, of the chain of being.

In chain, poets like Payne found a symbol that served at once to evoke the condition of slavery, which hemmed round and deformed the lives of all African Americans, and to suggest, in a completely different register, the flexible strength of a series of connections, a chain of affiliation rather than restraint. The chains of the coffle and the work gang were never far removed from the "golden chain" of transgenerational connection. The links of the former could be forged as quickly as those of the latter could be broken. The breaking of a chain could mean freedom or it could mean death. Frequently, freedom and death were conterminous. In "Death of a Favorite Chamber Maid," for example, slave George Moses Horton envisions death as being cut loose from "this cumb'rous chain," and in a later poem, "Imploring to Be Resigned at Death," he anticipates the afterlife of his spirit "cut loose from its chain."[48] In "Ode to Death," black publisher and abolitionist Alfred Gibbs Campbell blurs the distinction between a free life and a life of bondage, generalizing the condition of captivity and calling death the "Ultra Abolitionist,"

> Breaking chains as thou dost list!
> Stern emancipator, thou
> Layest petty despots low;
> Breakest every captive's chain.[49]

In "The Dying Slave," freeborn poet Joshua McCarter Simpson imagines the slave collapsing the literal and metaphorical significance of chain in his dying assertion: "My yoke and fetters, chains and all, / With this poor body here must fall."[50] For African-American elegists like Payne, Horton, Campbell, and Simpson, the metaphor of chain— their poetic control over chain as a symbolic instrument of the slaveholder's power—was central to their mediation between the worlds of the free and the unfree and the living and the dead.

One of Simpson's elegies, in particular, dramatizes the overturning of control with respect to chain as a symbolic instrument of the master.

"The Dying Slave-Holder" depicts a frightened and rueful master anticipating his fate in a hell of his own making, where, he foresees, he "shall writhe in endless pain, / And clank my *hot* and *sluggish chains*."[51] There is in Simpson's poem, as in others of its type, a mordant glee at this dramatic image of reversal—the exuberance of welcoming a justice long deferred, such as that commonly felt at the horror-stricken demise of Simon Legree at the end of *Uncle Tom's Cabin*. Like Stowe, other whites joined black authors in representing such scenes as expressions of solidarity with the oppressed, hostility toward slave owners and their agents, and rejection of the blackface assertion of slaves' attachment to their masters, as in Stephen Foster's famous minstrel song "Massa's in de Cold Ground" (1852).

Foster's biographer discerns an autobiographical element in this particular song, written by Foster after his father's incapacitation by stroke (he would die in 1855), making it a kind of elegy, "parricidal and anticipatory."[52] This prolepsis of mourning, transposed onto the plantation of the northern imagination, became a blackface retrospect on a beloved patriarch:

> Massa made de darkeys love him,
> Cayse he was so kind,
> Now dey sadly weep above him,
> Mourning cayse he leave dem behind.
> I cannot work before tomorrow,
> Cayse de tear-drops flow,
> I try to drive away my sorrow
> Pickin on de old banjo.[53]

Such popular and lucrative songs promoted fantasies of happy plantation life that assuaged anxiety among whites regarding the deadly-mindedness of slaves—slaves who would, if given the chance, hasten rather than mourn the passing of the master, and by extension white populations generally. In Foster's own song, hints of resistance and indecorum (traces, perhaps, of his own "parricidal" feelings) lurk in the lines about work stoppage ("I cannot work before tomorrow") and discordant gaiety ("Picking on de old banjo"). For the most part, though, Foster's success as a songwriter depended on his ability to turn misgiving into nostalgia.[54]

Occasionally, black writers were able to capitalize on the currency of minstrel-generated sentiment and restore white dread to visibility. In his novel *Blake* (1859–62), for example, Martin Delany unmasks the source of white anxiety in the scene of a meeting of black insurrectionists in New Orleans. Tib, a noisy latecomer to the meeting, is impatient for action, and as part of his apparent effort to motivate and mobilize his allies, he performs a send-up of Foster's song:

> Old master's dead and lying in his grave;
> And our blood will cease to flow;
> He will no more tramp on the neck of the slave,
> For he's gone where the slaveholders go!
> Hang up the shovel and the hoe—o—o—o!
> I don't care whether I work or no!
> Old master's gone to the slaveholders rest—
> He's gone where they all ought to go!

Tib's song turns racist sentiment into an anthem of mourning as militancy. In Delany's novel, though, the anthem leads not to insurrection but to arrest. The meeting place is surrounded by police, who themselves turn out to be the ones prompted to action by Tib's boisterous singing and by his concluding flourish, "'Insurrection! Insurrection! Death to every white!'" After a brief "inquisition" into the alarming extent of the thwarted rebellion, "the betrayer Tib" disappears from the narrative.[55]

The ambiguity of Tib's fate—was he the intentional "betrayer" of the uprising or an unwitting and possibly drunken one? would he be rewarded or punished for his betrayal? by whom?—may to some extent be an effect of conscience on the part of Delany, who fashioned Tib's song, which appears to be a send-up of Foster, out of a poem by Joshua McCarter Simpson published three years before Foster wrote "Massa's in de Cold Ground" and a decade before *Blake*. Published first in the Ohio newspaper *Concord Free Press* and later reprinted in Douglass's *North Star,* Simpson introduced the poem with the following notice:

> This piece of verse is not the true effusion of my own sentiments and feelings. The Muse has only authorized me to write as she presents a scene in Nature's forest in the South. I therefore only imagine myself secreted near a certain consecrated spot of merriment where the slaves are wont to as-

MOURNING OF THE DISPRIZED

semble, and spend their holidays in the usual manner; and hither I fancy I
see slaves resorting with their banjo instruments, to spend a few moments
of jollification over the death of an old tyrant master.[56]

Disclaimed by Simpson and later appropriated by Delany for a minor
and morally suspect character in his novel, the "effusion" of glee the
poem depicts seems bound up in a tradition of misgiving regarding the
power of such effusions to redress the losses they temporarily "jollify,"
that is, not the loss of the master but the losses the master has brought
about:

> He no more will hang our children on the tree,
> To be ate by the carrion crow;
> He no more will send our wives to Tennessee;
> For he's gone where the slaveholders go.

In the midst of "jollification" are perversity and horror: the staggering
image of a "family tree" on which children are literally hung, while
wives are sold away from their husbands. Such devastation makes the
"few moments" of glee at the master's death seem less like the exuberance of revenge than like the fleeting rictus of trauma. In his preamble
to "The Slaveholder's Rest," Simpson distances himself from this scene
of macabre enjoyment, and he seems furthermore to be signaling his
reluctance to invest in or fully play out the dramas of retribution he
nevertheless continues to hint at in his poetry. In one of his later poems
(written, it announces, to the tune of Foster's "Massa's in de Cold
Ground"), Simpson reminds white Americans, inattentive to black
misery and often blind to their own roles in perpetuating it, that "[t]he
day will come when you must die." One hears in this a powerful am-
plification of the vengeful trace in Wheatley's memento mori for white
folks—elegies in which her own losses were all but mutely registered.
The refrain of Simpson's poem "To the White People of America" poses
a question that shifts responsibility from the stifled black mourner to
the indifferent white listener: "Hear ye that mourning?"[57] The sounds
of inconceivable enormities of suffering awaited the penitent ear. Who
would listen for them? And what recompense could be imagined for
such losses?

The notion that the articulation of loss may lead to consolation and redress is at once a secular and a religious notion. Both law and theology sustain it, and elegy has made abundant use of both discourses even as in the modern era the foundations of faith in worldly and otherworldly justice alike have been radically unsettled.[58] Perhaps no modern constituency has been so isolated from the mechanisms of legal and spiritual redress as American slaves, who had no legal standing as persons (except when accused of a crime), whose opportunities for the preservation and transmission of African belief systems were substantially curtailed, and whose confidence in the operations of divine justice was constantly undermined by the hypocrisy of Christian slaveholders. Outside the law and often beyond the reach of religious solace, largely illiterate and commonly muzzled (literally or figuratively), the slave's complaint, the articulation of his grievance, and the expression of his woe have been among the most heavily suppressed and violently circumscribed in modern history.[59] The moral exhortation to "hear," as Simpson put it, "that mourning" is thus hard not to read also as an imprecation—the curse of an impossible labor that must nevertheless be essayed.

The primary font of audibility as well as the site of the principal challenge for shared audition of slave mourning was and is the spiritual—the religious folksongs that Du Bois called "sorrow songs" and that historians including Lawrence Levine have shown to be central to the expressive culture of antebellum slaves. Whether or not any individual songs were composed as occasional pieces for particular deaths, spirituals (often referred to by white observers as "hymns" or "chants") were an important and affecting part of burials and funerals in the slave states, as one may reasonably infer even from the scant surviving documentation of such events. At a nighttime slave burial on her husband's Georgia plantation, for example, Fanny Kemble found that the "first high wailing notes" of a spiritual "sent a chill through all my nerves."[60] In Virginia, Frederick Law Olmsted observed a slave burial during which there appeared

> an old negro, with a very singularly distorted face, who raised a hymn, which soon became a confused chant—the leader singing a few words alone, and the company then either repeating them after him or making a

response to them, in the manner of sailors heaving at the windlass. I could understand but very few of the words. The music was wild and barbarous, but not without a plaintive melody. A new leader took the place of the old man, when his breath gave out (he had sung very hard, with much bending of the body and gesticulation), and continued until the grave was filled, and a mound raised over it.[61]

Olmsted's account squares with others in which condescension ("a confused chant") vies with admiration for unconstrained and in this case strikingly embodied mourning ("in the manner of sailors heaving the windlass"; "much bending of the body and gesticulation").

Higginson experienced a similar reaction listening to his black corporal, Adam Allston, lead the singing at the funeral service for Lieutenant R. M. Gaston:

> the closing hymn "Jesus live & reign forever" was really magnificent, led by Uncle Adam Allston one of our saints & a splendid leader in these songs—often he is too excited, but today the emotion sobered him & he stood waving his arms & gesticulating with the music, he was wonderfully graceful & solemn.[62]

In the camps of his black regiment, Higginson became one of the earliest transcribers and collectors of slave songs. Several dozen appear in the essay on "Negro Spirituals" he published in 1867, including one—a funeral hymn for an infant called "The Baby Gone Home"—that he specifically refers to as "occasional."[63]

That same year, William Francis Allen and two coeditors published *Slave Songs of the United States,* which drew on material collected by Higginson and others. Of all the songs, one in particular—the one Higginson called "I Know Moon-Rise," which both William Howard Russell and Charles Tyler Trowbridge reported hearing sung at black funerals[64]—appealed strongly not only to Higginson but also, later, to Du Bois, who included it in *The Souls of Black Folk*:

I walk through the churchyard
　　To lay this body down;
I know moon-rise, I know star-rise;
I walk in the moonlight, I walk in the starlight;
I'll lie in the grave and stretch out my arms,

I'll go to judgment in the evening of the day,
And my soul and thy soul shall meet that day,
When I lay this body down.[65]

William Allen and his coeditors were suspicious of the authenticity of Higginson's version of this song, but printed it anyway. Others, too, suspected he was trying to make the spirituals more literary. Not only did he ignore the music, but according to James Harrison Wilson, Higginson "'finished' out a good many . . . with a good deal more of elaboration than the Negroes sang them."[66] Du Bois writes in *Souls* of his attraction to "I Know Moon-Rise," and he cites approvingly a remark of Higginson's on the fifth line: "I'll lie in the grave and stretch out my arms." "Never, it seems to me," wrote Higginson, "since man first lived and suffered, was his infinite longing for peace uttered more plaintively than in that line."[67] Du Bois interpolates Higginson's voice, allowing the latter to speak for him, in effect, regarding the pathos of that favorite line. Yet Du Bois also decided to edit out any traces of Higginson's efforts to capture the sounds of plantation speech. Where Higginson wrote "dis," Du Bois wrote "this"; for Higginson's "de" and "I go," Du Bois substituted "the" and "I'll go." He seems to have wanted to go Higginson one better in transforming them into something more like the literature of the day, something more like the fragments of elegiac and apocalyptic verses by Symons, Lowell, Fitzgerald, Barrett Browning, Sharp, and Swinburne that head various chapters of his book. The final chapter, called "The Sorrow Songs," is the only one to be headed by the lyrics of a spiritual, as if their literary transformation were, with that final flourish, accomplished.

Others would demur. For example, following Zora Neale Hurston, Lawrence Levine seeks to qualify Du Bois's "sorrow songs" term, opining that in these songs sorrowful feelings "were rarely pervasive or permanent."[68] Hurston herself is blunter: "The idea that the whole body of spirituals are 'sorrow songs' is ridiculous. They cover a wide range of subjects from a peeve at gossipers to Death and Judgment."[69] Hurston further wants to dissociate what she calls "genuine Negro spirituals" from the "Negroised white hymns" used at funerals. "The Negro," Hurston insists, has created no songs for death and burials, in spite of the subject matter contained in some of the spirituals. Negro songs are one and all based on a dance-possible rhythm. The heavy interpretations have been added by the more cultured singers. So for funerals fitting white hymns are used.[70]

"Genuine spirituals" have, in other words, been rewritten, rearranged, and inflected with melancholy sound effects in a distortion of black culture that makes it sound pervasively funereal, even to blacks themselves. In contrast, "white hymns" have been "Negroised" in a black-voice performance that consecrates, in the context of mourning, the more generalized exclusion, or social death, of African Americans. The common view of spirituals as "sorrow songs," Hurston implies in her 1934 essay, confirms blacks' identification with death—what Susan Mizruchi has called the "stigma of mortality" attaching to blacks in the late nineteenth and early twentieth centuries.[71]

But the distinction Hurston draws between "dance-possible rhythm" and "heavy interpretations" is too sharp, as if the affective traces of slave song and performance—unevenly gathered and imperfectly transcribed—could be so neatly distinguished, even by the most sympathetic observer. Du Bois himself was more subtle in his characterization of these songs. He called them the "the music of an unhappy people," but in them he also heard the "minor cadences of despair change often to triumph and calm confidence"—confidence in the consolations of life as well as death and in the redress of worldly and otherworldly justice.[72] Du Bois imagined a deep background for these songs: African melodies transported with slaves since the seventeenth century, adapted and added to by generations, retaining Africanisms, absorbing Judeo-Christian theology and texts, and finally altered and conventionalized by transcribers. Ronald Radano calls the transcriptions a "memorial in text" to that which precedes and exceeds entextualization. "It was through this process of mediation," Radano continues, "that America as a whole could 'hear' its collective slave past. And it is from this same intersubjective space that African Americans would begin to listen back, to recover a realm of awareness that had been denied to them as slaves."[73] In this vein, Du Bois called them "the sifting of centuries," implying a long history of selection and transmission, and further implying that the sifting process both reflected and contributed to the nature of the songs.[74]

It would surely be mistaken to compare this sifting process too closely to the text-based, socially sanctioned preservation and transmission of Puritan broadside elegies discussed in chapter 1. But the intergenerational (oral) transmission, modification, and ritual use of the slave songs and their later selection, transcription, and interpretation constitute a response to traumatic loss, such as the songs themselves quite variously thematize. Neither authentic in the transhistorical sense that Hurston sought to defend nor spurious in the manner of Foster's plantation melodies, the inscribed slave songs of the nineteenth century were the consequence of a transformative collaboration between the genealogical imaginations of slaves, who had created and preserved this tradition orally, and those whites and blacks who succeeded in recording—complete with their own misapprehensions and imaginative projections—slave song and performance as a written lyric heritage for post–Civil War America.

Even as printed texts, these lyrics are not the equivalent of European-American elegies. But in their dynamic consolidation and dissemination of the voiced bereavement and longing of millions, the spirituals were touchstones for the grieving imagination and for the development of expressive forms of mourning across what Jahan Ramazani calls the "ethno-generic divide" (as were the blues, later).[75] Du Bois himself highlights the affinities as well as the differences of sorrow songs and elegies. At the head of his chapter on the death of his son in *The Souls of Black Folk*, he sets both a fragment of musical notation from the song "I Hope My Mother Will Be There" and the final stanza of Swinburne's "Itylus" (1866). Paul Gilroy makes the generalizing observation that at the head of every chapter in *Souls* such a song fragment "both accompanied and signified on the Euro-American romantic poetry that comprised the other part of these double epigraphs."[76] For the chapter "On the Passing of the First-Born," Du Bois selected a song sung in the voice of a son and his mother, anticipating their reunion in heaven:

> I hope my mother will be there,
> In that beautiful world on high.

That used to join with me in pray'r,
In that beautiful world on high.
Oh, I will be there. Oh I will be there
With the palms of victory,
Crowns of glory you shall wear
In that beautiful world on high.[77]

In subsequent verses, the exchange is repeated with his sister, his brother, and finally his "Saviour." It is, like so many spirituals, a song about what Du Bois calls "longing toward a truer world."[78] It predicts the posthumous reconstitution of familial relationships in a realm beyond the reach of slavery's dissevering power over natal ties.

The selection from Swinburne, however, is a much more melancholy and disturbing poem of child loss. It is based on the ancient myth of Procne and Philomela, in which Procne murders her son Itys (Itylus) and feeds his boiled flesh to her husband, Tereus, to avenge his rape and mutilation of her sister, Philomela. Tereus then attempts to murder the sisters, but they are all three transformed into birds. In Swinburne's poem, the elegizing nightingale (Philomela) addresses the swallow (Procne) and reproaches her apparent forgetfulness, as in the final stanza, which Du Bois quotes:

O sister, sister, thy first-begotten,
The hands that cling and the feet that follow,
The voice of the child's blood crying yet,
Who hath remembered me? who hath forgotten?
Thou hast forgotten, O summer swallow,
But the world shall end when I forget.[79]

It is difficult not to hear in this passage sounds of the estrangement that grew between Du Bois and his wife, Nina, after the death of their son Burghardt, as if, in the voice of the nightingale, a grief-stricken Du Bois were accusing Nina of killing their son and then of failing to mourn him adequately. Arrogating the greater grief to himself, Du Bois then pledges eternal remembrance with Swinburne's final line, which may be read two ways. It is, in the first place, an extravagant figure for the compass of his own life: he will only forget when "the world shall end," that is, when he shall die. But it is also a way of figuring what he feels to be the incalculable power of grief itself, as if his memory of his son is all that keeps the very world from ending.

Beyond whatever private reproach against his wife (or against himself) may linger in these lines, there is also a plaint about the national refusal—from Georgia, where Burghardt died, to Massachusetts, where he was buried—to acknowledge the significance of African-American losses, including the deracination foregrounded here as "the passing of the first-born." Northern and Southern regions are conflated in Du Bois's wrenching account of the bigotry encountered by his grieving family. Whether on the streets of Atlanta or in the Berkshire Hills, the fact of Burghardt's death is met with race hatred, polluting the pastoralism of his father's grief-stricken fancy and suggesting to him a form of consolation that returns him directly to the world of antebellum slave songs:

> Blithe was the morning of his burial, with bird and song and sweet-smelling flowers. The trees whispered to the grass, but the children sat with hushed faces. And yet it seemed a ghostly unreal day,—the wraith of Life. We seemed to rumble down an unknown street behind a little white bundle of posies, with the shadow of a song in our ears. The busy city dinned about us; they did not say much, those pale-faced hurrying men and women; they did not say much,—they only glanced and said, "Niggers!" . . . .
>
> All that day and all that night there sat an awful gladness in my heart,— nay, blame me not if I see the world thus darkly through the Veil,—and my soul whispers ever to me, saying, "Not dead, not dead, but escaped; not bond, but free."[80]

This "awful gladness," at a child having been freed by death from a future of racial oppression and cruelty, is centuries old—a gladness born of the Middle Passage that lurks even after slavery in the "shadow" of the slave songs, which commonly express a preference for death. Du Bois's "not dead, but escaped" is the logic and the consolation of many spirituals. "Befo' I'd be a slave," goes the song "Oh Freedom," "I'll be buried in my grave."[81] A handful of other titles signals the perennial theme: "Ain't Going to Tarry Here," "I Can't Stay Behind," "Lay This Body Down," "Give Up the World," "Lord I Can't Stay Here By Myself," "Wish I's in Heaven Settin' Down," "Tryin' to Get Home." By the dozens, and in a range of tones from defiant to weary to jubilant, these songs are the record of a people's negotiations with mortality, and they include the memory of those who consciously chose to give life up. Their iterations of a preference for death would be misconstrued as evidence merely of black identification with whites' hatred and fear of the people they persecuted. For, while such pathological incorporations undoubtedly occurred, the motive and meaning of the longing for death seem in these songs by and large to have been the opportunity for escape, rest, and safety; they figure suicidality not chiefly as aggression turned inward but as the rejection of depersonalization, the assertion of will, the exercising of choice.

Pain, grief, and desperation drove untold numbers of slaves to take their own lives.[82] Some believed that after dying they would return to their homelands. Some were fleeing intolerable punishment and degradation. Some were acting out of defiance. Others, like Frederick Douglass and Charles Ball, contemplated suicide on multiple occasions but kept deciding against it.[83] Ignatius Sancho, whose father had committed suicide rather than endure slavery, came close to following his example. According to Joseph Jekyll, his eighteenth-century biographer, suicide would in Sancho's case be "sanctified as hereditary."[84] This ugly irony, lost on Jekyll, would continue to plague slaves and slave families down the smashed and severed generations. Slave children who had inherited the condition of their parents (usually, though not invariably, of their mother) could not expect any other sort of legacy, if indeed they even knew who their parents were. The most generous-souled parent might be the one willing to murder a child facing a life of slavery. Even in a post-slavery world, Du Bois found solace for his grief in the realization that his son would not grow "choked and deformed" by racism.[85] Under slavery, to submit to a child's destruction was in some minds to save that child. To bring about one's own destruction was a form of self-emancipation. To crop a lineage by killing oneself was not only to free oneself from bondage but also to prevent one's doomed potential progeny from coming to life. Thus, in a sense far from Jekyll's, suicide was "sanctified" as a tradition of last resort in the literature of slave experience—in accounts of the Middle Passage, in slave narratives, in fiction, in the spirituals discussed above, and in elegy.

Steal Away

Near the end of William Wells Brown's novel *Clotel; or, The President's Daughter* (1853), its eponymous hero, pursued by slave-catchers, commits suicide by leaping into the icy waters of the Potomac River (see Figure 8). The chapter in which this occurs, titled "Death Is Freedom," concludes with an elegy for Clotel that Brown adapted from Grace Greenwood's poem "The Leap from the Long Bridge: An Incident at Washington." Brown's alterations are relatively minor, except for the stanza he adds at the end, which reimagines the woman's fate in a startling way. In Greenwood's poem, the despairing slave relinquishes herself to the river's current, and as she is borne away, her "drowning voice" grows fainter and fainter, until "her cries have ceased for ever." Greenwood's final stanza pictures her spiritual form in heaven, lifting up to God her "unmanacled hands."[86] Brown truncates this pacifying vision of posthumous freedom and substitutes for it the grisly unsentimental image of the woman's corpse being swept down the river for miles and finally disgorged upon a bank near Mt. Vernon, within view of Washington's tomb—there, symbolically, to speak once again:

To tell of the freedom he won for our land.
A weak woman's corse, by freemen chased down:
Hurrah for our country! hurrah!
To freedom she leaped, through drowning and death—
Hurrah for our country! hurrah![87]

What the resurfaced corpse may "tell" and what the revisionary poet writes seem to merge as the poem ends by sounding off, in those acid cheers, against the solemnity of Greenwood's original ending ("And her sorrow and bondage are o'er").[88]

Brown's rewriting of Greenwood's poem helps illuminate the wide range of multiple and contradictory identifications that get expressed in and through antislavery elegies by slave, free-black, and non-black poets. It exemplifies, for instance, the liberal borrowings among these poets, who supported, copied from, and collaborated with one another on many projects, including the antislavery songbooks edited by Jairus Lincoln and George W. Clark that inspired Brown to compile his own similar anthology in 1848.[89] The fact that Brown does not acknowledge

THE DEATH OF CLOTEL. *Page* 218.

Figure 8. "The Death of Clotel," frontispiece, William Wells Brown, *Clotel; or, The President's Daughter* (London: Partridge & Oakley, 1853). Courtesy of Documenting the American South (http://www.docsouth.unc.edu), University of North Carolina at Chapel Hill Libraries, Rare Book Collection.

Greenwood's primary authorship of the poem in *Clotel* may or may not have been an act of aggressive expropriation directed at a white author. Because so many antislavery poems circulated widely, in numerous variant texts in both print and manuscript form, Brown need not have known Greenwood to be the author of "The Leap from the Long Bridge." Many such poems escaped attribution and existed in a shared idiom of antislavery protest that was drawn on by diverse authors.[90]

Yet, whether or not Brown knew who the poem's original author was, the dramatically different ending that he attaches to it highlights incommensurate points of view. Whereas Greenwood's poem reflects an attitude of resignation that affirms the unworldliness of Christian consolation and its deferral of justice to the afterlife, Brown's rewritten ending adopts a stance of inconsolate embitterment against the deadly hypocrisy of the nationalist discourse of freedom and its sacred object of mourning, the slaveholding George Washington. Brown's version rebels against both of antebellum America's most widely disseminated compensatory discourses: that of Christian submissiveness and that of patriotic propaganda. He throws down the slave's drowned corpse at the nation's feet as if it were a gauntlet, simultaneously opposing Christian complacency by refusing to relinquish the corpse to the decorous sublation it undergoes in Greenwood's ending to the poem.

At variance, though, with this opposition is Brown's identification with Greenwood in his sympathetic treatment of the suicide, who breaks with the Christian prohibition against self-murder even as the symbolic dimension of her act ("Death Is Freedom") subverts the idealization of American liberty. Brown and Greenwood join in their approval of the act, in part by casting it in the language of individuated achievement: the escape from bondage through an assertion of will. Also, despite their very different treatments of the corpse, both versions of the poem affirm that the slave's soul is "returned to its God."[91] They both, that is, offer an implicit assurance of divine as well as human forbearance for the slave who kills herself.

Traditionally in the Christian West, the suicide's provocation to God is the flouting of Mosaic law, as in the Augustinian reading of the sixth commandment.[92] The human or social provocation is much more complex, perhaps nowhere more so than in the context of chattel slavery, with its distortions to thinking about law, will, sacrifice, sanity, and self-possession. Against the argument that slaves were something other, something less than human, slave suicide was a potentially devastating rebuttal, a definitive assertion of mastery over one's own life and one's own body, a stunning proof of humanity. Yet suicide could also be regarded as the completion of the process of dehumanization initiated by enslavement, a final self-demotion to the level of beast or thing, as Immanuel Kant argues in his *Lectures on Ethics*.[93] Slave owners, anxious to protect the value of what was acknowledged by statutory law to be their property, tried to discourage suicide by mutilating corpses and by denying burial rites to slaves who killed themselves. Abolitionists depicted slave suicides as what Emile Durkheim would call altruistic or fatalistic, rather than egoistic or anomic, in order to generate sympathy for slaves both living and dead.

By the mid-eighteenth century, American attitudes toward suicide

in general were softening from what they had been during the first
century of English settlement. The vehemence of the Christian pro-
scription against self-murder, severe posthumous sanctions against the
suicide's corpse (such as burial at a crossroads), and the legal finding
of felo-de-se had largely given way to the less punitive medical and juridical determination of non compos mentis. Moral culpability was no
longer taken for granted. Indeed, by the turn of the century, as Howard
Kushner reports, "a postrevolutionary consensus had emerged that suicide was an action that resulted from forces beyond an individual's will
or control."[94]

Yet American slaves, like the *coloni* of the Roman Empire or the
serfs of medieval Europe, remained subject to stricter prohibitions of
suicide than other classes—prohibitions that reinforced the property
rights of *domini,* lords, and masters. Aboard the slaver or on the plantation, where those most likely to kill themselves had no legal claim
to property in anything, even their own bodies, suicide had in some
sense to remain a matter of personal responsibility or willfulness, for
the purposes of slave management. Slaveholders still credited the otherwise dehumanized slave with the quintessentially human capacity for
self-chosen death, a capacity that, as a threat to their private property,
needed to be guarded against and punished severely. Charles Ball, writing of life on a South Carolina plantation in his 1836 memoir, observes
that slave suicide

> is regarded as a matter of dangerous example, and one which it is the busi-
> ness and the interest, of all proprietors to discountenance, and prevent.
> All the arguments which can be devised against it, are used to deter the
> Negroes from the perpetration of it; and such as take this dreadful means
> of freeing themselves from their miseries, are always branded in reputa-
> tion after death, as the worst of criminals; and their bodies are not allowed
> the small portion of Christian rites, which are awarded to the corpses of
> other slaves.[95]

The suicide destroys the slaveholder's property by killing himself, and
he potentially compounds his master's losses by serving as a dangerous
example of self-liberation to other slaves. A slave who "escaped" via
suicide was irretrievable.[96] Ball himself admits to having seriously contemplated suicide on more than one occasion. While in Maryland, he

writes, "I longed to die, and escape from the hands of my tormenters; but even the wretched privilege of destroying myself was denied me; for I could not shake off my chains, nor move a yard without the consent of my master." Later, in South Carolina, he "seriously meditated on self-destruction, and had I been at liberty to get a rope, I believe I should have hanged myself at Lancaster. It appeared to me that such an act, done by a man in my situation, could not be a violation of the precepts of religion, nor the laws of God."[97] Such is the conclusion of both Grace Greenwood and William Wells Brown regarding the Long Bridge suicide.

Elegiac depictions of slaves' preferences for death are a common feature of antislavery poetry. Sometimes the preference is overtly suicidal, as in Theodore Dwight's "Picture of African Distress" (1789), in which a "raving mother" throws herself into the sea after losing her two children to slave traders.[98] Similar scenes in other poems depict anguished mothers killing their children along with themselves. One such poem, the pseudonymously published "Monimba: A True Story" (1791), is worth quoting in full, as it enables a range of observations that bear on the suicide theme in antislavery elegy:

Monimba, pride of Afric's plain,
The beauty of the burning zone,
Was led to Hymen's holy fane,
By Zanga, prince of Ebo's throne.
Six moons revolving saw them blest;
The seventh, a life commercial band,[99]
Lodg'd the cragg'd ball in Zanga's breast,
And sever'd love's united hands.
In vain the widow's piteous wail;
Nor heard her soul distressing cries;
Borne passive on the pinnion'd gale,
To distant climes the mourner hies.
There doom'd to rounds of endless toil,
Her life was soon to waste away,
On curst Port Royal's torrid soil,
Amid the fires of blazing day.
Her child—the tender babe unborn,
Must share its mother's iron fate:
Doom'd ere it saw the rising morn,

To horrid slav'ry's death like weight.
Monimba, own'd a feeling mind;
Oft had she wept at mis'ry's tale;
The tender heart by love refin'd,
With firmness bids misfortune, hail.
Confin'd below in bolted chains,
Deep musing o'er a world of woes,
The sudden gush of spouting veins,
At once announce parturient throes.
Rais'd to the deck—she ey'd the wave,
Plung'd with her babe beneath the flood,
And buried in a watry grave,
Escap'd the madd'ning sons of blood.[100]

One of the salient themes of antislavery elegy is the curtailment of mourning, either through direct suppression or as a consequence of general privation. Monimba has much to mourn during her brief, Jamaica-bound viduity: not only the murder of her husband and the uprooting of her life but also the "world of woes" she and her unborn child yet face. But she has been deprived of all customary contexts in which to manage her grief and any attendant ambivalence: "In vain the widow's piteous wail; / Nor heard her soul distressing cries." In such circumstances, suicide becomes not only the last avenue of escape but also, horribly, the last available form of mourning.

This "True Story" of Monimba's suicide may be related to contemporary lore about comparative suicide rates among slaves from different regions of Africa. Zanga, Monimba's consort, is "prince of Ebo's throne," which suggests that Monimba is Igbo, from the Bight of Biafra (now Bonny), or present-day southern Nigeria. According to Michael Gomez, the perception in certain slave states and parts of the Caribbean was that the Igbo were "more disposed to suicide than any other group." In the poem, the slaver that bears Monimba away is bound for Jamaica's Port Royal, and in Jamaica, writes Gomez, Igbo slaves were regarded as "prone to suicide if mistreated." "The unfavorable assessment of the Igbo," Gomez continues, "began even before they landed in the New World and centered on their behavior during the Middle Passage."[101] Gomez links suicidality among enslaved Igbo to their democratic disposition and to their strong attachment to a civil society distinguished by political liberties. A cultural predisposition to suicide among enslaved Igbo women in particular may, he feels, be further related to the relative freedom women enjoyed in Igbo society.[102] Monimba refuses to be "[b]orne passive," whether by slave-traders or by incommunicable grief. Her suicide completes in a last definitive act the merger of political and affective registers of extreme resistance.

In its depiction of that merger, the elegy sows seeds of identification. For, apart from her suicidality, what distinguishes Monimba most vividly is her sensibility. We are told she "own'd a feeling mind" and that she had been in the habit of putting it to use in the manner of a certain kind of eighteenth-century reader—a reader such as Lucretia, in John Whaley's brief poem "On a Young Lady's Weeping at Oroonooko":

> At Fate's approach whilst OROONOOKO Groans,
> *Imoinda*'s Fate, undaunted at his own;
> Dropping a gen'rous Tear *Lucretia* Sighs,
> And views the Heroe with *Imoinda*'s Eyes.
> When the Prince strikes who envy's not the Deed?
> To be so Wept, who wou'd not wish to Bleed?[103]

Like Lucretia (the namesake of a famous female suicide), Monimba is characterized by her capacity to identify with imagined sufferers as well as with potential readers: "Oft had she wept at mis'ry's tale." This reflexivity has the unsettling effect of suggesting to the reader that such identifications draw down their own misery—that readers, too, may bleed as well as weep, may bleed *because* they weep.

Blood itself is charged with an awful doubleness in the poem. It is both the blood of parturition (gothically exaggerated as the "sudden gush of spouting veins") and the gore of slavery, set flowing by the murderous "sons of blood" from whom the just-delivered Monimba saves herself and her newborn. Monimba and her baby, quickly "[r]ais'd to deck," would both still bear bloody traces of the birth. One pictures their blood marking the skin and clothing of their captors—and mixing there, perhaps, with the blood of other wounded, tortured, or murdered slaves. Literally and metaphorically, blood links the labor of childbirth and the violence of slavery. From the reproductive life of slaves comes the blood that fuels slavery's perpetual cycle of violence. Monimba's sacrifice of herself and her child saves them both from becoming the sexual thralls of the "sons of blood" and perpetuators of that cycle.

The phrase "sons of blood" further works to split and to unite this crowd of bloody forms. The compounded genitive—of possession (blood's offspring) and material (men covered in or made of blood)—lends Monimba's captors a range of mythological associations, from Ovidian manlike creatures spawned from the dripping gore of gigantomachy and gods overthrown, to the figure of Jesus Christ. It evokes the Johannine distinction between those "born of blood" and those "born of God." It is a reminder that all human offspring are born "of blood"—Monimba and her child no less than their captors. This commonality, this human consanguinity, is part of the doubling effect. Because we are all bags of the same red blood, bloodletting violence may unmask as well as repudiate shared humanity.

The revelation through violence of consanguinity highlights the potential for identification. "Monimba: A True Story" makes infanticide and suicide conceivable and even laudable in the face of other inevitable forms of violence and privation the poem compels the reader to imagine. To identify with Monimba's "feeling mind," her capacity for sympathy ("Oft had she wept at mis'ry's tale"), and the refinement of her "tender heart" may be to risk surrendering cherished convictions regarding the limits of the reader's own capacity for desperate action. For the sympathetic reader, the final three stanzas of the poem are a measure of the short distance between sensibility and insanity—between "a feeling mind" that suffers others' pain and the "madd'ning" effect of slavery. As a modifier of "sons of blood," the adjective "madd'ning" may be read in two ways. It may mean that their cruelty drives victims like Monimba mad. And it may mean that the "sons of blood" themselves are growing increasingly deranged as a result of their practice of slavery. In other words, the final three stanzas chart an ambiguous course to suicide through a mental landscape in which, once again, Monimba and her captors appear doubled as well as divided. Does Monimba commit suicide to escape from the madness of others, or from the madness into which slavery would plunge her? Is her suicide evidence that she is already mad, driven involuntarily to commit acts from which a reasoning mind would shrink? Are her captors, too, acting in some sense involuntarily as the deranged agents of a slave system that murders reason itself?

Antislavery elegists were for the most part sympathetic to those who committed suicide under the intense and prolonged stresses of slavery and racism. Even those who shrank from condoning suicide were nevertheless reluctant to condemn someone like Stephen Rodden, a free black who killed himself in Maryland after being sentenced to a long term of imprisonment for possessing antislavery literature. "Not for self-murder would I plead," writes William James Stillman in his elegy for Rodden,

> Yet pity claims my falling tear,
> When the poor captive or the slave,
> Driven to madness by despair,
> Seeks for deliverance in the grave.

Stillman pities Rodden's solitary end. Far, however, from being a self-isolating or self-enclosing act, Rodden's suicide, in his "dungeon red with gore," promises to have generative consequences for the forces of the reckoning to come. Stillman twice refers to Rodden's blood as that of a "patriot" and insists that "Where'er the patriot's blood is spilled, / One drop is never spilt in vain." To such "sacred spots," he says, come "[f]resh strugglers for the truth and right." Overturning the racist "one-drop" principle of polygenetic theorists, Stillman envisions a kind of parthenogenesis by means of which another patriot in the cause of liberty would spring up from each drop of Rodden's blood, as serpents sprang up from drops of the Gorgon's. He borrows from the discourse of patriotic propaganda ("voice of Liberty," "laurel wreath," "Freedom's altar") to imagine a new lineage of heroes. Instead of having destroyed the progeny he might have helped, had he lived, to create, Rodden's death, as Stillman imagines it, will help to augment and radicalize antislavery generations to come. The blood that will be spilled at last, Stillman promises, is that of the pro-slavery "tyrants" to whom the elegy is addressed. Eventually, the violence that people like Stephen Rodden turn against themselves will be turned outward instead:

> Patience must surely fail at length,
> Waiting for rights too long withstood,

And maddened suffering taught its strength,
Wipe out the fearful score in blood.[104]

These final lines forecast insurrection and the fatal settling of accounts. Blood cries out for blood. Like "Monimba," Stillman's elegy for Rodden ends with a violent image that blurs rather than sharpens the difference between "white" blood and "black" blood. One pictures the "fearful score" as a tally written down somewhere in the blood of slavery's victims, which will then be "wipe[d] out" or erased with the blood of the slaveholders and their apologists. The score will be settled when the racist logic of polygenesis and the inscription of the score itself are no longer legible, and blood dissolves into blood.

Despite his opposition to suicide, Stillman memorialized Rodden's act as an index of undeserved suffering and as a token of righteous rage to come. Other elegists found certain cases of suicide to be righteous in themselves, particularly if the suicide had altruistic features. For example, S. H. B. Smith's "The Negro Girl" is written in the voice of an unnamed slave child who kills herself to avoid having to give up information regarding her mother's whereabouts (her mother having escaped from their owner). She begins by considering the renewed punishments her mother would have to endure were she caught and brought back. In several ensuing stanzas she recalls instances of her mother's selfless caretaking and protectiveness. These memories strengthen her resolve to reciprocate in the only way available to her: by killing herself so as to ensure that she will not falter under reproof or torture and give her mother away:

O, it is fearful thus to die—
Yet, in that brighter world on high,
May some sweet angel plead for me,
Dear mother, that I died for thee![105]

Another case of altruistic suicide is rendered in Frances Harper's elegy "The Tennessee Hero," about an unnamed slave whipped to death by terrified whites amid the slave insurrections of late 1856 in Tennessee, Kentucky, and Missouri. Rather than give up the names of his comrades—those "men who would be free"—he "resolve[s] to die," relinquishing himself to "a death of pain." "Sweeter far to meet it thus," he reasons, "Than wear a treason stain."[106] One finds in these elegies by Smith and Harper an unconstrained affirmation of the slave girl's imitation of Christ ("I died for thee") and the political martyrdom of the "Tennessee Hero."

A more conflicted view characterizes a pair of elegies on slave suicides by Julia Ward Howe. The first was for a slave named Lewis, who died under disputed circumstances in Clarke County, Virginia, on August 20, 1851. His owner, Stephen Castleman, and Stephen's father, James, were indicted for Lewis's murder but acquitted at trial. Lewis had died after being whipped by the Castlemans on suspicion of theft. After forcing a confession from Lewis, they went in search of his supposed accomplice, leaving Lewis in a warehouse attic secured by a chain that was wound around his neck and then fastened to a ceiling joist. The Castlemans left a white employee to guard Lewis. That employee testified that Lewis had asked for his assistance to kill himself, either by providing a box off of which he could jump to hang himself or by providing him with a knife with which he could cut his throat. The employee ignored Lewis's pleas, waited half an hour, and then left. The Castlemans later found Lewis hanging dead from the chain to which they had fastened him. At trial, doctors testified that Lewis could not have fainted before he strangled, strongly implying that he had committed suicide, thus helping to exonerate the Castlemans in the eyes of the jury.[107]

Howe probably read about the case in *The National Era,* where it was written up at length in early November. Her elegy, "The Death of the Slave Lewis," was published in the same paper two months later, drawing on details from the earlier account. She begins the poem by imagining the night of August 20, its peaceful calm violated by a "shriek, / As of a soul in Hades." She vividly depicts Lewis's torture at the hands of the Castlemans, leaving no doubt of its severity and inhumanity. Then, when the Castlemans leave,

> They set a man to watch him, they aver,
> Who, as men will, forsook his misery;
> But while he staid, unless his statement err,
> Not rest nor healing craved the sufferer,
> But, "Can you lend me any help to die?"

Blind Nature has an instinct to be free;
Despair is mighty, though her hands be tied;
Howe'er he bowed the head and bent the knee,
(The action has a dark sublimity,)
The black man gathered up his strength, and died.
They left thee, Lewis, with thy wounds all warm,
But when they came, to heap thy measure o'er,
Free in the fetters hung thy passive form.
Oh! theirs the crime, if in hate's wildest storm,
Thy soul, unbidden, sought th' eternal shore.[108]

The incongruous formality of Lewis's request to his guard is one sign of Howe's ambivalence regarding suicide. She has him ask, "Can you lend me any help to die?" as if in the manner of the defeated hero of a chanson de geste, who asks to be killed by another so as to avoid the dishonor of killing himself.[109] The difference may be one of mere form, but it matters to Howe, who seeks to preserve a sense of doubt regarding the apparent suicide. It seems most likely that, left alone, Lewis killed himself by letting his knees and head fall forward, choking himself with the suspended chain. But Howe's description of this action is phrased as if it were a posture of supplication before God: he "bowed the head and bent the knee." In the beautifully dignified line, "The black man gathered up his strength, and died," she implies a death that is self-willed but not self-executed. Lewis wanted to die and die he did, but he did not kill himself. And finally she asserts that even "if" Lewis did kill himself, the Castlemans would nevertheless be culpable.

Still unresigned to Lewis's death, Howe extends the elegy another forty-five lines, which consist primarily of her vehement denunciations of the Castlemans and the Southern citizens who acquitted them. She envisions Lewis crying out to God with his "wound-mouths, never to be sealed," inspiring God's vengeance against his tormenters, whom Howe now addresses directly:

The curse of Cain shall hunt thy wandering thought,
To frantic haste, to fainting weariness.
Lookest thou earthward, blood is there unsought;
Skyward, the clouds th' avenging hue have caught,
And mock, like crimson monsters, thy distress.[110]

The blood of slavery is everywhere, splashed across heaven and earth by the Castlemans' betrayal of fundamental kinship with Lewis. To the slaveholders of the South, Howe transfers the "curse of Cain" commonly used by Bible-toting defenders of slavery to justify their racism. And she continues her condemnation of Christian slaveholders through to the elegy's penultimate stanza, followed, finally, by the most generous valediction she can muster:

> Ev'n though thou babble from the mystic book,
> And taste the sacred symbols of thy creed,
> Let Christ's black brother from the altar look,
> Faint, falter, 'neath his withering rebuke—
> The heav'nly food can poison too, at need.
> I pause, unwilling further to rehearse
> Thy meeds, or shut thee from God's clemency.
> Rather, I'll weep, and wish thee nothing worse
> Than that, returning blessing for thy curse,
> Thy victim's soul may plead with God for thee.[111]

Howe's "pause" may signal a measure of regret or distaste at the work of vilification her elegy has so extensively performed. It is not that she disavows that work, but rather that she seems at the end of the poem to reconsider what sort of statement of religious principle, whether of wrath or forgiveness, she wants it to be. And she pauses also to consider and make room for the figure of Lewis the suicide in the role not of lost soul but of righteous intercessor, the one who can, on behalf of all, return blessing for curse. "The Death of the Slave Lewis" is a long elegy, written in hasty stanzas shortly after the event, relying on a newspaper transcript of the court proceedings, yet imagining the contest in terms of biblical, rather than strictly local, coordinates. It is a religious declaration by someone devoted to the liberal Christianity of New England Unitarianism, and it is a social indictment by someone committed to a related doctrine of good works. And the most urgent question it poses may be: What sanction should suicide have in the fashioning of a better or transcendent world?

Within a few years, Howe had come to feel it should have none. The pivotal event may have been the suicide of one of her closest friends, Horace Binney Wallace, who killed himself in Paris a little more than a year after Lewis's death. By the time she wrote the poem "Slave Suicide" some years later, the ambivalence she had expressed in her elegy for Lewis was gone. The "Roman" way, she concluded, was the wrong way. "Slave Suicide" begins not with the individuated circumstances of a particular slave's death, as in her elegy for Lewis, but rather with a moral and philosophical question abstractly posed:

> Should one led up to death, or fearing worse,
> Those tortures that make dying a release,
> Anticipate the final boon of peace
> By taking on himself the murderer's curse?

Her answer is emphatically negative, and she swaps abstraction ("should one") for the first person to drive home the point:

> No! by my faith in God, I would not spare
> My flesh one blow prophetically due,
> Nor snatch a respite, nor for mercy sue,
> Lest I should wrong th' Omnipotence of prayer;
> Lest I should rob my soul of high repose
> Earned by such racking labor of the frame,
> Or spare a miscreant heart the bootless shame
> With which men see a victim's eyelids close.

In her masochistic identification with the tortured slave we likely hear traces of her feelings of both guilt and anger over Wallace's suicide. In the poem's figures of the Christian martyrs, of Jesus Christ, and most proximately of the slave, Howe finds examples of people who withstood the most terrible agonies—who bore their "martyrdom as God did mete." Subsumed within the figure of the slave, Wallace continues to haunt the poem in the figure of the "devoted friend" who should have borne rather than fled his sufferings:

> Smile then upon the scourge, devoted friend!
> There comes a glory, wreathed with every stripe,
> His meed who waits till his reward is ripe,
> And crown's God's perfect purpose in his end.[112]

Indeed, it would be truer to say that in "Slave Suicide" the figure of the slave has been subsumed within an idealization of patient suffering, appropriated as a symbol of self-control and Christian submissiveness that exceeds the already excessive requirements of grief for her friend. Such appropriations, arising out of identifications, are endemic to anti-slavery literature, which served audiences often "fascinated," as Karen Sánchez-Eppler has observed, "by the abuses they ostensibly oppose." "The valuation of depictions of slavery," she continues, "may rest upon the same psychic ground as slaveholding itself."[113] Howe's argument against suicide is an argument against its practice by slaves seeking to avoid or shorten the ordeal of pain. Needlessly perpetuating that ordeal is of course not Howe's design, but she would glorify physical endurance at the expense of self-determination. In "The Death of the Slave Lewis," self-annihilation is a claim to identity. In "Slave Suicide," that claim is denied not to save slaves' lives but rather to bolster a social prohibition against self-murder that had been too weak to save her friend.

None other than Abraham Lincoln made a contribution to the weakening of that prohibition when, as a twenty-eight-year-old lawyer, he published "The Suicide's Soliloquy" in an Illinois newspaper. The poem is steeped in a lugubrious postadolescent arrogance that imagines its own sorrows have no equal anywhere, not even in the tortures of hell, which the speaker in fact welcomes as potential anodynes. "Frightful screams, and piercing pains," he ventures, "[w]ill help me to forget."[114] Indicative, it would seem, of an early phase of Lincoln's lifelong struggle with depression, the poem is also of interest as a point on the continuum of suicidality and martyrdom that so many lives, in and out of slavery, traversed in the decades leading up to the Civil War. Some killed themselves, some forced others to kill them; there were those who committed themselves to dangerous causes, and those who relinquished themselves to perilous circumstances; some sacrificed themselves for others, while some merely abandoned lives they held to be worthless. In every case, the question of voluntarism arises—not only on the level of the individual but of the nation as well. In his 1838 Springfield Lyceum speech on "The Perpetuation of Our Political Institutions," Lincoln warned that if these institutions had any dangers to face, they would come not from abroad but from within: "If destruction be our lot, we must ourselves be its author and finisher. As a nation of freemen, we must live through all time, or die by suicide." Lincoln was speaking most directly of mob violence—including the murder of Elijah Lovejoy in nearby Alton, Illinois, less than three months earlier—which was making martyrs of blacks and whites all over the country as abolitionist fervor and opposition to it intensified. But Lincoln's warning was also more comprehensive, a warning "to the whole country" that national suicidality may go unrecognized in many forms of lawless passion and political ambition, whether of a Prosser or a Brown, a Vesey or a Turner, a Lovejoy or even a Lincoln.[115]

Rise, Mourner, Rise

Lincoln was preoccupied with thoughts of death, which he expressed not only in his poetry but in his political speeches as well, forecasting his own martyrdom in remarks both casual and grave. Upon his death, popular reaction confirmed him to be not only the self-sacrificing equal of George Washington—another father to his country—but also a Christ-like figure. His assassination on Good Friday inspired many such comparisons. Among African Americans, the sensation of loss was sharp, extensive, and frequently on display. According to Navy Secretary Gideon Welles, several hundred black women and children stood in front of the Executive Mansion "weeping and wailing their loss" through the cold wet morning of Lincoln's death.[116] "I was in Rochester," wrote Frederick Douglass,

> when news of the death of Mr. Lincoln was received. Our citizens, not knowing what else to do in the agony of the hour, betook themselves to the city hall. Though all hearts ached for utterance, few felt like speaking. We were stunned and overwhelmed by a crime and calamity hitherto unknown to our country and our government. The hour was hardly one for speech, for no speech could rise to the level of feeling.[117]

Nevertheless Douglass rose and spoke. Across the country in Sacramento, James Madison Bell read his newly written elegy for Lincoln to a "great public meeting of colored citizens" on April 18. A week later, New York's Common Council refused to let blacks participate in Lincoln's funeral procession through that city. But Alfred Gibbs Campbell was nevertheless inspired by the procession to write an elegy to the "Martyr of Truth and Right."[118] Bell, Campbell, and other African-American elegists—among them George Moses Horton, William Mallory, and

Jacob Rhodes—helped their white counterparts to commemorate both Lincoln's martyrdom and the lavish displays of sorrow it inspired.

Memorable and encompassing as that sorrow was, however, Thomas Reed Turner reminds us that "violent deeds and expressions" were also "at the heart of public reaction."[119] The assassination brought to a close the brief celebration of the end of the war. In its place came the unregulated pursuit of suspected or imagined conspirators. Ears were tuned to possible treasonous utterances. Violent reprisals, even against the innocent, went unprotested and unpunished. Supporters of a harsh reconstruction policy were emboldened. William Lloyd Garrison said that in Jefferson Davis's case he would be willing to make an exception to his stance against capital punishment. Anger was directed even at Lincoln himself, as a "rapid revulsion set in against what many people now considered to have been Lincoln's too lenient policy towards rebels and traitors."[120] Did Father Abraham bear some responsibility for his own assassination? Was there a sense of abandonment "at the heart of public reaction"?

Even before Lincoln's death, some extravagant hopes of African Americans had been sorely frustrated. During the war, slaves seized under the Confiscation Acts and runaways seeking the protection of Union forces were interned in "contraband camps," in many of which hunger, illness, and neglect kept spirits low and death rates high. In one such camp, at Benton Barracks near St. Louis, James Erwin Yeatman found that disappointment and ill-usage "have greatly disheartened the poor slave" and that "continued abuses sadden and depress him."[121] To many, "emancipation" itself was another traumatic upheaval. Of the French Caribbean in 1848, Frantz Fanon wrote: "Just as when one tells a much improved patient that in a few days he will be discharged from the hospital, he thereupon suffers a relapse, so the announcement of the liberation of the black slaves produced psychoses and sudden deaths."[122] Fifteen years later, in the American camps of newly freed slaves, as many as one in four would die. Elizabeth Keckley, working for the Relief Society in Washington, D.C., observed that emancipation and coming north were, in the absence of comprehensive assistance, but stages in yet another form of deracination. They are "wedded to associations," Keckley wrote of the displaced freedman and freedwomen, "and when you destroy these you destroy half of the happiness of their lives."[123] Walt Whitman, who logged countless hours in the gruesome army hospitals, could not bring himself to return to the contraband camps after just one or two visits. "There is," he wrote to his mother, "a limit to one's sinews & endurance & sympathies, &c."[124] Lincoln himself wished the nation could shed its black population. He was a zealous colonizationist and would have preferred to see more liberated blacks depart for new settlements in South America or Africa.

Lincoln's martyrdom helped to enhance his reputation as the "great emancipator" and his image as "Father Abraham." But his death left millions of blacks as they were before: without the consistent, reliable support of the national government. In a speech delivered at the unveiling of the Freedmen's Monument to Lincoln in 1876, Frederick Douglass described Lincoln as "preeminently the white man's President, entirely devoted to the welfare of white men." Addressing the white members of his audience, he said: "You are the children of Abraham Lincoln. We are at best only his step-children."[125] But in the immediate aftermath of the war, as Lincoln's white detractors were being beaten and hung in the streets of northern cities, such frankness was not possible. Any anger at the dead president had to be redirected, and his widow made a safe and convenient target, particularly for those who experienced Lincoln's death as a form of parental abandonment.

Among the members of the filial, exclusively male group that assembled at Lincoln's deathbed, Secretary of War Edwin Stanton was among the first to make Mary Lincoln the focus of his anger. Apparently, the intensity of her grief unsettled him—perhaps because he perceived in it the threat of emotional contagion—and eventually Stanton barred her from the room. In the weeks that followed, she offended many mourners by refusing to see them when they called at the White House. Prostrated by grief and thus unable to supervise the residence, which was rifled of many of the furnishings she had purchased for it, she would later be "widely condemned for having stolen government property." And her battle with the people of Springfield over the disposition of her husband's remains made her persona non grata in the Lincolns' Illinois hometown.[126] Like Victoria, she became one of the most famous mourners of the nineteenth century. Terminally committed to the public and private usages of that role, she became a figure not only of sympathy but of humor, distaste, and contempt as well.

Black attitudes toward Mrs. Lincoln are more difficult to trace, but there are some important exceptions. Foremost among them is Elizabeth Keckley's 1868 memoir, *Behind the Scenes,* which recounts her close personal and professional relationship with Mary Lincoln in detail. It is perhaps the most sympathetic portrait of Mary Lincoln as a mourner. Perhaps the most unusual is the poem "Mrs. Lincoln's Lamentation," one of three elegies George Moses Horton wrote for the slain president. All three were included in his 1865 volume *Naked Genius,* along with dozens of other poems that he composed at great speed while traveling with a Michigan cavalry regiment in the spring and summer of 1865.[127] As the title suggests, "Mrs. Lincoln's Lamentation" is reminiscent of the broadside elegy "Lady Washington's Lamentation for the Death of Her Husband," discussed in chapter 2. Like the earlier poem, Horton's depends for its effectiveness on the presidential widow's complex status as both public and private mourner. It acknowledges both the singular intensity of Mary Lincoln's grief and her representative role as the symbol of a nation in mourning.

If in some ways it would seem provocative for a recently liberated slave to speak in the voice of a white, socially elevated widow, there is nevertheless something starkly fitting about it. For the widow, like the slave, occupies a social position somewhere between life and death. She is both alive and not alive in the aftermath of her husband's demise. Sandra Gilbert notes that the word *widow*

> is from the Indo-European *widhewo-,* meaning "to be empty, be separated," to be "destitute" or "lack." Death has entered the widow, this etymology implies, and she has entered death, for she is filled with vacancy and has dissolved into a void, a state of lack or nonbeing that is akin to, if not part of, the state into which the dead person has journeyed.[128]

Horton's identification with Mary Lincoln may owe something to his experience of the social and civil deaths of slavery and his sense not only of the terrible privations of those liminal states but also of the intense accompanying desire to reach out to and reconnect with the dead. "In her grief and fury," Gilbert continues, "the widow wants only to speak to the dead one, to sustain and preserve him. But from the perspective of those outside her grief, her desirous speech is both awesome and awful."[129] Mary Lincoln's powerful desire to communicate with the dead—and thereby to reconstitute severed family ties—preceded her husband's assassination; she had been attending séances at least since the death of their son Willie in 1862. Her belief in spiritualism was strengthened by her friendship with Keckley, who regularly sought contact with her own dead son's departed spirit at Washington séances. As many as eight séances were held in the White House itself. When the president died, Mary Lincoln's first regret was that she had not been present at his deathbed to witness the "hovering" of his spirit.[130] Wanting only "to speak to the dead one, to sustain and preserve him," she had so unnerved a roomful of soldiers and statesmen with her keening that she was banished from her dying husband's side.

Written on the march through a world in ruin, Horton's elegy captures something of the awful extremity and threat as well as the more decorous pathos of the widow's grief. The poem opens onto scenes of mourning both pastoral and urban, in which "sylvan warblers" and "damsels of the city" alike announce their sorrow. Initially, Horton's Mrs. Lincoln articulates her grief both in the individuated terms of her marital role and in the collective terms of a national progeny to which she, like everyone else, belongs. She, too, addresses him as "Father Abraham," apostrophizing Lincoln on behalf of others as well as herself. But she is not content simply to mourn with others or to wait patiently for the day of their reunion. Rather, she seeks to join her husband right away: "Still we mourn, but we could not go with thee, / The lady of thy love aspires to thee." Images of spousal yearning and heavenly aspiration are conflated in her plea to "Abraham" that he "descend at once and open wide thy bosom." This plea combines a retrospective longing for restored intimacy and a prospective wish for the eternal fate of a righteous soul—a soul like that of Lazarus from the Lucan parable of Dives and Lazarus to which the poem alludes.

The central movement of the poem is an imaginative flight taken by Mrs. Lincoln toward her husband and toward death—a flight of thanatic as well as erotic longing. As the angels lift her up, however, she is distracted by a spectacle of retribution:

Let me look down on the sulphurous gulf,
And view the rich man with his blistered tongue,
The damned, the infernal homicide of peace,
While loud he calls and beckons for relief!
O, father Abraham, send down one drop
Of cooling water to appease the wound,
But ah! too late, the fratrid murderer cries,
My friend, my father Abram, bears me home;
I'm on my way, I'm on my way to heaven.
But oh! the scene is closed and leaves me drear,
Imagination's dream has passed away,
And I awake again, alas! to weep!

The narrative details and some of the language in this passage are familiar from Luke 16. But the "homicide of peace" and "fratrid murderer"
are also coordinates of a present ravaged by civil war and assassination.
In her representations of the rich man's desperate cries, Mrs. Lincoln's
own language becomes difficult to distinguish from his. It is as if she
were not only pleading for her husband's killer but identifying with
him. Nevertheless, the bid goes unanswered, Mrs. Lincoln's dream is
interrupted, and she is reawakened to grief.

This dream about the failure of sympathy helps constitute Horton's
own identification with Mary Lincoln as an ambivalent achievement.
It raises the possibility, for instance, that sympathy for another, such
as Mrs. Lincoln's for the rich man, may not only fail to secure relief for
the other but may also extend one's own suffering, just as Mrs. Lincoln,
abandoned by her heavenly escort, is returned to her painful viduity in
the mortal world. Furthermore, she finds the world itself diminished
upon her return. Before the dream, mourning is sociable: bards lament
pensively, orators declaim loudly, and the "damsels of the city weep."
But after the dream, Washington is void of sociability. The mourners
have withdrawn:

And desolation spreads the city around.
The theatre's gloomy where he fell,
With doors and windows closed.

Asleep, the city no longer stands for a community of mourners but for
a "benighted hemisphere" that needs to be rekindled to an enlightened

view of Lincoln's death. What that view would encompass, however, is left unspoken, as the poem ends with an image of the myriad viewers themselves, "[t]he blaze of day thrown back on every eye." The line makes the dawning day sound less like an illumination and more like a return of fire. One feels the recoil of the line itself in its return to perfect iambic pentameter after the irregular line that precedes it. This "blaze of day" suggests more than the mere glitter of April sunshine. It suggests a conflagration to come, a blaze that might punish rather than warm, blind rather than illuminate—the widow's rage, the ex-slave's "fire nex' time."[131]

Horton was probably aware of the elaborate provisions made for the public viewing of Lincoln's corpse, though he may not have known just how massive the response was. Millions of Americans viewed the body as it lay in state or watched the funeral train wend its way from Washington to Springfield, making stops in Philadelphia, New York, Chicago, and other cities. The public exposure of Lincoln's corpse, in particular, was unprecedented. Thanks to the new embalming techniques developed during the war, the corpse's visual integrity remained reasonably well preserved for almost three weeks, making public viewings possible up to the time of the interment at Oak Ridge Cemetery on May 4. In his funeral oration, Matthew Simpson observed that "[m]ore persons have gazed on the face of the departed than ever looked upon the face of any other departed man."[132] That so many people, black and white, might be able to look into the face of one dead man and see there an adequate reflection of all that had been lost and all that had yet to be regained was impossible. Others remained to be buried and mourned, and a new phase of national division and race hatred was just beginning. The violent deaths would continue to accumulate.

And so would the elegies for Lincoln. Hundreds of them would appear before the end of 1865, several dozen of them gathered in a three-hundred-page anthology published in Philadelphia. Other anthologies would be produced at intervals, as the steady stream of tributary and commemorative poems reached toward the century's end and beyond. Among the better-known Lincoln elegists, black and white, were William Cullen Bryant, Alice Cary, Frank Barbour Coffin, James D. Corrothers, Paul Laurence Dunbar, Timothy Thomas Fortune, Oliver Wendell

Holmes, Lucy Larcom, James Russell Lowell, Herman Melville, John James Piatt, Henrietta Cordelia Ray, Edmund Clarence Stedman, and Walt Whitman, to name but a few. Whitman alone wrote or attempted six elegies for Lincoln,[133] and he continued to lecture on Lincoln until his own death, reaffirming his conviction that there was, or at least could be, "a cement to the whole people . . . the cement of a death identified thoroughly with that people."[134] The martyred president was of course subject to a wide range of identifications and disidentifications, many of which found expression in the elegies mentioned above—all of them overshadowed, however, by Whitman's "When Lilacs Last in the Dooryard Bloom'd," an elegy in which death is as much solvent as cement, in which the body politic is only imperfectly comprehended by its representative figure, and in which the overriding fact of variability among persons is nothing to mourn.

CHAPTER 6

Retrievements out of the Night: Whitman and the Future of Elegy

> [B]y their very existence, lilacs and nightingales—where the universal net has permitted them to survive—make us believe that life is still alive.
>
> —THEODOR ADORNO

On a November evening in 1888, during one of his innumerable visits to Walt Whitman's Mickle Street home in Camden, New Jersey, Horace Traubel noticed something he had not seen before. "I stopped at the mantelpiece," he writes,

> to look at a strange little Washington-Lincoln photo. It represents Lincoln as being welcomed into the cloudlands and throwing his arms about Washington, who with a disengaged hand offers to put a wreath on Lincoln's brow. I spoke of it as "queer." W[hitman] laughed: "Everybody seems of the same mind—everybody but me: I value it: yet I could hardly tell why: probably because it made a favorable impression on me at the start. When I was in Washington I had it on my desk: the clerks got much frolic out of it: the chief clerk thought it was a cheap thing—the cheapest of things."[1]

In fact it *was* a cheap thing: a *carte-de-visite* photograph of a lithograph, published shortly after Lincoln's assassination in 1865 (see Figure 9). So many of these photographs were published and preserved that one can

Figure 9. George Washington welcoming Abraham Lincoln into heaven, ca. 1865.
Lithograph. Collection of the author.

inexpensively acquire them to this day. Yet Whitman makes his attachment to it seem anything but common. Indeed, it is a mark of his singularity. When Traubel calls it "queer," Whitman cheerfully informs him that everybody else thinks so too—"everybody but me." He recalls, genially, the ridicule of his fellow clerks in the office of the attorney general. Whitman, however, continues to value the photo more than twenty years later, although he says he can "hardly tell why."

Whitman's posture of bemused uncertainty or reticence regarding the source of his affection for this image is difficult not to read in relation to the intimate male contact it depicts. His appeal to the phenomenology of the "impression"—along with Traubel's fascination, the junior clerks' frolicsomeness, and the chief clerk's disparagement—marks the limits of expressibility at which nineteenth-century discourses of gender and sexuality had placed eroticized contact between males. Whitman sometimes used the nonce word *adhesiveness* (derived from the popular pseudoscience of phrenology) to characterize the drive for such contact. More often, though, he characterized this drive by the very descriptive inadequacy it highlighted—what, in "The Primer of Words," he called "words wanted."[2] The inarticulacy of homoerotic desire has a long history of enforcement by sanction, and the oblique, even defensive, rhetorical posture Whitman frequently adopts registers the long-lived religio-juridical terror of "peccatum illud horribile inter Christianos non nominandum," as well as the decorous or abstract language of mid-nineteenth-century sexual regimentation. Twenty years after the fact, the chief clerk's contempt for the Washington-Lincoln photo complicates the jocularity of the scene of recollection with Traubel. For in the assertion that it is "a cheap thing—the cheapest of things," Whitman ventriloquizes not just the midcentury lickspittle (who implicitly denigrates the photo's eroticism even as he seeks to demonstrate his own aesthetic connoisseurship) but also the impressionistic figure of his own ongoing struggle to reconcile attachment to the singularity (or queerness) of the mourned object with the revaluation of loss as a nationalizing, indeed democratizing, force.

Connoisseur of the common that he was, Whitman manifests no anxiety about the lack of aesthetic value emanating from this artifact of presidential kitsch. The strength of the impression made upon

Whitman by the chief clerk's reaction *does* suggest his own troubled alertness to the lack of definitive meaning emanating from the homoeroticism of nationalist iconography. However, the "favorable impression" made by the photo itself—a memento mori saved, cherished, and displayed—speaks to its value to Whitman as an emblem of his own eroticized attachment to both Lincoln and Washington—an attachment unnamed but inescapable in his writings. One journal entry in particular (for October 31, 1863) links Whitman's longing for an adequate affective language to his longing for Lincoln:

> Saw Mr. Lincoln standing, talking with a gentleman, apparently a dear friend. His face & manner have an expression & are inexpressibly sweet—one hand on his friend's shoulder, the other holds his hand. I love the President personally.[3]

Washington, too, is figured in scenes of longed-for contact, for example, in "The Sleepers," where Washington is seen bidding farewell to his officers:

> He stands in the room of the old tavern, the well-belov'd soldiers all pass
> through,
> The officers speechless and slow draw near in their turns,
> The chief encircles their necks with his arm and kisses them on the cheek,
> He kisses lightly the wet cheeks one after another, he shakes hands and
> bids good-by to the army.[4]

These and other comparable passages on the two presidents are figuratively united in the Washington-Lincoln photo, which draws on reigning motifs of spiritualism and the religion of civic sentiment to produce the striking visual effect of unobstructed male contact that Whitman sought, albeit with frequent unease, to articulate in his poetry.

In "The Centenarian's Story," for example, the voice of the poet interrupts the exchange between Revolutionary veteran and Brooklyn volunteer in order to insist explicitly upon his role as conjoiner of persons and generations:

> Enough, the Centenarian's story ends,
> The two, the past and present, have interchanged,
> I myself as connector, as chansonnier of a great future, am now speaking.
> (*Leaves of Grass*, 2:473)

These lines begin the final section of the poem, titled *"Terminus"* as if further to emphasize the discontinuity within the poem by which the poet's role as facilitator of continuity is marked (note, too, the strong caesura after the speech-canceling "Enough"). To account adequately for this rhetorical and tonal shift, one must first hear the familiar struggle recalled in the previous section's concluding lines. There, as the Centenarian describes his experience under Washington's command at the Battle of Long Island, he remembers, but cannot name, what he sees when he looks at Washington in defeat:

> Every one else seem'd fill'd with gloom,
> Many no doubt thought of capitulation.
> But when my General pass'd me,
> As he stood in his boat and look'd toward the coming sun,
> I saw something different from capitulation. (*Leaves of Grass*, 2:473)

At this point the poet breaks in ("Enough"), conscious of ambiguities, though "loath," as Kerry Larson observes, "to pursue them." These ambiguities are insufficiently characterized by Larson as belonging to prophecies of political integration.[5] The remainder, the excess, the "something different" away from which Whitman swerves here is echoed in Whitman's own glancing encounters with Lincoln, such as this one recorded in *Specimen Days*:

> I saw the President in the face fully . . . and his look, though abstracted, happen'd to be directed steadily in my eye. He bow'd and smiled, but far beneath his smile I noticed well the expression I have alluded to. None of the artists or pictures has caught the deep, though subtle and indirect expression of this man's face. There is something else there.

There was also some*one* else there, in the carriage with Lincoln, when Whitman locked eyes with him: Mrs. Lincoln, "dress'd," according to Whitman, "in complete black, with a long crape veil."[6] Mary Lincoln was still in deep mourning for their son Willie, who had died from typhoid fever the year before at age eleven.[7] According to her modiste and confidante Elizabeth Keckley, Lincoln himself was both devastated by Willie's death and fearful of what his wife's inconsolable grief would do to her mind. According to Keckley, during one of Mary Lincoln's "paroxysms of grief," Lincoln took her aside, pointed out the window at the new Government Hospital for the Insane (now St. Elizabeth's), and told her that if she could not control her grief she would end up there.[8] The regimentation of grief, like the regimentation of sexuality, in mid-nineteenth-century America was becoming increasingly medicalized. Excessive mourning was pathological as well as indecorous for the culture within which Whitman was attempting to figure the excess, the "something else," that characterized his own attachment to Lincoln.

Whitman's Civil War mourning has been located at different extremes on the erotic scale: from the almost thoroughly desexualized to the quasi-necrophiliac.[9] Robert Leigh Davis persuasively stakes out a middle ground with the following judicious characterization of Whitman's sexual identity as prompted by his work at Washington hospitals like Armory Square:

> What Whitman learned in the homosexual community of the hospitals— the "hospital wisdom" that confirmed his vision of democracy—was how to live a gay life in the midst of misunderstanding and misrepresentation.[10]

Davis is sometimes too quick to assimilate his image of Whitman to a quasi-liberationist, self-conscious, and pragmatically gay sensibility. Yet his fundamental reinterpretation of Whitman's nursing experience— of the uncertainties and delights of his contact with the soldiers in the hospitals—is a sensitive and eloquent account of Whitman's wartime sexuality, of his participation in what Davis calls "the complexity of a homosexual romance never wholly known, named, mastered, or made public."[11] It is, according to Davis, a homosexuality of negative capability, of open-endedness and of social moorings unloosed, of vitality always at risk, and of cherished flickerings of desire amid routine and appalling death. In the poetry of *Drum-Taps* and the prose of *Specimen Days,* Whitman practiced a writing of "remains," that is, a writing not just about unassimilable pieces or fragments of wartime experience, including erotic experience and memorable glances, but writing that is itself characterized by patchwork, discontinuity, and open-endedness. And it is also a writing of the remains of the dead, of corpses whole or damaged, and of possessions or other less palpable traces left behind. All of these "remains" contribute toward Whitman's fashioning of a language of mourning that in valuing the left over and the left out—

the dead soldier whose name no one knows, the unidentified bones on the battlefield, the murdered president whose democratic vision remains unfulfilled—discovers a moral substitute for statistical analyses of the costs of the war and for the forms of mourning—stoic, efficient, authoritative—that derive from such analyses.

Rising numeracy and the bureaucratization of reckoning activities during the antebellum period made the unprecedented losses of the war both more and less difficult to manage. Less difficult, because there was in the precision of numbers and official lists the solace of apparent certitude, the conviction that, vast as the losses were, they went only as far as the numbers indicated and no further. Statistics enabled detachment and psychically rewarded the habit of quantification that had emerged in the course of market revolution as a national characteristic.[12] But the scientific tallying of the dead also dramatized and even enhanced the difficulty of retrieving and conserving their identities for memorialization. Newspaper lists tantalized anxious families with names of soldiers "supposed killed," and battlefield cemeteries teemed with graves of the unknown. Collectivizing "the dead"—whether in trench graves or in published figures—redeemed unidentifiable and unlocatable bodies for a symbolic totality of otherwise immeasurable sacrifice, while at the same time highlighting the pace at which the war was outstripping both the psychic and the material resources of individuated mourning. Dismembered, decaying human flesh littered the country, and before it could be hidden away out of sight, a new generation of photographers rendered it visible even to those who never set foot on a battlefield. Images by Alexander Gardner, Timothy O'Sullivan, and others aroused such popular hunger for these graphic scenes of mayhem and gore that some photographers—alert to their market value—began staging shots by posing corpses for their cameras and by coaxing living soldiers into masquerading as the dead.[13] Gallery exhibitions, lavish albums, *cartes de visite,* and mail-order prints turned the immediacy of death into a marketable commodity and the exposed, anonymous corpse into a pervasive cultural presence (see Figure 10).

To live amid so many unassimilable deaths challenged ontological, as well as memorial, resourcefulness. Beginning in 1862, spirit photographers like William Mumler along with their unscrupulous battlefield

Figure 10. Timothy O'Sullivan, "A Harvest of Death," Gettysburg, Pennsylvania, 1863. *Gardner's Photographic Sketchbook of the War* (Washington, D.C.: Philip & Solomons, 1865–66). Courtesy of Annenberg Rare Book and Manuscript Library, University of Pennsylvania.

counterparts exploited the new technology's apparent grounding in the real to capitalize upon heightened uncertainty and fear. Grief-stricken clients gazed longingly at doctored images, and exhibit-goers searched the faces of repositioned and even disinterred corpses and of amateur actors playing possum for answers to their profoundest questions about the nature of death and their links to the dead. The uncanny impact of exhibits like Matthew Brady's "The Dead of Antietam" was captured (or was it invented?) by a visitor to Brady's gallery writing for the *New York Times* in the fall of 1862:

> You will see hushed, reverend groups standing around these weird copies of carnage, bending down to look in the pale faces of the dead, chained by

the strange spell that dwells in dead men's eyes. It seems somewhat singular that the same sun that looked down on the faces of the slain, blistering them, blotting out from the body all semblance to humanity, and hastening corruption, should have thus caught their features upon canvas, and given them perpetuity for ever. But so it is.

The redundancy of the phrase "perpetuity for ever" seems to betray the writer's uncertainty as to the future of the dead—whether the body's lost "semblance to humanity" bespeaks a humanity absolutely lost at the moment of death. These men no longer exist, except as "a confused mass of names," as a "jumble of type" in the morning newspaper, and, in a Broadway gallery, as "weird copies of carnage."[14] That last vivid phrase seems in some sense livelier, truer than the photographs themselves, given that many were falsified and that even the legitimate ones only fostered the illusion of presence.

Whitman, however, believed not only in the truth of photography—its ability to hold rather than merely mimic reality—but also in the perpetual existence of the dead:

> I do not think seventy years is the time of a man or woman,
> Nor that seventy millions of years is the time of a man or woman,
> Nor that years will ever stop the existence of me, or any one else. (*Leaves of Grass*, 1:153)

Whitmanian ontology affirms that what is *possible*—the intuition of what could be—is a feature of the actual world and gives it value. His response to the statistical imagination of the antebellum period was to boast, in "Song of Myself," that he "was never measured, and never will be measured" (*Leaves of Grass*, 1:74). And his response to the devastating statistics of the war was just as confident, if less boisterous: first, to acknowledge the rationalism and numeracy of "specimen days"—"went thoroughly through ward 6, observ'd every case in the ward, without, I think, missing one" (*Prose Works*, 1:35); "To-day, as I write, hundreds more are expected, and to-morrow and the next day more, and so on for many days. Quite often they arrive at the rate of 1000 a day" (1:45); "when these army hospitals are all fill'd, (as they have been already several times,) they contain a population more numerous in itself than the whole of the Washington of ten or fifteen years ago. Within sight of the capitol, as I write, are some thirty or forty such collections, at times holding from fifty to seventy thousand men" (1:66); "probably three-fourths of the losses, men, lives, &c., have been sheer superfluity, extravagance, waste" (1:75)—and then to turn from them to claim his place beside sick and wounded fellow immortals like Thomas Haley, shot through the lung and certain to die:

> I often come and sit by him in perfect silence; he will breathe for ten minutes as softly and evenly as a young babe asleep. Poor youth, so handsome, athletic, with profuse beautiful shining hair. One time as I sat looking at him while he lay asleep, he suddenly, without the least start, awaken'd, open'd his eyes, gave me a long steady look, turning his face very slightly to gaze easier—one long, clear, silent look—a slight sigh—then turn'd back and went into his doze again. Little he knew, poor death-stricken boy, the heart of the stranger that hover'd near. (*Prose Works*, 1:49–50)

To Robert Leigh Davis's valuable reading of this scene—of "an extravagance exceeding the reparative terms of the text," of "a realm of meaning only partly disclosed by the paragraph's dominant voice," of "an apprehensive, gently skeptical sympathy restrained by a recognition of secrecy, hiddenness, and erotic depth," of the "sudden 'turn,' that Whitman seems most to cherish as the countersign to an imminent death"[15]—there is little to add, except perhaps to note the slightly spectral quality Whitman affords himself, as if he were the authentic counterpart ("hover[ing] near") of the sham spirit of a Mumler photograph, surprised by the impression of being seen by someone who should not have been able to see him. In Whitman's telling, Haley seems to know he is there before he opens his eyes—seems to know where to look and ("without the least start") what to expect to see. Whitman has been a frequent visitor to Haley's bedside ("I often come and sit by him"), yet he refers to himself as a "stranger," a word paradoxically charged for Whitman with accumulated imaginings of a world of improved intimacies.[16]

The Calamus poem, "To a Stranger," speaks most magnificently, of all the short pre-war lyrics, to Whitman's universalist ontology of love:

> Passing stranger! you do not know how longingly I look upon you,
> You must be he I was seeking, or she I was seeking, (it comes to me as of
>   a dream,)
> I have somewhere surely lived a life of joy with you,

All is recall'd as we flit by each other, fluid, affectionate, chaste, matured,
You grew up with me, were a boy with me or a girl with me,
I ate with you and slept with you, your body has become not yours only
    nor left my body mine only,
You give me the pleasure of your eyes, face, flesh, as we pass, you take of
    my beard, breast, hands, in return,
I am not to speak to you, I am to think of you when I sit alone or wake at
    night alone,
I am to wait, I do not doubt I am to meet you again,
I am to see to it that I do not lose you. (*Leaves of Grass,* 2:392)

The valedictory charge is thrilling in the certainty with which it anticipates the fulfillment of an instant obligation—an obligation originating in nothing more than a fantasy of recognition and offered to the reader in an eroticized social spirit of generative mutuality. If we experience a sensation of confidence in this mutuality, it is because we, like Whitman, assume—and behave according to the assumption—that a great deal of psychic life and functioning is held in common. I understand, with what I believe to be similar excitement, the poet's exhilarating feeling of being bound not to lose the "passing stranger" he has projected onto me and that I, in turn, project onto this one or that one, leaving my ghostly trace in them as a creature of their reminiscence.

More than anyone else, Lincoln was Whitman's creature of reminiscence: the object of his cruising glance, the star of his national dramaturgy, the father of his family romance, and, to the end, his persistently ineffable loss. "The fit tribute I dream'd of," he told his last public audiences, "waits unprepared as ever" (*Prose Works,* 2:497). To our ears, this statement—coming from the author of one of the greatest elegies in the language—may at first sound merely disingenuous. But there is doctrine here as well as modesty. Indeed, there is the highly immodest doctrine of preparation that characterizes Whitman's wonderful, outrageous ontogeny in "Song of Myself":

Immense have been the preparations for me,
Faithful and friendly the arms that have help'd me.
Cycles ferried my cradle, rowing and rowing like cheerful boatmen,
For room to me stars kept aside in their own rings,
They sent influences to look after what was to hold me.
Before I was born out of my mother generations guided me,

My embryo has never been torpid, nothing could overlay it.
For it the nebula cohered to an orb,
The long slow strata piled to rest it on,
Vast vegetables gave it sustenance,
Monstrous sauroids transported it in their mouths and deposited it with
    care. (*Leaves of Grass,* 1:72)

The image of the Whitmanian embryo being carried gently toward the future between the crushing jaws of giant Mesozoic lizards is hard to resist, in part because it is proffered so sweetly to the rest of us as the image of our individual histories as well. "Preparations," for Whitman, are the intelligible workings of a universal temporality of becoming, in which death amounts to nothing: "I keep no account with lamentation, / (What have I to do with lamentation?)" (*Leaves of Grass,* 1:71). Relax, Whitman says, time is a conservator, not a thief.

Yet here, as is so often the case in Whitman's poetry, a strongly expressed conviction or wish ("I keep no account with lamentation") is qualified by a parenthetical remark that antagonizes or subverts the preceding sentiment rather than simply reinforcing it. "I keep no account with lamentation" is actually a very good, if overly pithy, characterization of Whitman's elegism. In "Lilacs," for example, he eschews the narrative "account" of the object of mourning one finds in many traditional elegies. He "makes no reference," as his friend John Burroughs observed in an early review of *Drum-Taps,* "to the mere facts of Lincoln's death—neither describes it, or laments it, or dwells upon its unprovoked atrocity, or its political aspects." And he also dismisses as irrelevant the numerical accountancy of his era's more unimaginative and officious mourners. "Hence the piece," wrote Burroughs, "has little or none of the character of the usual productions on such occasions."[17] As Burroughs recognized, Whitman sought in "Lilacs" (as in many of his other elegiac poems) to find a way to distinguish the unrealized possibilities of American elegy from their cruder approximations and popular distortions. Better still, he sought to make preparation for unrealized possibilities a more-than-consolatory elegiac aim. He wants to be open to the dissonance of loss and to be prepared for the creative possibilities it affords.

The musical theory of counterpoint thus provides a useful gloss on preparation in Whitman. It would be esoteric were it not for Whitman's devotion to Beethoven, Verdi, and other composers who boldly experimented with dissonance configurations. In part-writing, preparation means anticipating and softening the impact of dissonance by letting the dissonant note be heard as consonant in the preceding chord. In poetry, dissonance may be generated through counterpoint between meter and rhythm, as in the final two lines of Jones Very's elegy for John Woolman:

> And countless reapers, with their sickles stand,
> Reaping what thou didst sow with single hand.[18]

The trochaic substitution at the beginning of the final line is dissonant in that it generates a sensation of roughness or tension between the rhythm of the word "reaping" and the iambic meter of the poem. The impact of this dissonance is anticipated and softened by the consonance of the similar word, "reapers," which, in the previous line, comports with, instead of resisting, the iambic meter. This effect is particularly lovely in an elegy for the Quaker abolitionist Woolman in that it preserves a sense of the ambiguousness of the figure of the reaper: an image of both prosaic (agricultural) and appalling violence (Death wielding his sickle; the suggestion of castration) transmuted into an image of spiritual in-gathering and transcendence.

Whitman's so-called free verse does not preclude counterpoint. On the contrary, counterpoint in the absence of conventional meter is one of his virtuoso effects, audible in many places throughout "Lilacs," including its first couple of lines. The poem immediately alerts us to one of its central themes: the fecundity of liminal spaces. "When lilacs last in the dooryard bloom'd" is a hypometric line of iambic pentameter with a single pyrrhic substitution and a masculine ending on the stressed syllable, "bloom'd," establishing the long "o" sound as a conjunct of ideas of vigor and efflorescence. The second line departs dramatically from the relatively sonorous, conventional rhythm of line 1 with an opening pyrrhic followed by three consecutive stressed syllables. The "drooping" of the second syllable of "early" phonically anticipates the meaning of the next word, "droop'd," in which the long "o" sound is brought into a thematically discordant relation with the "bloom" of the previous line. The rhythm of line 2 is fitful; it struggles audibly to lift itself above the level of the drooping star in its final eight syllables ("in the western sky in the night"), which may be characterized metrically as the sequence anapest-iamb-anapest. The "preparation" in line 1 for the dissonance effect of line 2 tensely associates (rather than merely opposing) the word-pair "bloom'd" and "droop'd"—an antithetical pairing further recuperated for harmonic effect within line 5 and linked explicitly in line 6 for the first time with the object of mourning:

> Lilac blooming perennial and drooping star in the west,
> And thought of him I love. (*Leaves of Grass*, 2:529)

Every elegy is a love poem. The conjunction of death and love is where Western poetry begins, and the conjunction of mourning and sexuality is one of the enduring, demanding features of psychic life. In the early twentieth century, Karl Abraham and Sigmund Freud both began to investigate what they observed to be one of the most unsettling, but also very commonly experienced, sequelae of grief: an increase in libido and a heightened sexual need. To speak of grief as unambiguously anerotic is a poor way of speaking. Thus, even so erudite and sophisticated a treatment of elegy as that of Peter Sacks, with its stipulation of deflection of desire in mourning, seems at once brilliant and unsatisfactory. Deflection (and sublimation) of the drives is endemic to mourning, of course. But to read such deflections as both normative and uncontested is to miss the staggering pathos of erotic liberation that the elegiac tradition has made available to us through aesthetic experience. This is a recognition that Whitman brought to "Lilacs," though it has been misrecognized or defensively denied in virtually all of the published criticism.

The "misunderstanding and misrepresentation" of Whitman's poetics, yet sustained in some quarters by generations of sexually normativistic interpretation, have been strongly and persuasively confronted most extensively by Michael Moon in *Disseminating Whitman*. Yet Moon, like Sacks before him (whose de-eroticizing interpretation of the poem Moon ventures to critique), refrains, as he acknowledges, from "mounting a full-scale reading of 'Lilacs.'" In his book as in Sacks's—despite its analysis of Whitman's crucial revaluation of sexuality and loss in

Leaves of Grass and its 1867 edition specifically—"Lilacs" serves as a kind of threshold. It is where Sacks and Moon both stand as they pause on their way out—out of analysis, out of comprehensive narrative, out of difficulties. For Moon, the difficulties are largely avowed. He seeks chiefly to assimilate "Lilacs" to the "ongoing erotic program" of the first four editions of *Leaves,* thereby overriding interpretations of the poem that emphasize what Sacks calls its "castrative work of mourning."[19] Highlighting the elegy's numerous erotic evocations, Moon asserts that rather than renouncing sexuality, Whitman "relaunches a self through a poetic congeries of defiles of signified desire through which he has launched his earlier models of the self in the earlier editions of his book."[20] The launching pad, so to speak, is the infant's experience of the holding environment of the mother, the rupture of which initiates the subject into sexuality, the release from which enables the subject to "loose" or disseminate its affectionate presence in the world. But the maternal figure also reasserts itself, in Moon's reading, as terminal destination. It is where death is finally lodged, foreclosing, as Moon puts it in his concluding remarks, "possibilities of further lines of critique—for example, into the misogynistic implications of 'lodging' death with maternity and femininity." Thus Moon's book ends not only by discontinuing his reading of "Lilacs" but also by suspending the animation of the relaunched, libidinous figure of the poet: "Rather than seeing Whitman as simply abandoning his radical project at this point in his career, as some critics have done, I would argue that he had in a sense completed that project. . . . [H]e felt in the aftermath of the Civil War that newly emergent political realities demanded quite different strategies and practices."[21]

I would like to urge on readers of "Lilacs" a keener interest both in projects yet to be accomplished, such as the retrospect on Lincoln that continues to occupy such a prominent place in his later writings, and also in Whitman's projections of himself into the objects that help shape his experience of mourning. These objects include the lilac, evening star, and hermit thrush most clearly consecrated by Whitman with his own subjectivity. But they extend beyond this highly symbolic trinity to a whole range of objects that arrive in the poem, by design or by chance, to constitute the experience of mourning and the character of the mourner. In the opening lines of an earlier poem, "There was a Child Went Forth" (1855), Whitman describes the beginnings of a relation to the world that embraces the mutual articulation of the subject and its multiplying array of invested objects:

> There was a child went forth every day,
> And the first object he look'd upon, that object he became,
> And that object became part of him for the day or a certain part of the day,
> Or for many years or stretching cycles of years.
> The early lilacs became part of this child . . .

Lilacs come first in the long catalog of objects that comprises the rest of the poem—before the "grass," before "the song of the phoebe bird," before the "mire of the pond-side" and "the light-yellow corn," before the schoolmistress and the boys and girls, before even "[h]is own parents," his mother's "mild words," his father's "blows," and the "family usages" that the poet carries with him to the "horizon's edge," wondering "if after all it should prove unreal" (*Leaves of Grass*, 1:149–52). The "early lilacs" stand in this poem as a kind of threshold through which the child passes into the day, into the world. They are a symbol of the child's taking up what D. W. Winnicott calls "the perpetual human task of keeping inner and outer reality separate yet interrelated."[22] The child's range of interest expands, but along with that expansion come doubts—"the doubts of day-time and the doubts of night-time"—as to the reality of the world to which he is adapting himself. He asks, "is it all flashes and specks?" (*Leaves of Grass*, 1:151). The child goes forth every day to discover not the truth of the world but the deepening mystery of his own experience.

To "go forth" in Whitman's idiom is to encounter, as freely as possible, those objects both internal and external that facilitate his provision for the future. The child goes forth, "and will go forth every day," in order to place himself in the world, so that he can be placed by it later on—so that he may call upon the world, as it were, to evoke him. The potential enrichment from such mutual evocations—the sense of a world abounding in significance and, moreover, available for reciprocal transformations—is the reason the child goes forth. At first he does so unapprehensively; later, with a growing awareness that easy faith in an established reality is the cost of these everyday ventures ("the sense of what is real, the thought if after all it should prove unreal" [*Leaves of Grass,* 1:151]). Not the progressive establishment of meaning but a promiscuous letting loose, a rich unraveling, is the epistemology of Whitman's poetics, which patently reveals itself in the series of rich unravelings that, through its successive editions, constitutes *Leaves of Grass.*

Of course, Whitman was perennially anxious about the coherence and integrity of *Leaves.* He revealed some of his wartime anxieties in a letter to William O'Connor in January 1865, a letter in which he offers his high opinion of the recently completed *Drum-Taps,* in part, by favoring it over *Leaves.* Whitman tells O'Connor that the new book is "superior to Leaves of Grass" and that, unlike the earlier work, it is free of "perturbations" and "verbal superfluity." *Drum-Taps,* Whitman insists, is "certainly more perfect as a work of art, being adjusted in all its proportions, & its passion having the indispensable merit that though to the ordinary reader let loose with wildest abandon, the true artist can see it is yet under control."[23] Whitman's splitting of his genially figured lumpen-reader (the "you whoever you are" so frequently addressed, from the 1855 poem that would be called "A Song for Occupations," to "The Eighteenth Presidency" of 1856, to "Proto-Leaf" and the Calamus and Enfans d'Adam clusters of 1860, to "The Dresser" in *Drum-Taps* itself, to the postwar *Democratic Vistas* and the 1872 and 1876 prefaces) into "ordinary reader" and "true artist" suggests his own discomfort with the sensations of self-division brought on by the war and with his ambivalence regarding the book's appeal, through the more conventional versification of some of its poems, to a wider "ordinary" readership.

Whitman wanted the book to succeed commercially, but he resisted O'Connor's advice to turn it over to an established publisher. On April 1, 1865, he contracted with New York printer Peter Eckler to stereotype five hundred copies.[24] Lincoln was assassinated before the sheets could all be printed and delivered to the binder, and Whitman took advantage of the opportunity to compose and insert his first Lincoln elegy, "Hush'd be the Camps To-Day." But that short poem was not enough on its own to satisfy his sense of what the book should now encompass. The assassination not only created a new occasion for the poetry of the war, to which Whitman wanted to respond more fully, but it also meant that *Drum-Taps* was not yet ready, as he had boasted to O'Connor, to "go to the world verbatim & punctuation." Now, to "go forth," the book had further to adapt itself to the latest disorienting loss. By the end of the year, the original sheets were bound together with their own testament of doubtful completion, the appended *Sequel to Drum-Taps,* which included two more Lincoln elegies: "O Captain! My Captain" and "When Lilacs Last in the Dooryard Bloom'd."

Among the notebook jottings Whitman made in the aftermath of the assassination—many of them eventually contributing to the composition of "Lilacs"—are descriptions of Brooklyn and Manhattan shortly after the news of Lincoln's death reached New York. He notes the blackness of the sky, "long broad black like great serpents slowly undulating in every direction"; the houses "festooned with black"; the "black clothed men"; the "horror, fever, uncertainty, alarm in the public"; the weather "sulky, leaden, & dripping continual[l]y moist tears" (*Notebooks*, 2:762–64). At one point in his passage up Broadway he observes, among all the closed shops and offices, a "large & fashionable picture store, all shuttered up close, except a broad square plate glass, in which hung a small grinning picture frame, vacuous of a picture" (*Notebooks*, 2:765). The impression is uncanny—Whitman seems to register this with the adjective "grinning"—as if the negative space, framed and seen through the second, larger frame of the window, were the rictus of a death's-head. "Vacuous" conjures an empty head as well as the empty frame. A death's-head would be literally empty, devoid of matter. Whitman may be feeling that his head, too, is, in the immediate aftermath of immeasurable loss, a space of idleness, devoid of meaningful thought and expression. One thinks of the plaint that opens section 11 of "Lilacs": "O what shall I hang on the chamber walls? / And what shall the pictures be that I hang on the walls, / To adorn the burial-house of him I love?" (*Leaves of Grass,* 2:533). That empty frame on Broadway seems to have struck Whitman, and stuck with him, as an emblem of ineffable grief. The scene at the window seems a powerful emblem, too, of the reflexive position of the elegist, setting out to fill the emptiness of the memorial frame with an adequate image not only of the departed but also of the mourner himself. Whitman may be catching his own reflection in the glass, superimposed over the space within the frame, though he does not say so.

Michael Moon has identified a fascination with frames as a hallmark of Whitman's poetics. Beginning with a reading of the early short story "The Child's Champion," Moon develops a theory of Whitmanian substitution:

> Inventing a story which incorporates one's self/body into a compelling "picture" bears obvious resemblances to the process I have described as being fundamental to the *Leaves of Grass* project, that of attempting to provide actual (male) physical presence in a text—while actually being able only to produce metonymic substitutes for such presence. A desire for phantasmatic passage into the liminal space of a picture, and a concern with the means by which one's body might be "translated" or incorporated into the medium of a (visual or literary) text, is central to both "The Child's Champion" and *Leaves of Grass*.[25]

The "liminal space" of the text doubles the limens to which Whitman keeps returning: the window, the mirror, the door frame, the surface of the body, the shoreline, the river's embouchure, sunrise or the close of day, the moment of parting, a grave, mouths, this minute. Each limen of each poem is a space in which there may be an opportunity to audition substitutes in what Joseph Roach calls "the doomed search for originals."[26] These "originals," from a psychoanalytic perspective, include the parental object choices that remain the unconscious goal of erotic pursuits, and behind them, so to speak, at their origin, the unconscious remembrance of the holding space of the maternal world and the "primary, archaic forms of the libido" that Jacques Lacan maintains always remain to be dreamed.[27] I take the limens in Whitman's poetics of substitution to be sites of longing for a referentiality that would somehow restore the subject to these points of departure. That is, they are sites both for regression and for creativity, for conservation and for protest.

If one learns anything from studying elegy, it is that the genre is laced with rage—that is, with the more or less distorted echo, turned toward the world's ear, of what is in the history of the mourning subject an ancient grievance over unfulfilled aspirations of erotic life. I have found no direct indication that Lacan ever read "When Lilacs Last in the Dooryard Bloom'd." But when, in his seminar, he comes to the topic of sublimation, he makes room for a very fine description of Whitman's pastoralism of the erogenous zones. Whitman, as what we might call the elegist of erotic life, becomes for Lacan an opportunity to

> imagine what as a man one might desire of one's own body. One might dream of a total, complete, epidermic contact between one's body and a world that was itself open and quivering; dream of a contact and, in the distance, of a way of life that the poet points out to us; hope for a revelation of harmony following the disappearance of the perpetual, insinuating presence of the oppressive feeling of some original curse.[28]

Emblematic of this "oppressive feeling" in Whitman's Civil War writings, from his notebook scrawls to "Lilacs" itself, is the "insinuating presence" of blackness, a presence such as that of the great black serpents he sees "undulating in every direction" in the sky above New York. Serpents are archetypal creatures of an "original curse," and their movement "in every direction" places their point of origin, the origin of their blackness, at the center of things. There, at the center of things—for Freud the source of instinctual life and thus the basis for Winnicott's "perpetual human task of keeping inner and outer reality separate yet interrelated"—is a profound antagonism. It is the antagonism between the energy of a binding instinct (which Freud called "Eros") and that of an undoing instinct (which Freud called "destructiveness" but which has come fittingly to be called "Thanatos"), living on and expressing itself in the instinctual history of the subject, its longings and frustrations, devotions and reprisals.

Mourning is the inevitable consequence of instinctual life. We are built to grieve. But griefs are not equal among us, just as we are so frequently unequal to our griefs. Mourning is a particular form of striving, and elegy is a very specialized form of mourning. Whitman's regard for this specialization—his acknowledgement of its traditionality, his participation in its received conventions—is to some extent the source of the strength of his ambition to bestow himself, as well as Lincoln, upon the genre's future. In referring to the future of elegy, I mean to evoke not only a prospect, from Whitman's time, of its continuing cultural transmission as a genre, but also the concepts of futurity that elegy, as a specialized form of striving within Whitman's culture, itself sustains. For many of Whitman's antecedents in the genre—that is, for the largely Protestant cohort of American elegists in whose historical company this book places him—the future was to be anticipated with religious patience. The future existed as a temporal mode of understanding the completion of divine intention. In the interim, the question, "What should the world be like?" mattered as the key to a differential technique of spiritual resolution. As the Calvinist eloquence promoting this technique faded from the world, the task of articulating the future through alternative narratives of becoming fell to more secular voices. To the question, "What should the world be like" was added the question, "How, in a post-Christian era, is the cultural burden of signifying the future to be borne?"

Lightly, it would seem, to the Whitman of "Chants Democratic" (1860), whose chipper response, in the poem that would come to be called "Song at Sunset," is to "sing to the last":

> I sing the endless finales of things,
> I say Nature continues—Glory continues,
> I praise with electric voice,
> For I do not see one imperfection in the universe,
> And I do not see one cause or result lamentable at last in the universe.
>   (*Leaves of Grass*, 2:304)

Here is no utopian vision of completed intention (heaven on earth), no assertion of a moral imperative (an obligation to generations to come), but rather a revelry of optimism. William James gently mocked this passage as indicative of a temperament "incapable of believing that anything seriously evil can exist."[29] Yet Whitman's apparent insistence upon the perpetuity of the good, here and in many other such moments of lyric exuberance, is not a statement of timeless ethical principles but the inscription of a mood. And that mood has less to do with a predisposition to ignore evil than with the anxious projection of contemporaneity. To see the future as an endless continuation of the present good is to postpone endlessly the reckoning of that good—to refuse the question, "What should the world be like, *now*?" But this is hardly Whitman's most characteristic mood. Submitting himself to a stance of openness as to what might come next, Whitman passes through various states of receptivity and defensiveness with unprecedented self-consciousness. He was not waiting to discover evil the day Lincoln was killed.

The morning after the assassination, Whitman and his mother, along with his brothers and their families, did their best to assimilate the news, reading the papers and extras as they came in. According to Whitman, little was eaten and little was said (*Prose Works*, 1:31). Later in the day, Whitman ventured forth from family life into civic space, crossing the East River and walking up Broadway in the rain, observing lower Manhattan's somber transformation:

> I had so often seen Broadway on great gala days, tumultuous overwhelming shows of pride & oceanic profusion of ornament[at]ion & deck'd with rich colors jubilant show crowds, & the music of a hundred bands with marches & opera airs—or at night with processions bearing countless torches & transparencies & gas lanterns covering the houses.
>
> The stores were shut, & no business transacted, no pleasure vehicles, & hardly a cart—only the rumbling base of the heavy Broadway stages incessantly rolling. (*Notebooks*, 2:764)

The journey from the Whitman home on North Portland Avenue in Brooklyn to the pleasures of Broadway recollected in this passage had been a frequent one for Whitman in the late 1850s and early 1860s. In the months leading up to the war—dispirited, strapped for cash, and wearied by the vexations of life in the Brooklyn household—he began spending time at Pfaff's, a Broadway beer cellar and rendezvous for bohemians like Henry Clapp, Fitz Hugh Ludlow, Adah Isaacs Menken, and Artemus Ward. He also continued to cruise the streets, parks, docks, and lumberyards of New York, and to spend countless hours ("forenoons and afternoons—how many exhilarating night-times") riding up and down Broadway with the "strange, natural, quick-eyed and wondrous race" of his beloved stage drivers (*Prose Works*, 1:18). By the early 1860s, Whitman was spending many hours, as well, at the bedsides of sick and injured drivers at the Broadway Hospital, where he first developed the medical expertise and rapport with the ill with which he would serve so many so well—first the drivers and, later, in the same hospital, sick soldiers passing through New York. By December 16, 1862—the day he set out for Washington to search for his brother George, who had appeared on the casualty lists—Whitman was well prepared to resume his nursing activities in the hospitals and hospital tents of the war, where he began more intensely to imagine what Robert Leigh Davis calls "the homosexual democracy of [his] postwar career."[30] Whitman looks ahead, in other words, from the reparative and affectional achievements of the hospitals to a future of new forms of solidarity.

Whitman's wartime experience found him moving, literally and figuratively, among the relativized solidarities of the Whitman household, of Pfaff's, of the streets and omnibuses, and of the hospitals. Going forth from the Whitmans' Brooklyn home, he trailed skeins of dependence that contrasted sharply with new urban modes of elective intimacy and also with the very different relations of dependence established between Whitman and the men of the hospitals. In these relations, and in the writing they helped to shape, Whitman significantly revised the nationalist, republican faith in paternal power he inherited from his own paternal line, the North American roots of which could be traced back to the early seventeenth century. His grandfather had fought in the American Revolution, and his father was born on the very day the French Revolution began. Walter Whitman Sr. named three of Walt's brothers for national patriarchs—Andrew Jackson Whitman, George Washington Whitman, and Thomas Jefferson Whitman—and he trained them all up to revere his hero, Tom Paine (who, like the Whitmans, was proud of his Quaker antecedents).

It was, ironically, a generations-long patrimony of democracy, dissent, and heresy from which Whitman, as he later put it, "radiated" (*Prose Works*, 1:5). But his father's alcoholism, financial failure, and early death (only days after the publication of the 1855 *Leaves*) heaped a burdensome load upon him as well, including a large, now fatherless family to support. It was partly to escape from the privations of that household setting that he so assiduously cultivated, first in New York and then in Washington, alternative identities of belonging. But in going forth Whitman also brought the psychic life of his family into civic space, where it remained in touch with his expanding and accumulating allegiances. Roy Morris Jr. suggests that in the wards of the Broadway Hospital, Whitman, "the son of an alcoholic," was particularly upset by the patients suffering from delirium tremens.[31] And in one of his many letters from Washington home to his mother, he told her of a young soldier from Tennessee named John Barker—"one of the most genuine union men & real patriots I have ever met"—who had impressed Whitman deeply and "somehow made me think often of father" (*Correspondence*, 1:147). For months prior to his transportation to Washington, Barker had clung fiercely to his patriotic principles as a prisoner in Georgia and Virginia, refusing to join the Confederacy, even though "his little property [was] destroyed, his wife & child turned out." The sacrifice that Barker had made—not only of his health and freedom, but also of his property and even the well-being of his family—may have reminded Whitman of his father's own sacrifices of health, property, and family in a very different context of patriotism.

Whitman was also absorbed, of course, by the figure of another sacrificer of sons, Abraham Lincoln—Father Abraham as he was commonly called, both out of respect for the political symbol of paternal power and in fear of the sacrifices he was willing to make to preserve the patriarchal order of a unified nation. Lincoln's terrible burden was to lead millions of Isaacs to the war's Mount Moriah. Prepared to sacrifice the sons he had improbably acquired, devoting them to a future so many of them would not live to possess, Lincoln's conduct signified for Whitman the utmost possibilities and trials of secular faith. How that faith would be defined, and how sustained, were for Whitman questions indissolubly bound to his own improbable acquisition of sons and lovers—to his own experience of the torment of a passionate father's suffering, in the absence of any overriding illusions about the consolatory power of stringently anerotic Christian frameworks of mourning. He brought to the composition of "Lilacs" an Isaac-like wonder at the father's fear and trembling and an Abraham-like tenacity for that which he was at the same time only too ready to relinquish—not simply his son but his own ineluctably worldly prospect on the reanimation of desire.

"Lilacs" is the story of a secret culture of desire. But the aim of its secrecy is the release, rather than the evasion, of an unmastered expressivity. My aim in the reading that follows is to anatomize that secret culture and to interpret the carefully plotted story of its creative elaboration in a way that will not reinscribe the defeat of the erotic subject of mourning—a defeat commemorated in so many other readings of the poem. Helen Vendler, for example, in what is perhaps the most inflexibly anerotic reading of "Lilacs," insists that the "'plot' of the elegy is a long resistance on Whitman's part to the experience of the swamp."[32] But without the normative presumption of progressive deeroticization in mourning, what looks like resistance or evasion can be recognized more clearly as a practice of generative engagement. Whitman lingers upon the experiential threshold of the swamp not as the thrall of traumatic repetition but in order to equip himself for a more creative dreamlike movement. Vendler herself eloquently observes that "nothing is more touching in the poem than the reprise in it of Whitman's earlier work."[33] But I take this to mean, in a way that Vendler does not intend, something other than the mere recurrence of symbolic elements from earlier poems, such as the "early lilacs" from "There was a Child Went Forth." Instead, Whitman's poetics of reprise resembles more closely what Christopher Bollas describes as the "evasion of organized consciousness" that enables unconscious symbolic elaboration through a structure he names "psychic genera."[34] Genera, like trauma (its opposite), begins with the ego's acquired disposition toward the actual world. We learn from our early experiences how to fashion a psychic reality:

> trauma-developed psychic processes will be conservative, fundamentally aiming to control the psychic damage, desensitizing the self to further toxic events. . . . The child who internalizes fundamentally generative parents—who contribute to the evolution of his personal idiom—aims to develop such inner processes and to seek excitation and novelty as means of triggering personal growth. As such, genera link up with the life instincts which aggressively seek the procreative combinings of self with object.[35]

We need not be, like Bollas, psychoanalysts with our patients to experience our own unconscious associations elaborating the discourse of another. And we need not be, as readers, overly concerned with pinpointing our early experiences, or the poet's, as authentic sources of our discoveries about a poem. No descent into the psychology of the creative individual is recommended here. Instead, I am concerned with how in Whitman's elegy the mediation of intersubjective fantasies occurs in and through the object of mourning. I want to stipulate, with the clarifying assistance Bollas provides, that the experience of mourning as figured in "Lilacs" is a genera-developed as well as trauma-developed psychic process, neither exclusively conservative nor purely creative. Thus, the elegy involves both a submission of grief to a transformation by decorum and an apprehension of grief as an incentive to promiscuous achievements of combination.

I have already observed that the opening of "Lilacs" establishes liminal spaces as generative, while also submitting, initially, to the rhythmic decorum of the iambic pentameter line. The rhythm breaks loose in line 2 and initiates the counterpoint through which the vigor of blooming and the impotence of drooping are conjoined as symbolic adjuncts to the objectivizing trope of "thought":

1
When lilacs last in the dooryard bloom'd,
And the great star early droop'd in the western sky in the night,
I mourn'd, and yet shall mourn with ever-returning spring.

Ever-returning spring, trinity sure to me you bring,
Lilac blooming perennial and drooping star in the west,
And thought of him I love.

2
O powerful western fallen star!
O shades of night—O moody, tearful night!
O great star disappear'd—O the black murk that hides the star!
O cruel hands that hold me powerless—O helpless soul of me!
O harsh surrounding cloud that will not free my soul.
(Leaves of Grass, 2:529)

Eschewing the familiar metrical composure of the English poetic line, "indelibly stained," in Allen Grossman's vivid formulation, "by the feudal contexts of its most prestigious instances,"[36] Whitman nevertheless predicts a future of mourning that will be heroic in its faithfulness: "I mourn'd, and yet shall mourn with ever-returning spring." Yet the tonal balance of retrospect and prospect in section 1 is short-lived, yielding, in section 2, to a performance of the agonizing and constrained vigilance of sleepless, unending nights of mourning. The histrionic grief of section 2 is converted, behind night's "black murk," into a life sentence: "O cruel hands that hold me powerless—O helpless soul of me! / O harsh surrounding cloud that will not free my soul." The exaggerated emotionality of this section of the poem stages a common dynamic in Whitman's poetry: he becomes overwhelmed by the very stimulation he seeks. While he welcomes, in section 1, the reappearance of the beloved in the recurrent springtime trinity of mourning, the poet finds, in section 2, that the "thought of him I love" is the source of a distress that accompanies but is not equivalent to grief. His fear of the "black murk" and the "harsh surrounding cloud" is, in part, a displaced fear of the beloved's specifically sexualized power. All of the critical giggling that has gone on in reaction to Harold Bloom's perfectly reasonable suggestion that, in section 2, "a failed masturbation is the concealed reference" is just so much unreasonable embarrassment at the unspoken inference that Lincoln may be the object of, rather than the obstacle to, the poet's erotic fantasy.[37]

The other fearful dimension in section 2 has to do with the impression of a more general alarm at the possibility that fantasies taken for memories might—in the manner of the "black murk that hides the star"—occlude, rather than sustain, their treasured objects. Thus, section 3 begins by cleansing this image of what Whitman refers to elsewhere in *Sequel to Drum-Taps* as a "soil'd world" (*Leaves of Grass,* 2:556), reverting (it would not be inappropriate to say regressing) to the pastoralized landscape of childhood (viz. "There was a Child Went Forth"), circumscribed not by "black murk" but by "whitewash'd palings," and animated by one of the chief symbolic conventions of pastoral elegy, the plucking of a flower:

> 3
> In the dooryard fronting an old farm-house near the white-wash'd
>   palings,
> Stands the lilac-bush tall-growing with heart-shaped leaves of rich green,
> With many a pointed blossom rising delicate, with the perfume strong
>   I love,
> With every leaf a miracle—and from this bush in the dooryard,
> With delicate-color'd blossoms and heart-shaped leaves of green,
> A sprig with its flower I break. (*Leaves of Grass,* 2:529–30)

Hyphenated compound words are one of Whitman's linguistic fortes, commonly found throughout his poetry. But the fact that this scene of rupture contains more of them than any other section of "Lilacs" except section 14 (which is nine times as long) seems specially intended to announce the choreography of division and union that will characterize the rest of the poem as well. Michael Moon has demonstrated, through his interpretive collation of editions one through four of *Leaves of Grass,* Whitman's "intensified awareness . . . of the insuperable difficulty of simply overruling division and difference."[38] Here, at the opening of his elegy, Whitman asserts the reparative aspiration of his poetics—his need to dress the wounds and visibly heal the breaches to which elegiac tradition helps alert him.

These conventional wounds are displayed vividly and with rich allusiveness in section 4, where Whitman nods once again to the strict metrical tradition he disavows through an oblique reference to Philomela in his description of the singing thrush—Whitman's emanation of the lyric figure of the elegist:

> 4
> In the swamp in secluded recesses,
> A shy and hidden bird is warbling a song.
>
> Solitary the thrush,
> The hermit withdrawn to himself, avoiding the settlements,
> Sings by himself a song.
>
> Song of the bleeding throat,
> Death's outlet song of life, (for well dear brother I know,
> If thou wast not granted to sing thou would'st surely die.)
> (*Leaves of Grass,* 5:530)

This self-reflexive observation ("well dear brother I know") on intense expressive urgency implies that for the poet, as well as for the thrush, survival requires not just a voice but also a way of using that voice, a way of singing that can transmute the danger of suppressed grief into structured performance. Yet these lines hide the agency of that transmutation. Who or what "grants" the thrush to sing? The passive construction ("If thou wast not granted") seems to confirm an innate capacity (the thrush is a songbird, it is in its nature to sing) in which the poet recognizes his own vocation. But it is the poet's interpellation by poetic tradition that enables that recognition in the first place. The poet knows the thrush needs to sing because he has been trained by other poets to hear in the voice of the North American songbird an indigenous version of the ostensibly melancholy utterance of its European counterpart, the nightingale, which substitutes for the unutterable grief of the mutilated Philomela. Whitman was probably familiar with Coleridge's rejection of this culturally transmitted figure of natural melancholy in his poem "The Nightingale":

> A melancholy Bird? O idle thought!
> In nature there is nothing melancholy.
> —But some night-wandering Man, whose heart was pierc'd
> With the remembrance of a grievous wrong,
> Or slow distemper of neglected love,
> (And so, poor Wretch! fill'd all things with himself
> And made all gentle sound tell back the tale
> Of his own sorrows) he and such as he
> First nam'd these notes a melancholy strain:
> And many a poet echoes the conceit.[39]

Whitman neither merely "echoes the conceit" nor fully renounces his resemblance to the "night-wandering Man." Instead, he parenthetically (which in Whitman almost always means aggressively) asserts his knowledge of an authentic melancholy in nature even as he announces his effort to account as fully as possible for his own melancholy—and possibly "profane," in Coleridge's sense—acquiescence in the formal elegiac tradition he has chosen to engage. Moreover, as he will demonstrate later in the poem, the benediction that Coleridge bestows upon his infant son Hartley at the end of "The Nightingale"—"that with the night / He may associate Joy!"—has, as it were, descended upon Whitman as well.[40]

The poem's internal account of Whitman's relation to elegiac tradition continues in section 5 with an impressively hieratic interruption or postponement of the thrush's song—a postponement effected by a shift of focus to the American landscape and, by section 6, to a new articulation of the dynamics of voice. In the single, long, periodic sentence that constitutes section 5, the landscape's salient feature—the coffin that moves through it—seems buoyed by the poet's voice, positively lifted syntactically by the lovely descriptive periods that precede its appearance. When it does at length appear, at the very end of the sentence, it does so as something whose movements are as unencumbered as those of the "violets" and "yellow-spear'd wheat" that are its heralds. As the coffin continues, in section 6, to pass "through lanes and streets, / Through day and night," the murk and darkness of section 2 seem to reassert themselves weakly in the conventional trappings of mourning custom: "the cities draped in black" and "the show of the States themselves as of crape-veil'd women standing."

> 5
> Over the breast of the spring, the land, amid cities,
> Amid lanes and through old woods, where lately the violets peep'd from
>   the ground, spotting the gray debris,
> Amid the grass in the fields each side of the lanes, passing the endless
>   grass,
> Passing the yellow-spear'd wheat, every grain from its shroud in the dark-
>   brown fields uprisen,
> Passing the apple-tree blows of white and pink in the orchards,
> Carrying a corpse to where it shall rest in the grave,
> Night and day journeys a coffin.

> 6
> Coffin that passes through lanes and streets,
> Through day and night with the great cloud darkening the land,
> With the pomp of the inloop'd flags with their cities draped in black,
> With the show of the States themselves as of crape-veil'd women standing,
> With procession long and winding and the flambeaus of the night,
> With the countless torches lit, with the silent sea of faces and the unbared
>   heads,
> With the waiting depot, the arriving coffin, and the somber faces,
> With dirges through the night, with the thousand voices rising strong and
>   solemn,
> With all the mournful voices of the dirges pour'd around the coffin,
> The dim-lit churches and the shuddering organs—where amid these you
>   journey,
> With the tolling bells' perpetual clang,
> Here, coffin that slowly passes,
> I give you my sprig of lilac. (*Leaves of Grass*, 2:530–31)

Amid the blackness that descends—descends now into the specifically ritual elements of the poem's occasion—the poet's terrible private protest of pain in section 2 is displaced by the collective voices of the mourners who line the route of the journeying coffin: "the thousand voices rising strong and solemn . . . the mournful voices of the dirges pour'd around the coffin." The ebb and flow of mourning voices, "rising" and "pouring" like powerful tides, are Whitman's naturalistic image of the nationalization of individual mourners in these compounded scenes of local mourning. Amid this ebb and flow, the poet signals his presence in the scene not as a voice but as a gesture: "I give you my sprig of lilac."

Section 7 exposes the tension between objectification and occultation in Whitman's relation to Lincoln's coffin, his object of address, as its function shifts from that of a metonymy for Lincoln, at the end of section 6, to that of a synecdoche for "coffins all." For with this shift in the object of mourning comes a reassertion of the poet's voice, wresting itself away from the rising and pouring voices of the massed mourners of section 6, and supplementing the silent or phatic gesture of giving the sprig of lilac—itself a symbol of violence transmogrified into a traditional and consoling aesthetic. The parenthetical enclosure of section 7 marks grammatically as digression what is also a passage of compounded aggression:

> 7
> (Not for you, for one alone,
> Blossoms and branches green to coffins all I bring,
> For fresh as the morning, thus would I chant a song for you O sane and
>   sacred death.
>
> All over bouquets of roses,
> O death, I cover you over with roses and early lilies,
> But mostly and now the lilac that blooms the first,
> Copious I break, I break the sprigs from the bushes,
> With loaded arms I come, pouring for you,
> For you and the coffins all of you O death.) (*Leaves of Grass*, 2:531–32)

First, the poet rescinds the offering to Lincoln ("Not for you") made in the concluding line of section 6. In its generalization of the object of mourning—from "one alone" to "coffins all"—the passage turns from paying tribute to the slain president to an aggrandizement of the poet as the agent or emissary of all mourning—performer of "copious" and continuous breakings of the symbolic bloom, loading not "coffins" nor even "death" so much as himself with the broken sprigs as tokens of his own expressive power. In its more than generalizing abstraction of the object of attention and praise from Lincoln to death itself, the passage also wills a generic break from elegy to ode. "I am no longer content with my role," the poet seems to say. "Not only will I forgo the role of the moribund memorialist, who subordinates himself to the sham vivacity of the dead, but I'll also refuse to channel social sympathy among my fellow mourners along conventional lines. I admire not the dead, but Death, so that's what I'll trope into life!"

Yet even before section 7 concludes, we start to see signs of just how difficult such aspirations will be to sustain for a poet who desires so strongly to experience in solitude the triumph of eroticized communion. "With loaded arms I come," he announces, "pouring for you, / For you and the coffins all of you O death." "Pouring" takes no definitive object here; it could be the "sprigs from the bushes" or the poet himself if "pouring" is to be read intransitively. But it does take an object in the previous section of the poem: the "dirges pour'd around the coffin" by the pooled, nationalized voices of Whitman's fellow mourners. Whitman, as it were, pours himself back, syntactically, into that pool of voices—of voices figured as dirges or even as tears—from which he has just seemed to enact his differentiation.[41]

Through the poem's many voicings, Whitman projects his fantasy of a collective aspiration to share a singular experience of mourning so as to tame and unify the wild, riven subjectivities of the traumatized, the suspicious, the detached, and the resigned. But he also remains alert to the possibility that a superabundance of conviction in the ability to speak for others might actually weaken his power to do so. This alertness is one of the things that helps inform his choice of a "participation without belonging" in the tradition of pastoral elegy. It also keeps before us the image of a desiring personality, tense and exhausted with longing, as in the hypomanic self-assertiveness of section 7 and in the lover's wistful retrospect in section 8:

8

O western orb sailing the heaven,
Now I know what you must have meant as a month since I walk'd,
As I walk'd in silence the transparent shadowy night,
As I saw you had something to tell as you bent to me night after night,
As you droop'd from the sky low down as if to my side, (while the other
    stars all look'd on,)
As we wander'd together the solemn night, (for something I know not
    what kept me from sleep,)
As the night advanced, and I saw on the rim of the west how full you
    were of woe,
As I stood on the rising ground in the breeze in the cool transparent night,
As I watch'd where you pass'd and was lost in the netherward black of the
    night,
As my soul in its trouble dissatisfied sank, as where you sad orb,
Concluded, dropt in the night, and was gone. (*Leaves of Grass,* 2:532)

The intimate colloquy recalled here is reminiscent of some of Whitman's oblique encounters with Lincoln, as recorded in *Specimen Days* and elsewhere—encounters of vividly remembered glances and cherished wishes. One thinks not only of those savored, occasional glimpses of Lincoln himself but also of Whitman's moodier sketch of "The White House by Moonlight," dated February 24, 1864. No orb, not even the "western orb" of Venus in "Lilacs," ever received from him such dazzling treatment as does the moon here in its splendent diffusion:

A spell of fine soft weather. I wander about a good deal, sometimes at night under the moon. To-night take a long look at the President's house. The white portico—the palace-like, tall, round columns, spotless as snow—the walls also—the tender and soft moonlight, flooding the pale marble, and making peculiar faint languishing shades, not shadows—everywhere a soft transparent hazy, thin, blue moon-lace, hanging in the air—the brilliant and extra-plentiful clusters of gas, on and around the façade, columns, portico, &c.—everything so white, so marbly pure and dazzling, yet soft—the White House of future poems, and of dreams and dramas, there in the soft and copious moon—the gorgeous front, in the trees, under the lustrous flooding moon, full of reality, full of illusion—the forms of the trees, leafless, silent, in trunk and myriad-angles of branches, under the stars and sky—the White House of the land, and of beauty and night—sentries at the gates, and by the portico, silent, pacing there in blue overcoats—stopping you not at all, but eyeing you with sharp eyes, whichever way you move. (*Prose Works,* 1:40–41)

It is as if the White House itself were an effect of moonlight, made of moonlight—not the newly repainted and respectable White House of Matthew Brady's 1861 photograph but an otherworldly White House "of future poems, and of dreams and dramas." It is a trysting place for sublunar romance, where Whitman goes to think about the president and the aura that surrounds him, a place of possibility where even the uniformed armed guards evoke the cruising glances of "To a Stranger."

In section 8 of "Lilacs," Whitman revisits his earlier nightwalking self and a scene of missed understanding not only in self-recrimination for wrongly interpreting a portentous sign but also in an effort to preserve the sense of lost erotic opportunity: the signal not picked up on ("Now I know what you must have meant"), the singular companionship of the bright planet that "droop'd from the sky low down as if to my side," the troubled premonition doubling as unrecognized erotic excitation ("something I know not what kept me from sleep"), and, finally, the dissatisfactions and identifications associated with departure ("As my soul in its trouble dissatisfied sank, as where you sad orb, / Concluded, dropt in the night, and was gone").

"Concluded," as a term for the sad orb's departure, suggests at once rhetorical alignment (the orb concludes like the poet's single sentence comprising section 8) and consensus (they have reached an understanding). It further suggests the encompassing figure of planetary orbit. The orb drops off the horizon, to return again and again in its orderly revolutions. Its orbit describes a kind of hortus conclusus, a cosmic pastoral enclosure of the world, in which the poet's thoughts now naturally return, in section 9, to the tryst that awaits him in the swamp:

> 9
> Sing on there in the swamp,
> O singer bashful and tender, I hear your notes, I hear your call,
> I hear, I come presently, I understand you,
> But a moment I linger, for the lustrous star has detain'd me,
> The star my departing comrade holds and detains me. (*Leaves of Grass,*
> 2:532)

The poet returns in this section to detailing his protracted approach to the swamp, the lyric center of the poem, not as a series of eruptions of phobic resistance but as the appreciative pauses of a cultivated temperament slowly relinquishing itself to a more refined and therefore uncertain knowledge of his relation to the world. On the way, epistemological apprehensiveness keeps pace with the domestication of wildness. "Bring your sills up to the very edge of the swamp," Thoreau exhorts in his essay on "Walking," published just a few years before "Lilacs."[42] Whitman complies, starting at the farmhouse dooryard in section 1 and pushing its threshold slowly and self-consciously toward the edge of the swamp. In sections 9 and 13, he performs the spells or interludes of detainment—allowing himself to be held back by the "lustrous star" (*Leaves of Grass*, 2:532) and the "mastering odor" of the lilac (*Leaves of Grass*, 2:534)—that enable the further enrichment of his secret culture of desire. Loss—the legacy of uncertainty so lavishly bestowed upon us by loss—is, paradoxically, the source of this enrichment. "What we come to know," writes Bollas,

> as we mature into more sophisticated creatures is that we add new psychic structures that make us more complex, increase our capacity for the dream work of life, and therefore problematize the sense we have of an established reality, a world of psychically meaningful convention, available to us for our adaptation. As we age we know that our destiny is a rather paradoxical psychobiological unraveling.[43]

This unraveling process helps to unshroud and to challenge the cognitive and representational powers exercised with increasing confidence in the second half of the poem. Cognitive power takes the form of psychological tropes of mastery: understanding, thought, knowledge. Representational power takes the form, in sections 10 through 12, of a self-colloquy on how to write an elegy and on how to reevaluate the poet's status as one mourner among many:

10

O how shall I warble myself for the dead one there I loved?
And how shall I deck my song for the large sweet soul that has gone?
And what shall my perfume be for the grave of him I love?

Sea-winds blown from east and west,
Blown from the Eastern sea and blown from the Western sea, till there on the prairies meeting,

These and with these and the breath of my chant,
I'll perfume the grave of him I love.

   11
O what shall I hang on the chamber walls?
And what shall the pictures be that I hang on the walls,
To adorn the burial-house of him I love?

Pictures of growing spring and farms and homes,
With the Fourth-month eve at sundown, and the gray smoke lucid and
   bright,
With floods of the yellow gold of the gorgeous, indolent, sinking sun,
   burning, expanding the air,
With the fresh sweet herbage under foot, and the pale green leaves of the
   trees prolific,
In the distance the flowing glaze, the breast of the river, with a wind-
   dapple here and there,
With ranging hills on the banks, with many a line against the sky, and
   shadows,
And the city at hand with dwellings so dense, and stacks of chimneys,
And all the scenes of life and the workshops, and the workmen homeward
   returning.

   12
Lo, body and soul—this land,
My own Manhattan with spires, and the sparkling and hurrying tides,
   and the ships,
The varied and ample land, the South and the North in the light, Ohio's
   shores and flashing Missouri,
And ever the far-spreading prairies cover'd with grass and corn.

Lo, the most excellent sun so calm and haughty,
The violet and purple morn with just-felt breezes,
The gentle soft-born measureless light,
The miracle spreading bathing all, the fulfill'd noon,
The coming eve delicious, the welcome night and the stars,
Over my cities shining all, enveloping man and land. (*Leaves of Grass,*
   2:533–34)

Beginning with the question, "How shall I warble myself for the dead
one there I loved?" Whitman suggests that he will continue to identify
with the thrush through poetic competition. "Warble," for instance, is

not only an image of voice that emphasizes artifice and stylized performance. It is also, of course, a distinctly avian image of voice—and the warbler, it could be argued, is a far more characteristically North American family of birds than the thrush.[44] The placement of the pronoun "myself" speaks to the reflexiveness of mourning song, for it implies both the poet's subjective voice as an elegist ("How shall I do my warbling?") and his characteristic role as self-warbler ("How shall I warble myself, as well as Lincoln, into my song?").

The extended answer to the question, in sections 10 through 12, is redolent with conviction in the consolatory power of a specifically American landscape and with confidence, enabled by the reprise of earlier works, in the poet's ability to picture scenes of farm and forest, ship and workshop, prairie and ocean. Transcontinental gusts are literally his inspiration, and images of western prairies, of the commerce and industry of cities, and of the amplitude of states and rivers that give each other their names suggest to Whitman a comprehensive response to loss that he is more than capable of figuring. The fluency of cadences of memory also enables the newly energized solicitation of the thrush in section 13:

13
Sing on, sing on you gray-brown bird,
Sing from the swamps, the recesses, pour your chant from the bushes,
Limitless out of the dusk, out of the cedars and pines.

Sing on dearest brother, warble your reedy song,
Loud human song, with voice of uttermost woe.

O liquid and free and tender!
O wild and loose to my soul—O wondrous singer!
You only I hear—yet the star holds me, (but will soon depart,)
Yet the lilac with mastering odor holds me. (*Leaves of Grass*, 2:534)

The beautiful dalliance of unloosed impulse here—the pull exerted on the solitary thrush to "pour" forth his song, the pleasure of identification ("dearest brother"), the paradoxical rhythmic enthusiasm of the "voice of uttermost woe," indeed the transformation of histrionic "woe" into the exclamatory and delighted "O"s of praise, the flirtations and devotions—anticipates the consolidation of the poet's secret culture of desire in the final three sections of the elegy, beginning with the prelude to the thrush's song in section 14:

14
Now while I sat in the day and look'd forth,
In the close of the day with its lights and the fields of spring, and the farmers preparing their crops,
In the large unconscious scenery of my land with its lakes and forests,
In the heavenly aerial beauty, (after the perturb'd winds and the storms,)
Under the arching heavens of the afternoon swift passing, and the voices of children and women,
The many-moving sea-tides, and I saw the ships how they sail'd,
And the summer approaching with richness, and the fields all busy with labor,
And the infinite separate houses, how they all went on, each with its meals and minutia of daily usages,
And the streets how their throbbings throbb'd, and the cities pent—lo, then and there,
Falling upon them all and among them all, enveloping me with the rest,
Appear'd the cloud, appear'd the long black trail,
And I knew death, its thought, and the sacred knowledge of death.

Then with the knowledge of death as walking one side of me,
And the thought of death close-walking the other side of me,
And I in the middle as with companions, and as holding the hands of companions,
I fled forth to the hiding receiving night that talks not,
Down to the shores of the water, the path by the swamp in the dimness,
To the solemn shadowy cedars and ghostly pines so still.

And the singer so shy to the rest receiv'd me,
The gray-brown bird I know receiv'd us comrades three,
And he sang the carol of death, and a verse for him I love.

From the deep secluded recesses,
From the fragrant cedars and the ghostly pines so still,
Came the carol of the bird.

And the charm of the carol rapt me,
As I held as if by their hands my comrades in the night,
And the voice of my spirit tallied the song of the bird. (*Leaves of Grass,* 2:535–36)

The envelopment of loss, which descends once again in the form of a black cloud, now seems to bear a sense of social force, the reassurance of an available experience of commonality that the poet figures as a loving companionship of three.

When commentators inquire into the nature of these companions, they generally engage in a slightly irritating appeal to the flatly conceptual: for example, thought of death is "loss," knowledge of death is "process";[45] or the division of thought and knowledge is the antagonism of "experience" and "understanding";[46] or the poet mediates "between the general knowledge and the particular thought, the point at which Aristotle speculates that poetry originates."[47] But none of these is Whitman's "thought" or Whitman's "knowledge." Indeed, *knowledge* is a relatively rare word in Whitman, and when it does appear, it tends to be expressive of organic sensation ("My knowledge my live parts" [*Leaves of Grass,* 1:36]), satisfaction with immediacy ("knowledge, not in another place but this place, not for another hour but this hour" [1:97]) and with the embodied self ("The full-spread pride of man is calming and excellent to the soul, / Knowledge becomes him, he likes it always, he brings everything to the test of himself" [1:127]). The claim to "know" most frequently operates as a kind of epistemological come-on ("Knowing the perfect fitness and equanimity of things, while they discuss I am silent, and go bathe and admire myself" [1:4]) or sly flirtation with the reader ("I am the mate and companion of people, all just as immortal and fathomless as myself, / (They do not know how immortal, but I know)" [1:8]). Thoughtfulness, too, typically characterizes the opportunism of desire ("This moment yearning and thoughtful sitting alone, / It seems to me there are other men in other lands yearning and thoughtful" [2:393]) and the dream of contact ("And that my soul embraces you this hour, and we affect each other without ever seeing each other, and never perhaps to see each other, is every bit as wonderful. / And that I can think such thoughts as these is just as wonderful, / And that I can remind you, and you think them and know them to be true, is just as wonderful" [1:154]). In "Lilacs," the figure of the poet hastening into the swamp is a figure for whom the generative possibilities of loss have taken fresh hold of his imagination.

Of course, the oxymoronic quality of "fled forth" is a sign that apprehensiveness has been freshly accommodated rather than over-ruled. Nevertheless, his new companionship with the "thought of death" and the "knowledge of death" precipitates his entrance into the swamp, where the shyness of the thrush (a figure of inhibited desire) is overcome, finally, to the point of audibility and intelligibility in the poet's tallying voice. To tally is to mark as well as to correspond, and the material sense of marking is reinforced by Whitman's later decision to italicize the words of the thrush's song, which were not italicized in its initial publication in *Sequel to Drum-Taps*. Yet, rather than show-casing the thrush's song as the chief distillation of the poet's elegiac ambitions, the italicization helps us to see it as the least essential, most decorative part of the poem, a floated carol truly:

Come lovely and soothing death,
Undulate round the world, serenely arriving, arriving,
In the day, in the night, to all, to each,
Sooner or later delicate death.

Prais'd be the fathomless universe,
For life and joy, and for objects and knowledge curious,
And for love, sweet love—but praise! praise! praise!
For the sure-enwinding arms of cool-enfolding death.

Dark mother always gliding near with soft feet,
Have none chanted for thee a chant of fullest welcome?
Then I chant it for thee, I glorify thee above all,
I bring thee a song that when thou must indeed come, come unfalteringly.

Approach strong deliveress,
When it is so, when thou hast taken them I joyously sing the dead,
Lost in the loving floating ocean of thee,
Laved in the flood of thy bliss O death.

From me to thee glad serenades,
Dances for thee I propose saluting thee, adornments and feastings for thee,
And the sights of the open landscape and the high-spread sky are fitting,
And life and the fields, and the huge and thoughtful night.

The night in silence under many a star,
The ocean shore and the husky whispering wave whose voice I know,
And the soul turning to thee O vast and well-veil'd death,
And the body gratefully nestling close to thee.

Over the tree-tops I float thee a song,
Over the rising and sinking waves, over the myriad fields and the prairies
  wide,
Over the dense-pack'd cities all and the teeming wharves and ways,
I float this carol with joy, with joy to thee O death. (Leaves of Grass,
  2:536–37)

With so much left to say, is it reasonable to think that the poet would content himself with the passing chirp of a bird? Kerry Larson is right to observe that in itself "the song of the hermit thrush is largely unremarkable, being for the most part a reworking of material handled with more dramatic urgency in the *Sea-Drift* cycle."[48] It is the same urgency that Michael Moon suggests is resolved in "Lilacs" at the expense of a misogynistic lodging of death "with maternity and femininity"—with the "dark mother" and "strong deliveress." But this is not where maternal influence ends in the poem. It ends, not with death, but with dreaming.

Whitman does not fall asleep in the concluding sections of "Lilacs." Indeed, he is at pains to differentiate his visionary state from actual dreaming through the assertion of analogy ("I saw as in noiseless dreams"). Why is it that the recollection and interpretation of the experience of loss are figured finally as being akin to the experience of dreaming? Part of the answer lies in those "primary, archaic forms of the libido" that always remain to be dreamed, in the unconscious remembrance of the holding space of the maternal world. "To be in a dream," Bollas writes,

> is thus a continuous reminiscence of being inside the maternal world when one was partly a receptive figure within a comprehending environment. Indeed, the productive intentionality that determines the dream we are in and that never reveals itself (i.e. "where is the dreamer that dreams the dream?") uncannily re-creates, in my view, the infant's relation to the mother's unconscious, which although it does not "show itself," nonetheless produces the process of maternal care. In this respect the dream seems to be a structural memory of the infant's unconscious, an object relation of person inside the other's unconscious processing, revived in the continuous representation of the infantile moment every night.[49]

Thus, we all flee forth to "the hiding receiving night," which is Whitman's image for the holding environment of the dream, compassionately encompassing, protectively absorbing. But if indeed the dream is "a structural memory of the infant's unconscious," then it is also a return to the site of the first appearance of the matricidal drive, of the first sensation of the need to lose the mother, of the consequent eroticization of that loss, and thus of the self's dissemination as an affectionate, creative presence in the world. To flee forth to "the hiding receiving night" is to relinquish oneself to a fundamental ambivalence regarding the achievement of that presence and the perpetual rediscovery of that presence in the world's multiplying array of invested objects—objects, all of them, subject to loss. The figure of the dream in "Lilacs" is the sign of that willing relinquishment, transformed through the experience of loss into the acceptance of new love, the anticipation of new power.

Dreams open outward as well as inward; they reveal social as well as psychological imperatives. In Whitman, dream motifs are redolent of privacy, the isolation of sleep, and the inscrutability of unconscious knowledge. Yet they are also charged with the expressive power of what, in "The Wound-Dresser," he twice calls "dreams' projections," that is, projects of the waking mind as well as retrievable artifacts of the psyche ("retrievements out of the night," in "Lilacs") that can be shared and that may in fact help facilitate new kinds of intersubjective relationships. Sleeping and dreaming are pervasive motifs in Whitman in part because they are universally experienced states that help him limn the contours of an ideal world in which social and even somatic differences (such as race and gender) continue to exist and to signify, but in which they no longer threaten survival (for example, in the forms of misogyny and racism). "The diverse shall be no less diverse," he maintains in "The Sleepers," but

> The laugher and weeper, the dancer, the midnight widow, the red squaw,
> The consumptive, the erysipalite, the idiot, he that is wrong'd,
> The antipodes, and every one between this and then in the dark,
> I swear they are averaged now—one is no better than the other,
> The night and sleep have liken'd them and restored them. (*Leaves of Grass*, 1:118)

Whitman's paring away of somatic difference in his portraits of the sleepers suggests a break or discontinuity with the confinements and privations of social life, even as he evokes the confinement of the tomb: "A shroud I see and I am the shroud, I wrap the body and lie in the coffin, / It is dark here under ground, it is not evil or pain here, it is blank here, for reasons" (*Leaves of Grass*, 1:113). "The Sleepers" bases its analogizing between sleep and death on irrepressible surmise: because sleep mimics or presages death, its obvious continuities with waking states also reinforce contemporary philosophical and scientific uncertainties regarding the temporality of death and dying and the nature of death's disruptions to sensation and consciousness. Whitman not only leaves this existential dilemma unresolved ("it is blank here, for reasons") but also foregrounds it in a representation of dream work, in which manifestations of contrary concepts, like "particular" and "general," are not experienced as contradictory.

For the speaker of the poem, as well as for the sleepers he visits, adjacency becomes identity through the mechanism of dreaming: "I dream in my dream all the dreams of the other dreamers, / And I become the other dreamers (*Leaves of Grass,* 1:110). The hypnotic ease with which this sympathetic crossing occurs—figured in the condensed and effortless-seeming lexical transformations from "dream" (verb) to "dream" (noun) to "dreams" to "dreamers"—anticipates the aspiration, in "Lilacs," toward further promiscuous achievements of combination, such as the triune figure of eroticized companionship and the trio's appreciation of the reinvigorated song of the thrush in section 15:

15
To the tally of my soul,
Loud and strong kept up the gray-brown bird,
With pure deliberate notes spreading filling the night.

Loud in the pines and cedars dim,
Clear in the freshness moist and the swamp-perfume,
And I with my comrades there in the night.
While my sight that was bound in my eyes unclosed,
As to long panoramas of visions.

And I saw askant the armies,
I saw as in noiseless dreams hundreds of battle-flags,
Borne through the smoke of the battles and pierc'd with missiles I saw them,
And carried hither and yon through the smoke, and torn and bloody,

And at last but a few shreds left on the staffs, (and all in silence,)
And the staffs all splinter'd and broken.

I saw the battle-corpses, myriads of them,
And the white skeletons of the young men, I saw them,
I saw the debris and debris of all the slain soldiers of the war,
But I saw they were not as was thought,
They themselves were fully at rest, they suffer'd not,
The living remain'd and suffer'd, the mother suffer'd,
And the wife and the child and the musing comrade suffer'd,
And the armies that remain'd suffer'd. (*Leaves of Grass,* 2:537–38)

The silent pictures of the war and its aftermath, screened, so to speak, to the accompaniment of the thrush's song, suggest not only the achievement of memorial piety but also the improved sociability that begins with the recognition of the grievances of the living.

Yet this vision is also scored with the traces of isolation and aggression. To see "askant," for instance, is not only to see obliquely but also potentially to register distrust and disapproval—much as a soldier might view his enemy from an imperiled vantage of momentary safety and composure. The vision of battle recalls figural as well as literal violence. For example, the staffs of the battle-flags (the flags themselves emblems of bodies "pierc'd," "torn," and "bloody") are "splinter'd and broken" in a way that evokes the sprigs of lilac that the poet himself has so copiously broken. The word *suffer'd* becomes a kind of refrain, chanting the persistence of disruption, even as the poet anticipates his withdrawal from this scene of vigilant mourning.

The poem's final section announces its already accomplished revision of the thrush's song and the poet's readiness to leave behind this emblematic text of mourning in order to depart from the world of the poem:

16
Passing the visions, passing the night,
Passing, unloosing the hold of my comrades' hands,
Passing the song of the hermit bird and the tallying song of my soul,
Victorious song, death's outlet song, yet varying ever-altering song,
As low and wailing, yet clear the notes, rising and falling, flooding the
   night,
Sadly sinking and fainting, as warning and warning, and yet again
   bursting with joy,

Covering the earth and filling the spread of the heaven,
As that powerful psalm in the night I heard from recesses,
Passing, I leave thee lilac with heart-shaped leaves,
I leave thee there in the door-yard, blooming, returning with spring.

I cease from my song for thee,
From my gaze on thee in the west, fronting the west, communing with
   thee,
O comrade lustrous with silver face in the night.

Yet each to keep and all, retrievements out of the night,
The song, the wondrous chant of the gray-brown bird,
And the tallying chant, the echo arous'd in my soul,
With the lustrous and drooping star with the countenance full of woe,
With the holders holding my hand nearing the call of the bird,
Comrades mine and I in the midst, and their memory ever to keep, for
   the dead I loved so well,
For the sweetest, wisest soul of all my days and lands—and this for his
   dear sake,
Lilac and star and bird twined with the chant of my soul,
There in the fragrant pines and the cedars dusk and dim. (*Leaves of Grass,*
   2:538–39)

Whitman figures here a now attenuated sense of his own implication in the ongoing urgency of grief's "warning and warning" and its
paradoxical, concomitant "bursting with joy." To "pass," to "leave," to
"cease"—to find, in other words, a sufficient culmination for grieving
at the threshold of grievance is the final aspiration that Whitman be-
queaths to the reader of his poem.

For Whitman and his contemporaries, it was difficult to be sure
what the grievance was that survived and outlasted Lincoln's power to
adjudicate, or that survived beyond his unsatisfactory adjudication. It is
terrible to experience loss as the condition of being trapped in grief on
the verge of articulation, as Herman Melville dramatized most forcibly
in his Lincoln elegy "The Martyr" (1866). "The Martyr" is manifestly
a threat, a prologue to vengeance that augurs further violence in every
pulse of its refrain:

There is a sobbing of the strong,
And a pall upon the land;
But the people in their weeping
Bare the iron hand:

Beware the People weeping
When they bare the iron hand.[50]

Yet with each pulse, or beat, the poem's lines—here in the refrain and throughout the elegy—insist audibly upon a complex but quite regular rhythm. Precise metrical and stanzaic arrangements, end-rhymes, and other formal elements of repetition order the dispersive "Passion of the People" of which the poem, in its subtitle, claims to be "Indicative." Indeed, the very presence of a refrain (literally, the repetition of a breaking-off) figures the regimentation of disruptive energy. Melville's elegy is about the marshaling of unexpended force and thus hearkens back to rallying, militaristic verses from earlier in the war—poems such as Whitman's "Beat! Beat! Drums!" in which the beating of the drums is fully antagonistic to mourning decorum (Whitman there directs the drums to "Make even the trestles to shake the dead where they lie awaiting the hearses" [*Leaves of Grass*, 2:487]). In "The Martyr," however, the threatening force announced in the rhythmic beating of its lines turns out to be something more like the "pall" of melancholy, the "harsh surrounding cloud that will not free my soul" in section 2 of "Lilacs." "The Martyr" threatens revenge but crucially equivocates the object of address. Who must "beware"? Who, after all, is the focus of the "People's" vengeful passion? And why is the form of the threat presented as an efficacious conjunction of sorrow and rage—not the conversion of grief into anger but rather their convergence?

As an occasional poem, "The Martyr," like "Lilacs," depends for its intelligibility upon its embeddedness in the historical present. The Christological analogizing (Lincoln is identified as "Martyr," "redeemer," "Forgiver") challenges the reader's interpretation of historical context rather than displacing it. Nor is the agency of the martyrdom, the "crime" of Lincoln's assassination, delinked from the history of sectional conflict. Nevertheless, Melville alters and pluralizes the killer in the frequently repeated phrase "they killed him," occulting most obviously Booth's individual agency as Lincoln's assassin. Less obvious tensions between objectification and occultation occur in relation to the object of address. For the audience being called upon to "Beware the People" is at once the audience of killers and the audience aligned with the poet, speaking for "the People," from whom the killers ("they") are seemingly distinct. Formally, the poem's stanza-refrain structure suggests the polyvocal performance of singer and chorus; goaded by the singer of the stanzas, "the People" are heard in the refrain, responding, as it were, *in* as well as *to* their own voice. The warning thus voiced rebounds upon the structurally implied controlling voice of the poet in what reads as an inwardly as well as outwardly directed threat. Melville's passional fusion of voices in the militancy of "the People" never fully commands a poem that is also about how mourning overmasters expression—about how mourning may canalize and frustrate psychic articulation into an orgy of recrimination.

The terrible vigilance of a people desperate for but unable to find a language of amnesty that would correspond less damagingly to the voice of mourning is also the subject of an astonishing elegy written just days after the assassination by the young Emma Lazarus—an elegy not about Lincoln but about Booth, his killer, as he seeks to elude, "all the sleepless night," his vengeful pursuers:

> "To sleep! What is sleep now but haunting dreams?
> Chased off, every time, by the flashing gleams
> Of the light o'er the stream in yonder town,
> Where all are searching and hunting me down!
> Oh, the wearisome pain, the dread suspense
> And the horror each instant more intense!
> I yearn for rest from my pain and for sleep,—
> Bright stars, do ye mock, or, quivering, weep?"[51]

Booth never mentions killing Lincoln. Indeed, Lazarus's elegy ends up seeming less like a poem about a killer on the run than a meditative drama about the struggle to relinquish the burden of vigilance one's own aggressions and their objects enforce. He is dogged by the imperative of alertness to a degree that overturns elegiac convention: even the stars—conventional emblems of the immortalization of the deceased, as in "Lilacs" itself—become pursuers, possible avengers of the mourned.

Lazarus's Booth is also pursued by a choral voice—"all Nature's voices"—that punctuates his lamentations with the following refrain:

> Go forth! Thou shalt have here no rest again,
> For thy brow is marked with the brand of Cain.[52]

Here is the familiar elegiac regimentation of aggression through form. Yet Lazarus's elegy for Booth makes a startling (and, as far as I have seen, anomalous) appearance among Northern, abolitionist, and pro-Union responses to Lincoln's death because it makes explicit the identification between elegist and assassin that so many other Lincoln elegies suggest obliquely. In addition to rendering Booth audible through ventriloquization, the poem's narrative voice is sympathetic and sentimental, figuring Booth as a victim, as a kind of hunted stag, ultimately released by death from the suffering inflicted by, not on, his pursuers:

> All sorrow has gone with life's fitful breath.
> Rest at last! For thy brow bears the seal of Death.[53]

Yet these final lines also challenge the poem's own appeal to sympathy for individual suffering. Is it merely Booth's "sorrow" that ends with his death? Or does the poem also envision the end of a shared, collective sorrow, soothed and dissipated by knowledge of the assassin's death? Is mourning over, and the need for vigilance passed, because Booth is free from his own subjection to extreme vigilance? Is the force of Lazarus's unexpected and provocative sympathy for Booth extinguished with his life? Or do the poem's final lines recall the reader to his or her own ongoing, burdensome task of vigilance, ensuring the final displacement of Booth as an object of mourning in order that the proper object—Lincoln—may be restored to view?

Much has been made of Lincoln's absence from view in "Lilacs" as a symptom of historical evasiveness. Mutlu Blasing, for example, insists that the elegy's opening stanza is a "grand evasion" in which "the particular, historical present is unspoken for."[54] But to what extent was it necessary to speak for it, in the detailed, realistic manner whose absence from the poem Blasing treats as evidence of a kind of counterreferential pathology of mourning? As an occasional genre, elegy signals—indeed, it depends for its intelligibility upon—its embeddedness in the historical present, even as it troubles (rather than defensively "evading") the historical present by combining temporalities of tradition (e.g., reliance on elegiac conventions) and futurity (e.g., asseverations of perpetual mourning, which are themselves, of course, conventional to the genre). Timothy Sweet goes even further than Blasing, reading "Lilacs" as

Whitman's recovery of a fundamentally counterhistorical pastoralism, "a poem that is minimally about Lincoln's death as a historical event, and is scarcely at all about the Civil War."[55] Such assessments speak with some value to Whitman's relatively light reliance on historicizing detail in "Lilacs," as compared to many other contemporary Lincoln elegies. Yet Sweet's own language of approximation—"minimally about," "scarcely at all about"—gestures toward a more accurate characterization of "Lilacs" as an occasional poem that opts to see askance what is already in plain view—not Lincoln merely, nor the war in general, but also the feature of the conflict that was its most fundamental representational problem.

In section 15, the dreamlike vision evokes the reality of black suffering as another element of the historical present—an element evoked chiefly by the trope of whiteness. In the history of mourning arts, white is commonly a classicizing, funerary color—dramatically voiding flesh, pain, decay, and blood. It also suggests peace after death and is linked to the lunar light of Whitman's "comrade lustrous." But it would be a mistake to conclude that the trope of whiteness has a firmly settled relation of distance from the materiality of death and of the human body in particular. The image of the "white skeletons of young men" in section 15 of "Lilacs," for example, shares with the large number of similar images throughout Whitman's Civil War writings a metonymic relation to contemporary, anxious fantasies of death's complexion.

As Whitman knew from his firsthand experience with the war dead, the ability to sustain the illusion of a lifelike corpse was significantly enhanced during the war by the development of effective embalming techniques. Yet while embalming mitigated the effects of putrefaction, it did not prevent them. As Lincoln's own embalmed corpse wended its way west, it began to show signs of decay, including darkening of the face—a "blackening" that had to be covered up by crude cosmetics during the journey so that the body could continue to be displayed. In his oration at Oak Ridge Cemetery, Matthew Simpson spoke of the almost talismanic effect of Lincoln's corpse during its transcontinental viewing: it obliterated pernicious personal distinctions and promoted unity among mourners.[56] Yet it also provoked underarticulated anxieties about racial confusion and, ultimately, about the reality of integral distinctions among persons. Occasionally, these anxieties erupted in contemporary war reporting, as in the following passage from a *Harper's Weekly* article in the aftermath of Antietam:

> The faces of those who had fallen in the battle were, after more than a day's exposure, so black that no one would ever suspect that they had been white. All looked like negroes, and as they lay in piles where they had fallen, one upon another, they filled the by-standers with a sense of horror.[57]

The easy conflation here of the twin horrors of mass death and racial instability reflects a widespread tendency to conflate death, blackness, and national instability.[58]

In this light, Whitman's paling of death is difficult not to read, in "Lilacs" and elsewhere, as a reaction in part to the "horror" of the on-lookers at Antietam. Whitman rewrites contemporary tensions over racial and existential categories in his poems and, in this way, on the bodies of the dead. He moves among the dead in many of his poems not like the nurse of the hospital but like a version of the newly professionalized American undertaker, perfuming and blanching. He marks the faces of the dead soldiers: "faces so pale" (*Leaves of Grass*, 2:511), faces of "beautiful yellow-white ivory" (2:496), faces "white as a lily" (2:494). He insists upon the marmoreal impress of death as he insists upon the impress of his kisses:

> For my enemy is dead, a man divine as myself is dead,
> I look down where he lies white-faced and still in the coffin—I draw near,
> Bend down and touch lightly with my lips the white face in the coffin.

If in these lines the synecdoche of the white face seems to fall in some dehistoricized realm between Christology and fetishism, the poem in which they appear is itself an elegy for the times, lamenting that the "war and all its deeds of carnage must in time be utterly lost." Furthermore, it makes its lament under the aegis of the title-theme of "Reconciliation"—a reconciliation to be effected by death's cleansing of "this soil'd world" (*Leaves of Grass*, 2:555–56). The poem's linked motifs of cleansing, whiteness, and reconciliation once again evoke what seems to be the specter of Whitman's Civil War poetry: the "dark" figure—the corpse, the mother—lying beyond the salient, neatly morally differentiated categories of its culture. The transfigured corpse, like the "transfigured scene" of the war to which Henry James referred "every sort of intensity," functions most crucially as a figure not for racism but for the ambivalent goal of self-differentiation through mourning.[59]

Henry James begins his 1865 review of *Drum-Taps* by stressing that reading and writing about Whitman's book has been for him a "melancholy task," inviting the reader to ask: What, then, is the unspoken, ungrievable thing on which James's review turns? In a frequently exasperated tone, James characterizes Whitman as a self-absorbed seducer who writes elegies about the scenery of war that are preoccupied with his own sexuality. "For a lover," James complains, "you talk entirely too much about yourself." This charge seems motivated by James's ambivalence over masculinity and its centrality to the ambition he shares with Whitman to be "possessed" by the "idea of your country's greatness."[60] James's use here of the trope of possession, with its many cultural as well as psychological associations in the postbellum United States, speaks more precisely to James's own lifelong conflict over whether or not to try to limn the contours of his masculine identity. Yet, as James recognized, Whitman too was constantly doing battle with his own urge both to obscure and to specify the limits of variability in sexual terms. In a much later review of Bucke's edition of Whitman's "Calamus" letters to Peter Doyle, James writes of the "beauty of the particular nature" revealed in Whitman's "illiterate colloquy":

> To call the whole thing vividly American is to challenge, doubtless, plenty of dissent—on the ground, presumably, that the figure in evidence was no less queer a feature of Camden, New Jersey, than it would have been of South Kensington. That may perfectly be; but a thousand images of patient, homely, American life, else indistinguishable, are what its queerness—however startling—happened to express.

In the uncompromised and inaccessible singularity of Whitman and Doyle's relationship ("the whole thing"), James discovers—and delights in discovering—a combination of the "queer" and the "homely" that makes Americanness seem a kind of erotic consolation for what, to James at least, are the otherwise "indistinguishable" and therefore otherwise ungrievable privations of his own American life:

Whitman wrote to his friend of what they both saw and touched, enormities of the common, sordid occupations, dreary amusements, undesirable food; and the record remains, by a mysterious marvel, a thing positively delightful. If we ever find out why, it must be another time. The riddle meanwhile is a neat one for the sphinx of democracy to offer.[61]

The real "enormities"—the assassination, which Doyle witnessed, and the love for Doyle that Whitman so famously, so pitiably renounced in his 1870 notebook (*Notebooks*, 2:887–89)—remain unspoken. But their ephemeral traces, the letters, have escaped abandonment. This is what James takes pleasure in, just as the "cheapness" of the surviving token of libidinal investment was an affluent source of Whitman's pleasure in the "little Washington-Lincoln photo."

The image of Lincoln, both queer and homely, helped bring Whitman, as Lawrence Buell puts it, "to the threshold of canonicity" in his own time.[62] It was not "Lilacs," however, but "O Captain! My Captain" that enjoyed overwhelming popularity in the decades following the war. That elegy's weak capitulation to contemporary prosodic standards and mourning styles itself became a source of lamentation for Whitman later on. He told Traubel that although the poem had its "reasons for being," he was "almost sorry" he had ever written it.[63] His "almost sorry" may sound a bit cagey in light of his numerous recitations of the poem in tandem with his famous and lucrative lecture "The Death of Abraham Lincoln," in which he appropriated and embellished Doyle's eyewitness account. These performances, given in New York and Philadelphia between 1879 and 1890, were themselves a kind of consolation for Whitman, ill and financially dependent in his last years. Yet Whitman was not the only one who felt ambivalent about the popular success of this other artifact of presidential kitsch. Stuart Merrill, who attended one of the anniversary lectures in New York, heard Whitman recite ("sob" rather than "chant") "O Captain! My Captain!" and was appalled at the audience's applause, "which appeared to me an outrage to the grief of the poet." In relation to the tedious poem, Merrill assumes the farcical role ("I was in the presence of the sublime and I could only weep") of the late-Victorian aesthete— uncomprehending enemy of the very "noise of the crowd," "the impatient clanging of the tramcars," "the great roaring of steamboats" that had ignited Whitman's imagination and his desire.[64] Merrill colludes but semiconsciously with the sentimental valediction that was the substance of the final years of Whitman's public life. That long good-bye echoes in the schoolrooms where "Captain" is memorized and recited to this day. What those echoes yet sustain may be the still largely unexamined requirement for civic life of a certain ignorance as to the prodigality of pleasure in the experience of loss and the literatures of mourning.

AFTERWORD

Objects

He is present now as never before.
—JOHN BURROUGHS

I loved him living, and I love him still.
—ROBERT G. INGERSOLL

[S]omehow even this dead form reached up to me, as if for a last embrace, and I held it in my arms long and long and pressed it with a passion of love.
—HORACE TRAUBEL

On March 26, 1892, Whitman's death unleashed waves of sorrow, relief, anxiety, and other forms of libidinal expressivity. His survivors caressed and kissed him with their good-byes. They made casts of his face and hands. They washed his body and prepared it for viewing and for burial. Busily, they came and went from the Mickle Street house, exchanging their tears and sighs for Walt and nursing their jealousies of one another. They gathered his effects and plotted the dissemination of his praise. On the day of the funeral, unnumbered mourners appeared, "as if risen by instinct from all quarters of the wind, till a magic stream was in full play . . . [l]etter carriers, policemen, railroadmen, ferrymen, school children, merchants—who was not included?"[1] The great Shakespearean

I sat by your bedside, I held your hand:
Once you opened your eyes: O look of recognition! O look of bestowal!
From you to me then passed the commission of the future,
From you to me that minute, from your veins to mine,

.　　.　　.　　.　　.　　.　　.　　.　　.

O my great dead!
You had not gone, you had stayed—in my heart, in my veins,
Reaching through me, through others through me, through all at last,
　　our brothers,
A hand to the future.[7]

There is some of Whitman's poignancy here, if not his sophistication, as Traubel tries to articulate for himself the central Whitmanian question: where and how does lyric address meet cultural transmission? Elegy, he finds, is poised at this crossroads, where Whitman himself had encountered it.

Hand over hand, fresher and more energetic tributes came later, from Pound's oedipally obnoxious "A Pact"—published in 1913, the same year Apollinaire scandalized readers of the *Mercure de France* with his as-told-to account of Whitman's funeral ("Les pédérasts étaient venus en foule," etc.)[8]—to the randy sublimity of Ginsberg's "A Supermarket in California" (1955).

If there was anyone after Whitman who understood the prodigality of pleasure in the experience of loss, it was Ginsberg, whose grotesque and gorgeous elegy for his mother, "Kaddish" (1959), is one of the most powerful responses to "Lilacs" ever written. Indeed, there are many points in "Kaddish" where we may feel we are reading an elegy for Whitman himself—points where Ginsberg's experience evokes vivid scenes from Whitman's own life. For example, the hospitals scenes:

Over and over – refrain – of the Hospitals – still haven't written your
　　History;

the escape from family misery to urban refuge:

I left on the next bus to New York – lay my head back in the last seat,
　　depressed – the worst yet to come? – abandoning her, rode in torpor;

the pleasures of cruising his favorite New York street:

scholar Horace Howard Furness came to ask for a lock of Walt's ha
John Burroughs and Horace Traubel held hands as they gazed into tl
coffin for the last time. At the cemetery, they spotted Peter Doyle on
nearby hill, "twirling a switch in his hand, his tall figure and big soft ha
impressively set against the white-blue sky."[2] The mourners had heaped
Whitman's coffin with wreaths and blossoms so copiously that someone
later remarked "he slept beneath a wilderness of flowers."[3]

Whitman's friends worked hard to produce a funeral that would
express their own Whitmanian commitment to a certain kind of social
and political order, a funeral "attended with no form and little ceremony," inclusive of—indeed attractive to—all the elements of a democratic throng: workingmen, street urchins, mothers and ministers, city
officials, and "not a few artists."[4] An organized chaos, neither solemn nor
hilarious, giving place to intimates (such as Burroughs) and, with some
grousing, to the famous (particularly Richard Ingersoll), its management was also largely an affair of men. Mary Oakes Davis, Whitman's
housekeeper, "almost begged" for the privilege of washing the face of
the corpse (it was granted; his male nurse, Warrie Fritzenger, washed
the body). Whitman's sister-in-law, Louisa, was discouraged from taking an active role in planning the funeral ceremony; Richard Bucke
would not stand for her choice of eulogist.[5] Graveside, the five speakers
were all men. And the accounts of Whitman's death and burial were for
the most part either written or edited by Traubel.

Elegies, of course, were immediately forthcoming. On March 28,
Edmund Clarence Stedman wrote to Traubel from New York to say
that as he would be unable to attend the funeral, he was sending a
garland of flowers. "I have," he continued, "hastily written a few broken & all unworthy lines, which I trust you will permit to stay with
it."[6] Scribbled verses pinned to memorial wreaths gave way to more
deliberate compositions, unfurled from the days and years that followed. Many, such as the elegiac sonnets by Francis Howard Williams
and Robert Williams Buchanan, are mere unimaginative formalities.
Traubel's elegy, "Succession" (1894), is imitative of Whitman and egoistic
in the touching manner of an abandoned acolyte not knowing how else
to mourn but to aspire to the position of his priest. He exponentiates
himself as the new apostle of lyric circulation:

I walked on Broadway imagining Infinity like a rubber ball without space
  beyond;

the erotic dread of the mother's body:

Monster of the Beginning Womb;

as well as its idealization:

O glorious muse that bore me from the womb, gave suck first mystic life &
  taught me talk and music;

and, finally, the blooming profusions of elegy:

your Death full of Flowers.[9]

Naomi and Walt are both Ginsberg's "dark mother." They are, if you
like, his "thought of death" and his "knowledge of death." They are,
most importantly, inspiration for the elegist's perennial challenge: to
remain skeptical of normalizing conventions, while avoiding the imposi-
tion of a standard of eccentricity. In place of more decorous figures of
inheritance and succession, they are gods of sexual secretion and pel-
vic motion: "Creation glistening backwards" and the "Grinder of giant
Beyonds."[10] The libidinal oscillations of elegy, so often checked by fear
and misunderstanding, or by irreligious and hypocritical pieties, find
in Ginsberg, as in Whitman, their unchecked minister.

From the sheer tedium of Francis Williams to the scary magnificence of Ginsberg and beyond, generations of elegists have continued
more or less uncertainly to work through, in their various relations to
Whitman, both the fascination and the burdensomeness of the past as
a libidinal terrain. Mourning has a cryptic might, as Emerson might
say. It is not simply that we carry ashlike traces of the dead around
with us in the niches of some psychic vault. Memory is a columbarium only inasmuch as that columbarium points to the existence of a
full intrapsychic world—a world with other structures in it, structures
differently inhabited by those whom Longfellow called "the other living."[11] Unconscious communion with the other living makes conscious
memories of the dead unsatisfying—not because they remind us that
the dead are gone, but because they are proof of a kind of presence not

available to conscious experience. Memories ache, not because we have lost so irretrievably, but because we long so reasonably and so powerfully for a more direct experience, freer retrievements out of the night, of the objects we have made part of ourselves but know only, or mostly, as intrapsychic conflicts.

Behind every grief, there is the grievance: "I must die." How we handle that grievance determines to a great extent the way we live. A friend of mine who knew he would soon be dead told me that he was trying to "face it as a challenge rather than a curse." Automatically projecting my own fears onto him, I mistakenly assumed that by facing "it" he meant facing death as such. Years later, after he had died, I was able to listen to him more carefully.

I know that in those last months he still dreaded the prospect of a world that would no longer include him. We had often talked, in easier times, about our shared sense of what was most terrible about death. It meant we would not be around to discover how things, as he put it, "will turn out." Would there ever be a thinking machine? A palatable low-fat ice cream? Was the universe open or closed? Would there be a cure? We just could not stomach the thought of having to let go our claim on the world, so strong was our interest in what remained to be seen.

Even as my friend endured the final, often humiliating stages of illness, this particular form of egoism still kept hold of his imagination. Sometimes, it meant enduring his painful expressions of embitterment: "I hate it! You're all leaving me out!" And he was right. We had already become his mourners. Instead of keeping company with him through life, we now felt a more and more awkward sense of obligation to accompany him to death. And I regret to think how likely it is that he came to see himself as the victim of our efforts, as his mourners, to leave him behind—to deprive him, in effect, of his right to the life he was still living.

At other times, he seemed determined to show us he could buy back—in the form of creature comforts, sensual indulgences for flagging appetites—some portion of the present of which we were depriving him. He even bought a piece of the future by accruing phenomenal debts he never intended to discharge. He gloated over maxing out credit cards, and we giggled together over visions of enraged bank executives, years hence, forced to swallow his unpaid bills. As if, in all its selfish cruelty, the false hope peddled by the masters of the credit economy could be revisited upon them—could gouge *their* futures.

Conspiring with him in these indulgences was fun. Sometimes it really did feel like sharing the same quickened breath. But remembering these things without him is a more complex pleasure. D. A. Miller once touchingly memorialized a friend by recalling one of their most playful moments and warming to the memory of how "together [they] could be thus *easily* amused."[12] For me the pathos of this tribute lies in its ambivalence toward a rare moment of shared abandon. Miller's italicized "easily" holds that moment apart, turns it and beholds it in a number of ways: in delight (there *can be* such moments), in defense (it *was* that easy), in distaste (*too* easy to recall with perfect comfort). The word, slanting like a tombstone askew among ranks of upright graves, strains literally as well as rhetorically against the sentence that expresses the freedom of the recollected moment. How best to cherish our ambivalence about such moments and the persons who lived them? We were carried away together, Miller recalls, but I have returned, for now, to something less easy but superior—a superiority, indeed, that has everything to do with my efforts to measure the distances my friend and I have traversed.

And are traversing still. I have tried before to tell the story of a walk I took with my friend. What makes it a difficult story to tell is that he died several years before the walk took place. I do not consciously harbor belief in a personal afterlife, or in spooks, or in any other notion of plasmatic souls. It happened, though, that as I was walking to work in high spirits along a broad urban boulevard, I at some point knew myself to be hand in hand and conversing with my friend. There was nothing at all startling about it. On the contrary, it was all familiarity, complacence, quiet intimacy. I knew the touch of his hand without seeing it, recognized in some supersensory way the unmistakable profile of his head, the animated movements of talk, the contours of voice, without at all believing (or feeling the need to believe) that these things were actually present to me. In a few minutes I knew myself to be alone again, but without feeling like I had been left or bereft of something. The whole experience was like receiving an affirmative answer to an undisclosed question. It was a feeling of intense reassurance in I knew not what. And not knowing did not seem to bother me in the least.

Later, I thought of Whitman, in his Lincoln elegy, walking with the knowledge of death and the thought of death "as with companions, and as holding the hands of companions."[13] On some level, I must at the time have been daydreaming myself into that poem, for I had already begun to conceive of the book I would write, in which "When Lilacs Last in the Dooryard Bloom'd" would necessarily feature. Unconsciously, I had found my way inside the place of Whitman's desire, staged in his poem as the central element of a triune figure of unending companionship. I had chosen Whitman's poem, I reasoned, because of its congruence with some unconscious wish of mine—a wish that found expression in my conscious fantasy of walking hand in hand with my friend.

This meant, of course, that there were important sources of that congruence to discover elsewhere in the poem and in my associations to other mourned objects. Among them, as I later perceived, were the lilacs that hung over and perfumed my memories of some other, earlier losses. The hedge of lilacs that grew beside my childhood home had been consecrated by other readers of Whitman, readers in whose own griefs I was embowered long before I knew who Whitman was. Our earliest years, as Whitman discovers to us anew, are spent in search of an illusory but necessary feeling of congruence: the feeling that other people's sense of what is tolerable in life is commensurate with our own. Our later years, as Whitman also details so vividly, are spent accumulating knowledge of the unlikelihood of that commensuration. We tend to feel this unlikelihood most keenly when someone dies, not only in relation to the deceased but also as the condition of our relationships with the living. It often generates a sense of guilt that may itself become an affluent source of grief.

To fashion a poem (an artifact of address) out of such grief is to venture, it would seem, on the solicitation of a mute and indifferent object—precisely the sort of solicitation Paul de Man most famously and even more unpersuasively denigrates as "false" mourning, as if he believed it were impossible meaningfully to distinguish between material contingency and personhood.[14] Even an elegy can hardly seem to be a matter of complete indifference to its object, when the conviction that the dead live in and act through us takes so many forms and presupposes such a wide variety of transmissive mechanisms, including heredity, tradition, possession, and the psychoanalytic concepts of incorporation and introjection.

Lodging within us as objects, our lost ones participate in our designs on the world, bypassing for the most part our conscious acquiescence or resistance. I am their instrument as much as I am anything, usually dully aware of only the most painful manipulations. I am seized and often feel undone by them. Yet I hope for more alert and fluid relations, and I ask of them, in effect, how the burdensome feelings of indebtedness, remorse, and hostility might become more freely chosen allegiances, the kind of allegiance or affirmative incorporation best represented by the figure of the friend. My dead friend answers with another question—a question I try to hear as a challenge rather than a curse. He beckons, admonishes, flirts, and asks with side-turned look, "What are you afraid of?" It is in the work of mourning that our answers to this question arise.

Notes

Introduction

The epigraph at the chapter opening is from Walt Whitman, "Song of Myself," in *Leaves of Grass: A Textual Variorum of the Printed Poems,* ed. Sculley Bradley, Harold W. Blodgett, et al., 3 vols. (New York: New York University Press, 1980), 1:10.

1. This axiom is, in the broadest sense, my subject here. Among its crucial modern theorists, from Freud to Derrida, Zygmunt Bauman puts it this way: "Death is the ultimate condition of cultural creativity as such. It makes permanence into a task, into an urgent task, into a paramount task—a fount and measure of all tasks—and so it makes culture, that huge and never stopping factory of permanence" (*Mortality, Immortality and Other Life Strategies* [Stanford: Stanford University Press, 1992], 4). Bauman's industrial metaphor for culture ("huge and never stopping factory") is not the mark of a materialist analysis. Indeed, Bauman has been accused, for example, by Jonathan Dollimore in *Death, Desire and Loss in Western Culture* (New York: Routledge, 1998), 120–27, of failing to historicize social difference. But Bauman's book makes no claims to be the sort of cultural history of death to which Dollimore himself aspires. Its pertinence to the cultural history of American elegy derives from its analysis of the ways in which institutionalized social arrangements tend, in all their historical variability, toward the obviation of difference, with enlivening as well as devitalizing results.

2. Philip Freneau, "On Funeral Elogiums" (1790), in Philip M. Marsh, ed., *The Prose of Philip Freneau* (New Brunswick, NJ: Scarecrow Press, 1955), 268.

3. Lydia Huntley Sigourney, *Letters of Life* (New York: D. Appleton, 1866), 369–77.

4. My contention is that for many American poets of the eighteenth and nineteenth centuries, elegy was a crucial genre for developing specific cultural vernaculars to express new relations to old emplotments. From our contemporary retrospect,

genres such as elegy have been, as Virginia Jackson argues, "collapsed into the expressive romantic lyric of the nineteenth century." As this has occurred, Jackson continues, "the various modes of poetic circulation—scrolls, manuscript books, song cycles, miscellanies, broadsides, hornbooks, libretti, quartos, chapbooks, recitation manuals, annuals, gift books, newspapers, anthologies—[have] tended to disappear behind an idealized scene of reading progressively identified with an idealized moment of expression" (*Dickinson's Misery: A Theory of Lyric Reading* [Princeton, NJ: Princeton University Press, 2005], 7). In other words, we have "lyricized" such genres and, in the process, discounted the miscellaneous forms of circulation that constitute them as historically contingent genres in any given moment. The extensibility of Jackson's argument, which is grounded in a tour-de-force reading of what Emily Dickinson's readers learned to call "lyric," turns on how one defines the duration of the present. How far back does our "contemporary retrospect" begin? Jackson asserts that the lyricization of poetry begins in the eighteenth century, an assertion I would not dispute. But this does not mean that, even as late as Whitman's day, it no longer matters what kind of poem elegies are. As Jackson herself observes, "the process of lyricization [has been] an uneven series of negotiations of many different forms of circulation and address" (8).

5. The important critical works on elegy include John Draper, *The Funeral Elegy and the Rise of English Romanticism* (New York: New York University Press, 1929); Ruth Wallerstein, "The Laureate Hearse," in *Studies in Seventeenth-Century Poetic* (Madison: University of Wisconsin Press, 1950), 1–148; Ellen Zetzel Lambert, *Placing Sorrow: A Study of the Pastoral Elegy Convention from Theocritus to Milton* (Chapel Hill: University of North Carolina Press, 1976); Eric Smith, *By Mourning Tongues: Studies in English Elegy* (Ipswich, Eng.: Boydell Press, 1977); Lawrence I. Lipking, "Tombeau," in *The Life of the Poet: Beginning and Ending Poetic Careers* (Chicago: University of Chicago Press, 1981), 138–79; Peter Sacks, *The English Elegy: Studies in the Genre from Spenser to Yeats* (Baltimore: Johns Hopkins University Press, 1985); G. W. Pigman, *Grief and English Renaissance Elegy* (Cambridge: Cambridge University Press, 1985); Morton W. Bloomfield, "The Elegy and the Elegiac Mode: Praise and Alienation," in *Renaissance Genres: Essays on Theory, History, and Interpretation,* ed. Barbara Kiefer Lewalski (Cambridge: Harvard University Press, 1986), 147–57; Celeste M. Schenck, "Feminism and Deconstruction: Re-Constructing the Elegy," *Texas Studies in Women's Literature* 5 (1986): 13–27; Dennis Kay, *Melodious Tears: The English Funeral Elegy from Spenser to Milton* (Oxford: Clarendon Press, 1990); Louise O. Fradenburg, "'Voice Memorial': Loss and Reparation in Chaucer's Poetry," *Exemplaria* 2, no. 1 (1990): 169–202; Jahan Ramazani, *Poetry of Mourning: The Modern Elegy from Hardy to Heaney* (Chicago: University of Chicago Press, 1994); W. David Shaw, *Elegy and Paradox: Testing the Conventions* (Baltimore: Johns Hopkins University Press, 1994). Some related works of special importance to the study of elegy are Joshua Scodel, *The English Epitaph: Commemoration and Conflict from Jonson to Wordsworth* (Ithaca, NY: Cornell University Press, 1991); Esther Schor, *Bearing the Dead: The British Culture of Mourning from the Enlightenment to Victoria* (Princeton, NJ: Princeton University Press, 1994); Armando Petrucci, *Writing the Dead: Death and Writing Strategies in the Western Tradition,* trans. Michael Sullivan (Stanford,

CA: Stanford University Press, 1998); and R. Clifton Spargo, *The Ethics of Mourning: Grief and Responsibility in Elegiac Literature* (Baltimore: Johns Hopkins University Press, 2004).

6. Benjamin Franklin, "Silence Dogood, No. 7," in *Writings,* ed. J. A. Leo Lemay (New York: Library of America, 1987), 21–22. Further page references to this edition occur parenthetically in the text.

7. Mark Twain, *Adventures of Huckleberry Finn,* in *Mississippi Writings,* ed. Guy Cardwell (New York: Library of America, 1982), 726. Further page references to this edition occur parenthetically in the text.

8. Jahan Ramazani, for instance, in his discussion of "American Family Elegy," sweeps aside two centuries of elegy's "popularity and abundance" in America in his reference to "the elegy-by-recipe method satirized by Franklin and Twain" (*Poetry of Mourning,* 216), and in the voluminous *American Poetry: The Nineteenth Century* (New York: Library of America, 1993). Emmeline Grangerford's "Ode to Stephen Dowling Bots, Dec'd" almost entirely displaces the popular and abundant elegiac lyrics (most notably Lydia Sigourney's) to which it stands in parodic relation.

9. Nicole Loraux, *Mothers in Mourning,* trans. Corinne Pache (Ithaca, NY: Cornell University Press, 1998), 9–28 passim.

10. Nathanael Appleton, *The Great Man Fallen in Israel* (Boston: Bartholomew Green for Samuel Gerrish, 1724), 24.

11. Samuel Willard, *The Mourners Cordial against Excessive Sorrow . . .* (Boston: Benjamin Harris and John Allen, 1691), 42, 44.

12. *Acts and Laws Passed by the Great and General Court or Assembly of His Majesty's Province of the Massachusetts-Bay in New-England* (Boston: Bartholomew Green, 1721), 356. See also *Acts and Laws, of His Majesty's Province of the Massachusetts-Bay in New-England* (Boston: Bartholomew Green for Benjamin Eliot, 1726), 309; and *Temporary Acts and Laws of His Majesty's Province of the Massachusetts-Bay in New-England* (Boston: Samuel Kneeland, 1755), 22.

13. Loraux, *Mothers in Mourning,* 11.

14. Benjamin Wadsworth, *The Well-Ordered Family: or, Relative Duties,* 2nd ed. (Boston: Samuel Kneeland for Nicholas Buttolph, 1719), 29.

15. S[amuel] L. C[lemens], "In Memoriam. Olivia Susan Clemens," *Harper's New Monthly Magazine* 95, no. 570 (November 1897): 929–30.

16. Mark Twain, "Post-Mortem Poetry," *The Galaxy* 9, no. 6 (June 1870): 864.

17. See, for example, the unavowed (and seemingly unrecognized) disciplinary function of the special issue of *American Literature* (70 [1998]) called "No More Separate Spheres," with its near-exclusive focus on prose fiction—the genre commonly taken to provide, as Joseph Harrington observes, "a privileged access to history." Joseph Harrington, "Why American Poetry Is Not American Literature," *American Literary History* 8 (1996): 508. Subsequent critical enterprise has only fitfully begun to assimilate and to interpret early America's burgeoning poetic canon, which for the most part remains, as Mary Loeffelholz observes, "stubbornly locked in the category of anthologies and editions" (*From School to Salon: Reading Nineteenth-Century American Women's Poetry* [Princeton, NJ: Princeton University Press, 2004], 210n3).

18. Leslie Fielder, *Love and Death in the American Novel* (New York: Criterion,

1960), xvii. For a historical account of poetry's displacement from the field of Americanist criticism, see Harrington, "Why American Poetry Is Not American Literature," 496–515.

19. Neal L. Tolchin, *Mourning, Gender, and Creativity in the Art of Herman Melville* (New Haven, CT: Yale University Press, 1988); Mitchell Robert Breitwieser, *American Puritanism and the Defense of Mourning: Religion, Grief, and Ethnology in Mary White Rowlandson's Captivity Narrative* (Madison: University of Wisconsin Press, 1990); Julia A. Stern, *The Plight of Feeling: Sympathy and Dissent in the Early American Novel* (Chicago: University of Chicago Press, 1997); Susan L. Mizruchi, *The Science of Sacrifice: American Literature and Modern Social Theory* (Princeton, NJ: Princeton University Press, 1998). Despite what the studies by Tolchin and Stern in particular seem to suggest, the rise of the novel in America in the eighteenth and nineteenth centuries—what Cathy Davidson calls the American "revolution" of the word—does not simply displace elegy or render it irrelevant, except in our current critical retrospect. Indeed, one unexamined aspect of the novel's development in America (beyond the scope of this study) is its frequent functioning as a repository or memorial for elegy. From William Hill Brown's *The Power of Sympathy* (1789) to Nathaniel Hawthorne's *The Blithedale Romance* (1852) to William Wells Brown's *Clotel* (1853) to Elizabeth Stuart Phelps's *The Gates Ajar* (1868) to Herman Melville's *Billy Budd* (1891), American novels enshrine as well as compete with the at once popular and elite genre of the elegy as a literary site vested, as Davidson says of the novel, "with the voice (or voices) of authority." Cathy N. Davidson, *Revolution and the Word: The Rise of the Novel in America* (New York: Oxford University Press, 1986), 41.

20. See, for example, Harold Bloom, *Agon: Towards a Theory of Revisionism* (New York: Oxford University Press, 1982), 184; Sacks, *The English Elegy,* 316; Helen Vendler, "Whitman's 'When Lilacs Last in the Dooryard Bloom'd,'" in *Textual Analysis: Some Readers Reading,* ed. Mary Ann Caws (New York: Modern Language Association, 1986), 142; and Mark Edmundson, "'Lilacs': Walt Whitman's American Elegy," *Nineteenth-Century Literature* 44 (1990).

21. Edmundson, "'Lilacs,'" 465.

22. Betsy Erkkila, "Breaking Bounds," introduction to *Breaking Bounds: Whitman and American Cultural Studies,* ed. Betsy Erkkila and Jay Grossman (New York: Oxford University Press, 1996), 11.

23. I mean to invoke here the tradition of revisionary thinking about object relations from Freud and Melanie Klein to D. W. Winnicott and, most recently, Christopher Bollas.

24. See Charles Taylor, *Modern Social Imaginaries* (Durham, NC: Duke University Press, 2004).

25. [James B. Thayer], "Lowell's 'Under the Willows,'" *Boston Daily Advertiser,* Supplement, 5 December 1868, [2].

26. Matthew P. Brown, "'BOSTON/SOB NOT': Elegiac Performance in Early New England and Materialist Studies of the Book," *American Quarterly* 50, no. 2 (1998): 322.

27. Walt Whitman, "A Word Out of the Sea" (1860), in *Leaves of Grass,* 2:345.

28. Jacques Derrida, "The Law of Genre," *Glyph* 7 (1980): 206.

29. Allen Ginsberg, "Kaddish," in *Kaddish and Other Poems, 1958–1960* (San Francisco: City Lights Books, 1961), 7.

30. Nathaniel Hawthorne, *The Scarlet Letter: A Romance,* in *Novels,* ed. Millicent Bell (New York: Library of America, 1983), 144. On catharsis and compulsion in the reader's experience of genre, see Victoria Nelson, *The Secret Life of Puppets* (Cambridge, MA: Harvard University Press, 2001), 131–37.

31. Benedetto Croce, *Aesthetic as Science of Expression and General Linguistics,* trans. Douglas Ainslie, 1909 (New York: Noonday Press, 1953), 20.

32. Igor Kopytoff, "The Cultural Biography of Things: Commoditization as Process," in *The Social Life of Things: Commodities in Cultural Perspective,* ed. Arjun Appadurai (Cambridge: Cambridge University Press, 1986), 84.

33. Michael McKeon, ed., *Theory of the Novel: A Historical Approach* (Baltimore: Johns Hopkins University Press, 2000), 1.

34. Alastair Fowler, *Kinds of Literature: An Introduction to the Theory of Genres and Modes* (Oxford: Oxford University Press, 1982), 164–67. On the contemporary debate over the nature of species, see Marc Ereshefsky, *The Poverty of the Linnaean Hierarchy: A Philosophical Study of Biological Taxonomy* (Cambridge: Cambridge University Press, 2001).

35. Ereshefsky, *Poverty of the Linnaean Hierarchy,* 80.

36. Julia Kristeva, interview with Alain Nicolas, in Ross Mitchell Guberman, ed., *Julia Kristeva Interviews* (New York: Columbia University Press, 1996), 241; *Revolution in Poetic Language,* trans. Margaret Waller (New York: Columbia University Press, 1984), 13.

37. Fredric Jameson, *The Political Unconscious: Narrative as a Socially Symbolic Act* (Ithaca, NY: Cornell University Press, 1981), 130.

38. Henry Louis Gates Jr., *Loose Canons: Notes on the Culture Wars* (New York: Oxford University Press, 1992), 39, 37.

39. Paul de Man, "Anthropomorphism and Trope in the Lyric," in *The Rhetoric of Romanticism* (New York: Columbia University Press, 1984), 262.

40. Walt Whitman, "Vigil Strange I Kept on the Field One Night," in *Leaves of Grass,* 2:492.

41. Jacques Derrida, "The Deaths of Roland Barthes," 1981, trans. Pascale-Anne Brault and Michael Naas, in *The Work of Mourning,* ed. Brault and Naas (Chicago: University of Chicago Press, 2001), 56.

42. Fradenburg, "Loss and Reparation," 181; italics in original.

43. Henry Staten, *Eros in Mourning: Homer to Lacan* (Baltimore: Johns Hopkins University Press, 1995), xii–xiii.

44. Sigmund Freud, letter to Ludwig Binswanger, 11 April 1929, in *Essential Papers on Object Loss,* ed. Rita V. Frankiel (New York: New York University Press, 1994), 70.

45. Fradenburg, "Loss and Reparation," 182–83; italics in original.

46. Ibid., 184, 193; italics in original.

47. E. M. Cioran, "Mechanism of Utopia," in *History and Utopia,* trans. Richard Howard (Chicago: University of Chicago Press, 1998), 92–93.

48. Judith Butler, *Precarious Life: The Powers of Mourning and Violence* (London: Verso, 2004), 20, 22.

49. Ibid., 12.

50. Benedict Anderson, *Imagined Communities: Reflections on the Origin and Spread of Nationalism,* rev. ed. (London: Verso, 1991).

51. Sacks, *The English Elegy,* 312.

52. Ibid., 313.

53. Kenneth Burke, *The Philosophy of Literary Form,* 3rd. ed. (Berkeley: University of California Press, 1973), 6.

54. Sigmund Freud, "Mourning and Melancholy," in *Standard Edition of the Works of Sigmund Freud,* trans. James Strachey (London: Hogarth, 1957), 14:256.

55. Amy Clampitt, "The Dakota," in *The Kingfisher* (New York: Alfred A. Knopf, 1985), 29.

56. Following Ernesto De Martino's application of Freud's insight, Robert Pogue Harrison observes that "ritual lament submits the emotive spontaneity of grief to impersonal forms of expression" and wonders if it "was perhaps through grief that the human voice gained its first articulation" (*Dominion of the Dead* [Chicago: University of Chicago Press, 2003], 62).

57. Whitman, *Leaves of Grass,* 1:10; italics added.

58. Emerson's famous discouragement of Whitman's sexual frankness was motivated, as Elisa New observes, by more than the knowledge he had of "the prudery of the American public, perhaps by sharing it." "Whitman's unabashedly genealogical language," New writes, "is [to Emerson] not merely uncouth in pointing out the sexuality linking generation to generation. It is also, in Emersonian terms, theologically retrograde, reinstating an ancient determinism which shifted the burden of sin onto the shoulders of innocents down the generations" (*The Regenerate Lyric: Theology and Innovation in American Poetry* [Cambridge: Cambridge University Press, 1993], 97–98).

59. Breitwieser, *American Puritanism,* 8, 210.

60. Ibid., 16.

61. Ibid., 58.

62. As Richard Ford observes, "measure" never sheds its etymological origins in an evaluative term (metron) with moral force (*The Origins of Criticism: Literary Culture and Poetic Theory in Classical Greece* [Princeton, NJ: Princeton University Press, 2002], 18–19).

63. Herman Melville, *Mardi and a Voyage Thither,* in *Typee, Omoo, Mardi,* ed. G. Thomas Tanselle (New York: Library of America, 1982), 873.

64. The past decade has produced an unusually large number of such anthologies, particularly strong with regard to poetry by women. They include Cheryl Walker, ed., *American Women Poets of the Nineteenth Century* (New Brunswick, NJ: Rutgers University Press, 1992); Joan R. Sherman, ed., *African-American Poetry of the Nineteenth Century: An Anthology* (Urbana: University of Illinois Press, 1992); John Hollander, ed., *American Poetry: The Nineteenth Century,* 2 vols. (New York: Library of America, 1993); Paul Kane, ed., *Poetry of the American Renaissance: A Diverse Anthology from the Romantic Period* (New York: George Braziller, 1995); Robert Bain, ed., *Whitman and Dickinson's Contemporaries: An Anthology of Their Verse* (Carbondale: Southern Illinois University Press, 1996); William C. Spengemann and Jessica F. Roberts, eds., *Nineteenth-Century American Poetry* (New York: Penguin, 1996); Janet Gray, ed., *She*

Wields a Pen: American Women Poets of the Nineteenth Century (Iowa City: University of Iowa Press, 1997); Paula Bernat Bennett, ed., *Nineteenth-Century American Women Poets: An Anthology* (Cambridge, MA: Blackwell, 1998). On the history of American poetry anthologies from the 1790s to the 1990s, see Alan Golding, *From Outlaw to Classic: Canons in American Poetry* (Madison: University of Wisconsin Press, 1995), 3–40.

65. Sallie A. Brock. *The Southern Amaranth* (New York: Wilcox and Rockwell, 1869), v.

66. John Keese, preface to *The Mourner's Chaplet: An Offering of Sympathy for Bereaved Friends. Selected from American Poets* (Boston: Gould and Lincoln, 1844), iv.

1. Legacy and Revision in Eighteenth-Century Anglo-American Elegy

The epigraph at the chapter opening is from R. W. Franklin, ed., *The Poems of Emily Dickinson: Variorum Edition,* 3 vols. (Cambridge, MA: Harvard University Press, 1998), 2:542.

1. Robert Henson, "Form and Content of the Puritan Funeral Elegy," *American Literature* 32 (1960–61): 27. The sense of coherence Henson ascribes to American Puritan elegy is reinforced by a century of scholarship: John W. Draper, *The Funeral Elegy and the Rise of English Romanticism* (New York: New York University Press, 1929), 155–77; Roy Harvey Pearce, *The Continuity of American Poetry* (Princeton, NJ: Princeton University Press, 1961), 24–42; Kenneth Silverman, *Colonial American Poetry* (New York: Hafner Publishing, 1968), 121–32; Astrid Schmitt-v. Mühlenfels, "John Fiske's Funeral Elegy on John Cotton," *Early American Literature* 12 (1977): 49–62; Emory Elliott, "The Development of the Puritan Funeral Sermon and Elegy: 1660–1750," *Early American Literature* 15 (1980): 151–64; William J. Scheick, "Tombless Virtue and Hidden Text: New England Puritan Funeral Elegies," in *Puritan Poetry and Poetics: Seventeenth-Century American Poetry in Theory and Practice,* ed. Peter White (University Park: Pennsylvania State University Press, 1985), 286–302; Ivy Schweitzer, *The Work of Self-Representation: Lyric Poetry in Colonial New England* (Chapel Hill: University of North Carolina Press, 1991), 41–95; Matthew P. Brown, "'BOSTON/SOB NOT': Elegiac Performance in Early New England and Materialist Studies of the Book," *American Quarterly* 50 (1998): 306–39; Jeffrey A. Hammond, *The American Puritan Elegy: A Literary and Cultural Study* (Cambridge: Cambridge University Press, 2000).

2. The first accurate printing of this manuscript appears in *Proceedings of the Massachusetts Historical Society* 9 (1867): 298–342. It is also reprinted as "The History of Bacon's and Ingram's Rebellion, 1676" in *Narratives of the Insurrections, 1675–1690,* ed. Charles M. Andrews (New York: Charles Scribner's Sons, 1915), 43–98. Subsequent scholarship attributes authorship of the entire manuscript, including the two poems, to a Virginia planter named John Cotton; see Richard Beale Davis, *Intellectual Life in the Colonial South, 1585–1763* (Knoxville: University of Tennessee Press, 1978), 3:1352–54.

3. On the southern elegiac tradition, see Davis, *Intellectual Life,* 3:1401–19. On Cook and Lewis, see J. A. Leo Lemay, *Men of Letters in Colonial Maryland* (Knoxville:

University of Tennessee Press, 1972). See also Jack D. Wages, "Elegy and Mock Elegy in Colonial Virginia," *Studies in the Literary Imagination* 9, no. 2 (1976): 79–93.

4. Scheick, "Tombless Virtue and Hidden Text," 298.

5. For a reading of the "archive" of New England Puritan elegy that turns on the relation between material text and performance context, see Brown, "Elegiac Performance."

6. Michael Warner, *The Letters of the Republic: Publication and the Public Sphere in Eighteenth-Century America* (Cambridge, MA: Harvard University Press, 1990), 25–26.

7. *The New-England Courant*, 5–12 November 1722, 1.

8. *Cotton Mather's Verse in English*, ed. Denise D. Knight (Newark: University of Delaware Press, 1989), 51.

9. Joseph Roach, *Cities of the Dead: Circum-Atlantic Performance* (New York: Columbia University Press, 1996), 168.

10. *Cotton Mather's Verse*, 60–61.

11. See Sacvan Bercovitch, *The Puritan Origins of the American Self* (New Haven, CT: Yale University Press, 1975), 121.

12. Cotton Mather, *Magnalia Christi Americana: or, The Ecclesiastical History of New-England from Its First Planting in the Year 1620, unto the Year of our Lord, 1698. In Seven Books* (London: Thomas Parkhurst, 1702), 4:184–85. The Mitchell biography was initially published as *Ecclesiastes. The Life of the Reverend & Excellent Jonathan Mitchel . . .* (Boston: B. Green and J. Allen, 1697).

13. David S. Shields, *Civil Tongues and Polite Letters in British America* (Chapel Hill: University of North Carolina Press, 1997), 220.

14. Schweitzer, *Work of Self-Representation*, 43.

15. Silverman, *Colonial American Poetry*, 129.

16. *The New-England Courant*, 12 November 1722, 1.

17. *Boston News-Letter*, 30 May 1723, 1.

18. Shields, *Civil Tongues and Polite Letters*, 273, 249. On literary genres as "institutions," see Fredric Jameson, *The Political Unconscious: Narrative as a Socially Symbolic Act* (Ithaca, NY: Cornell University Press, 1981), 106.

19. *The New-England Weekly Journal*, 4 September 1727, 1.

20. *The London Magazine* 7 (July 1738): 357.

21. On the relationship between Byles and Green, see Shields, *Civil Tongues and Polite Letters*, 249–62.

22. *The London Magazine* 1 (November 1733): 579.

23. *The London Magazine* 6 (April 1737): 210.

24. Walter B. Norris, "Some Recently-Found Poems on the Calverts," *Maryland Historical Magazine* 32 (1937): 123.

25. Ibid., 125.

26. Ibid., 126.

27. *Pennsylvania Gazette*, 5 December 1734, 1. On the letter's attribution to Breintnall, see Lemay, *Men of Letters*, 181.

28. Benjamin Franklin, *Writings*, ed. J. A. Leo Lemay (New York: Library of America, 1987), 1331. Ironically, Keimer's *Elegy on the Death of Aquila Rose* has gone on

to become one of the most elusive and potentially most valuable items in the history of American printing. Worked off the press by Franklin and sporting a woodcut most likely carved by Franklin himself, what was advertised as the sole known copy was offered for sale in 2000 for $500,000. (The offering, which includes Keith Arbour's bibliographic description, was made in *Catalogue 50* [Philadelphia: Carmen D. Valentino, 2000]. I have not been able to trace the broadside's subsequent fate.)

29. Franklin, *Writings,* 1318.

30. Ibid., 879.

31. Warner, *Letters of the Republic,* 74.

32. Franklin, *Writings,* 91.

33. Ibid., 69.

34. Mitchell Breitwieser, *Cotton Mather and Benjamin Franklin: The Price of Representative Personality* (Cambridge: Cambridge University Press, 1984), 270.

35. Cotton Mather, *Bonifacius: An Essay upon the Good,* ed. David Levin (Cambridge, MA: Harvard University Press, 1966), 15.

36. Franklin, *Writings,* 1418.

37. Cotton Mather, *Small Offers Towards the Service of the Tabernacle in the Wilderness. Four Discourses, accommodated unto the Designs of Practical Godliness* (Boston: R. Pierce, 1689), 111.

38. Harry S. Stout, *The Divine Dramatist: George Whitefield and the Rise of Modern Evangelicalism* (Grand Rapids, MI: William B. Eerdmans, 1991), xx–xxi.

39. Growing confidence in a kinder, gentler afterlife was figured forth most dramatically, David Stannard notes, in a transformed iconography of death, as the ubiquitous winged death's-head of gravestones and broadside cuts was refashioned into the head of an angel (*The Puritan Way of Death: A Study in Religion, Culture, and Social Change* [New York: Oxford University Press, 1977], 156–57). Philippe Ariès calls this process of transformation "almost cinematic" (*The Hour of Our Death,* trans. Helen Weaver [New York: Oxford University Press, 1981], 340). See also Allan I. Ludwig, *Graven Images: New England Stonecarving and Its Symbols, 1650–1815* (Middletown, CT: Wesleyan University Press, 1966).

40. *A Hymn Composed by the Reverend Mr. Whitefield, To be sung over his own Corps* (Boston 1770).

41. Leonard W. Labaree et al., eds., *The Papers of Benjamin Franklin* (New Haven, CT: Yale University Press, 1959–), 5:475–76.

42. See Jon Butler, *Awash in a Sea of Faith: Christianizing the American People* (Cambridge, MA: Harvard University Press, 1990), 187. On the fetishizing of Whitefield's corpse, see Robert E. Cray, "Memorialization and Enshrinement: George Whitefield and Popular Religious Culture, 1770–1850," *Journal of the Early Republic* 10 (1990): 339–61.

43. *The Providence Gazette; and Country Journal,* 3–10 November 1770, 3.

44. See Stout, *Divine Dramatist,* 89.

45. *An Elegiac Poem; Sacred to the Memory of the Rev. George Whitefield . . .* (Boston: Isaiah Thomas, 1770), 6.

46. *The Massachusetts Gazette: and the Boston Weekly News-Letter,* 4 October 1770, 3.

47. Phillis Wheatley, *An Elegiac Poem, On the DEATH of that celebrated Divine, and*

eminent Servant of JESUS CHRIST, the late Reverend, and pious GEORGE WHITE-FIELD . . . (Boston 1770).

48. See Nancy Ruttenburg, *Democratic Personality: Popular Voice and the Trial of American Authorship* (Stanford, CA: Stanford University Press, 1998), 116–18.

49. George Whitefield, "A Prayer for a poor Negroe," in *The Works of the Reverend George Whitefield*, 7 vols. (London: Edward and Charles Dilly, 1771–72), 4:474. The original publication date of this prayer is unknown.

50. For an extended analysis of these changes, see Kirstin Wilcox, "The Body into Print: Marketing Phillis Wheatley," *American Literature* 71, no. 1 (1999): 1–29.

51. Phillis Wheatley, *Poems on Various Subjects, Religious and Moral* (London: A. Bell, 1773), 22–24.

52. Jane Dunlap, *Poems, Upon several Sermons, Preached by the Rev'd, and Renowned, George Whitefield, while in Boston* (Boston: n.p., 1771), 4.

53. "Elegy on the Death of a Late Celebrated Poetess," in *The Poems of Phillis Wheatley*, ed. Julian D. Mason Jr. (Chapel Hill: University of North Carolina Press, 1966), xvii–xviii. Further quotations are from this text.

54. See Daniel Cottom, "Captioning the Image of Tradition: Phillis Wheatley and Preposterous Authority," in *Ravishing Tradition: Cultural Forces and Literary History* (Ithaca, NY: Cornell University Press, 1996), 83–111.

55. Thomas Jefferson, *Writings*, ed. Merrill D. Peterson (New York: Library of America, 1984), 266–67.

56. Betsy Erkkila, "Phillis Wheatley and the Black American Revolution," in *A Mixed Race: Ethnicity in Early America*, ed. Frank Shuffelton (New York: Oxford University Press, 1993), 238.

57. Dennis Kay, *Melodious Tears: The English Funeral Elegy from Spenser to Milton* (Oxford: Clarendon, 1990), 4, 6.

58. *The New-England Courant*, 5–12 November 1722, 1.

59. Urian Oakes, *An Elegie upon the Death of the Reverend Mr. Thomas Shepard* . . . (Cambridge, MA: Samuel Green, 1677), 4.

60. Mather, *Magnalia Christi Americana*, 2:17.

61. *The Works of Anne Bradstreet*, ed. Jeannine Hensley (Cambridge, MA: Belknap Press, 1967), 189–91.

62. Celeste M. Schenck, "Feminism and Deconstruction: Re-Constructing the Elegy," *Tulsa Studies in Women's Literature* 5 (1986): 13–14.

63. "*A Lamentation &c. On the Death of a* Child," *The New-England Weekly Journal*, 30 July 1773, 1.

64. Cotton Mather, "An Elegy Upon the Death of Mrs. Mary Brown . . . ," *Cotton Mather's Verse*, 76.

65. Ibid., 74, 76.

66. Nicholas Noyes, *Upon the Much Lamented Death of That Pious and Hopeful Young Gentlewoman, Mrs. Mary Gerish* . . . (Boston: s.n., 1710).

67. John Danforth, *Honour and Vertue Elegized in a Poem Upon an Honourable, Aged, and Gracious Mother in Our Israel, Madam Elizabeth Hutchinson* . . . (Boston: s.n., 1713).

68. John Danforth, *The Divine Name Humbly Celebrated, on Occasion of the Translation to Heaven of the Bright Soul of the Pious and Vertuous, Madam Susanna Thacher . . .* (Boston: s.n., 1724).

69. Kenneth B. Murdock, ed., *Handkerchiefs from Paul* (Cambridge, MA: Harvard University Press, 1927), 22.

70. See Paul Connerton, *How Societies Remember* (Cambridge: Cambridge University Press, 1989), 72–104.

71. Edgar Allan Poe, *Essays and Reviews,* ed. G. R. Thompson (New York: Library of America, 1984), 19.

72. Franklin, *Writings,* 20–22.

73. Cheryl Walker, "In the Margin: The Image of Women in Early Puritan Poetry," in *Puritan Poetry and Poetics: Seventeenth-Century American Poetry in Theory and Practice,* ed. Peter White (University Park: Pennsylvania State University Press, 1985), 117.

74. John Winthrop, *The Journal of John Winthrop, 1630–1649,* abridged ed., ed. Richard S. Dunn and Laetitia Yeandle (Cambridge, MA: Harvard University Press, 1996), 271–72.

75. Mitchell Robert Breitwieser, *American Puritanism and the Defense of Mourning: Religion, Grief, and Ethnology in Mary White Rowlandson's Captivity Narrative* (Madison: University of Wisconsin Press, 1990), 18.

76. Two recent editions of eighteenth-century Anglo-American women's writing bring these networks dramatically into view: *Milcah Martha Moore's Book: A Commonplace Book from Revolutionary America,* ed. Catherine La Courreye Blecki and Karin A. Wulf (University Park: Pennsylvania State University Press, 1997); and *Only for the Eye of a Friend: The Poems of Annis Boudinot Stockton,* ed. Carla Mulford (Charlottesville: University Press of Virginia, 1995). See also Susan M. Stabile, *Memory's Daughters: The Material Culture of Remembrance in Eighteenth-Century America* (Ithaca, NY: Cornell University Press, 2004).

77. Mulford, *Only for the Eye of a Friend,* 5. See also Pattie Cowell, introduction to *Women Poets in Pre-Revolutionary America, 1650–1775: An Anthology* (Troy, NY: Whitston Publishing Company, 1981), 12–16.

78. The complex reciprocal relation between mourning and matrimony is a perennial theme of elegiac writing and may be traced in the related generic histories of elegy and epithalamion. Losses articulated, or even registered, only with difficulty often make their mark in elegy through marriage topoi, signaling a submerged relation between elegiac convention and unavowed grief work. Jeff Nunokawa has argued that Tennyson's deployment of epithalamic topoi in *In Memoriam* functions as "an elegy for earlier desire" ("*In Memoriam* and the Extinction of the Homosexual," *ELH* 58 [1991]: 429). Tennyson's representation of his mourning work for Arthur Hallam thus anticipates Judith Butler's discovery within heterosexuality of "an ungrieved and ungrievable homosexual cathexis" ("Melancholy Gender—Refused Identification," *Psychoanalytic Dialogues* 5, no. 2 [1995]: 171). Such cathexes seem frequently to give the discourse of friendship in early American writing an elegiac accent and may help illuminate the melancholy poetics of Stockton's intimacy with Fergusson.

79. Beginning in 1750, Hannah Griffitts, a Stockton contemporary, produced more than half a century's worth of annual elegies for her mother. Susan Stabile discusses this extraordinary cycle in *Memory's Daughters*, 178–89.

80. For a splendid particularist study of attitudes toward death and their relation to the experience of nationalism, see Claudio Lomnitz, *Death and the Idea of Mexico* (New York: Zone, 2005).

81. [Annis Boudinot Stockton], "An elegiack Ode on the 28th day of February [1782]. The anniversary of Mr. [Stockton's] death," *New Jersey Gazette*, 24 April 1782, 4. Reprinted in Mulford, *Only for the Eye of a Friend*, 112–14. The attribution of the note to Aaron Burr is Mulford's. Further quotations from the poem are cited parenthetically by line number within the text.

82. Annis Boudinot Stockton, "Aniversary Elegy on the Death of Mr Stockton the 28th of feb 1783," in Mulford, *Only for the Eye of a Friend*, 117.

83. Timothy Sweet, *Traces of War: Poetry, Photography, and the Crisis of Union* (Baltimore: Johns Hopkins University Press, 1990), 68.

84. Linda K. Kerber, *Women of the Republic: Intellect and Ideology in Revolutionary America* (Chapel Hill: University of North Carolina Press, 1980), 287.

85. Annis Boudinot Stockton, "Elegy inscribed to Richard J Stockton Esqr [Feb. 28, 1787]," in Mulford, *Only for the Eye of a Friend*, 143.

86. See Mulford, *Only for the Eye of a Friend*, 24; and Alfred Hoyt Bill and Constance M. Greiff, *A House Called Morven: Its Role in American History,* rev. ed. (Princeton, NJ: Princeton University Press, 1978), 39.

87. *Standard Edition of the Works of Sigmund Freud,* trans. James Strachey (London: Hogarth, 1957), 14:245.

88. Benedict Anderson, *Imagined Communities: Reflections on the Origin and Spread of Nationalism,* rev. ed. (New York: Verso, 1991), 24–25.

89. Zygmunt Bauman, *Mortality, Immortality and Other Life Strategies* (Stanford, CA: Stanford University Press, 1992), 113.

90. Thomas Paine, *Collected Writings,* ed. Eric Foner (New York: Library of America, 1995), 98.

91. In 1780, Franklin wrote to Joseph Priestly that "the rapid Progress *true* Science now makes, occasions my regretting sometimes that I was born too soon. It is impossible to imagine the Height to which may be carried, in a thousand years, the Power of Man over Matter. . . . all Diseases may by sure means be prevented or cured, not excepting even that of Old Age, and our Lives lengthened at pleasure even beyond the antediluvian Standard" (*Writings,* 1017). It is not so much "Matter" as consciousness of mortality that Franklin seeks to dominate in his fantasy of successive triumphs over particular "Diseases," exhibiting what Zygmunt Bauman calls the characteristically modern drive to "deconstruct mortality . . . to dissolve the issue of the struggle against death in an ever growing and never exhausted set of battles against particular diseases and other threats to life" (Mortality, 10, 97). Franklin's "regret" is occasioned by his dawning sense that death is a practical rather than existential problem.

92. *The Poems of Philip Freneau,* ed. Fred Lewis Pattee, 3 vols. (New York: Russell & Russell, 1963), 2:102.

93. Philip Freneau, "Lines occasioned by a visit to an old Indian burying ground," *The American Museum, or, Universal Magazine* 2 (1787): 515–16. Subsequent quotations from this text are identified parenthetically by line number within the text.

94. "To decipher religious myths about death and immortality, then, we need only recognize that the nexus of all spiritual imagery is the corpse; all narratives about life after death can be reduced to and derive their formal organization from a primal confrontation, which every culture and every individual repeats, with the bodies of the dead. The history of death, then, is the history of our organization, displacement, and metaphoric embellishment of this encounter, through language and funerary rituals." Alan Bewell, *Wordsworth and the Enlightenment: Nature, Man, and Society in the Experimental Poetry* (New Haven, CT: Yale University Press, 1989), 190.

95. *Thomas Gray and William Collins: Poetical Works,* ed. Roger Lonsdale (Oxford: Oxford University Press, 1977), 35.

96. See Phillip Round, "'The Posture That We Give the Dead': Freneau's 'Indian Burying Ground' in Ethnohistorical Context," *Arizona Quarterly* 50 (1994): 11.

97. Paine, *Collected Writings,* 572.

98. George Herbert, *The Complete English Poems,* ed. John Tobin (London: Penguin Books, 1991), 58.

99. See Ellen Zetzel Lambert, *Placing Sorrow: A Study of the Pastoral Convention from Theocritus to Milton* (Chapel Hill: University of North Carolina Press, 1976), xiii–xv.

100. *Poems of Philip Freneau,* 2:280.

101. John Milton, *Complete Poems and Major Prose,* ed. Merritt Y. Hughes (Indianapolis: Bobbs-Merrill Educational Publishing, 1957), 125.

102. Ibid., 124.

103. See, for example, his letter to Madison of December 20, 1787 (Jefferson, *Writings,* 917).

104. Roach, *Cities of the Dead,* 91.

105. Ernest Becker, *The Denial of Death* (New York: The Free Press, 1973), 7.

2. Elegy and the Subject of National Mourning

The epigraph at the chapter opening is from James Craik and Elisha C. Dick, "Gen. Washington's Illness," *Columbian Minerva* (Dedham, MA), 16 January 1800, 4.

1. *The Pennsylvania Gazette,* 28 April 1790, 3.

2. Thomas Jefferson, letter to Benjamin Rush, 4 October 1803, in *The Writings of Thomas Jefferson,* ed. Paul Leicester Ford, vol. 8 (New York: G. P. Putnam's Sons, 1897), 265.

3. Benjamin Vaughan, letter to La Rochefoucauld, 4 June 1790, in Gilbert Chinard, "The Apotheosis of Benjamin Franklin: Paris, 1790–1791," *Proceedings of the American Philosophical Society* 99 (1955): 441.

4. Julian P. Boyd, "Death of Franklin: The Politics of Mourning in France and

the United States," in *The Papers of Thomas Jefferson,* ed. Julian P. Boyd, vol. 19 (Princeton, NJ: Princeton University Press, 1974), 81.

5. Philip Freneau, "Stanzas, Occasioned by the Death of Dr. Franklin," in *The Newspaper Verse of Philip Freneau: An Edition and Bibliographical Survey,* ed. Judith R. Hiltner (Troy, NY: Whitston Publishing Company, 1986), 387.

6. Philip Freneau, "Verses from the other World, by Dr. Fr--k--n," in Hiltner, *Newspaper Verse,* 392.

7. In chapter 3 of *Sentimental Bodies: Sex, Gender, and Citizenship in the Early Republic* (Princeton, NJ: Princeton University Press, 1998), Bruce Burgett reads the intricate "logic of corporeal nationalism" in the Farewell Address and shows how the address helped set the terms for later struggles over Washington's memorialization.

8. Some of the larger exhibits mounted between 1998 and 2000 include, along with their venues: *George Washington: American Symbol,* Museums of Stony Brook, Long Island, and Museum of Our National Heritage, Lexington, Massachusetts; *The Great Experiment: George Washington and the American Republic,* Huntington Library, Los Angeles, and Morgan Library, New York City; *'His true & impressive image': Portraits of George Washington,* Mead Art Museum, Amherst, Massachusetts; *The Power and the Glory: George Washington and the Birth of Fame in America,* New-York Historical Society, New York City; *Treasures from Mount Vernon: The Man behind the Legend,* New-York Historical Society, New York City, Huntington Library, Los Angeles, Virginia Historical Society, Richmond, Atlanta Historical Society, and Chicago Historical Society; *Washington in Glory: America in Tears,* Fraunces Tavern Museum, New York City.

9. Thomas Pynchon, *Mason & Dixon* (New York: Henry Holt, 1997), 280. Pynchon's scene has its basis in fact: Washington did grow hemp at Mount Vernon, whence it was sold to rope and textile makers. For the license he takes, Pynchon may have found inspiration in Alfred Quiroz's 1994 painting, *George Washington Inspects the Hemp Crop,* in which Washington tokes up with two merry companions.

10. James Fenimore Cooper, *The Spy: A Tale of the Neutral Ground* (New York: Wiley and Halstead, 1821); William Makepeace Thackeray, *The Virginians* (New York: Harper and Brothers, 1859); Gertrude Stein, *Four in America* (New Haven, CT: Yale University Press, 1947); Gore Vidal, *Burr* (New York: Random House, 1973).

11. Michael T. Gilmore, "The Literature of the Revolutionary and Early National Periods," in *The Cambridge History of American Literature, Volume One: 1590–1820,* ed. Sacvan Bercovitch (Cambridge: Cambridge University Press, 1994), 593.

12. E. P. Thompson, "Commitment in Poetry," in *Making History: Writings on History and Culture* (New York: New Press, 1994), 339.

13. M. M. Bakhtin, *The Dialogic Imagination: Four Essays,* trans. Caryl Emerson and Michael Holquist (Austin: University of Texas Press, 1981), 5–8.

14. Julia A. Stern, *The Plight of Feeling: Sympathy and Dissent in the Early American Novel* (Chicago: University of Chicago Press, 1997), 3.

15. Elizabeth Barnes, *States of Sympathy: Seduction and Democracy in the American Novel* (New York: Columbia University Press, 1997), 63.

16. Of these many poems, a few survive in manuscript, some in the assembled

39. *Commercial Advertiser* (New York), 11 January 1800, 3.

40. Waldstreicher, *In the Midst of Perpetual Fetes,* 74.

41. John Adams, letter to Colonel Smith, 3 March 1800, Adams Papers, Massachusetts Historical Society, Boston.

42. John Adams, letter to Charles Love, 16 April 1800, Adams Papers, Massachusetts Historical Society, Boston.

43. Charles Love, letter to John Adams, 21 April 1800, Adams Papers, Massachusetts Historical Society, Boston.

44. The cultural work of elegy in the early national period is part of the history of what Richard Brodhead calls the "domestic-tutelary complex" in nineteenth-century America (*Cultures of Letters: Scenes of Reading and Writing in Nineteenth-Century America* [Chicago: University of Chicago Press, 1993], passim). Mary Loeffelholz extends Brodhead's prose-oriented analysis to include the "special role of poetry in both public and private arenas of instruction" during the same period analyzed by Brodhead in terms of the novel ("Who Killed Lucretia Maria Davidson? or, Poetry in the Domestic-Tutelary Complex," *Yale Journal of Criticism* 10 [1997]: 274).

45. Theodore Dwight, "Far, far from hence be satire's aspect rude . . . ," *Connecticut Courant* (Hartford), 6 January 1800, 3.

46. Eva Cherniavsky, *That Pale Mother Rising: Sentimental Discourse and the Imitation of Motherhood in 19th-Century America* (Bloomington: Indiana University Press, 1995), 11.

47. *Lady Washington's Lamentation for the Death of Her Husband* (Boston: Nathaniel Coverly, Jr., [1800]).

48. Stern, *The Plight of Feeling,* 31.

49. This grave is still open to visitors in New York City's Trinity Churchyard, where droves of Rowson's readers apparently used to congregate and weep.

50. Stern, *The Plight of Feeling,* 11.

51. See Betty Ring, *Girlhood Embroidery: American Samplers & Pictorial Needlework, 1650–1850,* 2 vols. (New York: Alfred A. Knopf, 1993); see also Sally Ripley, "Diary of Sally Ripley, 1799–1801," Women's History Sources, vol. 1, Collection 7671, 36–37, American Antiquarian Society, Worcester MA.

52. In a letter to his wife, Hannah, Thomas Dwight marks how sympathy's nationalizing power unravels amid the commodification of Washington's memory. While participating in Washington mourning ceremonies in Boston in late January, Dwight is mindful of the need to acquire souvenirs for his children and young relations: "Major [William?] Pynchon will carry you four Washington medals of white metal—one of which Miss Nancy Archbald presents to Mary—another is for my son John—another for Henry Bliss *my little son*—another for William B. Bliss, who I am sure will accuse his uncle of *barbarous* partiality, if forgotten in regard to the medal." Thomas Dwight, letter to Hannah Dwight, 29 January 1800, Dwight-Howard Papers, Massachusetts Historical Society, Boston.

53. "Lines on the Death of General Washington," *Bee* (New London, CT), 1 January 1800, 4.

54. *Commercial Advertiser* (New York), 4 January 1800, 2.

55. Charles Brockden Brown, review of Charles Caldwell, *An Elegiac Poem on*

the Death of General Washington, Monthly Magazine, and American Review (March 1800), 218.

56. Records of personal encounters with Washington—particularly by the French—are full of signs of admiration for his "external attributes" and "exterior form." Numerous assembled excerpts may be found in Rufus Wilmot Griswold, *The Republican Court; or, American Society in the Days of Washington* (New York: D. Appleton and Company, 1855); see also Gilbert Chinard, ed., *George Washington as the French Knew Him: A Collection of Texts* (Princeton, NJ: Princeton University Press, 1940).

57. Susanna Rowson, *Miscellaneous Poems* (Boston: Gilbert and Dean, 1804), 44. Further quotations from this poem will be identified parenthetically by line number within the text.

58. Ibid., 53.

59. Susanna Rowson, *Charlotte Temple,* ed. Cathy N. Davidson (New York: Oxford University Press, 1986), 5.

60. Lydia Sigourney, "The Mistletoe at the Tomb of Washington," in *Poems* (Boston: S. G. Goodrich, 1827), 217–18; Thomas Holley Chivers, "Washington," in *The Lost Pleiad and Other Poems* (New York: Edward O. Jenkins, 1845), 18; Samuel Bartlett Parris, "On a Sprig of Juniper, from the Tomb of Washington, Presented to the Author," in *Specimens of American Poetry,* ed. Samuel Kettell (Boston: S. G. Goodrich, 1829), 366–67; Hannah Gould, "Washington," in *Poems* (Boston: Hilliard, Gray, Little, and Wilkins, 1832), 207–9; John Pierpont, "Hark! 'tis the children of Washington pouring," in *Airs of Palestine, and Other Poems* (Boston: J. Munroe, 1840), 237–38; John Brainard, "On the Birthday of Washington," in *Poems of John Brainard* (Hartford, CT: S. Andrus & Son, 1841), 26–27.

61. John Bowlby, *Loss: Sadness and Depression* (New York: Basic Books, 1980), 96.

3. Taking Care of the Dead

The epigraph at the chapter opening is from Lester J. Cappon, ed., *The Adams-Jefferson Letters: The Complete Correspondence between Thomas Jefferson and Abigail and John Adams* (Chapel Hill: University of North Carolina Press, 1959), 467.

1. Lydia Huntley Sigourney, "The Mother of Washington," in *Select Poems,* 5th ed. (Philadelphia: Biddle, 1847), 290–92; Rosa [Jane Johnston Schoolcraft], "Invocation to My Maternal Grandfather . . . ," in *Schoolcraft's Ojibwa Lodge Stories: Life on the Lake Superior Frontier,* ed. Philip P. Mason (East Lansing: Michigan State University Press, 1997), 142–43. Four variants of Schoolcraft's poem, along with her elegies on other subjects, appear in Robert Dale Parker, ed., *The Sound the Stars Make Rushing Through the Sky: The Writings of Jane Johnston Schoolcraft* (Philadelphia: University of Pennsylvania Press, 2007).

2. Henry Wadsworth Longfellow, *The Seaside and the Fireside* (Boston: Ticknor, Reed, and Fields, 1850), 51. "Resignation" was also published in *The North Star* in 1849. According to Jean Baker, Abe and Mary Todd Lincoln read "Resignation" together when mourning their own children (*Mary Todd Lincoln: A Biography* [New York: Norton, 1987], 254).

3. Ralph Waldo Emerson, "Fate," in *Essays and Lectures,* ed. Joel Porte (New York: Library of America, 1983), 960.

4. Parke Godwin, ed., *The Poetical Works of William Cullen Bryant,* 2 vols. (New York: D. Appleton, 1883), 1:19. Further references to this edition, designated *Poetical Works,* occur parenthetically within the text.

5. Jahan Ramazani, *Poetry of Mourning: The Modern Elegy from Hardy to Heaney* (Chicago: University of Chicago Press, 1994), 8.

6. Cappon, *The Adams-Jefferson Letters,* 470.

7. Ibid., 487–88.

8. William M. Gouge, *A Short History of Paper Money and Banking in the United States* (Philadelphia: J. W. Ustick, 1833), 41–42.

9. On Jackson's assault on the money power, see Charles Sellers, *The Market Revolution: Jacksonian America, 1815–1846* (New York: Oxford University Press, 1991), 301–31.

10. [William Cullen Bryant], unsigned editorial, *Evening Post* (New York), 23 September 1833, 2. The *Post* serialized Gouge's *Short History* in 1834.

11. [William Cullen Bryant], "On the Happy Temperament," *North American Review and Miscellaneous Journal* 9, no. 24 (June 1819): 207.

12. Emerson, *Essay and Lectures,* 473.

13. Parke Godwin, ed., *Prose Writings of William Cullen Bryant,* 2 vols. (New York: Russell & Russell, 1964), 1:35. Further references to this edition, designated *Prose,* occur parenthetically within the text.

14. William Charvat, *The Profession of Authorship in America, 1800–1870* (New York: Columbia University Press, 1992), 109.

15. Ibid., 109.

16. William Cullen Bryant II and Thomas G. Voss, ed., *The Letters of William Cullen Bryant,* 6 vols. (New York: Fordham University Press, 1975–92), 1:320. Further references to this edition, designated *Letters,* occur parenthetically within the text.

17. [William Cullen Bryant], review of *Redwood, a Tale,* by Catharine Sedgwick, *North American Review* 20, no. 47 (April 1825): 251, 253.

18. Ibid., 253.

19. The revulsion Bryant reports feeling at his own verses contrasts with his account of his father's death scene. Peter Bryant's final moments, for which his son was present, must have been particularly gruesome, as he slowly suffocated on the blood that was filling his lungs. Yet, in a letter to his aunt two days later, Bryant offered a fairly clinical account, along with the following admission: "I never saw any body die before," the country doctor's son told her, "but judging as well as I am able I should think his death on the whole, more easy than is generally the case" (*Letters,* 1:91). Bryant's matter-of-fact description is suggestive of the sheer ordinariness of death in early-nineteenth-century rural New England. On the deathbed scene and the domestic setting for death and dying in the period, see Gary Laderman, *The Sacred Remains: American Attitudes toward Death, 1799–1883* (New Haven, CT: Yale University Press, 1996), 27–38. See also Sheila M. Rothman, *Living in the Shadow of Death: Tuberculosis and the Social Experience of Illness in American History* (Baltimore: Johns Hopkins University Press, 1995).

20. See also Bryant's "The Death of the Flowers," in which the occasion for the poem—the death of his beloved sister Sarah—figures in the final stanza as a kind of afterthought.

21. On the distinction between the rejection of neoclassicism and the myth of generic breakdown in British Romanticism, see Stuart Curran, *Poetic Form and British Romanticism* (New York: Oxford University Press, 1986).

22. Walt Whitman, *Complete Poetry and Collected Prose,* ed. Justin Kaplan (New York: Library of America, 1982), 988–89.

23. John Milton, *Complete Poems and Major Prose,* ed. Merritt Y. Hughes (Indianapolis: Bobbs-Merrill Educational Publishing, 1957), 120.

24. Despite loosening standards of versification, Augustan prejudices persisted in antebellum American criticism. For example, in the September 1836 issue of the *American Monthly Magazine* an anonymous reviewer upbraided the poet Nathaniel Parker Willis for his "constant violations of meter" (217). Citing what he felt was a particularly egregious instance of the "capital fault" of trisyllabic substitution, the reviewer maintained that "Pope's blood would have run cold at so gross a violation of all rule" (215). William Charvat discusses the criticism of poetic form in *The Origins of American Critical Thought, 1810–1835* (New York: Russell & Russell, 1968), pointing out "how late neo-classical principles lingered among the orthodox" (101). In England, too, certain prosodic theorists remained suspicious of trisyllabic substitution well into the nineteenth century. Paul Fussell outlines the transition from normative syllabism to the ascendance of accentual meter in his *Theory of Prosody in Eighteenth-Century England* (New London: Archon, 1954).

25. *The Poetical Works of William Wordsworth,* ed. E. de Selincourt and Helen Darbishire, 5 vols. (Oxford: Clarendon Press, 1940–49), 2:390–91.

26. Alexis de Tocqueville, *Democracy in America,* trans. Arthur Goldhammer, (New York: Library of America, 2004), 555.

27. Parke Godwin, *A Biography of William Cullen Bryant, with Extracts from His Private Correspondence,* 2 vols. (New York: D. Appleton and Company, 1883), 1:143–44.

28. Robert Blair, *The Grave. A Poem* (London: M. Cooper, 1743), 11.

29. Bryant took a lifelong interest in American painting and counted many painters among his friends and professional associates. Among them was Thomas Cole, for whom he wrote his best sonnet ("To Cole, the Painter, Departing for Europe") and with whom he appears standing on Table Rock in Asher Durand's iconic painting of American Romanticism "Kindred Spirits." In 1850, Durand's "Landscape, Scene from 'Thanatopsis'" was exhibited in New York at the National Academy of Design, where Bryant had often lectured, and subsequently at the American Art Union, where Bryant had been president from 1844 to 1846. Durand's painting (now in the collection of the Metropolitan Museum of Art, for whose establishment Bryant campaigned heavily) is not so much a scene from Bryant's poem as a baroque composite of extraneous elements, many of which—including a castle and a cathedral—are perhaps remotely evoked but nowhere described in "Thanatopsis."

30. Bryant did not name the poem himself. The untitled manuscript came, via Bryant's father, into the hands of the editorial staff of the *North American Review,* where it was published as "Thanatopsis" in 1817. Whoever coined the term is likely to

have been influenced by Henry Kirke White's poem "Thanatos," which appeared in an American edition of the author's work in 1811 (*Remains of Henry Kirke White,* 2 vols. [Philadelphia: J. & A. Y. Humphreys, 1811], 1:348–49).

31. Tocqueville, *Democracy in America,* 556–57.

32. Ibid., 557.

33. One recent sign of the enduring appeal of these lines is the position they occupy in Sherwin Nuland's best-selling book *How We Die: Reflections on Life's Final Chapter* (New York: Vintage Books, 1995). Nuland, professor of surgery and the history of medicine at Yale, sets out to "demythologize the process of dying. . . . to present it in its biological and clinical reality" (xvii). Yet after hundreds of pages of frank description in which he makes it quite clear that, for most of us, death will be anything but dignified, Nuland nevertheless ends his book by quoting the last nine lines of "Thanatopsis," as though they did not reinforce precisely those notions he means to dispel.

34. Herbert Marcuse, "The Ideology of Death," in *The Meaning of Death,* ed. Herman Feifel (New York: McGraw-Hill Book Company, 1959), 66–67.

35. According to Helen Trimpi, its sentimental aestheticism also looks forward to Melville's caricature of Bryant in *The Confidence-Man.* Bryant's taste for the melancholy and his reputed personal coldness are sent up, Trimpi argues, in the character of John Ringman, the "man with the weed" (*Melville's Confidence Men and American Politics in the 1850s* [Hamden, CT: Archon Books, 1987], 76–84).

36. Charles Eliot Norton, ed., *Letters from Ralph Waldo Emerson to a Friend, 1838–1853* (Boston: Houghton, Mifflin and Company, 1900), 35–36.

37. Lora Romero, *Home Fronts: Domesticity and Its Critics in the Antebellum United States* (Durham, NC: Duke University Press, 1997), 35.

38. The topos of pilgrimagic return by displaced Indians to sacred or memorial sites is pervasive in works of the white literary imagination of Bryant's day. Bryant employs it again at the end of his 1824 poem "Monument Mountain" (*Poetical Works,* 1:107). The history of Indian practices of sacred geography—from revisiting or ceremonially reconstituting sacred spots to more recent forms of toponymic research—is explored by Peter Nabakov in *A Forest of Time: American Indian Ways of History* (Cambridge: Cambridge University Press, 2002), 126–49.

39. See Peter M. Sacks, *The English Elegy: Studies in the Genre from Spenser to Yeats* (Baltimore: Johns Hopkins University Press, 1985).

40. Renato Rosaldo, *Culture and Truth: The Remaking of Social Analysis,* rev. ed. (Boston: Beacon Press, 1993), 70.

41. D. H. Lawrence, *Studies in Classic American Literature* (New York: Penguin Books, 1977), 90.

42. *The Complete Works of Ralph Waldo Emerson,* ed. Edward Waldo Emerson, 12 vols. (Boston: Houghton Mifflin and Company, 1903–4), 11:92.

43. [William Cullen Bryant], editorial, *Evening Post* (New York), 12 November 1832, 2.

44. Michael Paul Rogin, *Fathers and Children: Andrew Jackson and the Subjugation of the American Indian* (New Brunswick, NJ: Transaction Publishers, 1991), 121.

45. On "displacing the dead" in early American cemeteries, see David Charles

Sloane, *The Last Great Necessity: Cemeteries in American History* (Baltimore: Johns Hopkins University Press, 1991), 13–43.

46. *Shelley's Poetry and Prose*, ed. Donald H. Reiman and Sharon B. Powers (New York: W. W. Norton & Company, 1977), 103.

47. Barbara L. Packer, "'Man Hath No Part in All This Glorious Work': American Romantic Landscapes," in *Romantic Revolutions: Criticism and Theory,* ed. Kenneth R. Johnston, Gilbert Chaitin, et al. (Bloomington: Indiana University Press, 1990), 251, 259–60.

48. Ibid., 262; *The Collected Poems of Wallace Stevens* (New York: Alfred A. Knopf, 1954), 526.

49. Wordsworth, *Poetical Works,* 2:259.

50. See, for example, Crèvecoeur's description of frontier denizens in "What Is an American?" (*Letters from an American Farmer,* ed. Albert E. Stone [New York: Penguin, 1981], 72–73). The phrase "semi-barbarous citizens" comes from Jefferson's September 6, 1824, letter to William Ludlow, in Thomas Jefferson, *Writings,* ed. Merrill D. Peterson (New York: Library of America, 1984), 1496.

51. *The Collected Works of William Hazlitt,* ed. A. R. Waller and Arnold Glover, 12 vols. (London: J. M. Dent & Company, 1902–4), 1:214.

52. *The Addresses and Messages of the Presidents of the United States, from Washington to Harrison* (New York: Edward Walker, 1841), 398–99.

53. *Macbeth,* Riverside edition, ed. G. Blakemore Evans (Boston: Houghton Mifflin Company, 1974), 4.3.222–23; 4.3.216–19.

54. On the relationship between elegy and revenge tragedy, see Sacks, *The English Elegy,* 64–89. See also, John Kerrigan, *Revenge Tragedy: Aeschylus to Armageddon* (Oxford: Oxford University Press, 1995).

55. For a fascinating treatment of the complex mutuality of remembrance and forgetting on the eighteenth-century Pennsylvania frontier, see James H. Merrell, *Into the American Woods: Negotiations on the Pennsylvania Frontier* (New York: Norton, 1999), 179–224. On historical imagination and practice in Indian cultures, see Nabakov, *A Forest of Time.*

56. The term *prairie* had begun to appear in English by the late seventeenth century. But in 1815 it was still sufficiently novel for Robert Southey to question its propriety in a review of Lewis and Clarke's *Travels*: "If this word be merely a French synonime for savannah, which has long been naturalized, the Americans display little taste in preferring it. But perhaps it may designate open land in a woody country, whatever be the inequalities of the ground, whereas savannah (literally a sheet of land) can properly apply only to a level" (review of *Travels to the Source of the Missouri River, and across the American Continent to the Pacific Ocean . . . By Captains Lewis and Clarke, Quarterly Review* 12 [1815]: 326).

57. With regard to receding herds of buffalo and other game, Tocqueville notes: "I have been assured that this effect of the white man's approach can be felt in many cases two hundred leagues beyond his border. Thus the white man's influence affects tribes whose names he barely knows, tribes that suffer the evils of usurpation long before they become aware of who is responsible for them" (*Democracy in America,* 373).

58. Herman Melville, *Moby-Dick; or, The Whale,* ed. G. Thomas Tanselle (New York: Library of America, 1983), 962.

4. Elegy's Child

The epigraph at the chapter opening is from Harriet Beecher Stowe, *Uncle Tom's Cabin; or, Life among the Lowly* (1852), ed. Ann Douglas (New York: Penguin, 1981), 149.

1. Charles Sellers, *The Market Revolution: Jacksonian America, 1815–1846* (New York: Oxford University Press, 1991), 152–53.

2. Serge Leclaire, *A Child Is Being Killed: On Primary Narcissism and the Death Drive* (1975), trans. Marie-Claude Hays (Stanford, CA: Stanford University Press, 1998), 3.

3. Philippe Ariès, *The Hour of Our Death,* trans. Helen Weaver (New York: Oxford University Press, 1991), 536, 460.

4. Sellers, *Market Revolution,* 17, 157.

5. Ibid., 240.

6. Lydia Huntley Sigourney, *Letters of Life* (New York: D. Appleton, 1866), 368. Further references occur parenthetically in the text.

7. L. H. Sigourney, *Poems* (Philadelphia: Key & Biddle, 1834), 142–43.

8. With this phrase, Sarah Wentworth Morton refers to her dead son in her elegy "Memento, for My Infant Who Lived But Eighteen Hours" (*My Mind and Its Thoughts, in Sketches, Fragments, and Essays* [Boston: Wells and Lilly, 1823], 255–56).

9. Sellers, *Market Revolution,* 18.

10. Phyllis Cole, *Mary Moody Emerson and the Origins of Transcendentalism: A Family History* (New York: Oxford University Press, 1998), 10, 19.

11. Nancy Craig Simmons, ed., *The Selected Letters of Mary Moody Emerson* (Athens: University of Georgia Press, 1993), 314.

12. Ralph Waldo Emerson, "Man the Reformer," in *Essays and Lectures,* ed. Joel Porte (New York: Library of America, 1983), 137. Further references to this edition, designated *Essays,* occur parenthetically in the text.

13. *The Journals and Miscellaneous Notebooks of Ralph Waldo Emerson,* ed. William H. Gilman et al., 16 vols. (Cambridge, MA: Harvard University Press, 1960–1982), 5:415–16. Further references to this edition, designated *Journals,* occur parenthetically in the text.

14. B. L. Packer, *Emerson's Fall: A New Interpretation of the Major Essays* (New York: Continuum, 1982), 51.

15. *The Poetical Works of William Wordsworth,* ed. E. de Selincourt and Helen Darbishire, 5 vols. (Oxford: Clarendon Press, 1940–49), 5:73.

16. Ibid., 4:259–60.

17. Ralph Waldo Emerson, *Collected Poems and Translations,* ed. Harold Bloom and Paul Kane (New York: Library of America, 1994), 325. The merely physical manipulation of nature represented by telescopy is not sublime in the Kantian sense that applies to Emerson. But his emphasis here on the extensive power of sight anticipates the foremost instance of the Emersonian sublime, the transparent eyeball of *Nature,*

which looks through the world without the aid of desublimating technology. The tension here between limitation and overcoming is reinforced by the image of the sun itself. "Beneath this figure," writes Peter Sacks, evoking the history of its resignification in ancient and modern elegy, "there plays a heritage of powerful contradictions associated with the original positing of any imagery of light on the far side of darkness, or of presence in the space of an absence" (*The English Elegy: Studies in the Genre from Spenser to Yeats* [Baltimore: Johns Hopkins University Press, 1985], 34).

18. Emerson, *Collected Poems*, 326.

19. Ironically, Emerson anticipates here what Barbara Packer calls the "severest attacks on Emerson's character and sanity in this century . . . com[ing] from men who accuse him of harboring and fostering in others an infantile disregard for the realities of associated life. The untrammelled spiritual freedom he urges his hearers to cultivate, the reliance only on inner promptings, would result in anarchy and murder if actually applied to the world of natural and social relations" (*Emerson's Fall*, 92).

20. Wordsworth, *Poetical Works*, 4:279.

21. Ralph Waldo Emerson to Thomas Carlyle, 28 February 1842, in *The Correspondence of Emerson and Carlyle*, ed. Joseph Slater (New York: Columbia University Press, 1964), 317. Further references occur parenthetically in the text.

22. John Milton, *Complete Poems and Major Prose*, ed. Merritt Y. Hughes (Indianapolis: Bobbs-Merrill Educational Publishing, 1957), 125; Wordsworth, *Poetical Works*, 4:279.

23. "There is something pleasing," Emerson acknowledges in his 1835 lecture on Milton, "in the affection with which we can regard a man who died a hundred and sixty years ago in the other hemisphere, who, in respect to personal relations, is to us as the wind, yet by an influence purely spiritual makes us jealous for his fame as for that of a near friend" (*The Early Lectures of Ralph Waldo Emerson*, ed. Stephen Whicher, Robert E. Spiller, and Wallace E. Williams, 3 vols. [Cambridge, MA: Harvard University Press, 1960–72], 1:149).

24. This connection is suggested by Stanley Cavell, who fancies he finds in "Experience" an allusion to *The Winter's Tale*, in which, as he puts it, "the death of a son and a loving wife are the cost of a refusal to recognize contact with the reality of a birth" (*This New Yet Unapproachable America: Lectures after Emerson after Wittgenstein* [Albuquerque, NM: Living Batch Press, 1989], 98). Leaving aside the question of whether the word *reality* has quite the meaning in Emerson's essay Cavell ascribes to it, he performs an ingenious reading of "Experience" as a fantasy of male pregnancy, of autogenous birth, a birth that would be one's own. Yet the comparison of Emerson with Leontes is a caricature insofar as it suggests that uncertainty as such produces in Emerson the rhetorical equivalent of the Sicilian king's murderous anxiety. Emerson's dream of knowledge is a soft, not a turbulent, one.

25. In his *First Treatise of Government* Locke writes that "those who desire and design Children, are but the occasions of their being, and when they design and wish to beget them, do little more towards their making, than *Ducalion* and his Wife in the Fable did towards the making of Mankind, by throwing Pebbles over their Heads" (*Two Treatises Of Government*, ed. Peter Laslett [Cambridge: Cambridge University Press, 1988], 179–80).

26. *The New-England Primer Enlarged* (Boston: S. Kneeland, & T. Green, 1727), 9.

27. Benjamin Wadsworth, "A Sermon, Setting forth the *Nature of Early Piety,*" in *A Course of Sermons on Early Piety,* ed. Increase Mather (Boston: S. Kneeland, 1721), 10.

28. In "A Transcendentalist Father: The Child-Rearing Practices of Bronson Alcott" (*Perspectives in American History* 3 [1969]: 17), Charles Strickland offers the following passage from one of Alcott's manuscripts: "Of all the impious doctrines which the dark imagination of man ever conceived, this is the worst. This is, indeed, the sin, which is unpardonable—the belief in the original and certain depravity of infant nature. If man had set himself down to contrive an agency which would . . . most effectually degrade human nature, he could not have accomplished his foul purpose so effectually as by this." Alcott's various opinions regarding childhood and parenting are recorded in thousands of pages of observations on his daughters' early years, which Strickland reviews at length. Strickland points out that Alcott had a less than perfect understanding of Calvinist orthodoxy. Nevertheless, he was not alone in his opposition to currently held views on Calvinist theories of infant depravity. Peter Gregg Salter puts this opposition into historical perspective in *Children in the New England Mind: In Death and in Life* (Hamden, CT: Archon Books, 1977).

29. "Lidian [Emerson's second wife] came into the study this afternoon & found the towerlet that Wallie had built half an hour before, of two spools, a card, an awl-case, & a flourbox top—each perpendicularly balanced on the other, & could scarce believe that her boy had built the pyramid, & then fell into such a fit of affection that she lay down by the structure & kissed it down, & declared she could possibly stay no longer with papa, but must go off to the nursery to see with eyes the lovely creature; & so departed" (*Journals,* 5:480–81).

30. Emerson's own prose, with its combination of broken syntax (asyndeton) and repetition (anaphora), heightens the sublime effect. See *Longinus on the Sublime,* trans. W. Rhys Roberts (Cambridge: Cambridge University Press, 1899), esp. 43, 93, 101, 105, 137.

31. On oedipal reversal in the sublime, see Neil Hertz, "A Reading of Longinus," in *The End of the Line: Essays on Psychoanalysis and the Sublime* (New York: Columbia University Press, 1985), 1–21. See also Suzanne Guerlac, "Longinus and the Subject of the Sublime," *New Literary History* 16 (1985): 275–89, and the ensuing response from Frances Ferguson.

32. Stephen E. Whicher, *Freedom and Fate: An Inner Life of Ralph Waldo Emerson,* 2d ed. (Philadelphia: University of Pennsylvania Press, 1971), 45–46.

33. Packer, *Emerson's Fall,* 50–52.

34. James M. Cox, "R. W. Emerson: The Circles of the Eye," in *Emerson: Prophecy, Metamorphosis, and Influence,* ed. David Levin (New York: Columbia University Press, 1975), 72–73.

35. Discussing this allusion, Richard Poirier credits another version of the myth in which Zephyrus, jealous of Hyacinthus's love for Apollo, deliberately causes the boy's death by blowing the discus off course (*Poetry and Pragmatism* [Cambridge, MA: Harvard University Press, 1992], 60).

36. Emerson, *Collected Poems,* 117. Quotations from "Threnody" are henceforth identified by line number within the text.

37. Gay Wilson Allen, *Waldo Emerson: A Biography* (New York: Viking, 1981), vi–vii.

38. Viz. Virgil's lament for Daphnis in the fifth eclogue, Milton's for Edward King in "Lycidas," and Shelley's for Keats in "Adonais."

39. *The Poems of Edward Taylor,* ed. Donald E. Stanford (New Haven, CT: Yale University Press, 1960), 470.

40. *The Complete Poetry of Ben Jonson,* ed. William B. Hunter Jr. (New York: New York University Press, 1963), 20.

41. As a close student of Milton, Emerson perhaps knew of *excess* as a rare, archaic word for "sin." It is used this way, for example, in Milton's poem "Upon the Circumcision."

42. Immanuel Kant, *Critique of Judgment,* ed. J. H. Bernard (New York: Hafner Press, 1951), 113.

43. On "inexpressibility topoi," see Ernst Robert Curtius, *European Literature and the Latin Middle Ages,* trans. Willard R. Trask (Princeton, NJ: Princeton University Press, 1973), 159–62.

44. Margaret Alexiou, *The Ritual Lament in Greek Tradition* (Cambridge: Cambridge University Press, 1974), 12–13.

45. Sacks, *The English Elegy,* 35.

46. The *Poems and Fables of John Dryden,* ed. James Kinsley (London: Oxford University Press, 1962), 327.

47. *The Complete Works of Ralph Waldo Emerson,* ed. Edward Waldo Emerson, 12 vols. (Boston: Houghton, Mifflin, 1903–4), 9:452.

48. John McAleer, *Ralph Waldo Emerson: Days of Encounter* (Boston: Little, Brown and Company, 1984), 381. At the opposite extreme is the judgment of David Porter, who nevertheless holds Emerson to the same standard of sincerity, writing that "'Threnody' suffers demonstrably from a failure of feeling. It lacks emotional authority and convincing particularity in its portrayal of the son who died, of the relationship of the father to his son, and of the consequent grief" (*Emerson and Literary Change* [Cambridge: Harvard University Press, 1978], 30).

49. Allen, *Waldo Emerson,* 397.

50. Samuel Johnson, *Selected Poetry and Prose,* ed. Frank Brady and W. K. Wimsatt (Berkeley: University of California Press, 1977), 426.

51. "I know too well," she wrote to her nephew in characteristically exploded sentences, "those [joys?] of loving boys who[se] looks are of the soul & create new prophecies God alone who built yours can account for the calmness w'h masters your affliction—How you could write to me at such a time & with the poetry w'h belongs only to a world free from the sad mysteries of this." *The Selected Letters of Mary Moody Emerson,* ed. Nancy Craig Simmons (Athens: University of Georgia Press, 1993), 439. On Mary Moody Emerson's role as "priestess of mourning" to the Emerson household, see Cole, *Mary Moody Emerson and the Origins of Transcendentalism,* 261 and passim.

52. Kenneth Burke, "I, Eye, Ay—Concerning Emerson's Early Essay on 'Nature,' and the Machinery of Transcendence," in *Language as Symbolic Action: Essays on Life, Literature, and Method* (Berkeley: University of California Press, 1966), 186.

53. Mark Edmundson, "Emerson and the Work of Melancholia," *Raritan* 6, no. 4 (Spring 1987), 32.

54. Of course, for God there is no generative imperative—no "brute occasion" of physical need and no mortal dependence on propagation to ensure biological survival or to approximate immortality, a point Emerson is likely to have seen stressed in the 1825 translation of Milton's recently rediscovered *De Doctrina Christiana* (*A Treatise on Christian Doctrine, Compiled from the Holy Scriptures Alone,* trans. Charles R. Sumner [Cambridge: Cambridge University Press, 1825], 84–86). On the importance of this book to Milton's reputation in Unitarian Boston, see K. P. Van Anglen, *The New England Milton: Literary Reception and Cultural Authority in the Early Republic* (University Park: Pennsylvania State University Press, 1993), 81–108.

55. Milton, *Complete Poems,* 265.

56. "The deep Heart" begins the second part of the poem by asking the poet "'Weepest thou?'" (176), repeating the question several lines later. It is the same question twice asked of Mary Magdalene as she stands before Jesus' empty sepulchre in John 20. Emerson's journal testifies to his curiosity about mortal remains. A year after his first wife's death, he reports without elaboration that he "visited Ellen's tomb & opened the coffin" (*Journals,* 4:7). Equally reticent is his entry of July 8, 1857: "This morning I had the remains of my mother and of my son Waldo removed from the tomb of Mrs. Ripley to my lot in 'Sleepy Hollow.' The sun shone brightly on the coffins, of which Waldo's was well-preserved—now fifteen years. I ventured to look into the coffin. I gave a few white-oak leaves to each coffin, after they were put in the new vault, and the vault was then covered with two slabs of granite." *The Journals of Ralph Waldo Emerson,* ed. Edward Waldo Emerson and Waldo Emerson Forbes, 10 vols. (Boston: Houghton Mifflin Company, 1909–14), 9:102–3.

57. Thomas Weiskel calls the Romantic sublime "a major analogy, a massive transposition of transcendence into a naturalistic key" (*The Romantic Sublime: Studies in the Structure and Psychology of Transcendence* [Baltimore: Johns Hopkins University Press, 1986], 4).

58. Friedrich von Schiller, *Naive and Sentimental Poetry and On the Sublime: Two Essays,* trans. Julius A. Elias (New York: Frederick Ungar, 1966), 195.

59. Edmundson, "Emerson and the Work of Melancholia," 133, 136.

60. See Harold Bloom, "Emerson and Whitman: The American Sublime," in *Poetry and Repression: Revisionism from Blake to Stevens* (New Haven, CT: Yale University Press, 1976), 235–66.

61. John Guillory, *Cultural Capital: The Problem of Literary Canon Formation* (Chicago: University of Chicago Press, 1993), 108.

62. Wordsworth, *Poetical Works,* 2: 81.

63. Sharon Cameron, "Representing Grief: Emerson's 'Experience,'" *Representations* 15 (1986), 20.

64. Julie Ellison, "Tears for Emerson: *Essays, Second Series,*" in *The Cambridge Companion to Ralph Waldo Emerson,* ed. Joel Porte and Saundra Morris (Cambridge: Cambridge University Press, 1999), 140–61.

65. Alexis de Tocqueville, *Democracy in America,* trans. Arthur Goldhammer (New York: Library of America, 2004), 555.

66. Emerson, *Complete Works*, 9:335, 336.

67. Frederick Douglass, *My Bondage and My Freedom* (1855), in *Autobiographies*, ed. Henry Louis Gates Jr. (New York: Library of America, 1994), 151, 152, 157.

5. Mourning of the Disprized

The epigraph at the chapter opening is from Mary Prince, *The History of Mary Prince, a West Indian Slave. Related by Herself* (1831), ed. Sara Salih (New York: Penguin, 2000), 22.

1. For a sampling of accounts of slave funerals in the British West Indies, see Roger D. Abrahams and John Szwed, *After Africa: Extracts from British Travel Accounts and Journals of the Seventeenth, Eighteenth, and Nineteenth Centuries concerning the Slaves, their Manners, and Customs in the British West Indies* (New Haven, CT: Yale University Press, 1983), 163–79.

2. David R. Roediger, "And Die in Dixie: Funerals, Death, and Heaven in the Slave Community, 1700–1865," *Massachusetts Review* 22 (1981): 164–65.

3. Paul Gilroy, *The Black Atlantic: Modernity and Double Consciousness* (Cambridge, MA: Harvard University Press, 1993), 63.

4. Saidiya V. Hartman, *Scenes of Subjection: Terror, Slavery, and Self-Making in Nineteenth-Century America* (New York: Oxford University Press, 1997), 35–36.

5. Thomas Wentworth Higginson, "Negro Spirituals," *Atlantic Monthly* 19 (June 1867): 685, 686, 690, 694.

6. James Weldon Johnson, *The Book of American Negro Spirituals* (New York: Viking Press, 1925), 11; Ralph Waldo Emerson, "The Poet" (1844), in *Essays and Lectures*, ed. Joel Porte (New York: Library of America, 1983), 449; Jahan Ramazani, *Poetry of Mourning: The Modern Elegy from Hardy to Heaney* (Chicago: University of Chicago Press, 1994), 142; Higginson, "Negro Spirituals," 687.

7. Ramazani, *Poetry of Mourning*, 135.

8. Terry's poem "Bars Fight" seems to have been transmitted orally until the mid-nineteenth century, when it was transcribed and published in Josiah Gilbert Holland's *History of Western Massachusetts*, 2 vols. (Springfield, MA: Samuel Bowles and Company, 1855), 2:360.

9. George White, *A Brief Account of the Life, Experience, Travels, and Gospel Labours of George White, an African; written by himself and revised by a friend* (New York: John C. Totten, 1810), 53.

10. William Simonds, ed., *Our Little Ones in Heaven* (Boston: Gould and Lincoln, 1858).

11. J[ohn] G[reenleaf] W[hittier], "The Slave Poet of North Carolina," *The Non-Slaveholder* 4, no. 1 (January 1849): 16.

12. Orlando Patterson, *Slavery and Social Death: A Comparative Study* (Cambridge, MA: Harvard University Press, 1982), 6.

13. Ibid., 5.

14. [Margaretta Matilda Odell], "Memoir," in *Memoir and Poems of Phillis Wheatley . . .* (Boston: Isaac Knapp, 1838), 12–13.

15. Phillis Wheatley, "To the Right Honorable William, Earl of Dartmouth, His

Majesty's Principal Secretary of State for North-America," in *Complete Writings,* ed. Vincent Carretta (New York: Penguin, 2001), 40.

16. Phillis Wheatley to John Thornton, 30 October 1774, in *Complete Writings,* 159.

17. Vincent Carretta, introduction to *Complete Writings,* xxxv.

18. They include longtime pastor of Boston's Old South Church, Joseph Sewall; the American patriots' first martyr, twelve-year-old Christopher Snider, killed by a British soldier amid the tensions leading up to the Boston Massacre; son-in-law of Thomas Hubbard, Dr. Thomas Leonard; husband of Lucy Tyler, Dr. Samuel Marshall; daughter of Harvard treasurer and Old South Church deacon Thomas Hubbard, Thankfull Hubbard Leonard; daughter of Yale President Thomas Clap and sister-in-law of General David Wooster, Temperance Clap Pitkin; General Wooster himself; pastor of Boston's Church of Presbyterian Strangers, John Moorhead; infant son of Samuel Eliot, Charles Eliot; wife of Massachusetts lieutenant governor Andrew Oliver and sister-in-law of Thomas Hutchinson, Mary Sanford Oliver; and the pastor of Brattle Street Church, also the minister who baptized Wheatley, Samuel Cooper. The identification of Charles Eliot is made by Julian D. Mason Jr., *The Poems of Phillis Wheatley,* rev. ed. (Chapel Hill: University of North Carolina Press, 1989), 146n. The remaining subjects of Wheatley's known elegies are the unnamed son of a Mrs. Boylston; the brother- and sister-in-law of James Sullivan, and a child Avis; an infant, J. C.; the infant son of a "P. N. S. & Lady"; an unnamed "young Lady"; an unnamed "young Gentleman"; and an unnamed lady's "Three Relations."

19. Wheatley, "On the Death of J. C. an Infant," in *Complete Writings,* 50.

20. Wheatley, "To the Honourable T. H. Esq; on the Death of his Daughter," in *Complete Writings,* 52.

21. Wheatley, "On the Death of a Young Lady of Five Years of Age," in *Complete Writings,* 17.

22. Paula Bennett writes of the pathos with which Wheatley "positions her speaker as heavenly healer to the very people responsible for her 'woe'" in "Phillis Wheatley's Vocation and the Paradox of the 'Afric Muse,'" *PMLA* 113, no. 1 (1998): 71. For an excellent treatment of authority in the printed poems, see Kirstin Wilcox, "The Body into Print: Marketing Phillis Wheatley," *American Literature* 71, no. 1 (1999): 1–29.

23. Wheatley, "On the Death of Dr. Samuel Marshall," in *Complete Writings,* 46–47.

24. Wheatley, "On the Death of Doctor Samuel Marshall [variant 2]," in *Complete Writings,* 120.

25. Wheatley, "On being brought from Africa to America," in *Complete Writings,* 13.

26. Wheatley, "To His Honour the Lieutenant-Governor, on the Death of his Lady," in *Complete Writings,* 60–61.

27. Wheatley, "A Funeral Poem on the Death of C. E. an Infant of Twelve Months," in *Complete Writings,* 39; "To a Lady and her Children, on the Death of her Son and their Brother," in *Complete Writings,* 44; "To a Gentleman and Lady on the Death of the Lady's Brother and Sister, and a Child of the Name Avis, aged one Year," in *Complete Writings,* 45–6; "On the Death of J. C. an Infant," in *Complete Writings,* 50.

28. Odell, "Memoir," 23.

29. Horatio, "Elegy on the Death of a late celebrated Poetess," *Boston Magazine,* December 1784, 619–20.

30. John Willis Menard, "Phillis Wheatley," in *Lays in Summer Lands* (Washington: Enterprise Publishing Company, 1879), 81–82.

31. Horatio, "Elegy," 619.

32. Peter M. Sacks, *The English Elegy: Studies in the Genre from Spenser to Yeats* (Baltimore: Johns Hopkins University Press, 1985), 71.

33. Wheatley, "On the Death of J. C. an Infant," in *Complete Writings,* 49.

34. George Moses Horton, *The Poetical Works of George Moses Horton, the Colored Bard of North-Carolina. To Which Is Prefixed the Life of the Author, Written by Himself* (Hillsborough: D. Heartt, 1845), iii–iv.

35. Joan R. Sherman, introduction to *The Black Bard of North Carolina: George Moses Horton and His Poetry* (Chapel Hill: University of North Carolina Press, 1997), 15, 31–32.

36. Horton, *Poetical Works,* xiv–xvi.

37. George Moses Horton, "Eulogy on the Death of a Sister," in *Naked Genius* (Raleigh: William B. Smith, 1865), 93.

38. George Moses Horton, "On the Death of an Infant," in *The Hope of Liberty* (Raleigh, NC: J. Gales & Son, 1829), 10.

39. Phillis Wheatley, "To the Right Honourable William, Earl of Dartmouth . . . ," in *Complete Writings,* 40.

40. Wheatley, "To Maecenas," in *Complete Writings,* 10.

41. Alfred Gibbs Campbell, "The Doom of Slavery," in *Poems* (Newark, NJ: Advertiser Printing House, 1883), 68.

42. T. T. Purvis, "Ruth. A Ballad of '36," in *Hagar; The Singing Maiden, with Other Stories and Rhymes* (Philadelphia: Walton & Co., 1881), 141.

43. Joshua McCarter Simpson, "Onward and Upward," in *The Emancipation Car, Being an Original Composition of Anti-Slavery Ballads, Composed Exclusively for the Under Ground Rail Road* (Zanesville, OH: Sullivan & Brown, 1874), 152.

44. James Madison Bell, *The Poetical Works* (Lansing, MI: Wynkoop, Hallenbeck, Crawford, 1901), 124; see also Harriet A. Jacobs, *Incidents in the Life of a Slave Girl, Written by Herself,* ed. Jean Fagan Yellin (Cambridge, MA: Harvard University Press, 1987), 1.

45. Frederick Douglass, *Autobiographies,* ed., Henry Louis Gates Jr. (New York: Library of America, 1994), 40.

46. Daniel Alexander Payne, "Lines Occasioned by the Death of My Infant Daughter, Julia Ann Payne, July 12, 1848. Aged 9 months, 6 days, 5 hours," in *The Pleasures* (Baltimore: Sherwood, 1850), 34.

47. Samuel Johnson, "On the Death of Dr. Robert Levet," *Poems,* ed. E. L. McAdam Jr. (New Haven, CT: Yale University Press, 1964), 315; Percy Bysshe Shelley, "Adonais," *Shelley's Poetry and Prose,* ed. Donald H. Reiman and Neil Freistat (New York: W. W. Norton, 2002), 418.

48. George Moses Horton, "Death of a Favorite Chamber Maid," in *Poetical Works,* 27; "Imploring to Be Resigned at Death," in *Poetical Works,* 75.

49. Alfred Gibbs Campbell, "Ode to Death," in *Poems* (Newark, NJ: Advertiser Printing House, 1883), 16.

50. Simpson, *Emancipation Car,* 33.

51. Ibid., 69. Emphasis in original.

52. Ken Emerson, *Doo-dah! Stephen Foster and the Rise of American Popular Culture* (New York: Simon & Schuster, 1997), 185.

53. Stephen C. Foster, *Massa's in de Cold Ground, as sung by Christy's Minstrels* (New York: Firth Pond, 1852), 5.

54. On Foster, minstrel nostalgia, and the structure of racial feeling, see Eric Lott, *Love and Theft: Blackface Minstrelsy and the American Working Class* (New York: Oxford University Press, 1993), 187–201.

55. Martin R. Delany, *Blake; or the Huts of America* (Boston: Beacon Press, 1970), 105–6, 108.

56. Joshua McCarter Simpson, "The Slaveholder's Rest," *North Star* (7 December 1849), 4.

57. Simpson, *Emancipation Car,* 13–15.

58. See Sacks, *The English Elegy,* 64–89.

59. On the precarious survival of funeral rites in slave culture, see Eugene Genovese, *Roll, Jordan, Roll: The World the Slaves Made* (New York: Pantheon Books, 1974), 194–202; and Roediger, "And Die in Dixie," 163–83.

60. Frances Anne Kemble, *Journal of a Residence on a Georgian Plantation in 1838–1839* (Athens: University of Georgia Press, 1984), 147.

61. Frederick Law Olmsted, *A Journey in the Seaboard Slave States; with Remarks on Their Economy* (London: Sampson Low, 1856), 26.

62. Christopher Looby, ed., *The Complete Civil War Journals and Selected Letters of Thomas Wentworth Higginson* (Chicago: University of Chicago Press, 2000), 152–53.

63. Higginson, "Negro Spirituals," 689.

64. William Francis Allen, Charles Pickard Ware, and Lucy McKim Garrison, eds., *Slave Songs of the United States* (New York: A. Simpson, 1867), 19.

65. W. E. B. Du Bois, *The Souls of Black Folk,* in *Writings,* Nathan Huggins, ed. (New York: Library of America, 1986), 536.

66. James Harrison Wilson to Wendell Phillips Garrison, 11 June 1867, Field-Garrison Autograph Collection, Library of Congress, quoted in Dena J. Epstein, *Sinful Tunes and Spirituals: Black Folk Music to the Civil War* (Urbana: University of Illinois Press, 1977), 328–29.

67. Higginson, "Negro Spirituals," 689, qtd. in Du Bois, *Souls,* 543–44; James Weldon Johnson, too, cited Higginson's remark approvingly in his first *Book of American Negro Spirituals* (New York: Viking Press, 1925), 42.

68. Lawrence W. Levine, *Black Culture and Black Consciousness: Afro-American Folk Thought from Slavery to Freedom* (Oxford: Oxford University Press, 1977), 39.

69. Zora Neale Hurston, "Spirituals and Neo-Spirituals" (1934), in *Folklore, Memoirs, and Other Writings,* ed. Cheryl Wall (New York: Library of America, 1995), 870.

70. Ibid., 870, 872–73.

71. Susan L. Mizruchi, *The Science of Sacrifice: American Literature and Modern Social Theory* (Princeton, NJ: Princeton University Press, 1998), 280.

72. Du Bois, *Souls*, 538, 544.

73. Ronald Radano, "Denoting Difference: The Writing of the Slave Spirituals," *Critical Inquiry* 22 (1996): 526.

74. Du Bois, *Souls*, 538.

75. On the relationship of the blues to twentieth-century elegy, see Ramazani, *Poetry of Mourning*, 135–62.

76. Gilroy, *The Black Atlantic*, 90–91.

77. "I Hope My Mother Will Be There," in *Hampton and Its Students*, by M. F. Armstrong and Helen W. Ludlow (New York: G. P. Putnam's, 1874), 218.

78. Du Bois, *Souls*, 538.

79. Algernon Charles Swinburne, "Itylus," as qtd. in Du Bois, *Souls*, 506.

80. Du Bois, *Souls*, 509–10.

81. R. Nathaniel Dett, ed., *Religious Folk-Songs of the Negro, as Sung at the Hampton Institute* (Hampton, VA: Hampton Institute Press, 1927), 110.

82. The history of slave suicide has gone largely untold, receiving scant treatment in the voluminous literature on Atlantic slavery. An important exception is William D. Piersen, "White Cannibals, Black Martyrs: Fear, Depression, and Religious Faith as Causes of Suicide among New Slaves," *Journal of Negro History* 62 (1977): 147–59.

83. See Douglass, *Autobiographies*, 229, 268; and Charles Ball, *Slavery in the United States: A Narrative of the Life and Adventures of Charles Ball, a Black Man* (Lewiston, PA: John W. Shugert, 1836), 25, 49.

84. Joseph Jekyll, "The Life of Ignatius Sancho," in *Letters of the Late Ignatius Sancho, an African*, ed. Vincent Carretta (New York: Penguin, 1998), 6.

85. Du Bois, *Souls*, 510.

86. Grace Greenwood, *Poems* (Boston: Ticknor, Reed, and Fields, 1851), 82. Grace Greenwood was the pseudonym of Sarah Jane Clarke Lippincott.

87. William Wells Brown, *Clotel; or, The President's Daughter* (1853), ed. William Edward Farrison (New York: Carol Publishing Group, 1995), 222. Italics in original.

88. Greenwood, *Poems*, 82.

89. Jairus Lincoln, ed., *Anti-Slavery Melodies: For the Friends of Freedom* (Hingham: Elijah B. Gill, 1843); George W. Clark, ed., *The Liberty Minstrel* (New York: Leavitt and Alden, 1844); Brown acknowledges his indebtedness to these works in his preface to *The Anti-Slavery Harp: A Collection of Songs for Anti-Slavery Meetings* (Boston: Bela Marsh, 1848), [3].

90. The popular and widely reprinted 1788 elegiac ballad "The African," for example, was written by William Roscoe and James Currie, published anonymously, and, according to James G. Basker, "became a staple of such anthologies as Mavor and Pratt's *Classical English Poetry* (1801)" (*Amazing Grace: An Anthology of Poems about Slavery, 1660–1810* [New Haven, CT: Yale University Press, 2002], 200).

91. Brown, *Clotel*, 221.

92. "It is not without significance that, in the holy canonical books, no divine precept or permission can be discovered which allows us to bring about our own death, either to obtain immortality or to avert or avoid some evil. On the contrary, we must understand the Law of God as forbidding us to do this, where it says, 'Thou shalt not

kill.'" Augustine, *The City of God against the Pagans,* trans. R. W. Dyson (Cambridge: Cambridge University Press, 1998), 32.

93. Immanuel Kant, *Lectures on Ethics,* trans. Peter Heath (Cambridge: Cambridge University Press, 1997), 146–47.

94. Howard I. Kushner, *Self-Destruction in the Promised Land: A Psychocultural Biology of American Suicide* (New Brunswick. NJ: Rutgers University Press, 1989), 32.

95. Ball, *Slavery,* 49.

96. Slaveholders feared the possible effect on their slaves not only of other slaves' suicides but also of the supposed encouragement of abolitionists. On August 31, 1855, *Frederick Douglass' Paper* reprinted the following item from the pro-slavery *Kansas Herald* (Leavenworth): "Circumstances have transpired within a few weeks past in this neighborhood which have placed beyond doubt the existence of an organized band of Abolitionists in our midst. We counsel our friends who have money in slave property to keep a sharp look out lest their valued slaves may be induced to commit acts which might jeopardize their lives. Mr. Graffam Thompson of this place lost a valuable Negro about a week ago, and we have not the least doubt that she was persuaded by one of this lawless band to destroy herself rather than remain in slavery. In fact, one of this gang was heard to remark, 'that she did perfectly right in drowning herself,' and just as he would have done, or what any Negro who is held in bondage should do" (1).

97. Ball, *Slavery,* 25, 49.

98. Theodore Dwight, "Picture of African Distress," *American Museum* 6, no. 4 (October 1789): 328.

99. That is, a gang of slave-traders.

100. Belinda [pseud.], "Monimba: A True Story," *Massachusetts Magazine, or Monthly Museum* 3, no. 9 (September 1791): 573–74.

101. Michael A. Gomez, *Exchanging Our Country Marks: The Transformation of African Identities in the Colonial and Antebellum South* (Chapel Hill: University of North Carolina Press, 1998), 116–17. Gomez discerns some "potentially corroborative evidence" associating suicide with the Igbo in certain "flying African" folk traditions (117–20).

102. Ibid., 126–28.

103. John Whaley, *A Collection of Poems* (London: John Willis and Joseph Boddington, 1732), 92–93.

104. William James Stillman, "Verses, Occasioned by the suicide of Stephen Rodden," *North Star,* October 13, 1848, 4.

105. S. H. B. Smith, "The Negro Girl," *North Star,* July 20, 1849, 4.

106. Frances Ellen Watkins Harper, "The Tennessee Hero," in *Poems on Miscellaneous Subjects* (Philadelphia: Merrihew and Thompson, 1857), 33–34.

107. "Homicide Case in Clarke County, Virginia," *National Era,* 6 November 1851, 178–79.

108. Julia Ward Howe [Giuliana, pseud.], "The Death of the Slave Lewis," *National Era,* 8 January 1852, 5.

109. Georges Minois, *History of Suicide: Voluntary Death in Western Culture,* trans. Lydia G. Cochrane (Baltimore: Johns Hopkins University Press, 1999), 14.

110. Howe, "Death," 5.

111. Ibid.

112. Julia Ward Howe, "Slave Suicide," in *Words for the Hour* (Boston: Ticknor and Fields, 1857), 32–34.

113. Karen Sánchez-Eppler, *Touching Liberty: Abolition, Feminism, and the Politics of the Body* (Berkeley: University of California Press, 1993), 25.

114. Abraham Lincoln, "The Suicide's Soliloquy," *Sangamo Journal*, 25 August 1838; rpt. in Richard Lawrence Miller, "'What Is Hell to One Like Me?'" *American Heritage* 55, no. 4 (2004): 50–54.

115. Abraham Lincoln, *Speeches and Writings, 1832–1858*, ed. Don E. Fehrenbacher (New York: Library of America, 1989), 29.

116. *Diary of Gideon Welles*, 3 vols. (Boston: Houghton Mifflin, 1911), 2:290.

117. Douglass, *Autobiographies*, 809.

118. Campbell, "Abraham Lincoln," in *Poems*, 52.

119. Thomas Reed Turner, *Beware the People Weeping: Public Opinion and the Assassination of Abraham Lincoln* (Baton Rouge: Louisiana State University Press, 1982), 52.

120. Ibid., 23.

121. "The Negro and the War," *Valley Spirit* (Chambersburg, PA), 27 January 1864, 4.

122. Frantz Fanon, *Black Skin, White Masks*, trans. Charles Lam Markmann (New York: Grove Press, 1967), 220.

123. Elizabeth Keckley, *Behind the Scenes; or, Thirty Years a Slave, and Four Years in the White House* (New York: G. W. Carleton, 1868), 139.

124. Walt Whitman to Louisa Van Velsor Whitman, 7 July 1863, in *The Correspondence*, vol. 1, ed. Edwin Haviland Miller (New York: New York University Press, 1961), 115.

125. Douglass, *Autobiographies*, 917–18.

126. Jean H. Baker, *Mary Todd Lincoln: A Biography* (New York: W. W. Norton, 1987), 248, 250, 252.

127. Sherman, introduction to *Black Bard*, 29–30.

128. Sandra M. Gilbert, "Widow," *Critical Inquiry* 27 (2001), 564.

129. Ibid., 577.

130. Baker, *Mary Todd Lincoln*, 217–22, 245.

131. "I Got a Home in-a Dat Rock," in Johnson, *The Book of American Negro Spirituals*, 98.

132. Matthew Simpson, *Funeral Address Delivered at the Burial of President Lincoln at Springfield, Illinois, May 4, 1865* (New York: Carlton & Porter, 1865), 5.

133. Whitman published four elegies for Lincoln: "Hush'd be the Camps To-day" (1865), "When Lilacs Last in the Dooryard Bloom'd" (1865), "O Captain! My Captain!" (1865), and "This Dust was Once the Man" (1871). His unfinished manuscript elegies "Unveil Thy Bosom, Faithful Tomb" (1865) and "Thou West that gave'st Him to Us" (1865) appear in facsimile in *Walt Whitman's Drum-Taps (1865) and Sequel to Drum-Taps (1865–66): A Facsimile Reproduction*, ed. F. DeWolfe Miller (Gainesville, FL: Scholars' Facsimiles & Reprints, 1959), xxiv, xlii.

134. Walt Whitman, "Death of Abraham Lincoln," in *Prose Works*, 2 vols., ed. Floyd Stovall (New York: New York University Press, 1963–64), 2:508.

6. Retrievements out of the Night

The epigraph at the chapter opening is from Theodor Adorno, "The Essay as Form," in *Notes to Literature: Volume One,* ed. Rolf Tiedemann (New York: Columbia University Press, 1991), 11.

1. Horace Traubel, *With Walt Whitman in Camden,* vol. 3 (New York: Mitchell Kennerley, 1914), 134–35.

2. Walt Whitman, "The Primer of Words," in *Daybooks and Notebooks,* 3 vols., ed. William White (New York: New York University Press, 1978), 3:745. Traubel edited these manuscript materials and published them after Whitman's death as *An American Primer* (Boston: Small, Maynard & Company, 1904).

3. Walt Whitman, *Notebooks and Unpublished Prose Manuscripts,* 6 vols., ed. Edward F. Grier (New York: New York University Press, 1984), 2:539. Further references to this edition, designated *Notebooks,* occur parenthetically within the text.

4. Walt Whitman, "The Sleepers," in *Leaves of Grass: A Textual Variorum of the Printed Poems,* 3 vols., ed. Sculley Bradley, Harold W. Blodgett, et al. (New York: New York University Press, 1980), 1:115. Further references to this edition, designated *Leaves of Grass,* occur parenthetically within the text.

5. Kerry C. Larson, *Whitman's Drama of Consensus* (Chicago: University of Chicago Press, 1988), 215.

6. Walt Whitman, *Prose Works,* 2 vols., ed. Floyd Stovall (New York: New York University Press, 1963–64), 1:61. Further references to this edition, designated *Prose Works,* occur parenthetically within the text.

7. For William Wallace Lincoln, as for the younger memorialists of George Washington discussed in chapter 2, elegy writing was part of youth's tuition in sentimental citizenship. Four months before his own death, Willie sent to the *Daily National Republican* an elegy he had composed for Lincoln family friend Edward Baker, killed at the Battle of Ball's Bluff. Willie's poem is reproduced in Elizabeth Keckley, *Behind the Scenes* (1868), ed. Frances Smith Foster (Chicago: Lakeside Press, 1998), 82–83.

8. Keckley, *Behind the Scenes,* 88.

9. Representing the former extreme, Jerome Loving suggests that with the war Whitman's "'Calamus' feeling was becoming sweetly solemnized (if never completely anesthetized) by death" (*Walt Whitman: The Song of Himself* [Berkeley: University of California Press, 1999], 19); representing the latter extreme, Michael Moon suggests, in an essay on *Drum-Taps,* that "we may find in fetishes a broadly conceived means of extending our own bodies, as well as the bodies of our beloved dead, and in fetishistic practices further means of exploring and extending our relationships, including our sexual relationships, with the dead" ("Memorial Rags," in *Professions of Desire: Lesbian and Gay Studies in Literature,* ed. George E. Haggerty and Bonnie Zimmerman [New York: Modern Language Association, 1995], 237).

10. Robert Leigh Davis, *Whitman and the Romance of Medicine* (Berkeley: University of California Press, 1997), 40–41.

11. Ibid., 14.

12. See Patricia Cline Cohen, *A Calculating People: The Spread of Numeracy in Early America* (Chicago: University of Chicago Press, 1982).

13. On the manipulation of such images, see Timothy Sweet, *Traces of War: Poetry,*

Photography, and the Crisis of Union (Baltimore: Johns Hopkins University Press, 1990), 107–37.

14. "Brady's Photographs. Pictures of the Dead at Antietam," *New York Times,* October 20, 1862, 5.

15. Davis, *Whitman,* 91–93.

16. Few critics besides Davis have written as eloquently of these imaginings as Peter Coviello in *Intimacy in America: Dreams of Affiliation in Antebellum Literature* (Minneapolis: University of Minnesota Press, 2005), 127–55. See also Michael Warner, "Whitman Drunk," in *Breaking Bounds: Whitman and American Cultural Studies,* ed. Betsy Erkkila and Jay Grossman (New York: Oxford University Press, 1996), 30–43.

17. John Burroughs, "Walt Whitman and His 'Drum Taps,'" *The Galaxy* 2 (1866): 612–13.

18. Jones Very, "John Woolman" (1852), in *Jones Very: The Complete Poems* (Athens: University of Georgia Press, 1993), 274.

19. Michael Moon, *Disseminating Whitman: Revision and Corporeality in Leaves of Grass* (Cambridge, MA: Harvard University Press, 1991), 217; Peter M. Sacks, *The English Elegy: Studies in the Genre from Spenser to Yeats* (Baltimore: Johns Hopkins University Press, 1985), 317.

20. Moon, *Disseminating Whitman,* 219.

21. Ibid., 221.

22. D. W. Winnicott, *Playing and Reality* (1971) (East Sussex: Brunner-Routledge, 2002), 2.

23. Walt Whitman, letter to William D. O'Connor, January 6, 1865, in *The Correspondence, Volume 1: 1842–1867,* ed. Edwin Haviland Miller (New York: New York University Press, 1961), 246–47. Further references to this edition, designated *Correspondence,* occur parenthetically within the text.

24. F. DeWolfe Miller, introduction to *Walt Whitman's* Drum-Taps *(1865) and* Sequel to Drum-Taps *(1865–6)* (Gainesville, FL: Scholars' Facsimiles and Reprints, 1959), xxxiv.

25. Moon, *Disseminating Whitman,* 63.

26. Joseph Roach, *Cities of the Dead: Circum-Atlantic Performance* (New York: Columbia University Press, 1996), 3.

27. Jacques Lacan, *The Ethics of Psychoanalysis, 1959–1960,* trans. Dennis Porter (New York: W. W. Norton, 1992), 93–94.

28. Ibid., 93.

29. William James, "Is Life Worth Living?" in *Writings, 1878–1899,* ed. Gerald E. Myers (New York: Library of America, 1992), 480.

30. Davis, *Whitman,* 39.

31. Roy Morris Jr., *The Better Angel: Walt Whitman in the Civil War* (New York: Oxford University Press, 2000), 34.

32. Helen Vendler, "Whitman's 'When Lilacs Last in the Dooryard Bloom'd,'" in *Textual Analysis: Some Readers Reading,* ed. Mary Ann Caws (New York: Modern Language Association of America, 1986), 139.

33. Ibid., 133.

34. Christopher Bollas, *Being a Character: Psychoanalysis and Self Experience* (New York: Hill and Wang, 1992), 100.

35. Ibid., 71.

36. Allen Grossman, "The Poetics of Union in Whitman and Lincoln: An Inquiry toward the Relationship of Art and Policy," in *The Long Schoolroom: Lessons in the Bitter Logic of the Poetic Principle* (Ann Arbor: University of Michigan Press, 1997), 64.

37. Harold Bloom, "Whitman's Image of Voice," in *Agon: Towards a Theory of Revisionism* (Oxford: Oxford University Press, 1982), 189.

38. Moon, *Disseminating Whitman,* 89.

39. Samuel Taylor Coleridge, "The Nightingale," in William Wordsworth and Samuel Taylor Coleridge, *Lyrical Ballads and Related Writings,* ed. William Richey and Daniel Robinson (Boston: Houghton Mifflin, 2002), 47–48.

40. Ibid., 50.

41. These shifting enactments of voice in "Lilacs" have been parsed, or "tallied," by a number of the poem's readers, including Harold Bloom and Mitchell Breitwieser. Despite their very different conclusions about the poem, both favor the synesthetic term "image of voice" to describe its dynamic. For Bloom, Whitman's "image of voice" is an "interlocking" of the antithetical drives toward love and death, Eros and Thanatos, represented by the "bird's tallying chant" and its counterpart, the "broken lilac sprig" (Bloom, *Agon,* 190–91). Breitwieser, on the other hand, insists upon the incommensurateness of voices—upon the existence of two separate entities in the poem, each of which uses the pronoun "I." Rhetorically as well as linguistically, identity and even intimacy are illusions. For Breitwieser, Whitman's "image of voice" is deixis in writing: the "here" and "now" that haunt Whitman's efforts to designate what is ultimately an impossible condition of self-presence ("Who Speaks in Whitman's Poems?" in *The American Renaissance: New Dimensions,* ed. Harry R. Gravin [Lewisburg, PA: Bucknell University Press, 1983], 128, 133–35). Kerry Larson goes even further in his remarks on the first half of the poem and its "tenuous narrative voice," perceived as a static collection of "utterances . . . issuing from a splintered, centerless point of view." Yet for Larson this fragmentation is merely "a prelude to the triumphant fusion to be achieved in the final section" (*Whitman's Drama of Consensus,* 234–35).

42. Henry David Thoreau, "Walking," *Atlantic Monthly* 9, no. 56 (June 1862): 666.

43. Bollas, *Being a Character,* 61.

44. John James Audubon, for example, records more than four times as many species of warblers as species of thrushes in *Ornithological Biography, or an Account of the Habits of the Birds of the United States of America* (Edinburgh: Adam Black, 1831).

45. Betsy Erkkila, *Whitman: The Political Poet* (Oxford: Oxford University Press, 1989), 234.

46. Larson, *Whitman's Drama of Consensus,* 240.

47. Mark Edmundson, "'Lilacs': Walt Whitman's American Elegy," *Nineteenth-Century Literature* 44 (1990): 485.

48. Larson, *Whitman's Drama of Consensus,* 240.

49. Bollas, *Being a Character,* 14.

50. Herman Melville, *Battle-Pieces and Aspects of the War* (New York: Harper and Brothers, 1866), 141–42. On the contested valuations of violence and redemption in Melville's Civil War poetry, see Michael Warner, "What Like a Bullet Can Undeceive?" *Public Culture* 15, no. 1 (2003): 41–54.

51. Emma Lazarus, "April 27th, 1865," in *Poems and Translations* (New York: Hurd and Houghton, 1867), 38.

52. Ibid.

53. Ibid., 39.

54. Mutlu Konuk Blasing, "Whitman's 'Lilacs' and the Grammars of Time," *PMLA* 97 (1982): 32–33.

55. Timothy Sweet, *Traces of War: Poetry, Photography, and the Crisis of Union* (Baltimore: Johns Hopkins University Press, 1990), 71.

56. See Gary Laderman, *The Sacred Remains: American Attitudes toward Death, 1799–1883* (New Haven, CT: Yale University Press, 1996), 160.

57. "The Battle of Antietam," *Harper's Weekly* 6, no. 302 (October 11, 1862): 655. Quoted in Laderman, *Sacred Remains*, 102.

58. See Karen Sánchez-Eppler, *Touching Liberty: Abolition, Feminism, and the Politics of the Body* (Berkeley: University of California Press, 1993), 2–3.

59. Henry James, *Autobiography*, ed. Frederick W. Dupee (New York: Criterion, 1956), 415–16.

60. Henry James, "Walt Whitman's *Drum-Taps*," in *Literary Criticism: Essays on Literature, American Writers, English Writers*, ed. Leon Edel (New York: Library of America, 1984), 629, 633, 635.

61. Henry James, untitled review (April 16, 1898), in *Literary Criticism*, 662.

62. Lawrence Buell, "American Civil War Poetry and the Meaning of Literary Commodification: Whitman, Melville, and Others," in *Reciprocal Influences: Literary Production, Distribution, and Consumption in America*, ed. Steven Fink and Susan S. Williams (Columbus: Ohio State University Press, 1999), 131.

63. Horace Traubel, *With Walt Whitman in Camden*, vol. 2 (New York: Mitchell Kennerley, 1915), 304.

64. Stuart Merrill, *The White Tomb: Selected Writings*, ed. Edward Foster (Jersey City, NJ: Talisman House, 1999), 158–59.

Afterword

The epigraphs at the chapter opening are from the following: Horace Traubel, *With Walt Whitman in Camden*, vol. 9, ed. Jeanne Chapman and Robert Macisaac (Oregon House, CA: W. L. Bentley, 1996), 614; Robert G. Ingersoll, untitled eulogy, in *In Re Walt Whitman*, ed. Horace L. Traubel, Richard Maurice Bucke, and Thomas B. Harned (Philadelphia: David McKay, 1893), 452; and Traubel, *With Walt Whitman in Camden*, 9:622.

1. Traubel, *With Walt Whitman in Camden*, 9:616–17.

2. Ibid., 9:619–22.

3. Horace Traubel, "At the Graveside of Walt Whitman," in *In Re Walt Whitman*, 438.

4. Ibid., 437.

5. Traubel, *With Walt Whitman in Camden*, 9:602, 609.

6. Ibid., 9:613.

7. Horace L. Traubel, "Succession," *The Conservator* 5, no. 4 (June 1894): 57.

8. Guillaume Apollinaire, "Funérailles de Walt Whitman racontées par un témoin," *Mercure de France,* 1 April 1913, 658.

9. Allen Ginsberg, *Kaddish and Other Poems, 1958–1960* (San Francisco: City Lights, 1961), 13, 15, 16, 24, 29, 35.

10. Ibid., 33, 36.

11. Henry Wadsworth Longfellow, "Morituri Salutamus," in *Poems and Other Writings,* ed. J. D. McClatchy (New York: Library of America, 2000), 621.

12. D. A. Miller, "Anal Rope," *Representations* 32 (Fall 1990): 131.

13. Walt Whitman, "When Lilacs Last in the Dooryard Bloom'd," in *Leaves of Grass: A Textual Variorum of the Printed Poems,* 3 vols., ed. Sculley Bradley, Harold W. Blodgett, et al. (New York: New York University Press, 1980), 2:535.

14. Paul de Man, "Anthropomorphism and Trope in the Lyric," in *The Rhetoric of Romanticism* (New York: Columbia University Press, 1984), 262.

Index

Max Cavitch is assistant professor of English at the University of Pennsylvania.

7917

7917